W · W · NORTON & COMPANY

NEW YORK · LONDON

BEETHOVEN
ON BEETHOVEN

Playing His Piano Music His Way

WILLIAM S. NEWMAN

Professor Emeritus, The University of North Carolina at Chapel Hill

FIRST EDITION

The text of this book is composed in Primer, with display type set in Garamond Old Style. Composition and manufacturing by the Maple Vail Book Manufacturing Group. Book design by Marjorie J. Flock.

Library of Congress Cataloging in Publication Data
Newman, William S.
    Beethoven on Beethoven: playing his piano music his way/by
William S. Newman.
    p. cm.
    Bibliography:p.
    Includes index.
    1. Beethoven, Ludwig van, 1770–1827   Piano music.   2. Piano music-
Interpretation (Phrasing, dynamics, etc.)   I.Title.
ML410.B4N45 1988
786.1′092′4—dc19   87-18756

ISBN 0-393-02538-1

W. W. Norton & Company, Inc., 500 Fifth Avenue, New York, N.Y. 10110
W. W. Norton & Company Ltd, 37 Great Russell Street, London WC1B 3NU

1 2 3 4 5 6 7 8 9 0

In memory of our son Craig

(1952–1983)

CONTENTS

CONTENTS

PREFACE

MY AIM in this book has been to explore at least the main interpretive problems that confront every serious performer, teacher, and student of Beethoven's piano music. I have concentrated on whatever firsthand information I could find, hoping thus to meet a conspicuous need in music literature.

The idea of writing the book originated about when the final volume in my *History of the Sonata Idea* first appeared, in 1969, at which time the prospect of further Beethoven studies—coming on the rebound, as it were—was most welcome. That idea took more tangible shape when intriguing problems beset four of us on the faculty at the University of North Carolina as we prepared to play Beethoven's "Thirty-Two Sonatas" in eight monthly recitals. Indeed, the gist of those problems appeared within a year in a little book that W. W. Norton published—*Performance Practices in Beethoven's Piano Sonatas* (1971). However, that preliminary book was only "An Introduction," as its subtitle indicates.

During the seventeen years between 1969 and 1986, I have investigated some twenty aspects of performance in Beethoven's music. The studies that have resulted (as listed in the Bibliography at the end) have facilitated a divide-and-conquer approach to the writing of the present book. Although the final product has become much more than an interconnected anthology of those studies, it does draw repeatedly on them, most often with revisions and updating. But readers who have troubled to read them should be cautioned that the information and conclusions in this book not only augment the findings in the preparatory studies, but sometimes differ from them appreciably.

During those same years, studies on this surprisingly fresh topic of "authentic" Beethoven performance have begun to appear from other writers, too, and in increasing numbers, though not nearly so abundantly as the studies on quite different kinds of Beethoven problems, especially his biography and his sketches. In many ways, these new performance studies have contributed significantly to the writing of this book.

A book on performance problems depends on the quotation of many examples from composers' works. Of these examples, a considerable number come from modern editions by the kind permissions of their publishers. Grateful acknowledgement of these permissions is made here and in the separate captions by the use of the following code (identified here by an asterisk): HV*, G. Henle Verlag in Munich; EA*, European American Distributors Corporation, agent for the Universal Edition in London; BL*, The British Library in London; BV*, Barenreiter Verlag in Kassel; and EH*, The Beethoven-haus in Bonn. Nearly sixty-five percent of these examples come from G. Henle Verlag, publisher of the ongoing, comprehensive edition of *Beethoven Werke* and of several other authoritative Beethoven editions. For their use, particular thanks are owing to the late Dr. Günter Henle and to the Verlag's present Director, Dr. Martin Bente.

Naturally, even with that many examples in the book, still more references have had to be made without the benefit of such illustrations. Hence, the reader with the fullest collection of Beethoven's piano music at hand—in the most reliable editions, and, not incidentally, with the measures numbered for ready reference—will be the best equipped to follow the discussions. Regarding the music examples that do appear in this book, those quoted from the modern publications ordinarily do not include any modern editorial insertions such as fingerings. They and the examples quoted from earlier sources are preceded when necessary by whatever authentic key and time signatures, tempo and expressive inscriptions, and dynamic signs are in effect at the moment the quotations begin. These indications by the composer are usually grouped in brackets.

Various Beethoven scholars in this and other countries have generously provided specific information and advice upon request (as acknowledged where their contributions are cited). Right here I should like to single out two distinguished, long-time friends who have contributed exceptionally from their wide experience as both performers and scholars: Max Rudolf, eminent conductor and author in Philadelphia, and Frederick Neumann, well-known violinist and author in Richmond. The constructive criticisms that each has made to my individual studies published previously have been incorporated at various points in the present book.

Furthermore, for all the timely assistance on the scene, the photocopies, the replies to written queries, and the other help that one could hope to get from large archives and libraries, it is my pleasure to thank the invariably co-operative music staffs of the Beethoven-Archiv in Bonn, the Österreichische Nationalbibliothek and the Gesellschaft der Musikfreunde in Vienna, the British Library in London, the Deutsche Staatsbibliothek in East Berlin, the Bayerische Staatsbibliothek in Munich, the Bibliothèque Nationale in Paris, the Library of Congress in Washington, the New York Public Library at Lincoln Center, the Boston Public Library in Copley Square, and the Music Library at the University of North Carolina in Chapel Hill.

And I should like to acknowledge several valued grants that I have received in support of the research and writing done on this book. These include a Senior fellowship in 1972–73 from the National Endowment for the Humanities to work abroad in the archives and libraries just named; a year's Fellowship in 1983–84 at the National Humanities Center in North Carolina's Research Triangle Park to further the book's completion; and two Grants-in-Aid from the American Council of Learned Societies, as well as several grants from the University [of North Carolina] Research Council to provide the research assistance of a number of able individuals over the years, most of them then graduate students at the University of North Carolina. These individuals include Ann Chan, Rudi Schnitzler, Mary Kolb, Georgia Peoples, Julie Smith, Penny Schwarze, and Joni Carter.

Moreover, warm thanks are owing to the staff of W. W. Norton & Co. in New York, especially to Claire Brook and Ray Morse. Their help has included not only their knowledgeable, conscientious work with the manuscript of this book, but exceptional patience and understanding during my first, uncertain efforts to produce a book on a word processor.

And while expressing warm thanks for exceptional patience and understanding, may I add that it has been another Claire, my highly resourceful wife, who, as so often in previous research and writing, has come to the rescue in one crisis after another.

Translations are mine unless otherwise acknowledged.

W. S. N. May 1987

BEETHOVEN
ON BEETHOVEN

CHAPTER *1*

ORIENTATIONS

Definitions and Elaborations

*I*N THIS BOOK'S SUBTITLE, playing Beethoven's piano music his way might be expanded to mean playing it according to whatever intentions on Beethoven's part can be documented or can be supported by reasoning and analysis in the primary sources for his music. In other words, the aim is to get as close as we can to the styles of performance Beethoven himself had in mind. Such styles— or performance practices, to use today's favored academic term—involve whatever decisions the performer still must make between acquiring the most authentic score available and actually performing it. Some of those decisions might involve choices among keyboard instruments, tempos, ornament realizations, rhythmic groupings, articulation styles, expressive directions, and pedallings.

But the point needs to be made at once that only infrequently can one document Beethoven's intentions with hard evidence—that is, with proof in the score itself, or a positive declaration by a trustworthy witness if not by Beethoven. Most of the time one must rely on circumstantial evidence of one sort or another—chiefly on deductions from analysis and reasoning, or from analogous practices in other circumstances. For example, one may hope to determine an appropriate tempo for a piano passage by finding an analogous passage in one of the chamber works that Beethoven marked with his own metronome tempos. But even the circumstantial evidence may be lacking, or may be too slim to accept. Then, since some decision has to be made before a performance can take place, the only answer that remains is an educated guess based on artistic intuition and experience!

The Scope and Plan of This Study

Traditionally, studies of performance styles have concerned detailed and local rather than generalized and over-all aspects of performance—they have concerned the trees rather than the forest. So it must be in this book. Our focus must be largely on the micro rather than the macro problems of interpretation. But, as will come up more than once, the performer constantly needs to bear in mind a widely-endorsed proposition (undoubtedly reinforced by Wagner's theory of the *Gesamtkunstwerk*): both the composer's and the performer's ultimate purpose is to unite all aspects of interpretation toward the attainment of the clearest and most meaningful projection of the music's total form. Put more simply, at our level of detail "every critical analysis is a more or less precise indication of how the work being analyzed should be performed."[1]

For our purposes Beethoven's piano music covers both solo and ensemble works. The richest interpretive challenges occur among the solo works in the sonatas and variations, of course, and among the instrumental ensembles in those duos, trios, and concertos in which the piano shares at least equally.

The limitation solely to Beethoven's piano music is justified here not only by the practicalities of size and feasibility, but by considerations inherent in the topic itself. The piano was the instrument on which Beethoven excelled. It posed the largest variety of problems and it enjoyed his greatest experimentation and his most enterprising exploitation, both technical and expressive. Besides, throughout his career it occupied his attention more consistently than any other instrument. In fact, on several occasions the piano inspired him to consider writing a *Klavierschule*, although he never got beyond the jotting down of a few ideas.[2]

We shall be proceeding through the performance questions that arise in the same order they might be considered by the performer, with each decision we reach helping us deal with the next. The starting point—in fact, a prerequisite—has to be a determination of the most authentic score available, since no subsequent decision can be any better than the foundation on which it is based. Next is likely to arise the question of which piano Beethoven had in mind while he was composing the work under consideration, since the answer could influence the resolution, say, of pedalling and tone-production problems. And next, for similar reasons, is likely to come the essential question of the most appropriate tempo, since

1. Quoted from the music aesthetician Leonard B. Meyer in Luoma/DYNAMICS 33 fn. 2. (Short titles are expanded in the full Bibliography at the back of this book.)

2. Cf. WEGELER & RIES *Nachtrag* 23; Goldschmidt/CRAMER 115 and 231 (fn. 108), 124–25; Breuning/SCHWARZSPANIERHAUSE 103 ff.; Anderson/BEETHOVEN III 1250 and 1279; Newman/SCHINDLER 409–410.

an adequate answer can influence nearly all further decisions. Thereafter, the best order remains less predictable, for it will depend more on the nature of the particular work than on any logic in the sequence. However, one ordinarily would expect decisions about articulation, also local rhythmic grouping and dynamic direction, to be made before those about ornament resolutions, tone projection, pedalling details, idiomatic techniques, and even the use of repeats.

To be sure, in the larger view these problems are all interdependent. Hence, the discussions of them must overlap at times and subdivide at others. The discussion of articulation divides, for instance, when it gets to *tenuto* (meaning, "held full value"). Although *tenuto* relates to articulation by being the opposite of staccato (Ch. 5), it relates even more here to legato and tone production (Ch. 8).

Some Background Information on Beethoven's Career

Certain details of Beethoven's career are summarized here because they bear on performance problems in his piano music. These concern important turning points, pianistic activities, health obstacles, composing habits, and professional associates. Also noted here are some posthumous references to Beethoven and his piano music.[3]

Born in Bonn, Germany in December 1770, Beethoven moved to Vienna in late 1792 and remained there until his death at age 56 in March 1827. His instruction before he left Bonn included that by the Singspiel composer and local court organist Christian Gottlob Neefe, who acquainted the youngster with J. S. Bach's *Well-Tempered Clavier* and Emanuel Bach's *Versuch,* among other landmarks of music. Probably it also included a meeting, if not a few actual lessons, with Mozart during a brief visit to Vienna in 1787. His lessons with Haydn, somewhat hampered by a clash of personalities, started soon after his move to Vienna and lasted only about a year. Whatever personal contacts and relationships Haydn and Mozart had with Beethoven, the influences they ultimately exercised on him were clearly overwhelming.

Beethoven seems to have achieved his reputation as a preeminent, virtuoso pianist during his relatively few further travels, in the later 1790s. On trips in those years to leading music centers (including Prague, Dresden, Leipzig, Berlin, and Pressburg) he displayed his solidly developing talents, in composition as well as in piano. By about 1802, already resigning himself to the fate of increasing deafness, he began to play less as he

---

3. GROVE BEETHOVEN, updating GROVE II 354–414, is a source for the information that follows and a recent, authoritative summary of Beethoven's life, output, and bibliography.

channelled his activities more and more into composition. He continued
to perform with diminishing technical mastery and refinement, up to about
1809. In 1814, he appeared as a piano soloist for the last known time, in
his own "Archduke" Trio, Op. 97.

The hearing problem, which must have begun to worry him well before
1802, kept worsening somewhat unpredictably during the next two
decades, with deafness closing in completely during the last five years of
his life.[4] It undoubtedly affected his performance conceptions and intentions, especially in later years, with regard to tone, texture, and instruments—all aspects of sound that he could no longer distinguish. But how
much and in what way the deafness affected his intentions in any specific work raise questions that we can answer only by guessing, for they
involve the volume, the range, the instrument, the use of pedalling, the
place and environment, the occasion, and much else. Furthermore, one
must remember that his hearing deteriorated unevenly. There were bad
days and good days; there were sounds that failed to penetrate and sounds
that came through. Of greater importance, as the physical hearing seemed
to regress, so the musical hearing seemed to advance. We can understand that Beethoven would remember the sounds he had heard while
he still could hear, yet we find it harder to understand how, as instruments developed and ranges increased, he could come to hear internally
many sonorities that he had never heard while his hearing still was satisfactory.

As mentioned earlier, Beethoven kept writing music for piano almost
without interruption from his earliest to his last creative years. In particular, he wrote solo piano sonatas and sonatinas, completing thirty-seven
in all throughout that span. He started composing at the latest by his
twelfth year, with his "Dressler" Variations (WoO 63),[5] and did not stop
until he had written three miscellaneous little pieces in 1825 (WoO 61a,
85, and 86). Only two main breaks occurred in that piano output, each
lasting about three years—one from 1806 through 1808 and the other
from 1811 through 1813.

From time to time we shall be touching on Beethoven's composing
habits for the light they may throw on particular performance intentions.
One such habit, for instance, was that of inserting his editorial markings
after he had completed the notation of a work.[6] Consequently, we are
generally more concerned here with final versions of his manuscripts
than with sketches or other preliminary sources. Other notable habits

4. Cf. Thayer & Forbes/BEETHOVEN *passim* (cf."deafness," pp. 1106–07, especially pp. 373–
74 and 811–13).

5. Three essential, modern publications concerned with Beethoven's early music are
Schiedermair/BEETHOVEN, KAFKA SKETCHBOOK, and Johnson/FISCHHOFm.

6. Cf. Mies/TEXTKRITISCHE 32 and 49–51.

were those of jotting down ideas during his customary nature walks, composing both at the piano and in his head, frequent working on several compositions concurrently, heeding associates' recommendations even for radical changes in his compositions, annotating some of his sketches as well as final autographs with performance advice, and setting tempos as a first step during initial readings of his works.[7]

Among Beethoven's associates were several who left miscellaneous but often useful comments on his own performance and performance intentions. Ferdinand Ries (1784–1838), son of the Franz Ries who had taught violin to Beethoven in Bonn, was closest to Beethoven during the latter's early and middle years. The comments that Ferdinand left are valuable and generally trusted. Most of them are of an anecdotal nature, as related in the *Biographische Notizen über Beethoven* by him and by the Bonn physician Franz Gerhard Wegeler published in 1838 (with a *Nachtrag* in 1845)[8] There are also some pertinent remarks in Ries's replies after moving to London in 1813, at which time Beethoven began asking him to oversee his English publications.[9]

It was as a precocious piano student of nine or ten, in 1801, that Carl Czerny (1791–1857) first met Beethoven. Worth noting was the first assignment that Beethoven gave to Czerny, which was to read Emanuel Bach's epochal *Versuch*. Czerny's considerable observations on performing Beethoven occur especially in his autobiographical reminiscences, in a fourth volume that he added to his piano method Op. 500, and in his editions of the master's music.[10] Those observations have commanded respect because Czerny knew his craft, played as a professional, and was honest, upright, and legendary in his industry. However, they are sometimes superficial and, because he eventually went his own way in a teaching career that extended a full generation beyond Beethoven's death, they sometimes became inconsistent.[11] His Op. 500 includes specific, if brief, remarks about details in each of the Beethoven solo sonatas, chamber works with piano, and piano concertos. Those remarks are naturally most important for at least thirteen of the solo sonatas that he performed

7. Cf. Meredith/OPUS 109 505–530; also, Solomon/CREATIVE, which sheds light on Beethoven's composition habits while it demolishes one of the most oft-cited accounts of his creative process.

8. WEGELER & RIES.

9. Cf. Tyson/RIES; Hill/RIES *passim*.

10. Czerny/ERINNERUNGEN; Czerny/SCHOOL; Czerny/BEETHOVENm. Most of Czerny's significant comments on Beethoven performance are compiled in Badura-Skoda/CZERNY. On Czerny's editions of Beethoven's sonatas, cf. the listings indexed under his name in Newman/CHECKLIST.

11. He is also said to have stretched the truth when he was challenged, according to Churgin/BEETHOVEN 33, fn. 43.

for, and presumably actually studied under Beethoven, including Opp. 13, 14/1, 14/2, 26, 27/2, 28/i, 31/2, 31/3, 53, 57, 81a, 101, and 106.[12]

Ignaz Moscheles (1794–1870), the excellent pianist, teacher, composer, and lifelong champion of Beethoven's music, arranged a vocal score of the opera *Fidelio* in 1814 and therewith enjoyed his closest and most frequent contact with the master. His observations on Beethoven performance are found mainly in three sources: the valuable autobiographical records compiled posthumously by his wife, annotations in the translation (1840–41) of the first edition of Schindler's biography of Beethoven, and his collected editions of Beethoven's piano sonatas, which include metronome markings for "the Author's [Beethoven's] Time of each Movement."[13]

The last of the four Beethoven associates who commented on his performance intentions was Anton Schindler (1795–1864). Schindler first met the master in 1814 (the same year that Moscheles enjoyed his most frequent contacts with Beethoven), but it is now thought that he was not close to him until Beethoven's last five years (with gaps), from 1822 to 1827.[14] During those years Schindler served primarily as Beethoven's unpaid domestic lackey, although it was as a pioneer biographer of Beethoven that he eventually made his historical niche. The first edition of his biography, in 1840,[15] was a hasty, careless compilation that reappeared almost unchanged as a second edition in 1845. A completely revised third edition, still frequently inaccurate, appeared in 1860.[16]

Unfortunately, Schindler's reputation as a trustworthy observer, which had been questioned sporadically right from his own day, has suffered severe damage during the last fifteen years or so. I should emphasize "unfortunately" because Schindler probably had more opportunities to learn about Beethoven's performance intentions, at least in the later years, and more to say about them in both quantity and relevance than any other contemporary commentator. The evidence that has accumulated against Schindler, most since 1977,[17] shows that in the early 1840s he deliberately added or altered nearly half (some 240) of his entries in the 137 extant Conversation Books that Beethoven started using with his friends in 1819 because of his deafness. A jealous, insecure man, Schindler evidently committed his forgeries to counteract real or imagined

---

12. Cf. Badura-Skoda/czerny 9 (indicating that Opp. 53, 57, and 106 do belong in this list) and 52–54; Newman/performance 29–30.

13. moscheles; Schindler/beethoven; Moscheles/beethovenm. Cf. Tyson/moscheles.

14. Cf. Newman/schindler.

15. Schindler/beethoven.

16. Schindler/1860.

17. For a summary, cf. Newman/schindler 400–401.

challenges to his claim to be the one true inheritor of Beethoven's artistic secrets and intentions. Similar statements in his biography have not yet been questioned so thoroughly. But as matters stand, almost every popular statement about Beethoven performance that has been ascribed to Schindler has become suspect unless corroboration is known in some other, more reliable source.

To what extent did Schindler qualify as a musician? Although he had sung in a boys' choir before entering law school in Vienna in 1813, he left no conspicuous mark as a performer, conductor, teacher, or composer.[18] What does seem conspicuous is the lack of any information about him as a pianist. After all, the playing and interpreting of Beethoven's piano music concerned him more than any other topic in his writing, and in the teaching that evidently filled much of his time during his last quarter century. In his forged, but only the forged, entries in the Conversation Books, he apparently wanted above all to establish that he had worked systematically through Beethoven's piano sonatas under the composer's own supervision.[19]

Schindler may also have forged some annotations attributed to Beethoven which were placed over twenty-one Etudes that Johann Baptist Cramer had written.[20] The only known source for these annotations is what Schindler himself identified as his own handwritten copy of them. He entered them individually over the name "Beethoven" in the first two volumes of an 1824 reprint containing all eighty-four of Cramer's Etudes in four volumes (Ex. 1/1). He also entered his own annotations, signed

18. Cf. MGG XI 1729 (Joseph Schmidt-Görg).

19. Cf. Newman/SCHINDLER 403–404.

20. Cf. Newman/CRAMER; Goldschmidt/CRAMER; Tyson/KANN (a review of the most recent printing of the 21 Etudes and their annotations); and Newman/SCHINDLER.

EXAMPLE 1/1 Opening of Cramer's Etude 24 with Beethoven's supposed annotation in Schindler's hand (from MS 35, 88 in the Staatsbibliothek of East Berlin)

"A. S.," over nearly all of the other sixty-three Etudes, "following my teacher's example."

In 1985 the two East German scholars who have done most to expose Schindler's forgeries in the Conversation Books, Dagmar Beck and Grita Herre,[21] completed a well-reasoned article that suggests why Schindler's meager information about Beethoven's authorship of the Cramer annotations is not to be trusted.[22] However, hard evidence as to whether the annotations are indeed further Schindler forgeries still cannot be found, not until a Beethoven source confirms their validity or a Schindler acknowledgment confirms the contrary. My own conclusion is that the annotations in Schindler's document could very well be forgeries, yet still be largely true to and derived from Beethoven's own performance practices and intentions.[23]

The specifics of Schindler's forgeries and supposed Beethoven annotations are brought up here especially in Chapters 4, 5, and 6, on tempo, articulation, and the incise and phrase. This much attention is given to Schindler because, to the extent that those specifics still can be validated today, they figure among the most significant contemporary remarks that we have on Beethoven's performance intentions regarding tempo and rhythmic, melodic, accentual, and dynamic details in passagework.

Observations by still other contemporaries—among them Cramer, the violinist Karl Holz, Beethoven's young friend Stephan von Breuning, and the conductor Sir George Smart—are introduced where appropriate in later pages.[24] Several further treatises or methods by pianists and teachers in Beethoven's sphere, including Milchmeyer, Clementi, Starke, and Hummel, will also be cited in later pages. In one of them, Starke's *Wiener Pianoforte-Schule,* Beethoven actually supplied original or different sources for his Bagatelles Op. 119 Nos. 7–11, the second and fourth movements of his Sonata Op. 28, and the finale of his Third Concerto Op. 37.

Beethoven's Output for Piano

The charts in the Appendix list nearly every Beethoven work that is scored for piano as a solo instrument or as an equal or predominating

21. Beck & Herre/SCHINDLER.

22. Beck & Herre/CRAMER (a preliminary report, kindly supplied to me by the late Harry Goldschmidt).

23. Cf. Newman/SCHINDLER 414–22.

24. Cf., respectively, Schlesinger/CRAMER, Platen/AUFFÜHRUNGSPRAXIS, Breuning/SCHWARZ-SPANIERHAUSE, Young/BEETHOVEN.

participant in an ensemble. Only a few very early and slight works are omitted (such as two little rondos composed about 1783, WoO 48 and 49).[25]

The works referred to and illustrated most in this book are naturally those that (1) raise the most questions about Beethoven's performance intentions, (2) reveal the most about those intentions, and (3) have survived with the richest assortment of sources. Because the solo sonatas are the most widely played of his piano works—perhaps of all his works—because they are the best known, the most taught and played, the most published, the most written about, and, by popular consensus, among the greatest of all his works, the reader will hardly be surprised to find them referred to and illustrated more than any others. But some purists searching for authenticity here may be surprised to find the most familiar of these works referred to at times by their popular titles (such as "Moonlight" Sonata), even when these titles did not originate with Beethoven. As the charts indicate, Beethoven himself gave very few titles to his instrumental works. In my experience, no harm is done by using the acquired titles when so identified (see Ch. 9), whereas some convenience is gained in ready reference.

In general, we learn more from Beethoven's later than his earlier scores, for two main reasons. First, more primary sources, especially the manuscripts, have survived for the later works, including both the scores and some documents about them. Thus, at least sixteen such sources, not including sketches or unauthorized early editions, are known for his last piano sonata, Op. 111.[26] And second, which is more important, Beethoven inserted fuller and more varied editorial indications into his later works, among them his only metronome markings in any of his piano works—that is, those in each movement of his "Hammerklavier" Sonata in B♭, Op. 106.

For similar reasons, we tend to learn more from those of Beethoven's works that have always enjoyed the most popularity—among the solo sonatas, the *Pathétique*, Op. 13, the "Moonlight," Op. 27/2, the "Tempest," Op. 31/2, and the "Appassionata," Op. 57; among the ensemble works, two duos, the "Spring" Sonata, Op. 24 and the "Kreutzer" Sonata, Op. 47, and two trios, the "Ghost," Op. 70/2 and the "Archduke," Op. 97. These works have received the most attention, including the most performances, and the most comments by Beethoven's contemporaries.

---

25. WoO refers to a "work without opus number" as listed in Kinsky & Halm/BEETHOVEN and Dorfmüller/BEETHOVEN.

26. Timbrell/NOTES 204–205 lists 15, of which 2 are currently missing ("N" and "O"); on p. 213, fn. 31, he mentions a sixteenth source, yet to be made available.

The Sources of Information for This Book

The primary sources of information for this book have been, of course, Beethoven's own manuscripts of his music, or the copies and early publications of it that he supervised, plus whatever annotations and editorial markings he added later. The accessibility of the early editions and the extant manuscript sources, including published facsimiles, is discussed in our next chapter. As of spring 1987, the new BEETHOVEN WERKEm, which started to appear in 1959 from the Beethoven-Haus in Bonn, has grown to twenty of some thirty-five projected volumes, although only the volume with the first three piano concertos (III/2/I) contains its *Kritischer Bericht* thus far. Among the chief solo and ensemble piano works yet to appear in this new collected edition are the solo sonatas from Op. 78 to Op. 111, the fourth and fifth concertos, and all six piano trios in Opp. 1, 70, and 97. This edition is superseding the 19th-century BEETHOVEN GESAMTAUSGABEm and its 20th-century BEETHOVEN SUPPLEMENTEm, though the latter is still in progress.

Other sources include numerous statements made by Beethoven himself, especially in his letters to publishers and associates, in his annotations to his sketches, and in the infrequent written responses he entered into the Conversation Books. Since 1961 the fullest collection of the letters has been the English translation of them in three volumes by Emily Anderson. A new, still more complete, much needed collection in the original language, including more recent letters to Beethoven that have been found, is now underway at the Beethoven-Haus in Bonn.[27] A complete edition of the Conversation Books, edited by Karl-Heinz Köhler and others at the Staatsbibliothek in East Berlin, has now reached its eighth of ten or eleven projected volumes.[28] By the time its seventh volume had appeared (1977), the false entries by Schindler mentioned above had been discovered and were listed on an insert.

Next to these sources in importance and reliability are the comments written by associates in Beethoven's professional circles, other contemporary observers, and the close friends whom we met above. Although partial, somewhat haphazard collections of these comments have appeared in the past,[29] a complete documentary collection for Beethoven on a par with the collections already done for Bach, Haydn, Mozart, and Schubert has yet to get underway.

There are many modern, secondary sources that bear on this study

27. Cf. Anderson/BEETHOVEN; Alan Tyson in BEETHOVEN STUDIES II 1–19.

28. KONVERSATIONSHEFTE.

29. E.g., Kalischer/ZEITGENOSSEN, Kerst/BEETHOVEN, and Landon/BEETHOVEN.

(as the Bibliography at the end should reveal). Besides the collected editions already mentioned, there are the bibliographies of Beethoven's music, headed by the thematic index Kinsky & Halm/BEETHOVEN and the supplementary material in Dorfmüller/BEETHOVEN, the many biographies, of which Thayer & Riemann/BEETHOVEN and Thayer & Forbes/BEETHOVEN still dominate the field, although certain more recent biographies, among them Solomon/BEETHOVEN (1977), have enriched our understanding significantly. Unfortunately, a complete, organized, and up-to-date bibliography of the immense literature on all aspects of Beethoven and his music is still lacking. The documentary collection and the bibliography of writings on Beethoven remain two of the most conspicuous lacunae in the Beethoven literature.

The Bibliography of studies on Beethoven performance and of related publications at the back of this book is intended to be as current and complete as practical.

Prior to this book, no encompassing inquiry had been made into Beethoven's performance intentions. Closest to this goal with respect to the piano music are four quite different books. The first is Franz Kullak's little book, mainly on Beethoven's piano playing, tempos, articulation, and realization of trills, published originally as a preface to the 1881 Steingräber edition of Beethoven's five piano concertos; the second is a collection of 1966 containing three essays by Herbert Grundmann and Paul Mies, on Beethoven's pedalling, on his (and Mozart's) legato, and on his original fingering; the third is my introduction of 1971, which samples eight main kinds of performance problems in Beethoven's piano sonatas; and the fourth is a dissertation revised and published in 1972 by the excellent fortepianist Kenneth Drake.[30]

Finally, in this brief survey of sources of information for this book we must not overlook meaningful analyses of the music itself! After the composer's own markings and annotations have been examined and after the modern studies that evaluate these have been digested, there still will be much about the interpretation that only a resourceful analysis of the music will divulge (if anything will). Melodic, harmonic, textural, dynamic, syntactic, and structural analysis—each in its turn or all together can provide clues to Beethoven's interpretive intentions. But another kind of analytic tool often provides even surer clues, and that is the application of analogy. Many times in this book a reasonable solution to an interpretive problem will be proposed by establishing an analogy between it and a similar problem that Beethoven edited or wrote out more clearly elsewhere. Note,

30. Kullak/BEETHOVEN; Grundmann & Mies; Newman/PERFORMANCE; Drake/BEETHOVEN.

however, that logical relationships were not always Beethoven's way. He was quite capable of unexpected gestures—of surprise, whimsicality, startling contrasts—any of which might disappoint the expected analogy.

Some Relevant Philosophies and Perspectives

Historically speaking, performance practices have always been in a state of flux. In my opinion they were even more so in Beethoven's than in Bach's time. In that sense the performance questions in Beethoven's keyboard music have proved to be more problematic than those in J. S. Bach's. The difference reflects the greater participation, if not leadership, of Beethoven in the changing compositional styles of his time as against Bach's relative aloofness from those of his time.

Beethoven flourished right in the thick of the transition from light, five-octave forte pianos to heavier, wider-ranged instruments; from relatively few, standardized, somewhat circumscribed tempos to more numerous, more individualized, and more pliable tempos; from limited, somewhat unsystematized styles of articulation to more varied and meticulous styles; from less to more subtly organized ideas and syntax; from the priority of harmonic to that of melodic considerations in the realization of ornaments; from detached to legato as the "normal" touch; from less to more use of graduated dynamics; from no use to considerable use of pedals for sustaining tones, changing timbres, and influencing intensity; and from fewer to more extensive technical resources. In all these respects the interpretation of Bach's kind of keyboard music remained fairly stable (or unaffected) during his lifetime, whereas that of Beethoven clearly shared in those several changing styles of performance. It is no wonder that inquiring performers frequently must pause to ask what point in the transition Beethoven may have reached in any one instance.

Studies of performance practices in past music have matured considerably since Arnold Dolmetsch and a few others led the way early in this century. Not only have they fanned out both latitudinally and longitudinally from their original focus on J. S. Bach's music and on western European music of the 17th and early 18th centuries in general, but increasingly they have raised searching questions about the aesthetic purposes and values of such studies.[31] Here it seems sufficient simply to review some of these questions—especially those embodying certain qualifications and reservations—and to defer more specific reflections on them until later chapters.

31. E.g., cf. "New Thinking on Early Interpretation," pp. 27–83, that largely accounts for "new version" added to the title page of Donington/INTERPRETATION; also, the still more recent discussion, Taruskin et al./AUTHENTICITY.

An initial question concerns one's very reason for interpreting. Remembering Ravel's stern injunction, "Don't interpret my music!" (meaning: Leave it to my explicit notation.), we might well ask, why *do* we interpret a composer's music? My answer is still much like one I wrote nearly four decades ago (and as others surely must have written before then): We interpret to achieve a "meaningful projection of the [music's] total form."[32] But that answer does not wholly explain why we try to recapture the detailed practices and styles of another age—the choices between starting notes in a trill, or legato and nonlegato in a passage, or rolled and solid chords at a cadence. To that question my answer is that we strive to approximate the composers' intentions as an act of truth and fidelity. We assume they understood what they and their contemporaries wanted, we respect and prefer their judgment, and we acknowledge their right to set their own ground rules.

Whenever we find that we actually can determine Beethoven's intentions for the performance of his music in a particular passage, we next must face up to a central question that generates nearly all further questions: How literally do we want to carry out those intentions? Thus, should we be performing on the pianos of Beethoven's time because he had nothing better to use, or on some further developed piano that he seems to have had in mind as an ideal? (See Ch. 3.) Do we want to follow the exact metronome markings he provided for all four movements of his "Hammerklavier" Sonata, or markings that seem to allow more realistically for the physiological and aural contact with the instrument that Beethoven had lost by the time he wrote that work? (See Ch. 4.) Do we want to observe those slurs in the "Adagio" of the *Sonate pathétique* that today seem to start and stop illogically, or to substitute slurs that seem to implement the music's internal logic? (See Ch. 5.)

Deciding how literal we want to be depends on two closely related considerations. One of them is the viability of a performance solution. Is it practical? Is it effective? Most important, is it convincing as musical art? Beethoven treated his music as an art far more than as a science. But he was a practical artist, not a visionary. We can assume, then, that however the performer resolves a performance question, the resolution has to make musical sense to that performer. In other words, before a valid performance can occur there must be not only an ability to carry it out, but a sympathetic insight into the music itself. To state the point more emphatically, while the performance needs to occur in full cognizance of Beethoven's intentions, it can be a valid performance only to the extent that those intentions can be realized musically.

A corollary of that consideration is an argument advanced increas-

32. Newman/PROBLEMS 192.

ingly in recent years that unedited *Urtexts* (when such exist) are not likely to suffice for intelligent interpretations by most performers. All too often they still require decisions, choices, and even independent research that demand too much of the performer before the performing itself can begin.[33]

The other consideration affecting how literal we want to be is the historical timeliness of a solution. Tastes change from one era to the next.[34] Whatever the performer's resolution of a performance question from an earlier era, it still has to be reconciled with current tastes. This second consideration is more likely to be problematic for conscientious scholar/performers. Yet timeliness is part of any solution that is artistically convincing. It poses the chief problems when the image of tone quality or the limits of rhythmic freedom have changed radically from one era to the next. For instance, performers of today find it very hard to accept the extreme *rubato* in recordings that hark back to late 19th-century performance. To be sure, current tastes can be re-educated to allow for past tastes, but only within limits. On the other hand, in the foregoing observations should lie some justification for respecting a consensus of today's most widely respected performers as revealed by a comparison of their recordings. If many current recordings of the Beethoven piano works, especially the sonatas, only infrequently suggest research into "authentic" performance, they much more frequently suggest the essential skills and musicianship without which no music can become alive.[35]

All of which is to acknowledge frankly that at best primary, hard evidence can go only so far toward resolving the performance questions raised in this book. At that point the cultural context—the personal experience, exposure, aesthetic predilections, and even conjectural factors that add up to taste—must be recognized.[36] It takes that cultural context to fill out, qualify, and humanize each performance. It is no wonder that those most concerned with performance practices in past music have begun to shy away from the term "authentic," preferring a gentler term like "historically aware."

33. E.g., cf. James A. Brokaw in a review of new Bach keyboard editions, in NOTES XLII (1985–86) 392–95.

34. Friege/INTERPRETATIONS, a 1970 dissertation from East Germany, is a detailed, richly documented report of the changing performance of Beethoven's sonatas since his death.

35. Among studies of Beethoven recordings done with an eye to authenticity, cf. Braun/RECORDED; Goldstein/OP. 111.

36. Cf. Tomlinson/CULTURE.

CHAPTER *2*

SOURCE MANUSCRIPTS AND EDITIONS

Sketches and Autographs

EETHOVEN'S SKETCHES—their "history, reconstruction, inventory," and interpretation—have occasioned some of the most active Beethoven research since World War II.[1] Although the resulting studies have raised philosophical questions as to their ultimate value,[2] they do continue to derive useful analytic, interpretive, dating, and biographic information from the sketches. Yet, so far they have turned up but few clues to Beethoven's performance intentions, least of all as regards his piano music.[3]

The studies have not yielded more mainly because Beethoven ordinarily waited until his sketches had been converted into or replaced by

1. The quoted words comprise the subtitle of the comprehensive new reference work, BEETHOVEN SKETCHBOOKS, by Douglas Johnson (ed.), Alan Tyson, and Robert Winter. Gustav Nottebohm was the chief 19th-century pioneer in the study of the sketches, as in Nottebohm/BEETHOVENIANA and especially Nottebohm/ZWEITE. The relationships between Beethoven's manuscripts and printed editions are explored in Unverricht/EIGENSCHRIFTEN. At this point the reader will value reading the two chapters in Tyson/SKETCHES, which describe main stages in Beethoven's progress from sketches to publications.

2. E.g., cf. Johnson/SKETCHES; Kerman/CONTEMPLATING 136–41.

3. Some details of performance intentions were brought to light in 1937 in Prod'homme/BEETHOVEN, which cites and quotes many sketches for the solo piano sonatas. Further details occur in KAFKA SKETCHBOOK and Johnson/FISCHHOFm, which are studies and transcriptions of sketches for Beethoven's early piano music; and in, among other studies, Kramer/SKETCHES for the 3 Violin Sonatas Op. 30 (a Ph.D. diss. that includes "history, transcription, and analysis"), Lockwood/OP. 69 (a pathbreaking study and transcription of the first movement of Op. 69 in a prime source that is almost as much sketch as final autograph), Brandenburg/OP. 96, Meredith/OPUS 109 (including a list in vol. 1, pp. 3–4, of dissertations not yet completed in 1985 that are planned to explore other Beethoven piano sketches), and Drabkin/OP. 111.

final autographs—that is, until the notation was completed—before inserting articulation, expression, and other performance markings. Furthermore, his sketches are generally too fragmentary to present problems of performance practices. By way of infrequent exceptions, one finds tentative clues to his intentions regarding (1) tempo, as in some annotations and altered time signatures; (2) rhythmic groupings and articulation, as in some irregular, overlapping beams. Thus, in a section from an early, unfinished composition in D/d, Beethoven inserted the time signature $\frac{3}{4}$, but added "$\frac{3}{8}$ time is better here"; and in a sketch for the Sonata Op. 49/1, he used beams across (as well as during) the beats in measures 5 and 6 of the first movement, thus confirming the rhythmic groupings and slurs that are to be found in the subsequent, original edition.[4]

4. As in KAFKA SKETCHBOOK II 119 and 60.

Example 2/1   Sonata Op. 106/i: (a) mm. 223–28 (after the original Artaria edition); (b) mm. 225–28 (expanded) in an extant sketch (after Nottebohm/ZWEITE 126)

More frequent are the sketches that help corroborate or refute textual details that have proven to be uncertain and controversial in subsequent sources (granted that textual accuracy is only a prerequisite for performance practice). Much the best known examples are the two debatable sketches (one now lost) that have been used to argue for A♮ rather than A♯ in the first movement, measures 224–26, of Beethoven's "Hammerklavier" Sonata, Op. 106 (Ex. 2/1). Adding recently to what has become a sizable literature on that detail, Paul Badura-Skoda argues compellingly for A♮, finding support not only in the sketches, but in the notation, harmony, and structure, as well as in several analogies.[5]

Fewer final or near-final autographs by Beethoven have survived than sketches. Of those that have, most are of middle and of later works. None of the 13 solo sonata autographs are extant through Op. 22; 13 have survived, including only the first movement of Op. 81a, from the succeeding 19 sonatas.[6] In all, autographs are known to be extant for about 48 (or 44 per cent) of the approximately 110 compositions listed in the Appendix. Among them, a few are still owned privately, thus being out of public reach. Among the others, only 14 have been made available in published facsimiles and only half of those facsimiles were still in print as of early 1987. There is always the remote possibility that one or more of the missing autographs will still turn up. What important resolutions of performance questions might come to light, for example, if the lost autograph of that "Hammerklavier" Sonata Op. 106 ever turns up![7]

A number of the autographs are known or thought to have served as fair copies (*Stichvorlage*) for the engraver, including Opp. 28, 31, 33–35, 53, 54, and 57.[8] Alternatively, as the composer became more widely known, several *überprüfte Abschriften* served this purpose. These were manuscript copies prepared professionally from the autographs and proofread more or less closely by the composer. They often include comments, corrections, or clarifications by him that bear on performance questions.[9]

5. Badura-Skoda/OP. 106, with listings of previous literature and numerous examples. Cf., also, Newman/PERFORMANCE 23–24.

6. Cf. Tyson/SKETCHES 467–68. Tyson speculates that Beethoven tended to lose track of his earlier autographs by letting them serve as engravers' fair copies, since his earlier publishers lived mostly in Vienna where he could refer back to his autographs as necessary; but that as he began to deal more with foreign publishers he preferred to send copies away and keep his autographs at hand.

7. Op. 106 had to be left out of the planned study of Beethoven's last 5 sonatas, Schenker/LETZTEN, because its autograph was missing, although Schenker believed it still existed; cf. Kinsky & Halm/BEETHOVEN 292. One of Schindler's forged entries, in KONVERSATIONSHEFTE I 312, mentions tantalizingly what actually may have been the autograph of Op. 106; cf. Stadlen/FORGERIES 550.

8. Cf. Tyson/SKETCHES 467–68.

9. Cf. Tyson/SKETCHES 469–73.

When Beethoven's final autograph and a supervised manuscript copy of the same work are both extant, a comparison is likely to reveal advantages and disadvantages in each. On one hand, the autograph will convey a sense of authenticity, a ring of truth, especially in what has been called the psychological aspect of Beethoven's notation. Also, it may contain essential performance annotations, such as those on pedalling at the start and trilling at the end of the "Waldstein" Sonata autograph (Op. 53). And it may be the court of last resort for any disputed places in the text, if these were not revised in a later source, or if they were not simply careless errors,[10] or if his notation had not become illegible through haste or revisions. On the other hand, the supervised copy certainly will reveal clearer, cleaner notation and very likely some minor corrections if not revisions of the text, including some changed or new performance markings. But the copy also could well reveal new errors that crept in during the copying itself.

Textual comparisons that are made between these sources bring out differences that are typically fussy, as shown by two minutiae in the first movement of Beethoven's Sonata Op. 111. In the so-called Bonn autograph,[11] at measure 8, "sempre *pp* " appears, almost too faintly to be read, but in Wenzel Rampl's supervised copy of that autograph this essential inscription is missing and Beethoven failed to discover its absence;[12] in measure 95, at a scratched-out passage in the Bonn autograph, no portamento slur appears over the four right-hand notes analogous to that in measure 23, but Beethoven did insert it in Rampl's copy, though only over the last three notes.[13]

When one compares the notation of the great masters, its psychological nature in Beethoven's autographs seems exceptional. Sometimes that trait is attributed to his composition methods and to his isolation and introversion intensified by deafness.[14] The trait is largely absent, for example, in the autographs of Bach, Haydn, Mozart, and Schubert, individual and readily recognizable as these are. In effect, Beethoven not only recorded but experienced his music as he wrote it down. Thus, often when his phrases and subphrases swell and diminish, his notation slants forward and straightens up again, as on the opening page of the "Appassionata" Sonata Op. 57 (Ex. 2/2). When the tempo presses forward, so does the notation, as near the end of the first movement from Op. 111 in

10. Beethoven admitted making errors, but especially when he had to copy or proofread his own music (e.g., Anderson/BEETHOVEN I 234–35; II 919).

11. Schmidt/BEETHOVENHANDSCHRIFTEN no. 565.

12. Cf. Timbrell/OP. 111 19–20 and 72.

13. Cf. Timbrell/OP. 111 169.

14. Cf. Mies/TEXTKRITISCHE 28–31.

EXAMPLE 2/2 Sonata Op. 57/i/9–10 (after the autograph BEETHOVEN OP. 57m)

the "Berlin autograph" (Ex. 2/3); when the tempo holds back, again so does the notation, as at the "poco adagio" near the end of the "Poco Allegretto" finale from the Sonata for Piano and Violin Op. 96.[15] When the staccatos grow crisper and brighter, the dots tend to change gradually to strokes (as illustrated later, in Ex. 5/5, from Sonata Op. 26/i; see p. 127).

Sometimes the psychological nature manifests itself in the ingenuity of the notation, to be found in the early printed as well as the autograph sources. Thus, in the slow movement of the "Hammerklavier" Sonata Op. 106—referring to the original edition, since both its autograph and fair copies are missing—one can find pairs of tied sixteenth notes in place of single eighth notes that appear elsewhere, presumably to convey the "poco a poco" graduation of the "cresc." inscribed underneath (as at

15. BEETHOVEN OP. 96m, mm. 276–79.

EXAMPLE 2/3 Sonata Op. 111/i/144–46 (after the "Berlin autograph")

EXAMPLE 2/4   Sonata Op. 106/iii/36–38 (after the original Artaria edition)

mm. 36–38, Ex. 2/4).[16] The majority of these intriguing psychological indications are not transferable to the printed editions, yet may be the performer's only clues to particular interpretations.

As for the legibility of Beethoven's autographs, the first thing to say is that the notation frequently looks more indecipherable than it proves to be after moderate exposure to it. Even the conspicuous blotch throughout the autograph of the "Appassionata" Sonata Op. 57, reportedly caused by a soaking rain,[17] does not actually obliterate any notes beyond recall. In any case, the legibility varies from extensive crossing-out, obscurity of haste, and faintness of erosion, such as obtain in much of the Piano and Cello Sonata Op. 69 and the Piano Sonata Op. 110, to relative clarity, as in the Bagatelles for Piano Op. 33 and the Piano Sonata Op. 90. At the end of the "Waldstein" Sonata autograph, where Beethoven combines both notation and annotation to show how to play the finale's so-called Beethoven trills, we get an average, not exceptional, picture of the legibility problem (Ex. 2/5; cf. the transcription of this quotation in Ex. 7/44, p. 215).

In more than one letter Beethoven acknowledged that his handwriting, whether of music or words, was not easy to read.[18] Yet, in more than one letter he also asserted that his manuscripts were the most reliable sources for his music, and throughout his career he variously beseeched, cajoled, and berated his copyists and publishers in order to get more accurate results from them. Thus, protesting "a good plateful of misprints" in the original edition of his Sonata for Piano and Cello Op. 69, he added that in his experience, "the most correct engravings have been

16. Cf. Platen/NOTIERUNGSPROBLEM. A further reference to this passage appears in Chapter 8.

17. Cf. Thayer & Forbes/BEETHOVEN 407.

18. E.g., his letter of July 6, 1821, to the Berlin publisher Adolf Martin Schlesinger (Anderson/BEETHOVEN II 919; cf., also, II 926 and III 1319).

EXAMPLE 2/5 Sonata Op. 53, final page of autograph BEETHOVEN OP. 53m

made of those compositions of mine which were written out in my own handwriting."[19]

Early Editions

By early editions of Beethoven's music we mean editions published during his lifetime. An original edition refers to the first edition of a work published with his concurrence. A re-impression or a reprinting of an edition employs the same plates, but sometimes with minor changes, if only in the title page. But a different or new edition involves a fresh engraving of plates, unless the publisher simply re-used an earlier set of plates. In studies concerned primarily with bibliographic and textual distinctions these terms have been further refined and redefined,[20] but such further refinements do not come up in the present study of performance problems.

Closest to a full bibliography of Beethoven's early editions and reprints is Kinsky & Halm/BEETHOVEN, with its supplement in Dorfmüller/BEETHOVEN. About twenty percent of these sources are collected in Bonn's important Beethoven-Archiv, more than can be found in any other Beethoven library.[21] There are between two and ten early editions of each of Beethoven's solo piano works. An edition usually included whatever compositions were assigned to one opus number (e.g., the three sonatas under Op. 10). But collections of several opus numbers in one category rarely appeared during Beethoven's lifetime. When they did appear, they did so not in one volume but in a consecutive series of individual works with a common title page.[22]

In our dependence here on the most authentic score, our primary concern with regard to editions is to determine which ones actually benefitted from Beethoven's own supervision—that is, from his own proofreading and comments inserted in some preliminary copy, or from a separate list of corrections.[23] But to determine that supervision is more

19. Letter of July 26, 1809 (Anderson/BEETHOVEN I 234; cf., also, p. 246; Solomon/TAGEBUCH 228).

20. Cf. Kinsky & Halm/BEETHOVEN xvii and Unverricht/EIGENSCHRIFTEN 9–13.

21. My own library of them, which is going to the Ira F. Brilliant Center for Beethoven Studies in San Jose, California, is nearly complete as regards the solo piano sonatas, but is limited to photographic copies (made from the publications themselves in numerous public and private Beethoven collections in Europe and this country).

22. Cf. Newman/CHECKLIST.

23. This immediate discussion derives partly from Newman/AUTHORITATIVE.

readily proposed than achieved. Only infrequently does hard evidence exist. One or more of three procedures may help. First, if a work like Kinsky & Halm/BEETHOVEN fails to list any such proofs or correction sheets, then perhaps Beethoven's correspondence, Conversation Books, or other documents may bring to light at least his disavowal of a particular publisher (as of Karl Zulehner in Mainz in 1803[24]) or his endorsement of another (as of Breitkopf & Härtel in Leipzig in 1810.[25]) But one has to be wary of such disavowals and endorsements, especially the latter,[26] which seem to have more often masked a desire for the most advantageous business deal with the publisher than a genuine satisfaction with the quality of his publications.

The second procedure for determining Beethoven's possible hand in a particular edition is to compare that edition with whatever firsthand or supervised source preceded it most closely.[27] This procedure assumes that such a source is known and accessible, and that the chronological sequence (if not lineage ["filiation" or "stemma"]) of the works's manuscripts and editions has been determined. If an intelligible departure from the source turns up in the edition in question, then that departure could well have been superintended by Beethoven himself. For publishers during his lifetime rarely qualified, intended, or would have presumed on their own to edit a master's music in the sense of "improving" or expurgating it. They were still a far cry from the editors of the later 19th or early 20th centuries! Hence, as regards performance problems, Beethoven's publishers seldom either resolved or altered his indications knowingly. When they made unauthorized changes, they ordinarily made the inadvertent kind—that is, the errors that brought forth many heated responses from Beethoven, including his well-known opening in a letter of 1811 to that same Breitkopf & Härtel, "Mistakes—mistakes—you yourself are a unique mistake—"[28]

An oft-cited but rare exception to unofficious publishing in Beethoven's day was the four-measure subphrase that the Zürich publisher Nägeli seems to have added deliberately to his original edition of the Sonata Op. 31/1 (between measures 298 and 299 of the first movement). The autograph is now lost that he used as his fair copy, but he evidently could not resist changing the previous subphrase into a square eight-measure phrase.

24. AMZ VI (1803), Intelligenz-Blatt III; cf., also, Tyson/SKETCHES 481 fn. 2.

25. Anderson/BEETHOVEN I 284.

26. Cf., also, Anderson/BEETHOVEN II 526, 891, and 963.

27. Two studies based on this procedure are Tyson/ENGLISH and Leicher-Olbrich/ORIGINALAUSGABEN.

28. Anderson/BEETHOVEN I 320.

EXAMPLE 2/6 Sonata Op. 31/1/i: (a) mm. 296–303 in Simrock's corrected version; (b) mm. 296–306 with Nägeli's insertion

a. (Allegro vivace)

b.

Beethoven's rage over this editorial affront and the publisher Simrock's rectification in an "Editiou [!] tres [!] Correcte" are reported by Ries.(Ex. 2/6).[29]

Autograph versus Original Edition?

When that second procedure involves the comparison of an early edition and an autograph it raises a much discussed question as to which is ordinarily the more reliable source.[30] From Schindler to Otto Jahn, Otto

29. Cf. WEGELER & RIES 88–90.

30. For an excellent summary of both sides of this question, cf. Unverricht/EIGENSCHRIFT-EN 14–27.

Erich Deutsch, Max Friedländer, and Joseph Schmidt-Görg, one whole group of writers on Beethoven has favored the original edition, while still others—notably Schenker, Mies, and Unverricht in this century—prefer the autograph. But, considering the advantages and disadvantages already mentioned in comparing supervised copies with autographs, the recent consensus has been that neither the autograph nor the original edition is a consistently better source. Instead, for each work being questioned, each source—in fact, each textual question—must be weighed in its own right.

Thus, one textual consideration that favors an original edition rather than its autograph source occurs during the initial inscription in "Bagatelle" No. 6 from Op. 33. In the Viennese edition of 1803, this inscription reads, "Allegretto quasi Andante/Con una certa espressione parlante," whereas in the autograph it lacks its important qualifier, "quasi Andante."[31] A more frequently cited consideration (even though the manuscript source has disappeared) occurs in the slow movement of the Sonata Op. 106. It is the additional measure that Beethoven asked Ries to insert at the start, while Ries was shepherding the first English edition of Op. 106 through the press.[32] As Ries wrote later,

> Was my dear old teacher actually going off his balance? . . . To add [merely] two notes to such a huge, thoroughly realized work, already finished a half year ago!! But how my astonishment grew at the effect of these two notes . . . . I advise every art lover to try the beginning of this Adagio first without and then with these two notes that henceforth comprise the first measure and without doubt he will share my reaction.[33]

(Of course, these two notes also further the thematic relationships between movements, as discussed in Chapter 9 and illustrated in Ex. 9/12, p. 272.)

Conversely, an instance of a detail in an autograph that certainly surpasses its counterpart in the original edition—according to Beethoven himself, since the autograph is no longer extant—is that subphrase in the Sonata Op. 31/1 that Nägeli presumptuously expanded into a square phrase (as quoted in Ex. 2/6, above).

However, in the thick of this much concern about textual, especially editorial, authenticity, there needs to be interjected one of those acknowledgments that haunt performance-practice studies. In the coming chapters (especially near the end of Chapter 6), several of his contemporaries are cited to the effect that Beethoven was capable of belying his own repeated concern for textual authenticity. Evidently he did more or less

31. Tyson/english 42.

32. Letter of April 16, 1819 (Anderson/beethoven II 806).

33. Wegeler & Ries/beethoven 107–108.

in some of his playing than he notated or edited in his scores; or he even changed what he edited, from one performance to another. Of course, who would have more right to change Beethoven than Beethoven? His liberties with his own music can hardly justify the liberties of a Nägeli or of later editors and performers!

Trends in Editing Beethoven Since Beethoven

On several occasions during his later years (starting perhaps as early as 1803) Beethoven and one or another of his publishers projected what were to be complete, ideal editions of his works.[34] None of these editions materialized while Beethoven was still alive. Closest in time, size, and ideals was the partial edition of Tobias Haslinger in Vienna, which began with thirty of the solo piano sonatas during the first four years after Beethoven died.[35] Up to about 1860 the editions of Beethoven's piano music that did appear continued to introduce little if any editing in the later sense of amplification and interpretation. Except for Czerny and Moscheles, two who could claim firsthand exposure to Beethoven's own interpretations and instructions, editors were almost never named in those editions. And when either man did get named it was mainly because the edition was "metronomisée et doigtée" by one or the other.[36]

From about 1860, when a precipitate blossoming of Beethoven editions began, editors began to figure conspicuously—indeed, sometimes so conspicuously that the editor almost seemed to overshadow the composer. It became a point of honor for every celebrated performer or teacher to have edited his own "neue revidierte Ausgabe" and for every publisher to be able to display his own such edition in his catalog (as one tired reviewer already lamented in 1870).[37] Two main types of editor can be distinguished, although the types were not mutually exclusive.[38] One was the interpreter-pedagogue, the other the theorist-analyst. The interpreter-pedagogue is most familiar in the widely printed edition of Lebert and (especially) Bülow (from 1871),[39] with its copious verbal imagery, its

34. Deutsch/AUSGABE remains a main study of these projects; cf., also, Thayer & Forbes/ BEETHOVEN 339, 499, 659, 692, and 763. This section derives in part from Newman/ CHECKLIST.

35. Cf. Newman/CHECKLIST 510.

36. For further on Moscheles' edition cf. Tyson/MOSCHELES.

37. AMZ, 2d series, V (1870) 292–93.

38. Cf. Mies/TEXTKRITISCHE 9–12.

39. Cf. Newman/CHECKLIST 516.

often unauthorized markings of all sorts, its textual "improvements," and its practical suggestions for performance, all of which largely reflected Liszt's teaching of Bülow.[40] The theorist-analyst is most familiar in the once scarcely less popular edition of Hugo Riemann (from 1886),[41] with its principles of *Vierhebigkeit* and other syntactic units, its systematized articulation signs, and its harmonic and tonal exegeses.

Such editing, as well as the less personal editing of men like Louis Köhler (from 1869), started, at best, with the original editions, although some such subtitle as "new, corrected edition" soon became the rule rather than the exception. More often the editing simply depended on the transmission of the text from one publisher, edition, or editor to the next, implemented if not complicated by shifts of personnel, divisions and mergings of firms, and the sales and exchanges of old plates. A rare, evidently unprecedented exception in which an effort was made to collate some of the manuscript and earliest printed sources was the edition of Theodor Steingräber (from 1878, under the pseudonym of Gustav Damm).[42]

Since the turn of this century the trend has been reversed, leading toward the most authentic text as determined by increasing reference to the primary manuscript and published sources. The editor's comments have gradually been reduced to the listing of alternative readings. Beginning in 1901 Schenker's editions, "nach den Autographen rekonstruiert," began to appear, culminating in 1913–1921 with his "kritische Ausgabe mit Einführung und Erläuterung" of each of the last five sonatas except Op. 106.[43] This edition not only preceded but went beyond several editions that appeared with notable success between World Wars I and II, among them those of Casella, Schnabel, and Tovey. However, in these last the interpretive advices did become more objective and historically grounded than those in the late 19th-century editions, the purely pedagogic advices tended to disappear, the emphasis on a best source for the text increased (leading to that false notion, if not worship, of "the one" Urtext), and editors tried more conscientiously to distinguish their markings from the composer's.

Today, the best editions of Beethoven's piano music as regards authenticity of text and inscriptions are, in my opinion, those published by G. Henle Verlag and the Universal Edition by Schenker as revised by

40. Cf. NEWMAN LISZT 203–206.

41. Cf. Newman/CHECKLIST 518.

42. Cf. Newman/CHECKLIST 516, 517.

43. Cf. Schenker/KLAVIERSONATENm, Schenker/LETZTEN; also, Newman/CHECKLIST 520.

Erwin Ratz.[44] Whether authenticity alone will continue to be the primary criterion for the editing of top-ranked editions depends on how greatly the need for further, sophisticated editorial help is felt in order to fill out, qualify, and humanize whatever text has survived from the composer.

44. E.g., Wallner/KLAVIERSONATENm, Schmidt/KLAVIERSONATENm (only through Op. 57 to date); Schenker/KLAVIERSONATENm.

CHAPTER 3

BEETHOVEN AND THE PIANO: HIS OPTIONS, PREFERENCES, PIANISM, AND PLAYING[1]

First, Some Conclusions

S
INCE WE ARE CONCENTRATING on the performance of Beethoven's piano music in this book, one of our first discussions must focus on his use of the piano. Four main questions arise: (1) Which pianos did he actually use and prefer? (2) How well did they satisfy his preferences regarding sound and action? (3) What traits most distinguish his writing for them (or his "pianism")? (4) What qualities characterized his own playing, especially while he still ranked as an outstanding pianist?

My answers, which become this chapter's principal conclusions, might well be at least partially anticipated:

1. Contrary to statements prevalent in the past, Beethoven started with a distinct preference for certain Viennese pianos and, especially through his lifelong association with the Stein and Streicher families, maintained that allegiance to the end of his life.

2. The three pianos chiefly identified with Beethoven today (the Érard, Broadwood, and Graf) have been highlighted well beyond their musical

1. Various portions of Chapter 3 have been revised and updated from four separate studies by me published since 1970—Newman/PIANOS, -/RANGE, -/PEDALS, and -/PIANISM—(listed in full in the Bibliography). Permission to draw from these portions has been granted, respectively, by the *Journal of the American Musicological Society*, the editors of the forthcoming "Seventieth Birthday Tribute for Gwynn McPeek," Indiana University Press, and the *Piano Quarterly*.

value to him, to the extent of obscuring quite different preferences that he himself revealed in one way or another.

3. Not surprisingly, in his piano writing Beethoven was both more enterprising and more challenging than any of the three other greatest masters of piano composition who were his near contemporaries in Vienna and London (Haydn, Mozart, and Schubert).

4. At his best Beethoven played with great technical facility, though revealing some impatience with the perfection of technical details; he often exhibited a certain excess of animal spirits; he excelled in legato playing; and he commanded special attention for the depth of his expressive playing, particularly in slow movements. With a true creator's tendency to live chiefly in the present, he did some of his most inspired playing in his extraordinary improvisations.

A Consensus on Differences between Pianos Then and Now

Remarkably few historically minded persons have had the opportunity to live with pianos of Beethoven's time. These few, mainly performers and instrument makers, seem to agree without exception that differences between past and modern pianos can profoundly affect the music played on them.

Josef Mertin, Austrian maker of keyboard instruments and writer on performance problems in early music, states:

> A quite special touch has to be cultivated on Classic [Viennese keyboard] instruments, along with a complete reorientation according to other norms and expressive ranges. To be sure, one cannot maintain here that familiar modern piano concepts are not applicable to Classic music; there remain scarcely enough historical grand pianos to admit of such a conclusion, and [modern] replicas of them are generally inadequate and unsatisfactory. But the use of the modern piano has to be related to historical performance practices. Insofar as structural phenomena, tempo problems, and the performance of a work are concerned, the historical circumstances have conclusive significance.[2]

Irena Poniatowska, Polish author of a dissertation on the interrelation of Beethoven's piano writing and the pianos of his time,[3] writes that

> the reproduction, or rather the approximation of the tonal make-up of Beethoven's piano music . . . creates many problems, since the tone of the present concert grand differs markedly from [that of] the "Hammerklavier" of Beetho-

2. Mertin/KLAVIERE 92. But Mertin's statement about "historical grand pianos" must be qualified by the surprising number of Beethoven's works now recorded on early pianos, as listed in Basart/FORTEPIANO 22–57.

3. Cf. DMf XXVI (1973) 518.

ven's time. The materials have changed out of which the strings are produced and the hammers are covered. The intensity and duration of the tone have increased . . . . At the same time the number and intensity of the overtones have decreased today. Thus, today the tone is more obscure, more thick, and as regards tone color more uniform in all registers than in the instruments of Beethoven's epoch. Only in the middle register at a soft [level] does the tone color of the modern piano not differ from [that of] Beethoven's instrument . . . .[4]

The German musicologist Konrad Sasse, concerned about adapting the tone on Beethoven's instruments to that on modern instruments, gets more specific:

Since the striking area is smaller and the hammer head with its leather surface is harder on the historical than on the present grand piano, one can assume from the laws of acoustics alone that the formant characteristics of the historical piano lie between those of the harpsichord and the modern piano. Hence, especially in the bass register of the pianos in Beethoven's time, the figuration and full chords sound much less thick, syruppy, and ringing than on modern instruments. It follows that on a modern piano one ought to consider a portato rather than a legato in bass passages and figuration, and at a faster tempo even a quasi staccato, which amounts to a distinction between the playing style of the right and left hands. The full-chord playing in the left hand compels a difference in the attack force of the single fingers, which affects not only the dynamics but also the formant structure.[5]

Finally, Malcom Bilson, outstanding American performer and specialist on early pianos, protests a common view that Beethoven's pianos were but "limited" anticipations of an ideal found only in today's pianos. He endeavors to describe the tonal advantages and aesthetic qualities that modern proponents of the early instruments find in cultivating those instruments to play Beethoven's music. And, he adds, today's "pianos have large felt hammers that strike heavy steel strings" under the "enormous tension[s] permitted by the cast-iron frame," producing "a tone that starts slowly, develops to great richness, and tapers off gradually with a rather slow decay." Because of cross-stringing (or over-stringing), the bass gains enormous power, "but becomes muddy and virtually useless for clear passage-work"; whereas Beethoven's pianos "were all straight-strung . . . and had leather-covered hammers, a wooden frame, and much lighter stringing. The result was a sharper attack, less development of the tone, and a much quicker decay."

One of several musical works from which Bilson draws his illustrations is the slow movement of the Piano Sonata Op. 110, as sampled in Ex. 3/1. Bilson says that Beethoven

4. Poniatowska/INTERPRETATION 565.

5. Sasse/KLANGES 559.

put the weight of the suffering [in the slow movement] (at the "Arioso dolente") in the heavy left-hand chords into which, on a piano of his day, the performer could lean . . . fully. On a modern piano, these chords are simply too heavy when played full out; one is forced to lighten them, thereby reducing them to much more of an accompaniment than Beethoven conceived them to be. Leaning into these chords (not with loudness, but with depth, much as one would lean into the rich pianissimo chord in the bass register of a modern piano in the *Cathédrale engloutie* of Debussy) lends to this Arioso a heaviness and a depth of meaning that cannot be approached on any modern piano due to the necessary disparity in weight between the two hands.[6]

To be sure, the return to early instruments has introduced physical problems with the instruments themselves that have clouded the aesthetic considerations and aroused differences of opinion. Do we come closer to the composer's own ideal by reconstructing the early instruments, with all their mechanical hazards, or by making replicas and substituting the more dependable materials that modern technology has discovered and developed? Perhaps, as Robert Winter suggests,

It may well be that the Romantic historical performance movement may be best served over the next several years by withdrawing from the public spotlight and working towards the re-creation of the old technologies and standards that the exquisite external craftsmanship of these instruments suggests applied to

6. Bilson/BEETHOVEN 18–21. It is still pertinent to read of a comparison between the sound of the Érard of Chopin's and Schumann's time, one generation later, and that of the modern Steinway, reported by William and Phillippa Kiraly in PQ No. 117 (Spring 1982) 44–45.

EXAMPLE 3/1 Sonata Op. 110/iii/8–10 (after Wallner/KLAVIERSONA-TENm II 300; HV*)

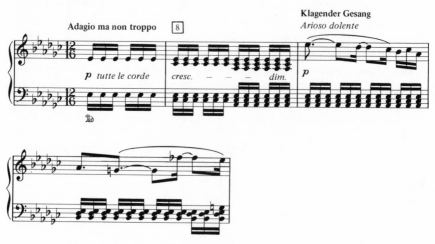

their sound as well. There will be continued debate over the virtues of restoring originals or producing replicas, though each kind of piano will clearly contribute lessons of its own. In either event the highest performance standards must finally begin to apply . . . .[7]

A Prevailing View About Beethoven's Preferences

If the instrument specialists seem to be unanimous about the main differences between the pianos of Beethoven's time and ours, there still is considerable confusion about which contemporary pianos Beethoven himself considered closest to his ideal. The confusion has been compounded by that preoccupation with the three Beethoven pianos that are still extant—the French Érard, now preserved in the Vienna Kunsthistoriches Museum; the English Broadwood in the Budapest National Museum; and the Austrian Graf in the Bonn Beethoven-Haus. Partly for the very reason that these are Beethoven's only known extant pianos (with the possible exception of the Vogel piano noted in the next section) and partly because they have received so much more attention than any other pianos identified with him, the emphasis on them has obscured quite different preferences that Beethoven did express.

Three samples may be quoted as typical of statements to be found in nearly every historical survey of piano music. In the first (1944) edition of the *Harvard Dictionary of Music*[8] we read that among the significant traits of the Broadwood piano are "a much heavier structure, allowing for a greater tension of the strings which thus become more sonorous; also the two pedals of the present pianoforte (patent from 1783); and an action, known as *English action*, which was much heavier than the Viennese action but also more expressive and dynamic. Small wonder that Beethoven much preferred his Broadwood to the Viennese instruments." In an article on the "Klavier" by Hanns Neupert,[9] we find, "Beethoven went over to the English system after he acquired a Broadwood piano in 1818, and, thanks to the growing predisposition to energetic playing, heavy tone production, and orchestral effects, this system eventually became universal, although the Vienna action still remained long in use in connection with such names as Ehrbar, Bösendorfer, etc." And in F. E. Kirby's *Short History of Keyboard Music*[10] we read, "It is noteworthy and characteristic that while Mozart praised the Stein piano for its lightness and delicacy

---

7. In Taruskin/AUTHENTICITY 25.

8. P. 576, but deleted for unstated reasons from the 2d (1969) and 3d (1986) eds.

9. MGG VII (1958) col. 1105.

10. New York, 1966, pp. 24–25.

..., Beethoven came to prefer the Broadwood piano, a much larger and more powerful instrument." That this view has continued to predominate is evident in several further publications, some still more recent.[11]

Beethoven's Pianos Summarized Chronologically

First, we need to assess the prevalent view that Beethoven shifted his allegiance from Austro-German to English pianos. An initial help is to review, chronologically insofar as possible, what pianos he is known actually to have used and sometimes owned. Although Beethoven may well have gotten his earliest keyboard experiences on the clavichord and harpsichord,[12] he encountered the fortepiano while he was still very young. His initial experiences with pianos paralleled Mozart's about a decade earlier, including the rejection of the Späth piano for the Stein, the visit to Johann Andreas Stein in Augsburg, and the eventual acquisition of a Walter piano. As early as 1783 he was reported as preferring the Stein to the Späth, and by 1788 (not 1787) he may have received a Stein from Count von Waldstein, there having been several such pianos at court in Bonn.[13] The Stein pianos that he tried in Augsburg in 1787 seem to have interested him as much as they did Mozart.[14]

We have only passing mentions of some pianos, among them a "pianoforte" on which he made monthly payments in 1792, whether for rent or purchase.[15] The next information comes in a letter of November 19, 1796, from Beethoven to Johann Andreas Streicher:

I received the day before yesterday your fortepiano, which is really an excellent instrument. Anyone else would try to keep it for himself; but I—now you must have a good laugh—I should be deceiving you if I didn't tell you that in my opinion it is far too good for me, and why?—Well, because it robs me of the freedom to produce my own tone. But, of course, this [criticism] must not deter you from making all your forte-pianos in the same way. For no doubt there are few people who cherish such whims as mine .... In regard to the sale of the fortepiano, I had conceived this idea long before you; and, moreover, I will cer-

11. Cf. Gábry/KLAVIER 381; Gill/PIANO 56 and 59 (the Broadwood being the only piano mentioned in connection with Beethoven).

12. Cf. Frimmel/KLAVIERSPIELER 219–22, but the evidence is only presumptive, especially the association of *Bebung* with Op. 110/iii, which is challenged in Ch. 10, below.

13. Schiedermair/BEETHOVEN 68, 88–89; Thayer & Riemann/BEETHOVEN I 234–35; MGG VII 1105 and XIV 148; Frimmel/KLAVIERSPIELER 219, 22.

14. Schiedermair/BEETHOVEN 187.

15. Thayer & Forbes/BEETHOVEN 135.

tainly endeavor to carry it out—With all my heart I thank you, dear St[reicher], for your kindness in being so obliging to me.[16]

Presumably the enigmatic joshing was intended as a compliment. We learn from this letter that Beethoven was borrowing another Stein piano, since Streicher, who had joined the firm of his late father-in-law, would not be developing the Stein piano under his own name until the son Matthäus Andreas Stein left the firm in 1802 to make pianos on his own. About 1801, when at age ten Czerny first played for Beethoven, he found a Walter piano in Beethoven's dwelling. Czerny called that Viennese instrument "the best [piano] at that time."[17] And in 1802 Beethoven wrote of "seeing myself compelled to display my art on Jakesch's piano,"[18] another Viennese make, which he may or may not have owned then. In a letter of November 23, 1803, to the publisher and dealer Breitkopf & Härtel in Leipzig, he endorsed two additional Viennese pianos, one made by "Herr Pohack" (or Bohack?) and the other by "Herr Moser."[19]

But it was already in 1803 that Beethoven was surprised, and his growing fame was recognized, by the unexpected gift of "un piano forme clavecin" from the celebrated Paris maker Sebastien Érard.[20] Although we shall see that Beethoven was unhappy with this instrument from the start, he evidently kept it with him until 1825, when he gave it to his brother in order to make room for the Graf piano.[21] By 1810 he was writing Streicher for another piano, presumably one built under Streicher's own name:

> You promised to let me have a piano by the end of October; and now we are already half through November and as yet I haven't received one—My motto is either to play on a good instrument or not at all—As for my French piano, which is certainly quite useless now, I still have misgivings about selling it, for it is really a souvenir such as no one here has so far honored me with . . . . All good wishes, if you send me a pianoforte; if not, then all bad wishes—[22]

16. Anderson/BEETHOVEN I 24.

17. Cf. Badura-Skoda/CZERNY 10.

18. Anderson/BEETHOVEN I 82–83.

19. Anderson/BEETHOVEN I 101; also, cf. Thayer & Riemann/BEETHOVEN II 336, 613, 622.

20. Thayer & Riemann/BEETHOVEN II 412–13; the Érard was not a gift from Lichnowsky, as had been reasoned in Frimmel/BEETHOVEN II 225.

21. Frimmel/KLAVIEREN 89.

22. Anderson/BEETHOVEN I 300. Supposedly the requested piano would replace a previous Streicher piano that had caused Beethoven to write earlier that year, "I do ask you to ensure that the instruments do not wear out so quickly—You have seen your instrument which I have here and you must admit that it is very worn out; and I frequently hear the same opinion expressed by other people—" (Anderson/BEETHOVEN I 271).

At least three more pianos seem to have come into and out of Beethoven's possession or use between 1814 and 1817. He received one made by S. A. Vogel from Pest in Hungary in 1814, then reportedly sold it the same year to another maker, Feiler. Beethoven is supposed to be seated at that Vogel in a miniature that is inadequately identified and described by Frimmel.[23] In 1982, the Smithsonian Institution in Washington acquired what was believed to be the Vogel in question, meaning—if the uncertainties can be resolved—that a fourth piano used by Beethoven may have survived![24] Then, there was the piano built by Wenzel Schanz about which he wrote in 1815, "I too possess one of his."[25] Haydn had admired the Schanz pianos above all others, but Beethoven reacted tersely, "*Schanz has sent me such a bad one that he soon will have to take it back again.*"[26] And there was a Kirschbaum piano recalled uncertainly by his little pupil Hirsch in 1817.[27]

Though hard evidence is lacking, it is sometimes assumed that Beethoven was first introduced to the Broadwood piano by Prince Louis Ferdinand during Beethoven's visit to Berlin in 1796.[28] At any rate, twenty-two years later—that is, by July 18, 1818—he received his own Broadwood, a second unsolicited gift of a piano (after the Érard) and a further sign of international recognition. Thomas Broadwood of the London firm, apparently inspired by a recent visit to Beethoven, had shipped the piano late in 1817. Beethoven's name was inscribed on a special plaque, followed by Broadwood's as donor and the names of several other prominent well-wishers then in London, including Kalkbrenner, Ries, and Cramer.[29] The honor and recognition indicated by the gift were made all the more conspicuous when the Austrian government took care of the duty before it finally found its circuitous way to Beethoven, after seven months in transit.[30] Beethoven had already conveyed his delight to Broadwood, writing in the faulty French he reserved for his English correspon-

---

23. Frimmel/BEETHOVEN I 22–23, II 233. Cf., also, Breuning/SCHWARZSPANIERHAUSE 90 fn.

24. Information kindly supplied by Mrs. Helen Hollis (then) of the music instrument collection at the Smithsonian Institution.

25. Anderson/BEETHOVEN II 505–6, 523.

26. Cf. Walter/HAYDN II (1969) 256–88; Anderson/BEETHOVEN II 507.

27. Frimmel/BEETHOVEN II 63.

28. Frimmel/BEETHOVEN II 225; Kalischer/ZEITGENOSSEN I 26–27.

29. Thayer & Riemann/BEETHOVEN IV 84–90; Gábry/KLAVIER 379–84; cf., also, Breuning/ SCHWARZSPANIERHAUSE 89–90.

30. Thayer & Riemann/BEETHOVEN IV 85–86; Anderson/BEETHOVEN II 754–55 and 763–64.

dents.[31] In the letter, he even promised to write one of his very next pieces for Broadwood.[32] In so doing, he was making but one of many such promises that he proved unable to keep. In any case, he could hardly have had either Op. 106 or its popular title in mind, as has been suggested.[33] Op. 106 was started well before Beethoven knew about the gift, completed largely if not entirely by the time the gift arrived, and intended evidently for Archduke Rudolph all along.[34] Moreover, the title "Hammerklavier" could not have been introduced in reference to the Broadwood, since it had already been used in reference to Op. 101, and then in letters of 1817 arguing, of course, not for the English but for the Germanic appropriateness of the term.[35]

By 1825 Beethoven acquired his last piano, or at least the lifetime loan of it. It was a Viennese Graf made to his requirements. Perhaps it was this instrument he alluded to in a letter of October 12 to his nephew Karl—"The chief thing is the pianoforte, for just now the weather is very fine and dry"—and presumably it was yet another piano he meant in the next sentence, "The Stein pianoforte can be attended to later."[36] Since Beethoven added that he would be paying for the Stein's repair later, it was probably in his keeping at the time. As for the Graf, further mention of that instrument will have to be qualified by Beethoven's almost total inability to hear it and by the imminent end of his composing for piano.[37]

In all, it has been possible here to identify fourteen of the pianos that Beethoven presumably owned or borrowed during his lifetime. There may well have been others. Eleven of these pianos came from Viennese piano makers, four being made by the Stein and Streicher families. Only the Vogel (from a Hungarian maker) and the two pianos honoring Beethoven from afar (the Érard and the Broadwood) came from makers outside of Vienna. Judging by remarks in Beethoven's letters, he actually may never have bought a piano, though he may have sold one or two pianos that came into his possession. Evidently it was no problem for him to persuade the piano makers to lend him their products, as one can tell from remarks in a number of his letters. Thus, in 1802 he wrote, " . . . the whole tribe of pianoforte manufacturers have been swarming around me in their anxiety to serve me . . . . Each of them wants to make me a pianoforte

31. Anderson/BEETHOVEN II 755–56.

32. Gábry/KLAVIER 382.

33. Gábry/KLAVIER 383.

34. Kinsky & Halm/BEETHOVEN 291–92.

35. Anderson/BEETHOVEN II 657, 660.

36. Anderson/BEETHOVEN III 1254–55.

37. For more on the Graf piano, cf. Wythe/GRAF, especially p. 458.

exactly as I should like it."[38] In 1810, in the letter quoted earlier asking Streicher to hasten the delivery of a piano, there is an implication that it was being borrowed when Beethoven added, "By the way, since my home is now in better order, your [instrument] will certainly suffer no damage."[39] In a letter of 1817 requesting Frau Nannette Streicher to have her husband make a piano "as loud as possible" for Beethoven's defective hearing, Beethoven wrote, "I have long been intending to buy one of your pianos, but at the moment that would be very difficult for me. Perhaps, however, it will be possible for me to do so later on. But until then I should like *to borrow* one of yours. Of course I don't want to do so without paying for it."[40] And as late as 1823 we find Matthäus Andreas Stein begging Beethoven to play once more in public, and on one of Stein's pianos instead of the one [?] Beethoven played.[41]

Actual Preferences and Ideals

It is important to acknowledge that Beethoven seems never to have been quite satisfied with the characteristics of any piano. A major, if somewhat illogical reason, may have been shortcomings that he found in the treatment of the piano by other performers, especially in their failure to play legato. At the age of twenty-six he wrote Streicher,

> There is no doubt that so far as the manner of playing it is concerned, the *pianoforte* is still the least studied and developed of all instruments; one often thinks that one is merely listening to a harp. And I am delighted, my dear fellow, that you are one of the few who realize and perceive that, provided one can feel the music, one can also make the pianoforte sing. I hope that the time will come when the harp and the pianoforte will be treated as two entirely different instruments.[42]

And in his last full year, after he had ended his writing for the piano except for the four-hand transcription (Op. 134) of his *Grosse Fuge* (Op. 133) for string quartet, Beethoven still expressed his dissatisfaction. Said he to Holz, "It [the piano] is and remains an inadequate instrument. In the future I shall write in the manner of my grand-master Handel annually only an oratorio and a concerto for some string or wind instrument, provided I have completed my tenth symphony (C minor) and my Requiem."[43]

38. Anderson/BEETHOVEN I 82.

39. Anderson/BEETHOVEN I 300.

40. Anderson/BEETHOVEN II 686.

41. KONVERSATIONSHEFTE IV 315.

42. Anderson/BEETHOVEN I 25–26.

43. Thayer & Forbes/BEETHOVEN 984; cf., also, Thayer & Riemann/BEETHOVEN V 123.

That kind of dissatisfaction was obviously more than just another of the many complaints in his last years about not being able to hear what he tried to play.

The documents confirm that all the favorable remarks Beethoven did make about pianos concerned only instruments made in Vienna according to Viennese practices. And most of those remarks, including his requests for pianos, concerned instruments made by the Stein and Streicher families. Thus, in the letter to Streicher of 1796, quoted above, Beethoven spoke of "your fortepiano, which is really an excellent instrument." In the letter to him of 1810 quoted above, he reinforced his request for one of Streicher's pianos with, "My motto is either to play on a good instrument or not at all." In July of 1817, about five months before his Broadwood was to be shipped to him from London, Beethoven again wrote Streicher, "Perhaps you are not aware that, although I have not always used one of your pianos, since 1809 [probably the first year he owned or borrowed a piano called a Streicher] I have always had a special preference for them—Only Streicher would be able to send me the kind of piano I require."[44] And in 1823 we find Czerny saying to an apparently sympathetic Beethoven, "I like only his [that is, Streicher's] instruments."[45] It may be added that it was to his lifelong friends, the Streichers, that Beethoven went even for improvements in the Broadwood after it came, and with whom he enjoyed a close relationship even after he sought help late in life from a rival piano manufacturer in Vienna, Conrad Graf.[46]

As for those three Beethoven pianos that remain best known because they are extant—the Érard, Broadwood, and Graf—the first two proved to be important to Beethoven almost solely for the honor and prestige they betokened, and the Graf, as we have seen, could have had no special meaning in any case, since by 1825 Beethoven could not hear it at all and would be writing little further piano music, anyway. Among Beethoven's early complaints about his Érard piano was that its English-type action was incurably heavy.[47] We have seen that by 1810 he was writing in a letter to Streicher that his "French piano" was "certainly quite useless now."[48] However, he evidently did keep the piano with him until 1825, when, as mentioned earlier, he gave it to his brother as no special act of kindness, but in order to make room for the Graf.[49]

44. Anderson/BEETHOVEN II 686.

45. KONVERSATIONSHEFTE IV 57.

46. Thayer & Forbes/BEETHOVEN 918–19.

47. Lütge/STREICHER 65.

48. Cf., also, Anderson/BEETHOVEN I 292.

49. Frimmel/KLAVIEREN 89.

Beethoven is not known ever to have thanked Thomas Broadwood after the Broadwood piano reached him. That he did appreciate at least the honor of the gift is suggested by a statement he is reported to have made to the poet Rellstab as late as 1825 (the year the Graf piano came to him). "It [the Broadwood] is a beautiful piano. I received it from London as a gift. Notice the names [inscribed] there . . . and it has a lovely tone."[50] But while the piano was in Vienna, still awaiting delivery to Beethoven, Streicher got the Englishman Cipriani Potter to try it, because Moscheles and others, although approving the tone, had found the English action too heavy (as with the Érard action) and Potter was used to that action.[51] Furthermore, by 1818, Beethoven probably found the Broadwood's six-octave range to be the disappointing limitation that Schindler implied rather than a new widening of the horizons that generally has been assumed.[52] Moreover, even the vaunted tone came into question, as we learn when Moscheles played at the Kärntnertor Theatre in late 1823 and obtained Beethoven's permission to use the Broadwood:

Moscheles wished, by using alternately at one and the same concert a Graf and an English piano, to bring out the good qualities of both. Beethoven was not exactly the player to treat a piano carefully; his unfortunate deafness was the cause of his pitiless thumping on the instrument, so that Graf—foreseeing the favorable issue of this contest to himself—generously labored to put the damaged English instrument into better condition for this occasion. "I tried," says Moscheles, "in my Fantasia to show the value of the broad, full, though somewhat muffled tone of the Broadwood piano; but in vain. My Vienna public remained loyal to their countryman—the clear, ringing tones of the Graf were more pleasing to their ears . . . ."[53]

When the harp maker Johann Andreas Stumpff visited during the next year, Beethoven told him that he owned a London instrument, but that it had not fulfilled his expectations for it.[54] He soon began to neglect its proper care. His "thumping" on the instrument was so great that the singing master Franz Hauser found all the upper strings already broken, in the early 1820s.[55] Others kept finding the instrument badly out out of tune, bringing a somewhat paranoid reply from Beethoven to Potter soon

50. Kerst/BEETHOVEN II 136.

51. Thayer & Riemann/BEETHOVEN IV 89; cf. MOSCHELES I 65.

52. Schindler & MacArdle/BEETHOVEN 372; cf., also, Thayer & Riemann/BEETHOVEN V 498.

53. MOSCHELES I 89; but cf. Schindler & MacArdle/BEETHOVEN 391 and KONVERSATIONS-HEFTE IV 315 and 328 for the possibility that another Viennese make, the Löschen, may have been used in place of the Graf.

54. Thayer & Riemann/BEETHOVEN V 127; also, p. 123.

55. Kerst/BEETHOVEN I 265. Cf., also, Friege/INTERPRETATIONS II 32 and 33.

after it arrived, "That's what they all say; they would like to tune it and spoil it, but they shall not touch it."[56] The one care Beethoven did give the Broadwood was to try repeatedly to have it made more audible in his deafness, as he had already tried with Stein in 1820.[57] It was probably in 1824 that Beethoven played for Friederich Wieck with the Broadwood on a "resonance plate" plus an ear trumpet fastened to the plate.[58] As we are reminded by several entries in the *Konversationshefte*,[59] the very purpose of the Graf piano that was made by 1825 especially for Beethoven was to provide him with an instrument that did make itself audible. Supposedly for this purpose it had quadruple-unison stringing and a special resonator,[60] although there is sufficient evidence that Graf had been making other pianos with four strings to a unison.[61] But the problem of Beethoven's deafness proved insurmountable.[62] And even those who could hear found the new piano made for Beethoven's use to be unsatisfactory.[63]

Knowing Beethoven's evident preference for Viennese pianos and knowing about when each of those pianos became available to him, we already have at least some bases for exploring certain of the performance problems to be raised in coming chapters. But simply to know that he preferred the light action and clear tones of Viennese pianos is not enough in itself. To exploit the information we have we need to consider the main characteristics of his pianos—especially their ranges, actions, and pedals. We will go further into tone quality and the use of the pedals in Chapter 8, approaching them differently from the discussions of those topics in this chapter.

The Range of Beethoven's Pianos

One of the initial signs of Beethoven's growing independence in his musical style was the increasing compromises he seemed obliged to make with the traditional five-octave range of the harpsichord and early piano (FF to f‴). A typical example may be noted already in the finale of the

56. Thayer & Riemann/BEETHOVEN IV 89.

57. KONVERSATIONSHEFTE II 65.

58. Thayer & Riemann/BEETHOVEN V 342–45, disagreeing with Wieck's recollection of the year 1826.

59. E.g., KONVERSATIONSHEFTE I 325, 332, 338; II 81–82; VI 247, 276; VIII 47, 288–89.

60. Frimmel/BEETHOVEN II 229–32.

61. Meer/PIANOFORTE 74; Wythe/GRAF 454.

62. Sonneck/BEETHOVEN 202; Breuning/SCHWARZSPANIERHAUSE 89–80 and 100.

63. Schindler & MacArdle/BEETHOVEN 385. Cf. F. Grünkhorn in *Musica* XVIII (1964) 167–68.

Example 3/2 Sonata Op. 2/1/iv: (a) mm. 2–3 and (b) mm. 51–52 (after beethoven werkem VII/2/I 12 and 13; HV*)

first of the three sonatas dedicated to Haydn (1796). In the first statement of the main theme the consequent figure rises a 5th, but before the exposition ends it is compelled by the five-octave range to drop a 4th instead (Ex. 3/2).

Granted that Beethoven lived at a time of noteworthy advances in all aspects of piano construction, it still seems significant that no such accomodations had proved necessary in the keyboard music of his principal 18th-century predecessors. J. S. Bach, far from straining the five-octave limit—which may not have been available on all his harpsichords, anyway—confined himself with apparent ease to no more than four octaves and a third (AA to c″′) in a work as brilliant as his "Italian Concerto." Haydn did make use of the full five octaves in his keyboard music. Yet he showed only a passing inclination, in his Sonata Hoboken XVI/50/iii (e.g., mm. 76–80), to exploit the added high notes (up to a″′) on the Broadwood piano lent to him during his second London visit (1794–95, perhaps four years before he actually completed the Sonata[64]). Mozart, who may never have been similarly exposed to upper extensions of the five-octave range, seemed to stop effortlessly at f″′, occasionally accommodating the fixed limit with subtle adjustments of his thematic material, but not with bold transpositions. (His use of a pedal board down to CC, never indicated in his scores, apparently was intended for enrichment and not any extension of range for his musical ideas.[65])

Apart from a very few extensions upward by one half- or whole-step, as in Op. 14/1/i/41, possibly available to him on the Walter piano he

64. Kramer/dating 168–69.

65. Cf. Badura-Skoda/mozart 13–15 and 204–205.

used,[66] Beethoven had to cope with the five-octave limit throughout his first twenty piano sonatas with opus numbers through Op. 49. Thus, in the first movement of *Sonate pathétique* he had to sacrifice the sense of peaking that he had created in the relative major key of the exposition (mm. 105–112) when he came to the corresponding measures in the tonic key during the recapitulation (mm. 257–64; Ex. 3/3). The reverse of this process may be seen in the analogous measures (97–106 and 278–86) of Op. 10/3/i, in which now the exposition has to interrupt its ascent to the peak whereas the recapitulation completes its ascent uninterrupted.

There is less evidence in those early sonatas that Beethoven found the bass range inadequate. In measures 268 to 273 (Ex. 3/4) of Op. 10/3/i, he had to be content with three single notes at the bottom of a scale obviously intended to continue in octaves throughout (cf. mm. 90–91). But as with Mozart, Beethoven's need to extend the bass range seems to have been more a matter of attaining a desired sonority than of maintaining or fulfilling the integrity of a theme.

66. Cf. JAMS XXIII (1970) 413–14 (M. E. Broyles) and 491 (W. S. Newman); Good/PIANOS 75 (referring also to Op. 15/i/172 and WoO 38/42, but incorrectly to Op. 1/2).

EXAMPLE 3/3 Sonata Op. 13/i: (a) mm. 105–112 and (b) mm. 257–64 (after BEETHOVEN WERKEM VII/2 145 and 148; HV*)

EXAMPLE 3/4   Sonata Op. 10/3/i/268–73 (after the early Simrock edition [1801], p. 32)

Throughout the composition of his first twenty sonatas, Beethoven showed no awareness of the high notes being added to some contemporary English pianos, partly to accommodate a new interest in four-hand playing. By August of 1803 he received his French Érard piano, on which the traditional five-octave range was increased by a 5th up to c''''. But he had already used that pitch earlier that year. He had used it in his Third Piano Concerto (as at Op. 37/iii/349) and by April he apparently had sketched a cadenza for the Concerto that reached the same c'''' and that he performed on an unknown piano.[67] In any case, by this time the range of German pianos, including Beethoven's eventual favorite in Vienna, the Streicher, was equalling and even surpassing that of the English pianos.[68] Only four years later, Beethoven used an e'''' to top one of the two cadenzas he wrote for the "Rondo" in the piano transcription of his Violin Concerto.[69]

Thereafter, Beethoven gradually extended the range of his piano music as the need arose and his preferred pianos permitted. However, prior to the loan of the Graf piano (by 1825), no piano known to have been at his disposal encompassed both extremes of the widest ranges he had required up to then—that is, the six-and-a-half octaves from CC to f'''' in his "Hammerklavier" Sonata, Op. 106. He had called for no extension of the bass range before his last five piano sonatas, from 1816. Then, realizing how innovative such extensions would be, he asked Tobias Haslinger (representing the publisher Steiner) to put letter names beside the new lower notes in the finale of Op. 101, in order to identify them for the performer,

67. Cf. Kramer/DATING 160–63.

68. Cf. Schindler & MacArdle/BEETHOVEN 193, fn. 91.

69. Cf. BEETHOVEN SUPPLEMENTEm X 73–74 (m. 15).

quite as he had done for himself in the autograph of this work.[70] Now the low range was needed for a deeper melodic foundation as well as for a fuller sonority. But unlike the higher and higher ranges that Beethoven, Cramer, Dussek, and other cultivators of the new piano had been advocating,[71] the lower ranges—only a 4th lower at most in Beethoven's time— had come into use more slowly, partly because composers had demonstrated less need and partly because current piano makers found the lower ranges a little more difficult to incorporate into their piano designs.[72]

The thematic compromises with range that Beethoven had to make in the first twenty piano sonatas diminished as the available ranges increased. At least in this respect there is little evidence in his late works of dissatisfaction with the piano. Since he did not seek increased range for novelty's sake, as, for example, Dussek did on occasion, his (or his publishers'?) few remaining compromises were mainly minor concessions to different ranges in different piano makes. Thus, an *ossia* had to be supplied for the early English editions of Opp. 106 and 111 wherever the range exceeds c'''' (as in the first issue of Op. 106 published by the Regent's Harmonic Institution of London (1819; Ex. 3/5), although in this instance the added staff is the original and the regular staff is actually the *ossia*.

The question now arises, how does this discussion of available ranges concern today's performance practices and the interpretation of Beethoven? Mainly, it may help to answer another, not uncommon question: can today's knowledgeable performer justifiably eliminate those changes

---

70. Cf. Anderson/BEETHOVEN II 660. The letters appear at the bottom of p. 24, mm. 223–228, in the autograph of Op. 101 and, reduced to the lowest letter, on p. 15 of the original Steiner ed.

71. Cf. Walter/HAYDN 269–70.

72. Loesser/PIANOS 226–27.

EXAMPLE 3/5 Sonata Op. 106/i/46–47, after the Regent's first issue (1819)

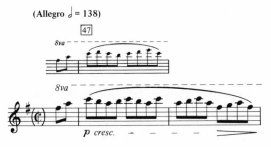

in the earlier works that Beethoven seemed compelled to make by the more restricted ranges? In his later years Beethoven considered one reason for a new edition of his works to be the possible removal of those compromises.[73] In other words, he considered recomposing the compromised sections in order to take advantage of the wider ranges that had become available. But, as we have seen, he never quite realized that new edition. And subsequently both Czerny and Schindler wrote against any posthumous modifications, mainly on the grounds of stylistic inconsistency with the five-octave range.[74] On the other hand, Streicher had seen a practical advantage in having Beethoven himself modify the sections in question. He argued that by this means and the injection of a few new, little pieces Beethoven could be assured of selling the new edition to those who had already bought the old one![75] In any case, Beethoven asserted more than once and demonstrated in practice that if any arranging or rearranging had to be done, only the composer was qualified to do it.[76]

Piano Actions—English, French, and Viennese

Beethoven probably never saw or tried either of two chief innovations in piano construction during the first half of the 19th century, the half century that witnessed the virtual perfection of the piano as we now know it. There is every reason to believe he would have welcomed both. Insofar as these innovations can be attributed to a particular year and maker, they are Érard's double-escapement action, introduced in its nearly modern form in 1821, which facilitated more rapid repetition and lighter action; and John Isaac Hawkins' one-piece cast-iron frame, introduced in Philadelphia in 1825, which enabled greater string tensions and bigger sounds.[77] The main distinction in piano construction that concerns the present discussion has remained that between the so-called German (or Viennese) and the English actions. The German system was distinguished especially by its individually hinged keys, each with a separate hammer and escapement mechanism; by a shallow, light, fast, responsive touch; and consequently by a highly controllable, songful, clear, yet somewhat frag-

73. Cf. Deutsch/AUSGABE.

74. Badura-Skoda/CZERNY 26; Schindler & MacArdle 402–403, 444.

75. Thayer & Riemann/BEETHOVEN V 119.

76. E.g., cf. Anderson/BEETHOVEN I 74–75.

77. More details appear, of course, in Harding/PIANO-FORTE and in the updated and new information in GROVE XIV, article on "Pianoforte." Cf., also, three more recent, informative discussions—Derek Adlam's lucid account and illustrations in Gill/PIANO 23–27 and Ch. 3 on "Beethoven and the Growing Grand" (with emphasis on technological changes) in Good/PIANOS; and Kiraly/ÉRARD.

ile tone. The English system was distinguished by the suspension of its keys from a common rail; by its heavier, deeper, more sluggish touch; and consequently by a rounder, fuller, yet somewhat muffled tone of wider dynamic range. In Beethoven's time both systems still used leather- rather than felt-covered hammers.[78]

Although Beethoven maintained his allegiance to Viennese pianos, he did persist in requesting a sturdier instrument, with a sturdier action and bigger tone, undoubtedly because he needed an instrument capable of withstanding his animal energies, of projecting his more intense feelings, and of compensating for his growing deafness. Yet no evidence could be found here that he ever realized his ideal in the Broadwood or other English pianos, or in the French pianos, which were modeled so closely after the English types.[79] From the standpoint of piano actions, even without the further evidence presented here, one would need only to recall the light, rapid finger work required in the finale of Op. 81a and the second movement of Op. 106 to guess that Beethoven still had the Viennese pianos in mind late in his life.

We learn more about Beethoven's preferences in piano actions from a valuable article of 1927 by William Lütge on Andreas and Nannette Streicher,[80] based on correspondence from 1800 to 1807 in the files of Breitkopf & Härtel. That publishing firm joined with Beethoven in getting Streicher to make, in addition to the double-strung instruments with lighter actions that he had been making, some triple-strung pianos with heavier actions, producing a bigger tone and including the action-shifting pedal, although even these pianos were never quite to satisfy Beethoven in his growing deafness. However, Streicher stopped short of converting to the actual English action, partly because Breitkopf & Härtel concluded that there was no market for English pianos in Germany and partly because Streicher himself was not convinced of the English mechanism's superiority. (Not until the mid-century did that mechanism come to prevail internationally.)

One letter in particular, addressed by Streicher to Härtel in 1805, deserves quoting almost in full. It is a response to a letter from Härtel that mentioned preferences by both Clementi and some amateurs for a bigger tone and heavier action, welcoming such critical comments and asking Härtel

78. Jander/ORPHEUS 204–205 provides an excellent description of the sort of Viennese six-octave fortepiano for which Beethoven probably wrote his Fourth Concerto Op. 58, including its range, stringing, heaviness of construction, dynamic capabilities, and pedals.

79. No support could be found, for example, for the undocumented statement in Sakka/KLAVIERE 335 to the effect that Beethoven was inspired by a Broadwood piano he saw (in Prince Louis Ferdinand's possession?) during his obscure visit to Berlin in 1796.

80. Lütge/STREICHER.

to write without reservation all that the amateurs find fault with on my instruments and [all] that they would wish to have [built in them] externally and internally. I would not ask you this favor if I were not convinced that you can differentiate exactly between the possible and the impossible and can separate easily the [pointless] caprices of music amateurs from legitimate demands . . . . There is one remark in your letter with which I cannot concur, namely [that regarding] the heavier action and deeper [key] fall of pianos such as Clementi demands. I can assure you from twofold experience that a pianist can become accustomed much sooner to a poor tone, dragging, sticking of the keys, and all kinds of [other] evils than to the heavy action and even less to deep fall of the keys. This summer I too have manufactured some of such instruments [the action of] which, however, is far from the action demanded by Mr. Clementi, and now I have every reason to regret it. To be sure, the English pianos gain an advantage over ours if we construct the keyboard [action?] according to their way, and this [way] also seems to be Clementi's goal. Only it is also certain that then the fortepiano surely will not be the universal instrument any longer, whereby at least nine-tenths of the keyboard amateurs will have to give up their playing.

Beethoven certainly is a strong pianist, yet up to now he still is not able properly to manage his fortepiano received from Érard in Paris, and has already had it changed twice without making it the least bit better, since the construction of the same does not allow a different mechanism. On several instruments I have taken a middle road between light and heavy [action,] but also have been forced to leave this [course] as well, since not only local but also foreign amateurs have protested it . . . .[81]

Four years later, in a travel report dated February 7, 1809, in Vienna, composer-critic Reichardt reported the progress Streicher had made in his efforts to attain the best of both worlds:

Streicher has left the soft, the excessively pliant, as well as the bouncing rolling of the older Viennese instruments, and—upon Beethoven's advice and request—has given his instruments more resistance and elasticity so that the virtuoso who performs with strength and significance has power over the instrument for sustaining and supporting [the tone?] and more sensitive pressure and release [of the key?]. Through this [change] he has given his instruments a greater and more diverse character so that more than any other instruments they will satisfy the virtuoso who seeks more than easy glitter in performance.[82]

But by comparison and as noted earlier, recall that when the Broadwood arrived in 1818, its action still seemed too heavy, deep, and sluggish.

---

81. Lütge/STREICHER 65–66. For more on the tone of the Streicher piano, cf. Fuller/STREICHER.

82. Reichardt/BRIEFE I 311.

The Pedals Available on Beethoven's Pianos

The following relatively brief discussion concerns which pedals were available to Beethoven on the pianos he used rather than the uses to which he put them. (Those uses are explored in Chapter 8 on "Further Expressive Factors.") The name Broadwood is commonly linked with the early incorporation of pedals on the fortepiano because of that firm's 1783 patent for both dampening and damper pedals.[83] But as with the expansion of ranges, there is no need to look to the English for precedents, since well before Beethoven was ready for them, all the basic types of devices and controls—whether hand-, knee-, or foot-operated—were available on various pianos of German and French as well as English manufacture. Those devices were often built into the instrument to suit the buyer.[84]

Basically there were three main types of devices: damper raising, whether divided into separate bass and treble controls or combined in a single control; action-shifting, permitting the striking of but one or two strings of triple-strung keys, and of but one string of double-strung keys; and dampening, achieved through a piece of cloth, leather, or other material interposed between hammers and strings or laid on the strings, either to make the tone softer or to give it a special color such as "flute" or "bassoon." Hand, knee, or foot controls were the usual means, too, of introducing extraneous effects, like the bells, triangles, and drums Dussek called for on occasion (as in his Op. 45). Thus, one Streicher piano made in 1816—a six-octave instrument double-strung in the bass and triple-strung in the treble—had four pedals: action-shifting, bassoon, damper, and piano-or-lute by dampening; and it could also produce kettle-drum and bell effects through two knee controls[85] (notwithstanding Streicher's aversion to all special effects or *Mutationen*).[86]

The question as to what pedals Beethoven had at his disposal may seem largely academic, since he never called for any controls but those for damper-raising (to sustain the tones) and action-shifting (to sound only *una corda* or *due corde*). Yet, knowing what other controls he had at hand reveals what he chose not to use and therefore must have regarded as extraneous. We can only be sure what pedals are on the three extant

83. Cf. H. Neupert in MGG II 329. Technical descriptions of the pedals on Beethoven's Érard, Broadwood, and Graf pianos appear in ÖMZ PEDAL, especially the article by Kurt Wegerer.

84. Cf. the illustrations in Hirt/KLAVIERBAUS 31, 47, 48, 334, 342, *et passim*.

85. Huber/BEETHOVEN 83.

86. Cf. Lütge/STREICHER 63–64.

pianos that do not seem to have represented his preference in pianos. We know the Érard piano has four pedals (that is, foot controls). From left to right, they are a "lute" pedal (with the lute being simulated by the insertion of leather thongs between the hammers and the strings), a damper pedal (as on today's pianos), a dampening pedal (achieved by inserting a cloth fringe between the hammers and strings), and an action-shifting pedal (as on today's grand pianos). The Broadwood has two pedals, the left for action shifting and the right for damper control. But the Broadwood's right pedal is itself divided so that its left half can be depressed independently to control the dampers from CC to b and the right half from c' to c''''. The Graf has three pedals, the left being action-shifting, the middle dampening, and the right damper control.[87]

It is worth noting that Beethoven showed an interest in damper and action-shifting controls and showed his awareness of the split damper pedal several years before he consistently requested damper and action-shifting pedals in his scores. Thus, in a sketch dating from 1790–92 he wrote "mit dem Knie" (with the knee) for the dampers to be raised during a series of repeated chords[88] (this request being the earliest known for a damper control in any composer's score, from two to seven years earlier than a request by Haydn for "open Pedal" in his Sonata Hoboken XVI/50/i/73). But not until about 1795, in the manuscripts of his first two piano concertos (e.g., Op. 15/ii/91–93 and Op. 19/i/281–284) did he start to call for the damper controls a little more regularly.[89]

In a letter of November 1802 Beethoven made clear that he already knew about the *una corda* control, for he inquired about a Walter piano that would include a "Zug mit einer Saite" (pull [or knob] with one string).[90] His first requests in his scores for this control came three to four years later in his Fourth Piano Concerto (Op. 58/ii/55–56 and 60–72) but not again until his last five piano sonatas. Finally, at least fifteen years before his Broadwood with the split damper pedal arrived (1818), he revealed that he knew about that type of pedal in a note that appears at the beginning of his autograph of the "Waldstein" Sonata Op. 53: "N.B. Where [the designation] Ped[al] occurs, the entire damper [apparatus] should be raised[,] from bass as well as treble. [The symbol] O means to

---

87. For an illustration of each piano and its pedals, kindly provided by Dr. Keisei Sakka of Tokyo, see Newman/PERFORMANCE 36–39. A clearer picture of the Broadwood's divided damper pedal appears in Sakka/KLAVIERE between pp. 328 and 329 (but the left pedal is not also subdivided, although it would seem to be in the illustration).

88. Cf. KAFKA SKETCHBOOK II 132 and 287.

89. Cf. Hans-Werner Küthen in BEETHOVEN-WERKEm III/2 *Kritischer Bericht* 83–84.

90. But the translation cannot be "the tension with one string," as in Anderson/BEETHOVEN I 82.

let it fall again." In other words, he knew about the split pedal, but at least in this instance rejected its use. Did this rejection also represent his preference in all his other exposures to the split damper pedal, or did it apply only to Op. 53, suggesting that that device might be exploited at other times? We do not know for sure, but in my opinion—since no other reference by Beethoven to the split damper pedal is known—this rejection did represent his general preference.

Czerny says that while Beethoven still used a knee-lever damper control, his term for raising the dampers (removing them from the strings) was "senza sordino"[91] (not "sordini," although the meaning was plural, without dampers). His term for lowering, or restoring, them was, as expected, "con sordino" (with dampers). When he started to use the true (foot) pedal, he began using the abbreviations "Ped." for raising the dampers and "O" for restoring them. He did this from about 1801–1802 at the start of Op.31/2, in the "Kreutzer" Sonata Op. 47 for piano and violin, and at one point in a sketch for the "Eroica" Variations Op. 35.[92] All these uses occurred well before the Érard's arrival, though they are not yet found in the Third Piano Concerto, Op. 37, whose composition began in 1800.[93] Beethoven indicated *una corda* and *tre corde*, or *tutte le corde* as U.C. and T.C. when he did not write them out. With slight variations, he indicated the progression from one to the other as he did in the "Hammerklavier" Sonata, Op. 106/iii/87–88—"poco a poco due et allora tre corde" (or its converse). But that gradual progression cannot be duplicated today (and could not even then on certain pianos), because the modern "una corda" pedal can shift the action only between two and three, or one and two, strings.

The Pianism of Beethoven Compared with That of Haydn, Mozart, and Schubert

Among the four great Viennese masters who flourished in the rich half century from the 1770s to the 1820s, Mozart and Beethoven excel in their "pianism," while Haydn and Schubert must be ranked only average by comparison. Such seems to be a prevailing view among today's per-

91. Badura-Skoda/CZERNY 51. This term is not to be translated "without the use of the damper pedal" as in Schindler & MacArdle/BEETHOVEN 94; cf., also, pp. 422 and 447–48.

92. Cf. Kramer/DATING 163–64.

93. As will be noted more fully in Chapter 8, Czerny was wrong if his mention of the foot pedal under Op. 53 (Badura-Skoda/CZERNY 51) was meant to imply that Beethoven had not called for it earlier.

formers.[94] By "pianism" I mean the way these men wrote for piano, or, more explicitly, their compositional exploitation especially of the techniques, idioms, expressive means, and sounds of the piano. The differences in their pianism are easy enough to explain. Mozart and Beethoven were frontrank pianists in their own right; Haydn and Schubert were experienced orchestral musicians, but with no more than an average ability to play the piano. Mozart and Beethoven not only understood better how to write for their instrument, but they took a much more active interest in its problems. Both men knew very well the athletic capabilities of the hand at the keyboard as well as the musical capabilities of the early Viennese piano, and both treated these capabilities with rare sympathy, resourcefulness, and imagination. As in everything else musical, Mozart was perhaps the most natural among great composers—which is to say, the most fitting and fluent—in his pianism. Beethoven was perhaps the most enterprising and challenging. Mozart accepted the limitations of hand and instrument, just as he did the five-octave range, and stayed comfortably within them. Beethoven challenged those limitations from the start, repeatedly making demands that seem to imply superhuman potential.

Haydn and Schubert wrote for the piano more as a convenient, if not expedient, vehicle for their ideas than as a source of musical pleasure in its own right. To be sure, they wrote with reasonable understanding of the idiom. Yet their understanding was more the comprehensive background of the professional composer than the ingenuity of the professional pianist. When their treatment of the keyboard was unidiomatic, it was inadvertent—in Schubert's case, perhaps somewhat indifferent, too. Haydn's unidiomatic writing can be awkward to manage; so can Schubert's, which sometimes can be thick and less well-balanced in sound.

Haydn's chief athletic exploitations of the piano keyboard occur in his late piano works, above all in his piano trios, and they occur at moderate to fast tempos, largely in the right hand. Except for the inadvertent difficulties such as an awkward, fast scale in double-thirds,[95] his exploitations are generally not more than the standard techniques of the times—for instance, scalewise and chordal passages, octaves, occasional trills, hand crossing, rapid hand alternation, and repeated notes (as already in evidence by about 1766; Ex. 3/6). Haydn's most imaginative writing for

---

94. More details and illustrations will be found in Newman/PIANISM. For Beethoven, cf., also, Schmid-Lindner/KLAVIER 40–45. In a solid new study of Haydn's keyboard music that reached me just before this book was going to press—Brown/HAYDN's, especially Essays 2 and 5—evidence is adduced for a somewhat greater interest in the keyboard on Haydn's part than may be suggested here. As regards his pianism, or idiomatic treatment, my comparative evaluation of the four composers remains the same.

95. E.g., Trio H[oboken]. XV/30/iii/37–41.

EXAMPLE 3/6 Haydn's Sonata in E♭ No. 29/iii/14–28 (as numbered by Christa Landon; after the Wiener Urtext I 148–49; EA*)

keyboard has less to do with ingenious and idiomatic uses of the hand than with orchestral or color contrasts of sonorities and ranges.[96]

Mozart's pianism appears at its finest in his later piano concertos. Compared with Haydn's, his writing fits more aptly and consistently the special nature of the keyboard, delves considerably further into the tech-

96. E.g., in Robbins Landon's numbering, Trio 41/ii/106–113.

nical challenges of the day, and exhibits greater resourcefulness in its applications. Thus, Ex. 3/7, from the finale of Mozart's Concerto K. 449 in E♭, lies well for the hands, yet requires more intricate finger work, greater hand extensions, and wider sweeps of the five-octave keyboard. Examples that fit the hand so well are evidence in themselves of Mozart's deep understanding of keyboard idioms. So are his careful, polished uses, with impeccable voice-leading, of the prevailing, stock keyboard devices, including hand crossing, skips, and even the newly popular "um-pah-pah-pah" accompaniment (as in his Sonata for Piano and Violin K. 526/iii/111–115).

Schubert's most developed pianism occurs in his later sonatas, in the "Wanderer" Fantasy, in certain shorter pieces for solo piano, and in his chamber duos, trios, and "Trout" Quintet. Although he followed closely in Beethoven's footsteps, his music does not reveal a further cultivation

EXAMPLE 3/7 Mozart's Piano Concerto K. 449/iii/102–113 (after *Wolfgang Amadeus Mozart, Neue Ausgabe sämtlicher Werke* V/15/4 50–51; BV*)

of either the resources or the reaches of pianism. He does seem to have presupposed an advanced level of technical experience throughout his compositional career, for any one of his large-scale piano works, early or late, is likely to provide a good cross-section of the standard keyboard techniques as they were then being exploited. Thus, in scarcely four measures the finale of his late Sonata D. 959 exhibits wide-ranging scales, skips, and broken chords and octaves (Ex. 3/8). But, again, these works do not approach Beethoven's either in the ingenuity of their keyboard treatment or the extent and diversity of their technical challenges. As with Haydn, Schubert contributed most to piano writing not through idiomatic figurations or technical challenges but through his effective contrasts of range and his clear balance of sound (at least when his scoring is not too thick for transparent piano sound). Good examples of both range and balance occur in the "Con moto" of Sonata D. 850, where soft middle and high notes complement the songful melody in a kind of hocket; and in the opening of Sonata D. 960, where Schubert takes a characteristically Romantic delight in the mystical sound of the piano's lowest bass notes.

As for Beethoven, the differences between his and Mozart's piano writing are more obvious than between Mozart's and Haydn's. Furthermore, those differences are evident right from Beethoven's Op. 1 and in a broad cross-section of his piano writing, both solo and ensemble. They are evident not only in the writing itself, but in his chronic dissatisfaction

EXAMPLE 3/8 Schubert's Sonata D. 959/iv/160–64 (after the edition of Paul Mies and Paul Badura-Skoda II 279; HV*)

EXAMPLE 3/9 Sonata Op. 2/3/iv: (a) mm. 15–18, (b) mm. 30–31, (c) mm. 85–87, (d) mm. 272–76, (e) mm. 288–92 (after BEETHOVEN WERKEM VII/2/I 58–66; HV*)

with the power and range of pianos that seem to have satisfied Haydn and Mozart. The most demanding technical requirements and expressive challenges occur, of course, in Beethoven's late works. But already in the finale of the brilliant Sonata Op. 2/3 (Ex. 3/9), one can find new challenges in (a) unprecedented finger speeds, (b) stretched chordal accompaniments, (c) fast left-hand octaves followed by fast skips into double-thirds, (d) mixed double-notes, and (e) a trill that grows into a double- and then a triple-trill.

To be sure, the still greater technical challenges in Beethoven's late works may not all have been conscious or deliberate on his part. In his ultimately total deafness, did Beethoven realize the problems he was making for the balance and projection of sound? In his almost endless contacts with the keyboard did he realize the problems he was introducing in the athletics of technique? Whatever the answers, the resulting difficulties, premeditated or not, reached a level that hardly has been surpassed in piano writing, certainly not in music of comparable significance. Difficulties such as those in Ex. 3/10 from the "Diabelli" Variations are typical. They include (a) fast, close, interlaced finger work, (b) fast mixed chords and octave interchanges, and (c) fast legato double-notes.

Such challenges in Beethoven's piano writing exist because they grow out of, seldom because they contradict, idiomatic uses of the keyboard. When Beethoven reverts to the stock accompaniments of musical Classicism he not only glorifies them by integrating them thematically but he extends their technical reach. In the first movement of Sonata Op. 90

EXAMPLE 3/10 The "Diabelli" Variations, Op. 120: (a) XXVII/17–20, (b) XXVIII/12–20, and (c) XXVI/25–30 (after BEETHOVEN WERKEm VII/5/226–28; HV*)

(mm. 55–60), while the left hand inverts the initial motive in its lowest notes, it plays an Alberti bass in open position, spanning a 10th. Similarly, in the first movement of *Sonate pathétique* Op. 13, while the left hand recalls the main theme in its rising notes (mm. 195–219), it plays a murky bass that drives on to the point of testing physical endurance. Beethoven also writes more frequent and more extended passages in unbroken octaves than Haydn or Mozart had written—for instance, in the first movement of his Sonata Op. 54 (as in mm. 94–103). Occasionally, he does seem to miscalculate, if not defy, the keyboard idiom. Thus, when both hands

EXAMPLE 3/11 Sonata Op. 2/3/i/252–56 (after BEETHOVEN WERKEm
VII/2/I 50; HV*)

play broken octaves he usually has them oscillating in parallel motion
rather than in the contrary motion that would lend itself more naturally
to the opposed lie of the hands. One of many such instances occurs at
the end of the first movement of Sonata Op. 2/3 (Ex. 3/11). An infrequent exception to this parallelism occurs in the "Emperor" Concerto,
Op. 73/i/214–15 (and corresponding passages). To be sure, a similar
disregard of natural hand oppositions occurs in the writing of our other
three composers,[97] but not with comparable, simultaneous demands of
speed and power. Beethoven could be impractical on occasion, too, despite
his demonstrated fascination with technical keyboard problems (as in the
experimental exercises he left).[98] Thus, in the finale of his "Hammerklavier" Sonata, Op. 106, he wrote, among many difficult trills, a so-called
Beethoven trill that has no satisfactory realization at any tempo approach-

97. E.g., cf. Haydn's Piano Trio H. XV/16/i/144–47, Mozart's Concerto K. 503/i/372–80,
and Schubert's Sonata D. 784/i/57–58.

98. E.g., cf. forty such exercises as printed in Kann/CRAMER xi–xvi.

EXAMPLE 3/12 Sonata Op. 106/iv/112–14 (after Wallner/KLAVIER-
SONATENm II 261; HV*)

ing the stipulated ♩ = 144 (Ex. 3/12), whether the trill stops while each melodic note is struck by another finger of the same hand, or continues, as he presumably preferred. (See Chapter 7 on the performance of Beethoven-trills.)

Beethoven as a Performing Pianist

Beethoven's career as a performing pianist could be dated from his twelfth to his thirty-ninth years, or about 1782 to 1809.[99] After 1809, and especially after about 1814, he played only on isolated occasions, although there are reports of his improvising almost to the end of his life. His prominence as a pianist seems to have been from about 1796 to 1805. In 1783 Beethoven's teacher Neefe had already described his pupil as "a boy of . . . most promising talent. He plays the clavier very skillfully and with power, reads at sight very well, and . . . plays chiefly *The Well-Tempered Clavier* . . . [and connoisseurs] will know what this means."[100] By 1801 Beethoven may have reached something of a peak in performance, he himself being able to assert then that "My pianoforte playing . . . has considerably improved."[101] But his emphasis on performing began to decrease as his compositions drew more attention and as his hearing began to deteriorate alarmingly. A less well-documented factor may have been his near loss of a finger in 1808 (apparently to some sort of assailant).[102] And another factor, somewhat confusingly documented, may have been the concert of his works on December 22 of that year, which was reported in one source to be "defective in every respect";[103] it included his performance of his Fourth Concerto and Choral Fantasy.

After 1809 the reports of Beethoven's infrequent performances are mixed, but not often without some mention of deterioration. Thus, Spohr's autobiography mentions hearing Beethoven play in 1814 in the first

---

99. Nearly all the firsthand reports of Beethoven's piano playing are scattered throughout Thayer & Forbes/BEETHOVEN. Frimmel/KLAVIERSPIELER provides the fullest compilation of them. Kullak/BEETHOVEN provides a convenient summary and Friege/INTERPRETATIONS II (less accessible) provides nearly all the documents, frequently from secondhand sources. Additional information appears in Nohl/BEETHOVEN 9–49.

100. Thayer & Forbes/BEETHOVEN 66.

101. Anderson/BEETHOVEN I 65.

102. Thayer & Forbes/BEETHOVEN 430. Alan Tyson supplies further information and references in BEETHOVEN-JAHRBUCH X 192.

103. AMZ XI (1808–1809) 268–69. Cf. the several reports in Thayer & Forbes/BEETHOVEN 446–50; Landon/BEETHOVEN 223.

movement of his "new" Trio Op. 70/1 (actually his "Archduke" Trio in B♭ Op. 97?).[104] Spohr said, in brief, that Beethoven apparently was too deaf to hear that the piano was badly out of tune and he was obviously out of practice. He struck at the loud passages so heavily that the strings jangled and he played the soft passages so softly that whole groups of tones disappeared.

But, of course, such reports had nothing to do with Beethoven's artistry or musicianship. It was in 1812 that one of his remarkable keyboard transpositions was witnessed. The versatile Viennese musician Friederich Starke offered to play Beethoven's Horn Sonata with the master. Finding the available piano to be one-half step too low, Beethoven at once transposed its part up to F♯, playing "in a wondrously beautiful way; the passages rolled along so clear and fine that one couldn't believe at all that he was transposing. Beethoven also had praise for Starke because he had never heard the sonata performed with shading; he found the *pp* especially fine."[105]

Among still later, isolated reports, Moscheles wrote of Beethoven's playing in his "Archduke" Trio in 1814 that, "aside from its intellectual element, [it] satisfied me less, being wanting in clarity and precision; but I observed many traces of the *grand* style of playing which I had long recognized in his compositions."[106] The singer Franz Wild told of being accompanied in 1815 and 1816 by Beethoven in two of Beethoven's solo cantatas[107] and the Leipzig pianist Friedrich Schneider still had the highest praise for his improvising in 1819.[108] On one hand it is hardly surprising to find Schindler writing in a letter of 1855 or 1856 to Lenz that Beethoven "was no longer able to play his own sonatas from Op. 106 on [that is, by the time he wrote them, from 1818?]."[109] On the other hand, as late as 1822 there was a report of Beethoven improvising before a group of friends at the home of the Baroness von Puthon, at which time, "His

---

104. Cf. Spohr/LEBENSERINNERUNGEN 180–81 and 366. But the trio that most qualified as "new" in 1814 was Op. 97 and Beethoven was known to have played in that work (in what is usually called his last public performance as a pianist, except in accompaniments—cf. Thayer & Forbes/BEETHOVEN 577–78 and Landon/BEETHOVEN 256).

105. Thayer & Forbes/BEETHOVEN 526.

106. Thayer & Forbes/BEETHOVEN 578. Friedrich Nisle in 1808 was one of several others who found more satisfaction in the musicality than in the technical skill of Beethoven's playing (cf. Friege/INTERPRETATIONS II Doc. 27).

107. Thayer & Forbes/BEETHOVEN 610 and 641.

108. Thayer & Forbes/BEETHOVEN 739. On Beethoven's unsurpassed and universally acclaimed improvising, cf. Kross/IMPROVISATION, especially pp. 133–36.

109. Frimmel/KLAVIERSPIELER II 267.

playing was masterly, and showed that he still knows how to handle his instrument with power, enthusiasm, and love."[110]

At best, firsthand reports of the playing of great keyboardists before the later 19th century have provided little tangible information about such practical concerns to teachers and students as hand position, touch control, pedalling techniques, and rapid finger work. Of Beethoven, the fullest, most conscientious, and probably most reliable reports are several left by Czerny, even granting that some of that observer's own ideas may have inserted themselves unconsciously. In 1852, while writing at some length on Beethoven's remarkable improvising, Czerny said,

> Nobody equalled him in the rapidity of his scales, double trills, skips, etc.— not even Hummel. His bearing while playing was masterfully quiet, noble and beautiful, without the slightest grimace (only bent forward low, as his deafness grew upon him); his fingers were very powerful, not long, and broadened at the tips by much playing, for he told me very often indeed that he generally had to practice until after midnight in his youth. In teaching he laid great stress on a correct position of the fingers (after the school ["Essay"[111]] of Emanuel Bach, which he used in teaching me); he could scarcely span a tenth. He made frequent use of the pedals, much more frequent than is indicated in his works. His playing of the scores of Handel and Gluck and the fugues of Seb. Bach was unique, in that in the former he introduced a full-voicedness and a spirit which gave these works a new shape. He was also the greatest *a vista* player [sight reader] of his time (even in score reading); he scanned every new and unfamiliar composition like a divination and his judgment was always correct, but (especially in his younger years) very keen, biting, unsparing. Much that the world admitted then and still admires, he saw from the lofty point of view of his genius in an entirely different light.

> Extraordinary as his playing was when he improvised, it was frequently less successful when he played his printed compositions, for, as he never had patience or time to practise, the result would generally depend on accident or his mood; and as his playing, like his compositions, was far ahead of his time, the pianofortes of the period (until 1810), still extremely weak and imperfect, could not endure his gigantic style of performance. Hence it was that Hummel's purling, brilliant style, well calculated to suit the manner of the time, was much more comprehensible and pleasing to the public. But Beethoven's performance of slow and sustained passages produced an almost magical effect on every listener and, so far as I know, was never surpassed.[112]

Czerny threw further light on Beethoven's performance by comparing it with that by other distinguished pianists of the time:

110. AMZ XXIV (1822) 310, as transl. in Schindler & MacArdle/BEETHOVEN 413.

111. Bach/VERSUCH I 15–22?

112. As transl. in Thayer & Forbes/BEETHOVEN 368–69 from a Czerny document in the former Deutsche Staatsbibliothek (cf. Badura-Skoda/CZERNY 13, with fn.).

Clementi was able to unite brilliant bravura execution with tranquility and a regular position of the hands, solidity of touch and tone, great address and flexibility of finger, clear and voluble execution, correctness, distinctiveness, and grace of execution; and in his day he was always allowed to be the greatest Player on the Piano-forte .... The [English] Pianos of that day possessed for their most distinguished properties, a full Singing quality of tone; but as a counterbalance to that, they had also a deep fall of the keys, a hard touch, and a want of distinctness in the single notes in rapid playing; this naturally led *Dussek, Cramer,* and a few others to that soft, quiet, and melodious style of execution, [with] beautiful Cantabile, a fine legato combined with the use of the Pedals, [and] an astonishing equality in the runs and passages, for which they, and likewise their compositions, are chiefly esteemed, and which may be looked upon as the Antipodes of the modern, clear, and brilliantly piquant manner of playing. *Mozart[']s* style, which approached nearer to the latter mode, and which was brought to such exquisite perfection by Hummel, was more suited to those [Austro-German] piano-fortes which combined light and easy touch with great distinctness of tone, and which were therefore more suited for general purposes, as well as for the use of Youth; [thus, his style revealed a] distinct and considerably brilliant manner of playing, calculated rather on the Staccato than on the Legato touch; an intelligent and animated execution[; and the] Pedal seldom used, and never obligato [that is, required by a sign in the score?]. Meantime, in 1790, appeared *Beethoven,* who enriched the Piano-forte by new and bold passages, by the use of the pedals, by an extraordinary characteristic manner of execution, which was particularly remarkable for the strict Legato of the full chords, and which therefore formed a new kind of melody;—and by many effects not before thought of. His execution did not possess the pure and brilliant elegance of many other Pianists; but on the other hand it was energetic, profound, noble, with all the charms of smooth and connected cantabile and particularly in the Adagio, highly feeling and romantic. His performance[,] like his Compositions, was a musical painting of the highest class, esteemed only for its general effect. The means of Expression is often carried to excess [by Beethoven or by his subsequent interpreters?], particularly in regard to humorous and fanciful levity.[113]

In his memoirs Czerny enlarged on his comparison with Hummel when he wrote, "Whereas Beethoven's playing excelled in its extraordinary strength, character, and unprecedented bravura and fluency, Hummel's performance [was] the model of the highest purity and clarity, the most ingratiating elegance and delicacy."[114]

Most of the other reports of Beethoven as a performer generally confirm Czerny's observations. A few of these may be sampled, more briefly and in chronological order. In 1791, before his well-known encounter

113. Czerny/SCHOOL III 99–100; but readers should be cautioned that I have consolidated and combined passages from Czerny's two pages in order to eliminate considerable repetition.

114. As quoted in Frimmel/KLAVIERSPIELER II 247.

with the pianist Abbé Sterkel and according to Dr. Franz Wegeler, physician and life-long friend, Beethoven "had not [yet] heard a great or celebrated pianoforte player, knew nothing of the finer nuances in the handling of the instrument; his playing was rude and hard."[115] But, as the story continues, Beethoven was able immediately to mimic Sterkel's refined, ingratiating style when he did meet and hear him. In the same year of 1791, the dilettante composer Carl Junker wrote, "I have heard[the Abbé] Vogler upon the pianoforte . . . and never failed to wonder at his astonishing execution; but Bethofen [*sic*], in addition to the execution, has greater clearness and weight of idea, and more expression—in short, he is more for the heart—equally great, therefore, as an *adagio* or *allegro* player."[116] Schindler is the (not very reliable) source for three of four successive reports of Beethoven's playing that may define a trend in it. About 1799–1800, the fine pianist Johann Baptist Cramer faulted the lack of precision less than its inconsistency—"one day he [Beethoven] would play it [a composition] with great spirit and expression, but the next day it would sound moody and often muddled to the point of unclarity." About 1805–1806 the blunt Cherubini reacted with only one word, "rough." And about 1807 Clementi, as he recalled twenty years later, found that Beethoven's "playing was not polished, and was frequently impetuous, like himself, yet was always full of spirit."[117] Also in 1805, the young pianist and composer Camille Pleyel (son of Ignaz) had this to say:

At last I've heard Beethoven; he played a sonata of his composition and Lamare accompanied him. He has unlimited execution [technical flare? sweep?], but he has no [formal] schooling and his execution is not polished—that is, his playing is not unblemished. He has a lot of fire, but he pounds a bit too much. He manages diabolical difficulties, but he does not play them altogether precisely. However, his improvising gave me much pleasure. He doesn't improvise coldly as Woelf [Wölfl!] does; he plays whatever enters his head and he dares all. Sometimes he does astonishing things. Besides, he ought not be thought of as a pianist, because he is dedicated totally to composition and it is very hard to be at once a composer and a performer.[118]

115. WEGELER & RIES 17; cf. Thayer & Forbes 103–4.

116. As quoted in Thayer & Forbes/BEETHOVEN 105.

117. Schindler & MacArdle/BEETHOVEN 413. Cf. Thayer & Forbes/BEETHOVEN 209–210.

118. I am indebted to the late Rita Benton for sending me an article that contains not only Camille's letter but its correct ascription to Camille (rather than Ignaz as, for example, in Landon/BEETHOVEN 104): L-G. Mayniel, "Le centenaire de la Maison Pleyel," in *L'Art d'Écoratif* for May, 1909, p. 179 (Camille is also confirmed as the writer by J. G. Prod-'homme in the Guido Adler *Festschrift* of 1930, p. 192).

Beethoven's Teaching

It is too bad that Beethoven never wrote the piano method he kept hoping to write, as will be mentioned further in Chapter 6. But we do get some idea of his attitude toward performing from the things he emphasized most in his teaching. His longtime friend Ferdinand Ries wrote,

When Beethoven gave me a lesson, he was—contrary to his nature, I might say—remarkably patient . . . . Thus, he [would] let me repeat a piece ten times, sometimes still more. In the Variations in F, dedicated to the Princess Obescalchi (Opus 34), I had to repeat the last, Adagio variation seventeen times almost entirely; he still remained dissatisfied with the expression in the little cadenza, although I thought I played it as well as he . . . . When I missed something in a passage or struck notes and leaps falsely that he frequently wanted brought out, he rarely said anything. Only if I failed in the expression, in the crescendos and such, or in the character of a piece, did he get provoked, since, as he said, the former was an accident,[but] the latter [revealed] a lack of knowledge, or feeling, or care. The former happened to him very often, even when he played in public.[119]

Besides the lengthy excerpts from Czerny quoted above, two others from him may be added that pertain particularly to the instruction Beethoven gave him. In his memoirs he wrote,

At the first lessons Beethoven concentrated only on the scales in all keys, showing me the one correct position of the hands (still unknown then to most players), of the fingers, and especially the use of the thumb—rules whose applications I only learned to understand fully much later. Then he went through the exercises in the lesson book with me, making me aware particularly of the legato that he himself had mastered in such an incomparable manner and that all other pianists of the time regarded as unperformable on the fortepiano, for in Mozart's time the brittle and short staccato touch was [still] the [prevailing] style.[120]

There was also Beethoven's significant letter to Czerny of February 12, 1816, with the following sentence—" . . . you must forgive a composer who would rather have heard his work performed exactly as it was written, however beautifully you played it in other respects—"[121]

Finally in this chapter, among the contemporary pianists Beethoven most admired, three may be noted briefly here. According to Ries, Beethoven "singled out one pianist to me as outstanding, John Cramer. All

119. WEGELER & RIES 94–95. Some interesting information on Beethoven's teaching appears in Nohl/BEETHOVEN 71–84.

120. Badura-Skoda/CZERNY 11.

121. Anderson/BEETHOVEN II 560.

others he valued little."[122] Ries did not amplify this statement, but one clue to Beethoven's preference may lie in the attraction he seems to have felt later toward the textures and their rhythms in Cramer's skillfully constructed Etudes (as discussed here in Chapter 6). The Baroness Dorothea von Ertmann, who knew Beethoven from 1804, was a favorite performer of his music in private performances. Although evidences of his own and others' esteem abound, the specifics that survive about her playing may be summed up as fine, sensitive, compelling musicianship.[123] And Frau Marie Pachler-Koschak seems to have merited the same kind of praise, but there is still less specific information, mainly a short letter from Beethoven written in the summer of 1817, including the following (not atypical) paragraph: "I have never yet found anybody who plays my compositions as well as you do, not even excepting the great pianists, for they either have nothing but technique or are affected. You are the true guardian of my intellectual offspring—"[124]

122. WEGELER & RIES 99–100.

123. Cf. Thayer & Forbes/BEETHOVEN 412–13, 526, 668–69; Huber/BEETHOVEN 23–27.

124. As transl. in Thayer & Forbes/BEETHOVEN 685 (cf. pp. 684–86; also, Huber/BEETHOVEN 30).

CHAPTER 4

TEMPO: RATE AND FLEXIBILITY[1]

Its Elusiveness, Even with the Metronome

EVER SINCE Beethoven's own day, arriving at the "right" tempo has confronted musicians with one of the most elusive challenges in performing his music. It has occasioned many a heated debate and many a categorical criticism, as well as not a few enterprising studies. In this further effort to deal with his tempo, both the rate and flexibility must be considered, since they interrelate. But at least this effort can be confined to his instrumental music, for tempo is complex enough in itself, without the influence of a descriptive programme or a vocal text.[2] In the present chapter our primary aim is first to summarize previous writings on Beethoven tempo and then to propose some further approaches to that problem.

The elusiveness of the problem is reflected by Debussy's typically sarcastic observations in 1901 regarding different styles of conducting Beethoven's symphonies: ". . . some 'accelerate,' others 'ritard,' and it's this poor great old Beethoven who suffers the most. Serious, informed persons declare that this or that conductor knows the true tempo, which makes a fine conversation topic in any case. What makes them so sure of themselves? Do they receive communications from Heaven above?"[3]

1. Portions of this chapter are revisions and extensions of Newman/TEMPO. That article had undergone previous updating and revisions as "Das Tempo in Beethovens Instrumentalmusik—Tempowahl und Tempoflexibilität" (in DMf XXIII [1980] 161–83) after originating as a lecture (in English) honoring the retirement of Frederick Neumann at Richmond University in February 1977.

2. Beethoven makes a point of textual influences on "expression" in a letter of 1809 to the Scottish publisher George Thomson (Anderson/BEETHOVEN I 248).

3. Debussy/CROCHE 32.

With Beethoven, both the tempo and its flexibility became more crucial and more elusive than they had been with his predecessors. It underwent new refinements in the rate and new relationships between changes of tempo, within as well as between movements. As Beethoven wrote in December of 1826, in an oft-quoted letter to the publisher Schott, "We can have almost no further *tempi ordinari,* since one must [be free to] respond to the call of unconstrained genius."[4] This sentence generally is taken to mean that one could no longer be restricted to the standard tempos of the immediate past, typically five—very slow, slow, moderate, fast, and very fast—but that he now felt free to choose whatever gradation seemed appropriate to the character of a particular piece, such as "Poco Adagio quasi Andante" (Op. 66, Var. XI[5] "Allegro assai vivace" (Op. 115/ 17.[6])

Before getting into the nature and uses of those finer tempo gradations, we need to be sure we agree on our basic terms. In this book rhythm is the term encompassing the regular or irregular recurrence in time of some musical element or idea. Tempo is the rate of speed of the ongoing rhythm. Beat refers to rhythm's most basic element, a unit-beat being the primary unit by which a particular rhythm is divided (as declared in its time signature). The pulse that one actually feels and conducts may correspond to the unit-beat, or it may compound or subdivide the unit-beat, as in $\updownarrow$ and *alla breve* or as in the choice of a sixteenth note for a metronome marking in $\frac{4}{8}$ time. Meter refers to the organization of beats into measures.

On first thought, one might suppose that Beethoven would have resolved the more precise determination of his tempos through his celebrated, pioneer exploitation of Maelzel's new device, the metronome. That is, he would have done so insofar as either he or his close associates, especially Czerny and Moscheles,[7] actually left metronome markings for his music. Unfortunately, for many pianists those markings have raised more questions than they have answered. At the outset, the one thing we can confirm is Beethoven's primary, lifelong concern with a correct realization of his tempos, a concern revealed often in his editorial inscriptions, letters, and Conversation Books, and in the reports of those same close associates. To cite the evidence most often given (in spite of the

4. My translation from Leitzmann/BEETHOVEN II 230.

5. BEETHOVEN WERKEM V/3 161. On the 5 standard tempos, cf. Koch/LEXIKON 64.

6. BEETHOVEN WERKEM II/1 31. And David Fallows cites the bewildering inscription with which Beethoven's Mass in C, Op. 86, opens, "Andante con moto assai vivace quasi Allegretto ma non troppo" (GROVE XVIII 679).

7. Drake/BEETHOVEN 36–41 lists the markings recommended by both Czerny (2 versions) and Moscheles for Beethoven's piano sonatas, as well as those recommended later by Bülow and by Schnabel, for comparison.

source), Anton Schindler tells us, "When a work by Beethoven had been performed, his first question was always, 'How were the tempi?' Every other consideration seemed to be of secondary importance to him."[8]

There are three main reasons why Beethoven's tempos remain elusive even in the music for which he left metronome markings. First, we cannot be sure that the markings on his early metronomes correspond fully with those on modern metronomes. Second, we cannot be sure that he really meant what he thought he meant by those markings, anyway. And third, we have come to realize that no one tempo for a particular piece will prove ideal for every performance, each with its particular combination of circumstances. Brief comments on those three reasons will take us further into our topic.

The Beethoven scholar Gustav Nottebohm soon refuted Schindler's assertion that the same numbers indicated different tempos on two metronomes of different sizes that Maelzel had made.[9] He confirmed, in any case, what Beethoven himself must have understood as soon as he became interested in a "metrometer" (not later than 1812)[10]—that those numbers (like the ones used for most other early time-keeping devices) all indicated the number of beats per minute. In other words, 60 indicated, as it still indicates, one beat per second.[11]

8. Schindler & MacArdle/BEETHOVEN 423 fn. One recalls Mozart's remark in a letter to his father of Oct. 24, 1777, that "time" is "the most essential, the most difficult and the chief requisite in music" (as in Anderson/MOZART I 340).

9. Nottebohm/METRONOMISCHE 126–37; Schindler & MacArdle/BEETHOVEN 425–26. Schindler's assertion is still accepted in some recent writings, as in Goldschmidt/CRAMER 125.

10. The year is suggested by Beethoven's note to Zmeskall of Feb. 8, 1812, as translated in Thayer & Forbes/BEETHOVEN 528. By 1813 Beethoven was already signalled as a convert to Maelzel's metronome (Seifert/METRONOMISIERUNGEN 183).

11. Nottebohm/METRONOMISCHE 127 fn. reprints 2 explicit clarifications, from 1817 and 1818. Cf. Edgard Varèse's pertinent remarks in *Musik-Konzepte* VIII (April 1979), p.4, written somewhat sarcastically in the manner of Debussy's remarks quoted above. For a documented summary of the metronome's history as it concerned Beethoven, see Thayer & Forbes/BEETHOVEN 528, 544–45, 686–88, 932, and 1040.

Although the recent, highly controversial study Talsma/ANLEITUNG explores the subject of tempo in Beethoven's music resourcefully, I find myself quite unable to accept its basic premise, advanced in its initial chapter, to the effect that the note values in Beethoven's metronome markings for his fast movements (only) were meant to be understood at one half of their written value. Talsma argues, for example, that in an "Allegro" movement marked $\frac{4}{4}$ with a half note at 80, Beethoven actually meant a quarter note at 80 and used the half note rather to signify the value of the prevailing arsis-thesis (or tactus) complementation of two quarter notes. That premise not only exploits the common complaint of excessive speeds by going too far—indeed, further—in the other direction, but 1) it defies Nottebohm's reprinted clarifications as well as other practical evidences like those to be cited shortly from Quantz a half-century earlier and from Sir George Smart during Beetho-

As to whether Beethoven really meant quite the metronome markings he supplied, the uncertainty has persisted longer. It concerns his grasp of the practicalities of musical performance as late as 1817, the first year in which he supplied markings in any quantity.[12] How much contact had he lost with his instrument some eight years after ending virtually all professional activities as a pianist and after losing his hearing almost entirely? That question must be asked not only because of the well-known problems of scoring and sonority in Beethoven's late works, but because of metronome markings against which the majority of performers have rebelled, including not a few markings that have been regarded as outright errors of arithmetic or transcription.[13]

Two further assertions by Schindler have also been refuted. One is the obvious misstatement, contradicted by Schindler himself, that Beethoven left markings only for the Ninth Symphony and the "Hammerklavier" Sonata Op. 106.[14] As is well known, he also left markings for the other eight symphonies, the first eleven string quartets, and a half-dozen lesser works,[15] comprising nearly ninety separate movements and over 135 markings in all. And he seems to have had every intention of adding

---

ven's lifetime; 2) it fails to justify adequately its application only to fast tempos; 3) it largely disregards the similar complaints of excessive speeds in the "andante" and slower movements; 4) it overstates both the technical impracticality and the musical incomprehensibility of most of Beethoven's markings in movements with fast inscriptions; 5) it overlooks Beethoven's own exceptional technical dexterity (as reported in our previous chapter); 6) it generally sidesteps the many markings (with fast inscriptions) in which the value in the marking is the same as, not twice that of, the unit-beat in the time signature (e.g., a quarter note at 120 in $\frac{2}{4}$, in the finale of the String Quartet Op. 18/1); and 7) it rests not on any unequivocal, contemporary documentation, only on moot and conjectural statements. Among newer studies that derive from Talsma/ANLEITUNG, cf. Wehmeyer/INTERPRETATION. Among recent antidotes for Talsma's study, though without mention of it, is Malloch/MINUET (cited further below), in which Classic tempos, especially of many Beethoven minuets, are argued generally to have been taken decidely too slow, not too fast! Cf., also, ÖMZ XL (1985) 369–70 and XLI (1986) for further pros and cons.

12. In 1817 S. A. Steiner of Vienna and the Leipzig AMZ XIX 873–74 published Beethoven's markings for his first 8 symphonies. But Beethoven had supplied markings as early as 1815, unless a letter supposedly from him to Tobias Haslinger is wrongly placed in that year in Anderson/BEETHOVEN II 542.

13. E.g., cf. Paolone/AUTOGRAFO, especially pp. 188–89 and 194–95, on Beethoven's markings for Op. 106 in his letter to Ries of April 16, 1819, and on the extreme errors in those markings that crept into both the first London edition (not the Artaria edition in Vienna) and into WEGELER & RIES. Also, cf. Stadlen/METRONOME I 330–31; Frimmel/HANDBUCH I 408–411.

14. Schindler & MacArdle/BEETHOVEN 425.

15. A full list, complete with markings, appears in Beck/TEMPOPROBLEM 212–220, but arranged by tempo inscription rather than by the work. A full list of Beethoven's works not marked by himself but arranged by works and augmented by the markings of Czerny, Moscheles, Kolisch, and Leibowitz may be found in Riehn/ORIGINALE.

markings for many of his other works,[16] among them Opp. 109, 110, 111, the "Diabelli" Variations, and the Bagatelles Op. 126.[17] However, among all Beethoven's solo piano works as well as instrumental chamber works with piano, Op. 106 remains his only piano work for which his metronome markings are known today. Schindler's other false assertion is that Beethoven eventually renounced the metronome, doing so after realizing in disgust that he had provided two, often different, sets of tempos for the Ninth Symphony on two different occasions.[18] Except for Beethoven's characteristic reaction in 1826 to a metronome that had broken down— "the deuce take everything mechanical"[19]—the evidence shows that he retained his interest in the metronome's value up to his last days, *especially* as regards the Ninth Symphony.[20]

As it happens, that one set of markings for piano—that is, in Op. 106— contains some of the markings most often protested by performers. Mainly, they have seemed unreasonably fast, not just in one but in all four movements, and with regard not only to technical difficulties but to musical sense as well. One may get an idea of these speeds by listening to Artur Schnabel's faithful but often unsuccessful attempts to observe them literally—for example, the half note at 138 in the first movement.[21] Yet, there have been at least a few performers who have believed in holding to this tempo. Most notable among these is Liszt, who treated Beethoven's music with the greatest respect.[22] Indeed, the American pianist William Mason heard Liszt chastise an upstart pianist about 1853 for playing that first movement too slowly and failing to heed Beethoven's own marking.[23] Both Rudolf Kolisch and Hermann Beck have argued

16. E.g., cf. Anderson/BEETHOVEN III 1178, 1182, 1263, and 1273; Stadlen/METRONOME II 40.

17. Schindler/BEETHOVEN II 105 (although no evidence can now be found for Opp. 109 and 110); Stadlen/METRONOME II 40.

18. Schindler & MacArdle/BEETHOVEN 425–26.

19. Anderson/BEETHOVEN III 1295; cf., also, II 804 and III 1182 and 1249. And cf. Stadlen/METRONOME II 45–47.

20. Cf. Anderson/BEETHOVEN III 1314–15 and 1344–45, also 1273 and 1286. Regarding a transition passage in the String Quartet Op. 132/iii, Beethoven jotted down in 1825, "Metronome highly necessary" (KONVERSATIONSHEFTE VIII 27).

21. Angel GRM 4005. In all fairness, Schnabel had intended to redo this youthful product of idolatry, as also his inexperienced edition of Beethoven's sonatas (Artur Schnabel, *My Life and Music* [New York: St. Martin's Press, 1964] 130–31).

22. Cf. Newman/LISZT.

23. William Mason, *Memories of a Musical Life* (New York: Century, 1902) 103–106. Cf., also, Newman/LISZT 197–98. For speeds and timings of Op. 106/i in recordings by 9 present-day pianists (ranging from 74 to 120 per half note on the metronome) cf. Černý/OP. 106/i.

that today's performers simply fail to get the meaning of the music; suggests Beck, these performers often impede their fluency by trying to be too "pathetic."[24] The arguments of Kolisch and Beck will be discussed presently.

Yet Beethoven can hardly be said to have prepared his markings casually or to have disregarded their practicability in performance. Considerable evidence to the contrary exists. For instance, well before he resorted more fully to the metronome he had striven for more precise tempos. Witness his letter of 1810 to Breitkopf & Härtel designating more specific tempo terms for the String Quartet Op. 74, or his letter of 1813 asking whether the Scottish publisher George Thomson understood "andantino" to be faster or slower than "andante."[25] And more than ten years after he started using the metronome, in the letter of 1826 to the publisher Schott that was cited earlier, he was still attributing the success of a performance (the Ninth Symphony) "largely to the metronome markings."[26] He often made tempo changes after actual performances, sometimes increasing the speed, as in the three successive versions of the very last section in *Leonore-Fidelio*,[27] sometimes slowing it, as in the "Gloria" of the Mass Op. 86.[28] And in spite of his deafness he spent much time in rehearsals working out ideal tempos, as when his nephew Karl helped him set the metronome markings,[29] or when, in the words of violinist Joseph Böhm, Beethoven's "eyes followed the bows [of the string quartet with close attention so that] . . . he was able to judge the smallest fluctuations in tempo or rhythm and correct them immediately."[30]

Finally, there is that third reason why Beethoven's tempos remain elusive even with his metronome markings. No one tempo can suit all circumstances. It is not surprising that virtually every composer who has provided metronome markings in his scores has found a need to revise them from time to time. One only has to recall how the volume, the pedalling in piano music, the performer's disposition toward emotional and virtuosic display, the size of the hall and audience, the acoustics, the mood of the day, changing aesthetic attitudes, and even the weather—how any or all of those can affect the choice of tempo. To be sure, such variables are hardly subject to regulations (thank goodness!), but they can make a perceptible difference, nonetheless.

24. Kolisch/TEMPO 177–78; Beck/BEMERKUNGEN 41–42.

25. Anderson/BEETHOVEN I 285 and 406.

26. Anderson/BEETHOVEN III 1325.

27. Beck/TEMPOPROBLEM 86.

28. Anderson/BEETHOVEN I 378; cf. I 243 and II 542 for related changes.

29. Stadlen/METRONOME I 332–33 and Plate V.

30. Thayer & Forbes/BEETHOVEN 940–41.

Yet how great do such differences of occasion and circumstance ever become? As the experienced quartet leader Rudolf Kolisch remarked (his italics), *"What matters is always, of course, only a significant divergence which destroys the meaning—never mere nuances within the type."*[31] It is doubtful that a difference of circumstances ever actually changes the category of tempo. As examples of changed categories, one might listen to a recording of both *Soñate pathétique* Op. 13 and "Sonata appassionata" Op. 57 as played by the late Glenn Gould.[32] In Op. 13 he turns "Adagio cantabile" into "Andante" by playing at M.M. 84 the eighth note that Czerny had learned under Beethoven at 54 and that most artists take today at about 63 (as in a recording by Friedrich Gulda). In Op. 57 Gould turns the opening "Allegro assai" into "Allegretto" by playing the dotted quarter-note at 76 that Czerny took at 108 and that most artists now take at about 92 (as in a recording by Emil Gilels).[33]

Some Previous Studies of Beethoven Tempo (Beck)

In spite of the elusive aspects of Beethoven's tempos that continue to challenge performers, one initial conclusion has been coming to the fore: If his original metronome markings have the same clock values today and if they represent the composer's considered judgments, then by and large they should be taken at face value. This conclusion is important not only for the music that he did provide with markings but, by suitable analogies, for the music that he did not. To be sure, those markings still fail today to win universal acceptance among performers and scholars. They continue to arouse controversies, as revealed in a spate of new studies from the numerous conferences of the Beethoven sesquicentennial year of 1977.[34]

However, in the most extended study yet done of Beethoven tempo— the one by Beck shortly to be examined—the general validity of the markings is accepted, as it is here and in certain other studies to be noted. These modern studies, like the relatively few on tempo in the music of

31. Kolisch/TEMPO 180.

32. Columbia MS 7413.

33. Badura-Skoda/CZERNY 37 and 52; Musical Heritage OR-B119 and Deutsche Grammophon 2530 406, respectively.

34. It is not surprising that the Vienna Beethoven conference reported in BEETHOVEN-KOL-LOQUIUM 1977 was soon dubbed the "Metronom-Kongress," including Stadlen/METRO-NOME II and Seifert/METRONOMISIERUNGEN. Nearly all of MUSIK-KONZEPTE 8 (1979), dedicated to the late Rudolf Kolisch, concerns Beethoven's use of the metronome. For a review of the various Beethoven "metronome congresses" and publications around 1977–79, cf. BEET-HOVEN-JAHRBUCH X (1978–81) 374–84.

Beethoven's greatest Viennese predecessors, have at least one element in common: They all establish some link with absolute time values, metronomic or other, in order to support their conclusions. Although time-keeping devices had not yet been used by Haydn and Mozart, modern studies such as those by Isidor Saslav, Rudolf Elvers, and Max Rudolf[35] have had to start with 18th-century ancestors of the metronome or with tables that give exact time values to allegro and other standard tempo terms.[36] Some authors of those studies have started with the tempo table that Quantz published in 1752, which followed tradition in taking its beat from the heartbeat, but at a fast 80 per minute.[37] Others have started with a few Classic pieces written for musical clocks and music boxes, some of which still work; or with metronome marks added posthumously that may or may not trace back to tempos preferred by the composers themselves in performance.

That one most extended study of tempo in Beethoven's music is a German dissertation completed in 1954 by Hermann Beck, the essence of which appeared in the *Beethoven-Jahrbuch* for 1955–56.[38] Having begun by arguing for the general validity of Beethoven's metronome markings, Beck stresses that these, rather than the "tempi ordinari" or a single point of reference like the heartbeat, became necessary in order to accommodate the great refinements of tempo introduced toward the end of the 18th century. He then argues that a full understanding of these markings calls for the identification of each with a particular rhythmic *Bewegung*—that is, a characteristic rhythmic flow and feel, or what Rousseau had already perceived in 1768 as "le vrai Mouvement."[39] Beethoven himself sought to define a rhythmic character, as we read in another well-known letter by him on tempo and the metronome (addressed to the Viennese conductor Mosel in December of 1817):

I am heartily delighted to know that you hold the same views as I do about our tempo indications[,] which originated in the barbarous ages of music. For, to take one example, what can be more absurd than Allegro, which really sig-nifies *merry*, and how very far removed we often are from the idea of that tempo. So much so that the piece itself means the *very opposite of the indication*—As for those four chief movements, which, however, are far from embodying the

35. Saslav/HAYDN, Elvers/TEMPI, Rudolf/MOZART.

36. Cf. Zaslaw/TEMPO.

37. Quantz/VERSUCH 261; cf., also, pp. 263–71.

38. Beck/TEMPOPROBLEM and -/BEMERKUNGEN.

39. In his *Dictionnaire de musique,* under "Battre la mesure," as cited in Zaslaw/TEMPO 720. But by 1739 Mattheson had already cited what must have been a very early use of this term by Rousseau (as noted in Chapter 6 below).

truth or the accuracy of the four chief winds, we would gladly *do without them.* But the words describing the character of the composition are a different matter. We cannot give these up. Indeed the tempo is more like the body, *but these*[words] *certainly refer to the spirit of the composition*—As for me, I have long been thinking of abandoning those absurd descriptive terms, Allegro, Andante, Adagio, Presto; and Maelzel's metronome affords us the best opportunity of doing so. I now give you *my word* that I shall *never again* use them in any of my compositions.[40]

(It hardly needs be added that this promise was kept no better than so many other naive, well-meant promises from Beethoven!)

Beck says the *Bewegung*, or rhythmic character (as we shall call it hereafter), is determined collectively by three aspects of rhythm, each of which exerts its own type of influence. These are (1) the prevailing note values and patterns; (2) the time signature and its traditional tempo associations; and (3) the tempo inscription. All three had already been comprehended under "le vrai Mouvement" by Rousseau, as cited above, and in 1777 by J. P. Kirnberger and J. A. P. Schulz in Sulzer's *Allgemeiner Theorie der schönen Künste.*[41] Also, two of the aspects, the time signature and the tempo inscription, had been interrelated by Mozart in an oft-quoted letter of July 7, 1783, when he wanted to convince his father that Clementi played too slowly.[42] But Beck argues that all three aspects—note values, signature, and inscription—must be interrelated in order to arrive at the correct rhythmic character. Thus, although only one of the three aspects differs, the three-part rhythmic character is not the same for the opening of Beethoven's second quartet in Op. 18 as for the close of his Quartet Op. 74 (Ex. 4/1). The time signature, $\frac{2}{4}$, and the tempo inscription, "Allegro," are the same, but the note values and patterns are so different that Beethoven's metronome markings at those passages come out almost twice as fast for Op. 74 as for Op. 18/2. That is, as against a quarter note at 96 in Op. 18/2/i Beethoven has a half note at 84 at the close of Op. 74. One needs to hear these passages performed to perceive fully their contrast in rhythmic character. That kind of identification of tempo with rhythmic character, at least as regards time signatures and note values, appears to have been recognized consciously by Beethoven himself as early as 1790. As Richard Kramer has shown, Beethoven seems to have come to it at least partly through Kirnberger's writings.[43]

---

40. Anderson/BEETHOVEN II 727.

41. Beck/BEMERKUNGEN 27.

42. Anderson/MOZART II 850, as discussed in Zaslaw/TEMPO 721–22.

43. Kramer/EDUCATION 73–76. I am indebted to Richard Kramer for supplementary information by correspondence.

EXAMPLE 4/1 String Quartets (a) Op. 18/2/i/1–6 and (b) Op. 74/iv/ 186–88 (after BEETHOVEN WERKEM VI/3/I 27 and VI/4/II 123; HV*)

In order to classify each fast movement that Beethoven "metronomized," Beck prepared a series of tables arranged by tempo inscriptions, metronome markings, and "tempo [or metric] groupings." The first of these tables (Ex. 4/2) includes, near the tops of its second and fifth columns, the two allegro tempos already cited from Opp. 18/2 and 74 (Ex. 4/1). That table consists of all the fast movements in $\frac{2}{4}$ meter with metronome markings. Its three categories of tempo groupings correspond either to the upbeat of a single measure (e.g., the first and second quarter notes in one $\frac{2}{4}$ measure) or to the down- and upbeat of two successive measures (e.g., a half note each in two $\frac{2}{4}$ measures). The latter might also occur, of course, in one $\frac{4}{4}$ measure marked *alla breve* or lined ¢ (cut time, as in the Septet Op. 20/i/19 ff.). The tempo groupings find some support in Beethoven's frequent designation of a metronome marking for an entire measure (as in the markings for whole-notes in symphonies 4/i and 8/i). And they find further support in his grouping of measures by threes and fours, "ritmo di tre battute" and "ritmo di quattro battute," as in the second movement of his Ninth Symphony.

These groupings are important in any discussion of tempo to the extent that their character more than the actual pace may finally determine the tempo. Czerny said of the "Rondo" finale in Op. 31/1/1 (Ex. 4/3), "Since the 'Allegretto' is *alla breve*, the whole [movement] must be performed markedly fast (*allegro molto*). The lovely, melodious, expressive theme is to be played as *cantabile* as possible and the four-part harmony [is to be] projected through fully sustained tones."[44] But Schindler argued that

44. Badura-Skoda/CZERNY 46–47.

Example 4/2   Tabelle 1 in Beck/BEMERKUNGEN 39 (EH*).

	1.Tempogruppe	2. Tempogruppe		3.Tempogruppe
Bewegungs-gliederung	♩ ♩ ♩ ♩	♩ ♩ ♩ ♩	𝅗𝅥 𝅗𝅥	𝅗𝅥 𝅗𝅥
Allegro	♩ = 96 (op. 18, 2; 1. S.)	♩ = 120 (op. 18, 1; 4. S.) ♩ = 126 (op. 59, 1; 4. S.)	𝅗𝅥 = 69 (op. 18, 2; 2. S.)	𝅗𝅥 = 84 (op. 74; 4. S.)
In tempo d'Allegro		♩ = 132 (op. 68; 3. S.)		
A. ma non troppo			𝅗𝅥 = 66 (op. 68; 1. S.)	𝅗𝅥 = 80 (op. 60; 4. S.)
A. ma non troppo, un poco maestoso	♩ = 88 (op. 125; 1. S.)			
Allegro von brio			𝅗𝅥 = 72 (op. 92; 4. S.)	𝅗𝅥 = 108 (op. 67; 1. S.)
A. molto			𝅗𝅥 = 76 (op. 55; 4. S.)	
A. molto e vivace			𝅗𝅥 = 88 (op. 21; 4. S.)	
A. molto quasi presto			𝅗𝅥 = 92 (op. 18, 4; 4. S.)	
Presto	♩=116 (♪=116) (op. 55; 4. S.)		𝅗𝅥 = 92 (op. 59, 1; 4. S.)	

Example 4/3   Sonata Op. 31/1/iii/1–4 (after Badura-Skoda/CZERNY EA*)

Czerny had overlooked the influence of rhythmic character and quoted Czerny's first sentence—not, however, the qualifying second—asking, "Did Beethoven really have such a limited, schoolmaster-like notion of the *alla breve* measure that he would establish it, or any time signature, as the first law in interpreting a piece of music, rather than the particular character of the music itself? He himself played this rondo, and would have played it, 'at a comfortable pace.' The whole movement has much the character of a quiet narrative."[45]

Perhaps unwittingly, Schindler was also getting at a familiar psychological association with time signatures and prevailing note values. Given two meters with the same number of beats per measure but different values (e.g., $\frac{3}{4}$ vs. $\frac{3}{2}$), one tends to take the meter with the larger values more slowly. The most frequent psychological explanation is merely that the greater value looks simpler and "longer" (although the age-old, ever-changing relationships between time signatures and tempos have hardly proved to be that simple or predictable, what with proportional notation, tactus, *doppio movimento*, and other ambiguities.[46]

To be more specific, if one is unaided by any tempo inscription, one tends to choose a perceivably slower tempo for a measure of four half notes than for a measure of four quarter notes. And a corollary of that statement is that one tends to play slower when a measure of four quarter notes is marked $\frac{2}{2}$, *alla breve*, or ¢ rather than $\frac{4}{4}$ or C. The same tendency is evident in compound meters, causing $\frac{6}{4}$, for instance, to be taken slower than $\frac{6}{8}$. For that matter, there is a related tendency to think of compound meter in general as being livelier than simple meter, as in $\frac{6}{8}$ compared with $\frac{2}{4}$.

Unfortunately, Beethoven's responses to these tendencies seem to have vacillated, thus providing only very tenuous aids to the determination of any one tempo. When he changed to a slower tempo in the "Gloria" of his Mass Op. 86, he wrote explicitly, "I have altered C to ¢ , thus altering the tempo . . . A bad performance at which the tempo was too fast induced me to do this."[47] Yet, it was different when he wrote Ries on April 16, 1819, asking him to drop the "assai" from "Allegro assai" in the London edition of the "Hammerklavier" Sonata Op. 106 in order to accommodate the faster tempo (and more fluent character) that he evidently wanted. Then he included no request to change the ¢ to C.[48] Clearly, the effect of cut time in Beethoven's music has to be decided from case to case and,

45. Schindler & MacArdle/BEETHOVEN 422–23.

46. Cf. GROVE XVIII 675–85 (R. Donington & D. Fallows) and Zaslaw/TEMPO.

47. Anderson/BEETHOVEN I 378.

48. Cf. the letter as transcribed in Paolone/AUTOGRAFO 195; also, Brandenburg/TAKTVOR-SCHRIFTEN 42.

of course, not only by the time signatures and note values or patterns, but by the tempo inscriptions and by still other factors that, as will be argued presently, are needed to reinforce Beck's three-part rhythmic character.

With the score in hand, it is edifying to review the following instances

Instances of "Cut Time" in the Piano Sonatas

Opus	Inscription	Signature	Note values
2/1/i	Allegro [half = 104]	¢	qtr., 8th
2/1/iv	Prestissimo [half = 104]	¢	qtr., triplet 8ths
10/1/iii	Prestissimo [half = 96]	¢	qtr., 8th
10/3/i	Presto [half = 132]	¢	qtr., 8th
13/i	Allegro molto e con brio [half = 144]	¢	half, qtr.
13/iii	Allegro [half = 96]	¢	qtr., 8th
14/1/iii	Allegro comodo [half = 80]	¢	qtr., triplet 8ths
14/2/ii	Andante [qtr. = 112]	¢	qtr., 8th
27/1/i	Andante [qtr. = 66]	¢	half, qtr.
27/2/i	Adagio [qtr. = 54]	¢	qtr., triplet 8ths
31/1/iii	Allegretto [half = 96]	¢	half, qtr.
49/2/i	Allegro, ma non troppo [half = 104]	¢	qtr., triplet 8ths
53/iii	Prestissimo [coda] [whole = 88]	¢	qtr., 8th
81a/i	Allegro [half = 112]	¢	qtr., 8th
106/i	Allegro (half = 138) ["Allegro assai," originally]	¢	qtr., 8th
7/i	Allegro molto e con brio [dotted qtr. = 126]	6/8	dotted qtr., 8th
10/3/ii	Largo e mesto [8th = 72]	6/8	qtr., 8th
14/2/i	Allegro [qtr. = 80]	¢	8th, 16th
14/2/iii	Allegro assai [dotted qtr. = 80]	3/8	8th, 16th
22/2	Adagio con molto espressione [8th = 100]	9/8	8th, 16th
27/1/i	Allegro [dotted qtr. = 104]	6/8	8th, 16th
27/2/iii	Presto [half = 80]	¢	8th, 16th
31/1/ii	Adagio grazioso [8th = 116]	9/8	8th, 16th
57/i	Allegro assai [dotted qtr. = 120]	12/8	dotted qtr., 8th
101/i	Allegretto, ma non troppo [dotted qtr. = 72]	6/8	dotted qtr., 8th
101/ii	Vivace alla marcia [half = 76]	¢	half, qtr.
106/ii	Presto (half = 152)	2/4	qtr., 8th
106/iii	Adagio sostenuto (8th = 92)	6/8	dotted qtr., 8th
109/ii	Prestissimo [dotted half = 80]	6/8	dotted qtr., 8th
111/ii	Adagio [dotted 8th = 60]	9/16	dotted 8th, 16th

of "cut time" in his piano sonatas; and after these the instances that are
not in "cut time." (Two prevailing note values are included for each listing [qtr. = quarter and half=half note]; the metronome markings of
Beethoven are in parentheses, those of Czerny in brackets.[49]

Thus an extreme contrast occurs in the "Moonlight Sonata," Op.27/
2, with the use of ¢ for the "Adagio sostenuto" or opening movement, yet
unlined c for the "Presto agitato" finale. Of course, it is not the metric
relationship between these outer movements, but their individual rhythmic character and groupings that concern us here. Those groupings will
surprise not a few performers who, as Czerny's metronome markings
suggest, prefer to think in quarter notes in the opening movement and
half notes in the finale. With Czerny, as with Beethoven himself, the unit
used for the metronome beat often contradicts the unit-beat (or denominator) defined by the time signature.

In the foregoing tables a different contrast appears between the two
fast, outer movements of Op. 2/1, which are both marked $\downarrow$ = 104 by
Czerny. If the tempos are the same, what makes the "Prestissimo" finale
sound so much faster than the opening "Allegro"? This time the difference lies in the note values—in the rush of triplet eighth notes compared
with duple eighth notes. In the finale of Op. 14/2, should we give preference today to Czerny's recollection (in 1842?[50]) of the dotted quarter
note at 80 or to his reconsidered marking of 88 in the Simrock edition
(1856 and later,[51] which Moscheles also recommended?[52] In this instance
the answer depends to a considerable extent on our understanding of the
tempo inscription. To rephrase the question, does the "assai" in "Allegro
assai" mean "very," which is its more frequent interpretation, or "rather,"
which moderates the "Allegro" so that "Scherzo" in its movement's title
is more likely to convey a piquant than a fleeting rhythmic character? My
own recommendation in this instance would be for "very," based on an
extension of Beck's "rhythmic character" to include such traits as slow
harmonic rhythm and light texture (see pp. 104–110).

Beck's larger purpose was to show how his approach may be applied
by analogy to that majority of works for which Beethoven did not provide
metronome markings. In other words, once Beck had identified each

49. In this chart I have used Czerny's markings from his *Vollständigen theoretisch prac-
tischen Pianoforte-Schule Op. 500* IV/ii (as in Badura-Skoda/CZERNY); but except where a
marking is missing or is wrong or questionable in Op. 500 according to long-time consensus, the intention at this point is not to express preferences over other, sometimes different
(usually faster) markings that Czerny gave elsewhere for the same movements (as in Badura-Skoda's inserted "Kommentar").

50. Cf. Newman/SSB 180 and fn. 34.

51. Newman/CHECKLIST 511.

52. Drake/BEETHOVEN 37.

Example 4/4 Sonata Op. 10/2/i/1–6 (after BEETHOVEN WERKEM VII/2/I 106; HV*)

metronome marking with a particular rhythmic character, then he assumed that approximately the same marking, or tempo, would apply in other Beethoven works that dated from about the same period and revealed a similar rhythmic character. Thus, Beethoven's quarter note at 96 for that opening "Allegro" of String Quartet Op. 18/2 (Ex. 4/1 above) might be applied to the opening "Allegro" of Piano Sonata in F Op. 10/2 (Ex. 4/4), which dates from the same period and reveals a similar rhythmic character, but no original metronome marking. And this possibility of 96 might be compared with Czerny's earlier marking of 104 for Op. 10/2/i[53] and with a fairly recent recording by Emil Gilels at 100.[54] Since Beck was primarily interested in developing a methodology, he saw no need to pursue his rhythmic analysis and tempo tables beyond one range of tempos in Beethoven's music, that marked "allegro" or faster.[55] Although the largest number of refinements in Beethoven's tempo inscriptions do pertain to those fastest tempos,[56] from the practical standpoint of performance at least as many problems arise in his moderate and slower tempos.

Four Other Studies of Beethoven Tempo

Rudolf Kolisch included the full range of Beethoven's instrumental music in an article of 1943[57] that anticipated Beck's efforts to link Beethoven's metronome markings with different sorts of rhythmic character. But perhaps because Kolisch approached this problem less systematically, he defended his observations less convincingly, relying largely on intuitive considerations for many of the specific metronome markings that represent his conclusions.

53. Cf. Badura-Skoda/CZERNY 35.

54. Deutsche Grammophon 2530 406. Stadlen/METRONOME II 56 questions such analogies because they suggest the *tempi ordinari* that Beethoven rejected (cf. fn. 5 above). But the analogies are no more "ordinary" in their tempos than their prototypes.

55. Beck/TEMPOPROBLEM 83.

56. Cf. the lists before and after 1812 in Rothschild/MOZART 12–14.

57. Kolisch/TEMPO. The late Rudolf Kolisch, to whom MUSIK-KONZEPTE 8 is dedicated by virtue of his article, never got to complete his promised 2d installment of Kolisch/TEMPO.

In 1967 and 1982 two related studies were published by the English pianist and writer Peter Stadlen that evaluate selected uses of the metronome by Beethoven.[58] The first of these concentrates on a well-known error at the *alla breve* "Presto" in the "scherzando" movement of the Ninth Symphony and (less convincingly) on what to do about it. That study, which does not relate specifically to Beethoven's piano music, set a new standard of thoroughness in the documentary investigation of such errors. Stadlen's second study examines 66 of Beethoven's 136 certifiable metronome markings that seem to indicate tempos faster or slower than those of any reputable performers' recordings that Stadlen has been able to check. Of those 66, 62 are found to be faster and 4 slower. After making all manner of allowances—for possible variations in metronomes, for the viewing of the pendulum weight at misleading angles (parallax) or even at its bottom rather than its top, for an unconscious tempo increase when other instrumental parts are tested at the piano, and for any combination of these—Stadlen concludes that it is possible to bring all but 6 of Beethoven's markings within the realm of plausibility. (He supports his findings with extended charts that list works, recordings, performers, and metronome tempos.) In other words, the conclusion is implied, at least, that apart from a few clear errors, Beethoven's metronome markings, even those that seem questionable at first, are based on reasonable expectations and that these expectations become understandable when due allowance is made for possible flaws in his metronomes and confusion in setting or interpreting the markings.[59]

In a fourth study of Beethoven tempo, an article of 1966, Nicholas Temperley did not accept Beethoven's own metronome markings.[60] In fact, he dismissed them out of hand as being "almost useless as guides to performance speeds," chiefly because of the uncertainties that a flexible tempo could create. Instead, he preferred to get what tempos he could get indirectly from over-all timings of performances led by Sir George Smart during Beethoven's last dozen years. Smart, an eminent London conductor and early Beethoven champion, had a penchant for jotting down timings of works he conducted, including those of all nine Beethoven symphonies. Unfortunately, he seems not to have consulted Beethoven personally about his tempos until he visited Beethoven in Vienna in 1825, after he had jotted down most of his timings.[61] Therefore, except for any direct influence that Beethoven's London associates could have had, pri-

58. Stadlen/METRONOME I and -/METRONOME II.

59. Stadlen/METRONOME II 54.

60. Temperley/TEMPO 323.

61. Young/BEETHOVEN 8–17.

marily Ferdinand Ries and Ignaz Moscheles,[62] those timings have to be taken mainly as notable examples of practices contemporary with Beethoven.

Smart's timings pose tough questions at best, since most of them lump an entire symphony or other cyclic work in one over-all timing, leaving unclear how long each movement lasted, how much time occurred between movements, whether any movement or section was deleted, and whether any or all repeats were taken.[63] There is even doubt in not a few instances as to which symphony or other work was intended. With considerable ingenuity Temperley was able to resolve enough of those questions to conclude that the tempos then did not differ consistently in either direction from the tempos taken by leading conductors today. Temperley also concluded that Smart was more likely to observe repeats in Beethoven's than in Haydn's or Mozart's music, though mostly only the shorter repeats. His observations pertain to tempo primarily as the over-all structure may bear on it.

Applying Beck's "Rhythmic Character" to Moderate and Slower Tempos

Thus far in this chapter I have sought to summarize and evaluate four aspects or problems of Beethoven's tempo—its elusiveness in spite of his metronome markings, the validity of those markings, Hermann Beck's association of the markings with types of "rhythmic character," and some related findings in other past studies based on relatively objective information. The remainder of this chapter introduces five additional aspects of Beethoven tempo that seem just as necessary to consider. None has received much attention in modern writings and all have an appreciable bearing on either the choice or flexibility of Beethoven's tempos, if not both.

As we have seen, the consensus seems to favor the acceptance and application of Beethoven's own metronome markings, subject to qualifications such as Stadlen and some others have discussed. Furthermore, it is my opinion that Beck's methodology is well grounded both logically

---

62. Fascinating at this point is Schindler/BEETHOVEN II 104–112, although much of what Schindler says there about the metronome and about Moscheles has been discredited (as in Schindler & MacArdle/BEETHOVEN 322, 359–60, and 372–74).

63. Cf. Braun/RECORDED 67, fn. 5. These qualifying factors had not been considered at all when Czerny wrote a plea for accurate timings of masterworks as the best guides to correct tempos (Badura-Skoda/CZERNY 121).

and musically, whatever its flaws and shortcomings, and that we would do well to continue in the direction to which Beck has pointed. Therefore, working on these assumptions, we need first to extend Beck's methodology to Beethoven's metronome markings for moderate and slow tempos, including identifications of those markings with various types of rhythmic character. Only then, by analogy, can we hope to supply further, acceptable markings to the whole range of Beethoven's piano music.

Second, we need to define more fully the nature of rhythmic character itself through the consideration not only of the three external factors—note values, signature, and inscription—but of pertinent internal factors such as harmonic rhythm and textural density. Third, we need to make some allowance for the particularly elusive question of tempo flexibility, which Beck scarcely mentioned, but which Temperley and a few others have regarded as a main reason for rejecting metronome markings. For instance, as noted above, Temperley has preferred to derive Beethoven's tempos by averaging whatever over-all timings of early performances are known today. Fourth, we should be taking note of the seldom mentioned but considerable influence of structure and dimension on tempo. And as our fifth, final aspect of Beethoven tempo to introduce, we need to bear in mind the effects on tempo of changing aesthetic attitudes over the two centuries since his composing began.

A full extension of Hermann Beck's methodology to moderate and slow tempos must await further, equivalent tabulations and comparisons by some other investigator. Here it must suffice to test that methodology on one moderate and one slow tempo. For metronome markings besides those in his Piano Sonata Op. 106 we must turn to Beethoven's instrumental works not for piano. An orchestral movement that specifies a moderate tempo and poses one of the conductor's most familiar problems is the second movement of Beethoven's Fifth Symphony. This movement, in $\frac{3}{8}$ meter, is inscribed "Andante con moto" and marked ♪ = 92. Most conductors prefer a little slower tempo—for example, Karajan about 84 in a recent recording[64] and others still slower—presumably because of the varied divisions of the unit-beat into sixteenth, triplet-sixteenth, and thirty-second notes. However, when we seek an analogy in a movement without Beethoven's own metronome marking, we immediately discover a limitation to extensions of Beck's methodology. The "Andante con moto" in question happens to be Beethoven's only use of that inscription in $\frac{3}{8}$ meter without further qualification.[65] It is true that "Andante cantabile con moto" over the second movement of the First Symphony, also in

64. Deutsche Grammophon 2563 020, but Stadlen/METRONOME II 61 clocks Karajan at about 80.

65. Cf. Beck/TEMPOPROBLEM 189 and 191.

⅜ meter, is a similar inscription. But, as the added term "cantabile" may have been meant to suggest, this movement flows along at a decidedly faster tempo, with a marking of 40 for a dotted quarter note—that is, for an entire measure rather than for the time signature's unit-beat of an eighth note.

In any case, in that situation no satisfactory analogy can be proposed, since there is no other Beethoven piece in ⅜ meter with a similar inscription and no metronome marking. Indeed, sufficiently close analogies between works with and without metronome markings become somewhat harder to find at the moderate and slow tempos, given Beethoven's carefully differentiated tempo inscriptions and our exclusion of his vocal music. For instance, one hardly would expect to find more than the one inscription reading, "Un poco meno andante ciò è un poco più adagio come il tema," which heads Variation IV in the finale of Piano Sonata Op. 109.

This last inscription recalls Beethoven's query as to whether "andantino" meant faster or slower than "andante."[66] He must have arrived at no final answer, but contrary to Mozart's use of "andantino" (as concluded in an interesting discussion by Neal Zaslaw[67]) Beethoven's twenty-three uses of that term seem to interpret it more often as meaning faster instead of slower than "andante."[68] Similarly, when "assai" should mean "very" and when it should mean "rather" (moderately) must remain uncertain, although performers do not seem to allow sufficiently for the possibility that moderation rather than heightening of the tempo is intended.[69] In "Assai vivace" over the "Scherzo" of Op. 106 the term presumably means "very," but at the "Assai meno Presto" in the third movement of the Seventh Symphony the inscription itself as well as the sharply reduced metronome speed (84 for a dotted half note, down from 132) confirm that here "assai" must mean moderation of the tempo.

An analogy that is sufficiently close in the moderate (andante) range does occur between the "Andante cantabile" of String Quartet Op. 18/5 and the "Andante cantabile con variazioni" in Piano Trio Op. 1/3 (Ex. 4/5). Only the Quartet has metronome markings. Both movements have the time signature ²⁄₄, although Beethoven chooses the eighth rather than the quarter note for his metronome marking, at 100. Approximately the same tempo seems appropriate in the Piano Trio. If it were to differ at all it would be toward slightly more flow, hence speed. Although the rhythmic character as Beck defined it is essentially the same in the two move-

66. Cf. Anderson/BEETHOVEN I 406.

67. Zaslaw/TEMPO 722.

68. Cf. Beck/TEMPOPROBLEM 193.

69. Cf. GROVE I 659 "Assai" (D. Fallows).

EXAMPLE 4/5 (a) String Quartet Op. 18/5/iii/5–8 (after BEETHOVEN WERKEM VI/3/I 92; HV*) and (b) Piano Trio Op. 1/3/ii/5–8 103 (after Raphael & Klugmann/TRIOSM I; HV*)

ments—that is, insofar as the note values, time signature, and inscription are concerned—it begins to differ a little when the Quartet's internal traits are also considered, including its portato articulation, dotted figure, and ornamental turn. These have the effect of restraining the flow slightly, especially of stretching the cadence a bit and thereby encouraging flexibility. In representative recordings of these analogous movements, by the Bartók Quartet and the Barenboim Trio,[70] the performance of the Quartet movement proves, in fact, to be slightly slower (using Beethoven's original marking of an eighth note at 100) than that of the Trio movement (with its eighth note clocked at 104).

For an extension of Beck's analogical method to a slow tempo, we may compare the "Adagio molto" that introduces Beethoven's First Symphony with the "Adagio molto" in his Piano Sonata Op. 10/1 (Ex. 4/6). The Symphony has Beethoven's own marking of an eighth note at 88, although most conductors take it a little slower (Karajan at a flexible 76, for example).[71] The Sonata has only the posthumous markings by Czerny and Moscheles, indicating a still slower eighth note at 69–72,[72] which is also the tempo range taken by Friedrich Gulda.[73] But now we see that one of Beck's three external aspects of the rhythmic character is no longer

70. Qualiton SLPX 11425 and Angel 3771-1.

71. Deutsche Grammophon 2740 172.

72. Cf. Drake/BEETHOVEN 36.

73. Musical Heritage OR B-118.

EXAMPLE 4/6 From the openings of (a) the First Symphony, after the piano reduction in Edition Peters No. 196a/3, and (b) the slow movement in Piano Sonata Op. 10/1 (after BEETHOVEN WERKEM VII/2/I 98; HV*)

a. Adagio molto.

b. Adagio molto

the same in the two works. The time signature in the Symphony opening is c, or ⁴⁄₄, whereas that in the Sonata movement is ²⁄₄.

Two questions naturally follow. Shouldn't an eighth note in ⁴⁄₄ be equated with a sixteenth note in ²⁄₄, since each ⁴⁄₄ measure has twice the total note value of each ²⁄₄ measure? And if so, won't the use of an eighth note as the beat in both works cause the Symphony opening to sound only about half as fast as the Sonata opening? The answer has to be "no" to both questions. The use of an eighth- rather than a sixteenth-note pulse in the Sonata movement always seems to have been accepted without question by performers; and from measure 4 on in the Symphony, each measure of ⁴⁄₄ meter actually functions as two measures of ²⁄₄ meter, with a downbeat and its release (or arsis and thesis) in each pair of quarter notes, quite as in the Sonata. To be sure, prior to measure 4 of the Symphony there are a downbeat and its release in each pair of half- rather than quarter-note beats. In terms of a $\frac{2}{4}$ measure one might say that Beethoven was beginning his slow introduction with a "ritmo di due battute"! Otherwise, in slow music the tempo groupings that were discussed earlier are more likely to consist of single or divided unit-beats than of whole measures or other compounds of the unit-beat.

If it is agreed that the eighth note in Ex. 4/6 does represent the common denominator between the Symphony opening and the Sonata movement, the somewhat slower tempo in the Sonata must be attributed, as in our previous analogy, to internal traits that include the articulation, ornamentation, and dotted figures—also, in this instance, the faster harmonic rhythm. Furthermore, there is that tendency, suggested earlier, to play a shorter measure slower than a longer one, even when the unit-beat remains the same.

Extending the Meaning of "Rhythmic Character"

In the process of extending Beck's methodology from fast to moderate and slow tempos, it also has proved necessary to extend his tripartite definition of rhythmic character. One consequence, typical in the field of performance practice, is the increased subjectivity of any performance problem the moment one penetrates it beyond its external traits. Thus, Beethoven supposedly said of Cramer's Etude No. 9, "Since the character of the melody calls for a certain breadth, it [No. 9] should never be played fast."[74] That implied influence of melodic breadth suggests a relationship to tempo more subjective than that of Beck's note values, or time signatures, or inscriptions;[75] so do the details of articulation, ornamentation, dotted figures, and harmonic rhythm that were illustrated in Exx. 4/5 and 4/6.

It will be recalled that such internal components of the rhythmic character tend to slow the tempo more or less. They figure among still other enrichments by the composer that require appreciable added time to be digested fully. Those other enrichments are chiefly rhythmic and textural. Any irregularities in the rhythm that disturb or oppose the steady pulsation of the meter and any complications in the texture that impede the smooth flow of the lines are also likely to slow the music. Presumably

74. The reference is to Beethoven's annotations in the Cramer Etudes, which are discussed in Ch. 6 below.

75. A new study, Gelfand/TEMPO, makes "melodic content" a main tempo determinant in Beethoven's music. Although this study claims an approach that differs from the studies of Kolisch and Beck (p. 97, fn. 9), it depends in its own way on extending the meaning of rhythmic character.

EXAMPLE 4/7 Sonata Op. 110//iii/167–69 (after Wallner/KLAVIER-SONATENm II 306; HV*)

it was because of abrupt rhythmic and textural complications during Op. 110's fugal finale (Ex. 4/7) that Beethoven prescribed a slowing of the tempo. Such influences on the rhythmic character and ultimately on the tempo must be weighed against Beethoven's metronome markings that are generally regarded as being on the fast side and against his early reputation for unprecedented speed and agility in his own performance.[76] And they may go far to explain why certain performers of Beethoven such as Backhaus generally have preferred slower tempos than most others take.

In the "Rondo" theme of Beethoven's "Emperor" Concerto (Ex. 4/8), both the hemiola, which is pointed up by the two-note slurs, and the vigorous syncopation in the second measure conflict with the meter, hence tend to slow the over-all tempo (perhaps explaining the inscription "Allegro ma non troppo" rather than "Allegro" in some earlier sources). And these conflicts tend to slow the tempo even more when Christoph Eschenbach emphasizes them than when Arthur Rubinstein underplays them, in recordings currently available.[77] In this connection, one might

76. Cf. Friege/INTERPRETATIONS I 32–36, II docs. 7, 21, and 22 (among others).

77. Deutsche Grammophon 2530 438 and Dynoflex CRL7-0725, respectively.

EXAMPLE 4/8 The "Rondo" theme from the finale of Beethoven's "Emperor" Concerto (after Altmann/CONCERTOSm V 122)

recall Schindler's assertion that during Beethoven's teaching, it "was above all the rhythmic accent that he stressed most heavily . . . ."[78] Some confirmation of his concern with accents does exist both in remarks by Czerny[79] and in the fact, of course, of so many accent marks in Beethoven's own editing.

By way of Schindler, too, come the annotations about accenting, instrumental prosody, texture, and legato that Beethoven supposedly inserted for his nephew Karl's training in twenty-one of Cramer's Etudes.[80] These annotations, which are discussed in Chapter 6, are mentioned at this point because they suggest a strong preoccupation with further rhythmic minutiae that are likely to slow a performance, including applications of poetic feet. If we can believe Schindler, Beethoven might have wanted to bring out the three iambic "tone feet" that I have marked with horizontal brackets in the "Rondo" theme of his "Spring" Sonata, Op. 24, for piano and violin (Ex. 4/9). In the "Scherzo" of the same work there is a deliberate and very witty rhythmic conflict, or "contretemps," that creates a textural complication with a slowing effect (Ex. 4/10). To exploit this amusing passage a little more clearly, Clara Haskil and Arthur Grumiaux might have chosen a slightly more deliberate tempo in their recorded performance,[81] even though the inscription is "Allegro molto" and Beethoven's fast triple meters generally imply a whole-measure pulse (judging by his metronome markings for other movements).[82]

This consideration of internal traits that often contribute to rhythmic character could have included still other favorite Beethoven practices that might have a slowing effect, like abrupt dynamic shifts, or changing harmonies during a single application of the damper pedal (both discussed in Chapter 8). But except for one relatively extrinsic influence on rhyth-

78. Schindler & MacArdle/BEETHOVEN 416.

79. As in Badura-Skoda/CZERNY 42.

80. Cf. Newman/CRAMER; Goldschmidt/CRAMER.

81. Philips 6588 002.

82. The contention in Rothschild/MOZART 81 that Beethoven changed back to a smaller pulse in his last works (e.g., to the quarter note in $\frac{3}{4}$ meter) is largely speculative.

EXAMPLE 4/9 The "Rondo" theme from Op. 24/iv/5–6 (after BEETHOVEN WERKEM V/1/110; HV*g)

(Allegro ma non troppo)

EXAMPLE 4/10 Sonata for Piano and Violin Op. 24/iii/9–13 (after BEETHOVEN WERKEM V/1 108; HV*)

mic character yet to be noted, one more illustration should suffice here, starting this time with the performer and with his choice of a tempo that seems too slow.

In 1978, reviewing Anton Kuerti's generally fine recording of Beethoven's major piano works,[83] I suggested that certain slow movements in the sonatas were played too slowly. One of these was the "Largo e mesto" from Op. 10/3 and another that might well have been cited was the "Adagio sostenuto" from Op. 106 (Ex. 4/11). In both movements Kuerti takes the eighth note at about 54. Other recording artists time on the average at about 60 in Op. 10/3—for example, Alfred Brendel[84]—and at about 69–72 in Op. 106—for example, Charles Rosen.[85] The two movements have enough in common in their rhythmic character, including their § meters and their similar tempo inscriptions, note values, and general styles, to give us another plausible analogy in the category of slow tempos, even though they represent quite different periods in Beethoven's creative career (1796–98 as against 1817–18). With that analogy in mind, one would have some objective basis for advocating a faster tempo in Op. 10/3/ii, since Beethoven's metronome marking in the "Adagio sostenuto" of Op. 106 is an eighth note at 92.

To be sure, 92 is faster than any recognized performer is known to take either of these slow movements. But there are further reasons for

83. Newman/KUERTI, especially pp. 116–18.

84. Philips 6500 417. Czerny and Moscheles agree on an eighth note at 72.

85. Columbia M3X 30938. The average for the beginning of Op. 106/iii among 9 recording artists (not including Kuerti) who were timed in Stadlen/METRONOME II 71 is 73, the highest being 84 and the lowest 58. Stadlen lists Beethoven's marking of 92 as a possible "VE" (visual error, or parallax) for 80.

EXAMPLE 4/11 Sonatas (a) Op. 10/3/ii/1–3 and (b) Op. 106/iii/1–3 (after BEETHOVEN WERKEm VII/2/I/129 and Wallner/KLAVIERSONATENm II 244; HV*)

advocating a tempo in both movements at least as fast as today's norm, reasons that go back to the internal traits of rhythmic character. One of them is relatively slow harmonic rhythm, often lasting a full measure, which is longer than usual in Beethoven's slow movements. The slower the harmonic rhythm, of course, the greater will be the sense of flow and therefore the faster the tempo. Another reason is the breadth of the ideas, corresponding to the slow harmonic rhythm and to the number of Beethoven's slurs that last a measure or more throughout each movement. Indeed, my own inclination would be to feel two very slow dotted-quarter-note pulses in each measure rather than the single eighth-note pulses. Still another reason for advocating faster tempos than Kuerti takes is the sense of dramatic urgency and onward motion created in each movement, as by the driving crescendos prolonged over several measures (e.g., mm. 65–72 in Op. 10/3/ii and 160–66 in Op. 106/iii) or by the words added to the tempo inscription in Op. 106, "Appassionato e con molto sentimento."

    A relatively extrinsic influence on rhythmic character, and therefore tempo, is that of a few select dances, especially the minuet. Actually, two types of minuet of distinctly different character and tempo were still being danced and performed in the Classic era. One was a moderate if not slower piece that was kept from being faster by having "plenty of [sixteenth] notes," as Mozart put it in an enlightening letter written from Italy in 1770.[86] The other was an allegretto or even faster piece, in eighth- and quarter-notes. That the two types continued to stand apart throughout Beethoven's minuets is clear from pronounced differences in their inscriptions, character, and metronome markings (by Czerny when not by Beethoven).

The problem is that performers began to disregard these differences in the generation after Beethoven and generally have been disregarding them ever since. Indeed, most performers have played both minuet types in style and tempo as though there had been only the moderato type, whereas actually the faster minuet had been much more prevalent. Only recently have studies been published that should correct the misconceptions.[87] In any case, those who bear in mind that two types did exist will be able to distinguish them readily enough. Thus, compare two minuets—one gentle, poignant, moderato; the other bright, lively, allegretto—from the Sonata for Piano and Violin Op. 30/3 and the Piano Trio Op. 1/3 (as sampled in Exx. 4/12 and 4/13, respectively). Metronome markings typical of the distinction between these two types may be suggested: a quarter note at 116 for Ex. 4/12 (by analogy with Beethoven's marking in his Quartet Op. 59/3/iii) and a dotted-half at 58 in Ex. 4/13

86. Anderson/MOZART I 121. The stimulating discussion of dance "topoi" and their influence on tempo in Mozart's *Figaro* and *Don Giovanni*, in Allanbrook/GESTURE, is being extended to classic instrumental music by Dr. Allanbrook.

87. Two independent articles have investigated the minuet tempos, Rudolf/MINUETS and Malloch/MINUET. Malloch gets part of his evidence from restorations of musical clocks on which certain Haydn minuets were "recorded."

EXAMPLE 4/12 Sonata for Piano and Violin Op. 30/2/ii/51–55 (after BEETHOVEN WERKEM V/2 70; HV*)

EXAMPLE 4/13 Piano Trio Op. 1/3/iii/1–4 (after Raphael & Klugmann/ TRIOsm I 110; HV*)

(from Czerny[88]). Recall that the last of his "Diabelli" Variations is a nostalgic return—almost anachronistic, by 1823—to a graceful "Tempo di Menuetto moderato." To that title Beethoven added, "but not dragged," the same expression Czerny was to use about the "Tempo di Menuetto" quoted in Ex. 4/12.[89]

Flexibility in the Pulse Rate

In this chapter on tempo, flexibility is defined as elasticity in the pulse rate. Like tempo itself, flexibility reflects the prevailing rhythmic character, though at a more local level. And, it similarly responds to changes in the harmonic rhythm, texture, articulation, ornamentation, and rhythmic progress. Moreover, it also manifests itself predominantly by stretching rather than compressing the ongoing rhythm (a point seldom mentioned). For it likewise needs sufficient time to digest those changes in the rhythmic character.

One argument for performing Beethoven with flexibility is the number of his phrases or subphrases that end with a *fermata,* as at the deceptive cadence near the opening of the Sonata in A Op. 101 (Ex. 4/14). There is even evidence from Emanuel Bach and his successors that short rests were sometimes stretched out, judiciously, for expressive or rhetorical purposes in music at slow to moderate tempos.[90] But Schindler clearly went too far when he suggested that the quarter-note rests all "be extended to about double-length" in a fast, dramatic passage like that in the Sonata in C Minor Op. 10/1/i/13–21.[91] In any case, one soon realizes that flex-

88. Badura-Skoda/CZERNY 88.

89. Badura-Skoda/CZERNY 74.

90. Bach/VERSUCH 254; cf. Schwarz/PAUSEN 125–27, 128–30.

91. Cf. Newman/PERFORMANCE 54.

EXAMPLE 4/14   Sonata Op. 101/i/5–7 (after the autograph)

(Allegretto ma non troppo)

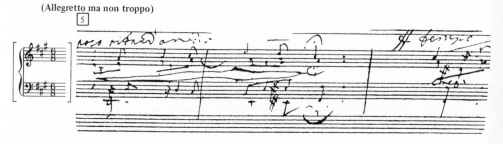

ibility does not literally mean a balance of push and pull on the tempo—
or robbing Peter to pay Paul, as modern *rubato* is sometimes explained.

By way of further illustration, we might take Brendel's recording of
the melodious "Andante" in Beethoven's Piano Sonata Op. 79,[92] a movement that suggests a Venetian barcarole. With a metronome set at Brendel's prevailing tempo of about 50 for a dotted-quarter note, we can readily
tell how often Brendel slows, though not accelerates, the pulse rate in
order to give momentary emphasis at each expressive peak, as at the
ornamental repetition of the phrase and at the half cadence on the dominant during measures 17–22 (Ex. 4/15).

What authority might we hope to cite for such flexibility? We tend to
think of Classic composers as preferring the dignity and drive of steady
tempos. Haydn left no comments known to us and few editorial markings
(chiefly cadential ritards) favoring flexibility,[93] although some flexibility
is expected, for example, at the return to a rondo refrain or during the
capriciousness that often infuses his music. Mozart revealed no more in
his editing than Haydn. Like his father, he did write more about tempo,

92. Philips 6500 417.

93. Flexibility is not considered in Saslav/HAYDN.

EXAMPLE 4/15 Sonata Op. 79/ii/17–22 (after Wallner/KLAVIERSONA-
TENm II 175; HV*)

though not about flexibility in the more modern sense.[94] If anything, he wrote against flexibility when he gave his clear definition of tempo rubato in the 18th-century sense, in a letter of 1777 to his father: "They all marvel that I always stay in strict time. They don't realize that tempo rubato in an adagio does not apply to the left hand."[95] Schubert, even in his songs, is authoritatively reported to have "always kept the most strict and even time, except in the few places [which prove to be remarkably few] where he expressly indicated in writing a ritardando, morendo, accelerando . . . ."[96] Furthermore, celebrated composer-theorist-pedagogs of his time, including Hummel and especially Czerny, were still insisting on strict time, with only minimal deviations.[97] Exceptional was Weber's statement in 1824, three years before Beethoven died, which disclosed a new, early Romantic spirit: "the beat, the tempo, must not be a controlling tyrant nor a mechanical, driving hammer; it should be to a piece of music what the pulse beat is to the life of a man."[98]

As for Beethoven, the surviving testimony, apart from the music itself, indicates that at least in principle he still favored a fairly strict, Classic tempo in his early career, but that he shifted toward more flexible tempo in later years as he increasingly embraced the new Romanticism. Thus, recalling the early period around 1800 and *Sonate pathétique,* Ries wrote, "Generally he [Beethoven] himself played his compositions very impetuously, yet for the most part stayed strictly in time, only infrequently pushing the tempo a little. Occasionally he would retard during a crescendo, which created a very beautiful and most remarkable effect."[99] And writing of the still earlier Piano Trio Op. 1/3, Czerny emphasized a recurring point that he presumably had derived from his study with Beethoven:

We must insert here the special observation, applicable generally, that there is a certain way to play melodious passages [subordinate themes] more restfully and yet not noticeably slower, so that the whole [movement] seems to move at one and the same tempo and [any difference] would only be realized if a metronome were beating. A conspicuous tempo change is not permitted except where the composer has indicated it expressly with a più lento, ritardando, etc.[100]

94. Flexibility is not considered in Elvers/TEMPI.

95. Bauer & Deutsch/MOZART II 83.

96. As quoted from Leopold von Sonnleithner in Newman/SCHUBERT 529–30.

97. Cf. Newman/SCHUBERT 542–44, with citations.

98. Weber's complete statement (added to full metronome markings for *Euryanthe*) was reprinted in AMZ L (1848) cols. 123–27.

99. WEGELER & RIES 106.

100. Badura-Skoda/CZERNY 87; cf., also, p. 30 and Hummel/ANWEISUNG 425–32, especially p. 428.

On the other hand, based on his closeness to Beethoven in his later years, Schindler wrote instead about tempo flexibility, seeing it as a main clue to Beethoven performance. Indeed, he wrote about it more abundantly than any other close associate of Beethoven's. Though he eventually recanted some of his earlier, most extreme statements,[101] in the third edition of his Beethoven biography he still promoted certain freedoms to a degree that raises doubts about his own musicianship.[102] Still, no connoisseur of Beethoven's later music can doubt that Schindler took his cue at least partly from Beethoven's own views. For example, Schindler's personal prejudices alone are not likely to explain two well-known statements in the Conversation Books of 1824 that Schindler is known to have falsely added about twenty years later, one implying that Czerny had played *Sonate pathétique* too inflexibly in tempo and one observing with an apparent sense of vindication that, according to others, Beethoven was taking his allegros slower than he had taken them fifteen to twenty years earlier.[103]

Beethoven's impassioned nature alone must have predisposed him toward tempo flexibility from the start. If he did not play his previously completed compositions with the same abandon that he revealed in his incomparable improvising,[104] he still exhibited that impetuosity reported by Ries and others.[105] Beethoven himself is not known to have used the term "tempo rubato," though he surely was well aware of it in the 18th-century sense employed by Mozart.[106] But he clearly knew its equivalent in the later sense, too, as when he wrote at the head of an autograph score of 1817, now missing, "100 according to Mälzel; yet this can only apply to the first measures, since feeling also has its beat, which cannot be conveyed wholly by a number (that is, 100)."[107] And he could well have been making the same point when he wrote Ries in 1825, "With pleasure I shall mark for you the tempos of *Christus am Ölberge* by means of the metronome, as uncertain [unsatisfactory?] as this time-keeper is."[108]

Lest such flexibility be interpreted too freely, one might counter with

101. Cf. Newman/SCHINDLER.

102. E.g., cf. Schindler & MacArdle/BEETHOVEN 418–22.

103. KONVERSATIONSHEFTE V 190 and 217. Both statements are among the forgeries listed in Beck & Herre/SCHINDLER.

104. Cf. Badura-Skoda/CZERNY 21–22.

105. WEGELER & RIES 106.

106. Bauer & Deutsch/MOZART II 83. Beethoven would have known its use in Bach/VERSUCH I/III/28 or by Neefe (cf. Thayer & Forbes/BEETHOVEN 37 and 371); cf., also, Marx/ANLEITUNG 68 (fn.).

107. According to Marx/ANLEITUNG 69, referring to the song "Nord oder Süd," WoO 148.

108. ". . . so wankend auch noch diese Zeitbestimmung ist" (Kastner & Kapp/BRIEFE 750).

Beethoven's recommendation in 1818 that students use the metronome so that they will not "*arbitrarily* sing or play out of time."[109] Whatever the flexibility, Beethoven apparently was stressing an aspect of his tempo that has been recognized too little: the need to establish and maintain a prevailing tempo.[110] In a letter from Milan of July 14, 1831, Mendelssohn reacted to the performance of two Beethoven sonatas by one of Beethoven's favorite pianists, Dorothea von Ertmann: " . . . often she exaggerates the expression a little, keeps dragging a good deal, then hurries again . . . ."[111] Was this freedom a reflection of Beethoven's own intentions while he was still alive, or of Ertmann's musical excesses as the years went by, or merely of Mendelssohn's vestigial Classicism?

Beethoven's own editing of his music supplies some primary evidence, though less than might be expected, for the flexibility of tempo that he seems to have wanted. His editing includes about two dozen terms or signs that either specify local tempo changes—for example, *rallentando* and *stringendo*—or at least imply them, as do *perendosi* and *appassionato*. A term like *marcando* might or might not affect the tempo. The same evidently applies to *calando*.[112] But Czerny's remark that *espressivo* "almost always" means *ritardando*[113] is supported in Beethoven's editing by several instances in which *espressivo* is followed by *a tempo*, as in the finale of his Sonata for Piano and Violin Op. 96 (Ex. 4/16),[114] (appropriately played in the recording by Haskil and Grumiaux.[115]) With that mention of Czerny and *espressivo*, it is worth quoting all eleven of his conditions under which a *ritardando* might be appropriate. Although Czerny was dispensing pedagogic generalizations at this point and not referring specifically to Beethoven's piano music, his words do reflect the influence of Mozart and Beethoven.

The *Ritardando*, according to the generally established rule, is much more frequently employed than the *Accelerando*, because the former is less likely to disfigure the character of the piece, than the too frequent hurrying on in the speed of the movement. We may retard the time most advantageously:

109. Anderson/BEETHOVEN III 1441–42 (cosigned by A. Salieri).

110. Cf. Stadlen/METRONOME II 54 (fn. 53).

111. Mendelssohn/REISEBRIEFE 194; cf., also, Schindler & MacArdle/BEETHOVEN 209–211.

112. Cf. Rosenblum/CALANDO.

113. Czerny/SCHOOL III 33–34.

114. This is one of several examples brought to my attention in a helpful article awaiting publication, "Tempo Flexibility in Conducting Beethoven's Symphonies," by the American educator and conductor Russell T. Waite. A similar example may be found in Piano Sonata Op. 109/ii/29–33.

115. Philips 6588-003.

EXAMPLE 4/16 Sonata for Piano and Violin Op. 96/iv/97–101 (after
BEETHOVEN WERKEM V/2 155; HV*)

a. In those passages which contain the return to the principal subject;

b. In those passages, which lead to some separate member of a melody;

c. In those long and sustained notes which are to be struck with particular emphasis, and after which quicker notes are to follow;

d. At the transition into another species of time, or into another movement, different in speed from that which preceded it;

e. Immediately after a pause;

f. At the Diminuendo of a preceding very lively passage; as also in brilliant passages, when there suddenly occurs a trait of melody to be played piano and with much delicacy;

g. In embellishments, consisting of very many quick notes, which we are unable to force into the degree of movement first chosen;

h. Occasionally also, in the chief *crescendo* of a strongly marked sentence, leading to an important passage or to the close;

i. In very humorous, capricious, and fantastic passages, in order to heighten the character so much the more;

[Czerny omitted the letter j. as was the custom then.]

k. Lastly, almost always where the Composer has indicated an *espressivo;* and also

l. At the end of every long shake which forms a pause or Cadenze, and which is marked diminuendo.

n[ote]: It is of course understood, that here, under the term *Ritardando*, we mean to comprehend all other equivalent expressions, which indicate a more or less marked slackening in the original degree of movement, as for Example: *rallent*[.], *ritenuto, smorzando, calando, &c;* as they are only distinguished from each other by the more or less degree of Ritardando.[116]

Czerny follows with his own examples and comments, conceding only rare, cautious instances of *accelerando.*

Beethoven's editing of his thirty-two solo piano sonatas provides the clearest evidence of his shift from less to more flexibility, because those sonatas provide both the most nearly continuous coverage of his composing and his most pliable medium for his flexibility. It is important to

116. Czerny/SCHOOL III 33–34.

remember that the medium itself affects the rate as well as the flexibility of the tempo. Said Schindler, "That orchestral music does not admit of such frequent changes of time as chamber music, is, of course, an understood fact."[117] As for the rate of tempo, in Beethoven's own arrangement for string quartet of his Piano Sonata Op. 14/1—the very arrangement about which he wrote that only the composer should arrange his own works[118]—he changed the "Allegro" inscription over the first movement of the Sonata to "Allegro moderato" in the Quartet, and "Allegro comodo" in the third movement to "Allegro."

In the earlier solo sonatas, the editorial terms indicating flexibility are not only less numerous, but less varied. They are confined largely to retards and focal points in the structure, whereas in the later sonatas they even include accelerations and extend to freer passages at other places in the music. Yet the total number of such terms is few enough—none in Op. 26 nor several other sonatas—to make highly plausible Czerny's implications and Schindler's declarations that Beethoven played and expected many more freedoms than he indicated.[119] At the same time, the terms suggesting flexibility are so rare in all but the last slow movements that one has to keep remembering the extent to which a dignified, Classic

117. Schindler/BEETHOVEN II 140.

118. Anderson/BEETHOVEN I 74–75.

119. E.g., cf. Badura-Skoda/CZERNY 42; Schindler & MacArdle/BEETHOVEN 397, 401, and 412.

EXAMPLE 4/17 Sonata Op. 106/iii/117–20 (after Wallner/KLAVIER-SONATENm II 251; HV*)

(Adagio sostenuto ♩ = 92)

steadiness still dominated Beethoven's concept of this movement type. Moreover, one has to keep remembering that Beethoven never lost track of a prevailing beat and tempo, no matter what the freedoms were, as is suggested, for example, by a remark in the score of his Ninth Symphony, at measure 8 of the finale, "Selon le caractére d'un recitative, mais in tempo." (An exception is his inscription "senza tempo" over a short piano cadenza in the first movement of his "Emperor" Concerto Op. 73 (mm. 371–72).

Sometimes Beethoven even wrote out his "freedoms" within a steady, underlying beat—that is, he indicated them through the notation rather than the editing. A choice illustration, recalling Mozart's rubato, is the Chopinesque cantilena marked "con grand' espressione" in the slow movement of the "Hammerklavier" Sonata (Ex. 4/17). But in any such intensely expressive music, performers also are likely to incorporate their own agogic inflections, the sort that are too subtle to be notated, as is true, for instance, in Kuerti's recorded performance.[120]

Structural and Historical Aspects of Beethoven Tempo

A full discussion of structural and historical influences on Beethoven tempo would take us beyond the scope of this book, but those influences warrant at least brief mention to keep the tempo problems in perspective. Regarding musical structure, the greater its size and complexity, the more likely will be its influence on tempo choice and flexibility. (In other words, the larger the forest, the more it must dominate the details of the individual trees.) Compared with the brevity and simplicity of Beethoven's bagatelles, the length and complexity of his "Diabelli" Variations require more care in choosing tempos slow enough to permit comprehension, yet fast enough to retain the attention; and tempos flexible enough to maintain interest, yet steady enough to maintain the continuity of the whole.

In short, the greater length and complexity increase the need for a clear balance of unity and contrast. Thus, the need for clear unity may itself require that that exceptionally long, complex slow movement of the "Hammerklavier" Sonata be played more nearly at Beethoven's metronome marking of 92 per eighth note and that it be played more steadily than in most recent recordings.[121] And the need for sharper contrasts

---

120. Aquitaine Records M4S 90371.

121. Referring to an earlier ed. of Newman/SCE 136 and 530, Paolone/OP 106, pp. 140 and 153–54 endorses as being close to Beethoven's intentions my own relatively fast timing of 36–37 minutes in numerous recital performances of the whole sonata (including iii); however, he rightly questions the accuracy of my timing of 17 minutes for the final "Largo" and fugue alone, which, in fact, should have read, "about 12 minutes."

may require that the seven movements of the Piano Trio Op. 38 be differentiated by tempos even more strategically opposed than those Beethoven had specified in the more colorfully scored movements of the Septet Op. 20. (When he arranged Op. 38 from Op. 20, he neither took over the markings from Op. 20 nor inserted new ones).

A method has yet to be found for determining and co-ordinating such structural influences. The timing of a complete performance, as in Temperley's investigations, reveals at best a prevailing tempo, but not the extent of any flexibility. A more basic relationship may exist between structure and metric grouping, as it does between structure and the shape of a musical idea. Whereas the shaping of the idea influences the shaping of the phrase that contains it, hence the period, the section, and finally the whole structure, so the choice of a metric grouping may influence the choice of measure—$\frac{2}{2}$ rather than $\frac{4}{4}$, for example—, the "ritmo di quatro battute," and ultimately, in its own way, the larger structural concepts. (The influential, 19th-century French theorist Mathis Lussy, whom we shall meet in Chapter 6, relates his primordial rhythmic groupings—masculine and feminine "incises"—to *A–B* and *A–B–A* musical structures.)[122]

To me, one shortcoming in Beck's valued dissertation is a failure to exploit the structural implications of his own tempo tables more fully. As each table progresses to faster tempos with more comprehensive beats, it also progresses to broader rhythmic units, which prove to define incipient structural levels. Thus, in Ex. 4/2 above, his table of $\frac{2}{4}$ meters progresses from a quarter note at 88 to a half note at 108 and from trochaic units (strong-weak) of one measure each to broader, trochaic structural units of two measures each. But Beck did go on to examine structural relationships in another respect. A decade after he wrote his dissertation, he wrote an article on proportional relationships in the contrasting tempos of the movements in a Beethoven cycle (as will be discussed in Chapter 9).

Finally, regarding changing historical attitudes, these reveal discernible trends less in the rate than the flexibility of the tempo. The usual supposition has been that tempos have been speeding up throughout the nearly two centuries since Beethoven began composing. This is a supposition that traces right back to Beethoven's own day. Türk wrote in 1802 that allegro had come to mean a much faster tempo than it had meant fifty years earlier,[123] A. B. Marx found the tempos in 1863 much "livelier" than in Mozart's day,[124] and a New York reviewer recently called

122. Lussy/EXPRESSION Ch. 5.

123. In the 2d ed. of Türk/KLAVIERSCHULE, as quoted in Rothschild/MOZART 8.

124. Marx/ANLEITUNG 62 (p. 105 in 1st ed.).

the new young pianists "louder and faster than ever." But the evidence is far from conclusive. Bärbel Friege's voluminous dissertation of 1970 on performance trends in Beethoven's piano sonatas since his own day establishes no metronomic bases for comparison, but leaves the impression of vacillating preferences, depending simply on personal tastes and technical abilities.[125]

Rothschild's evidence that the "Eroica" Symphony took an hour when Beethoven conducted, 52 minutes in a 1921 performance, and 46 now (1961) gives way to fuller evidence suggesting that the average may always have been around 50 minutes[126] and yields to the more general experience that many of Beethoven's metronome markings still seem, if anything, too fast, not too slow, for today's performers.[127] Even Liszt, who, as we saw, insisted on maintaining Beethoven's fast tempo for the first movement of the "Hammerklavier" Sonata, felt he had to reduce the tempo for its slow movement from 92 per eighth note to 84.[128] Perhaps Temperley's findings are the safest—that of no consistent differences in tempo then and now.[129]

There may have been more consistent trends in the flexibility of tempo, if only because strictness and freedom of tempo suggest objective and subjective approaches. These approaches have tended to alternate in the arts, somewhat in keeping with Curt Sach's cycles in *The Commonwealth of Art*.[130] If there has been any peak of tempo flexibility since Beethoven, it has been that prescribed in the widely circulated edition of his piano sonatas prepared by Lebert and Bülow, first published in 1871.[131] This edition reflects both the strong influence of Liszt and the general practice of the next quarter century or more.[132] It still must have prevailed when Xaver Scharwenka recorded the first movement of Op. 90 about 1905 on a Welte piano roll (subsequently transferred to a disc recording).[133] But even in Bülow's time there were objective editions that gave no encour-

125. Friege/INTERPRETATIONS *passim*.

126. Rothschild/MOZART 9; Temperley/TEMPO 330. My own tally of several "Eroica" recordings current around 1978 also yielded an average of about 50 minutes. Cf. the more detailed, often similar conclusions in Braun/RECORDED about historical tempo changes in Beethoven's Fourth Symphony.

127. Cf. Beck/TEMPOPROBLEM 56–57.

128. Cf. Newman/LISZT 197–198.

129. Cf. Temperley/TEMPO.

130. New York, 1946.

131. Cf. Newman/CHECKLIST 516.

132. Newman/LISZT 203–206.

133. The Classics Record Library WV 6633-2.

agement to such tempo flexibility. Among these was Theodor Steingräber's pioneer effort to prepare an Urtext from the earliest editions of the
sonatas.[134] One begins to suspect that individual artistic temperament
and athletic prowess have influenced the choice and flexibility of tempo
quite as much as historical attitudes have.

134. Cf. Newman/CHECKLIST 517.

CHAPTER 5

ARTICULATION: THE DEMARCATION AND CHARACTERIZATION OF BEETHOVEN'S MUSICAL IDEAS

Means, Uses, and Ways

ARTICULATION in music has been compared with some justification to facial expression in acting. It refers to the slurs, pauses, staccatos, accents, ornaments, and dynamic shifts that help to demarcate musical ideas, to stamp them with an inner character and distinction, and even to shape them. Slurs, pauses, staccatos, and accents are all discussed in the present chapter—slurs and pauses first, as main means of demarcating the ideas, then staccatos and accents as means of characterizing them. Ornaments, which often mark focal points in musical ideas, get a separate chapter (7). Dynamic shifts are discussed in chapter 6.

Articulation ranks with tempo and ornamentation in posing some of the performer's most frequent and vexing challenges. Generally, slurs and staccatos have presented the most problems, pauses and accents the fewest. Beethoven's slurs and staccatos often raise questions not only about their meanings but about exactly where the slurs start and stop and how the various staccato signs—dots, strokes, and wedges—may be distinguished. On the other hand, his pauses and accents have proved to be both clearer in their meanings and less ambiguous in their notation.

Keyboardists have to resort to articulation to achieve their expressive goals even more than other instrumentalists, mainly because their expressive resources, especially those of the pianists, are relatively fewer. Basically, pianists can control only the intensity and duration of tones. They lack several of the important controls regularly exploited by the other instrumentalists, and singers, too. Thus, they are unable to swell a tone or control its rate of diminution; they cannot choose from almost countless styles of bowing and blowing; they have no way to vary the timbre, do vibrato, or alter the intonation. To be sure, at broader levels pianists can extend the resources they do have by creating the illusion of controlling tone quality, even timbre—that is, by connecting or disconnecting tones, grouping them rhythmically and dynamically, pedalling in different ways, balancing textural strands appropriately, and employing agogics suitably (all discussed in Chapters 6 and 8).

Performers who prefer to consult the early music sources for their articulation indications should bear in mind two further considerations. First, in the Classic Era it was not necessarily expected that the composer would mark every instance of articulation in the score that was intended in performance. Instead, as we are assured by treatise writers from Emanuel Bach to Czerny, composers usually inserted essential markings only at the start of a stylistically uniform section and simply assumed that these would obtain through the rest of that section.[1] Sometimes the composer confirmed this assumption by adding such terms as "simile" or "sempre staccato" (as in Beethoven's Op. 28/ii/3).

But second, Beethoven was exceptional among his contemporaries in tending to complete more if not all of his markings in a section, or even a whole piece. However, because he was not consistent in this practice, when he did not continue the markings the performer is left with uncertainty as to whether their omission was deliberate or inadvertent. In Ex. 5/1, from the third movement of Sonata in D Op. 102/2 for piano and cello, there are slurs and staccatos that one would assume also apply to the unmarked passages that follow—for example, to measures 26–29— since the unmarked passages and context are similar. Yet there are other instances where Beethoven seems to have changed the articulation deliberately for valid musical reasons. An example is the change from one long

---

1. E.g., cf. Bach/versuch I 126, Türk/school 344, Czerny/school I 189.

Example 5/1 Sonata for Piano and Cello Op. 102/2/iii/14–15 (after beethoven werkem V/3 129; HV*)

(Allegro fugato)

(sempre piano)

EXAMPLE 5/2 Sonata Op. 22/i/22–25 (after the original edition of Hoffmeister)

slur to two short slurs in the first movement of the Sonata in B♭ Op. 22 (Ex. 5/2). Unfortunately, we are still left in doubt, because the long slur becomes two short slurs in the equivalent measures (153–54) of the recapitulation.

Please note that the articulation markings are best checked in the primary manuscript sources when these are extant and accessible. Because of the frequent ambiguities in the slur and staccato markings, the original editions and the modern Urtext editions based on the early sources are only as reliable as the visual acuity and the musical experience of their engravers and editors. In other words, everyone with comparable vision and experience has the same chance of arriving at a right or wrong reading of the manuscript sources, but loses that chance upon turning to the printed sources.

Problems in Reading and Interpreting Beethoven's Slurs[2]

Beethoven marked slurs in his scores more extensively and more regularly than any other great master had done before him. Bach had marked slurs scarcely at all in his keyboard music, more in his string music, and still more in his vocal music, but with no clear, consistent rationale that has yet been determined (when his slurs start and end precisely enough to be considered at all).[3] Haydn and Mozart marked some slurs in about half of their keyboard music and more in their other music. But the rationale of their slurring seldom seems to go beyond an indication of prevailing legato and a demarcation of relatively small rhythmic groupings.

The performer who troubles to explore Beethoven's slurs in one of the early sources may need to overcome any of five difficulties before being able to determine the slurs' musical purpose: imprecision in their writing or printing, confusion with signs otherwise intended, inconsistency in their use, illogic in their meaning, and apparent omissions. Underlying

2. This section derives in part from Newman/ARTICULATION, with the kind permission of the publisher Wilhelm Hansen in Copenhagen.

3. Cf. Newman/BACH.

especially the imprecision and illogic is always this question: To what extent did Beethoven associate the slur with the span of a musical idea and hence with its start and end, or—in terms more functional for the performer—with its attack and release? The summary answer may be that he did so more than his predecessors Haydn and Mozart did, more where his ideas are motivic or fragmentary rather than complete, and more when his tempo is fast rather than slow.

However, in an article whose title might be translated as "Get Rid of Slurs to Indicate Phrasing," Schenker declared that the [Classic] masters knew "only one kind of slur, the legato slur: it means the connection of a series of tones."[4] He was saying no more nor less than can be found throughout the Classic treatises. But although the Classic masters seldom equated slurs with complete phrases in their scores, the slurs often seem to have meant something more finite by their slurs than an ongoing style of touch. After all, the original slurs—those inserted to regulate bowing, blowing, or singing—all defined points of attack and release. The difficulty is that those original slurs grew from the demands of technique rather than musical syntax. They had not necessarily defined the starts and stops of musical ideas. Indeed, we find an instance in Türk's treatise where he inserts rests to illustrate unmusical interruptions during an idea (that is, faulty syntax), then corrects those interruptions by inserting legato slurs in place of the very same rests![5] As he continues his innovative discussion of musical ideas, Türk does mention the need for attacks and releases, but not in any connection with slurs.

Imprecision in the writing or printing of Beethoven's slurs first becomes a problem when the start and end of the slur do not align clearly with specific notes (a problem that is even more pronounced in Bach's manuscripts). Thus, in the autograph of the Sonata in E Op. 109, the slur that begins over measure 5 of the third movement aligns so uncertainly with specific notes in the main theme that it has been aligned differently in each of three subsequent reproductions—in a copy of it that Beethoven supervised, in the original edition, and in the modern Schenker edition (Ex. 5/3). As a result, we have four quite different interpretations of the theme in those measures—different, that is, if one assumes that the slurs do have at least some bearing on attack and release.

Paradoxically, Beethoven showed on numerous occasions that the exact placement, start and end, of his slurs mattered very much to him, as in a statement from his letter to Holz of August 1825: "For God's sake please impress on Rampl to copy everything exactly as it stands . . . . The slurs

4. Schenker/PHRASIERUNGSBOGEN.

5. Türk, *Klavierschule* 340–341.

EXAMPLE 5/3 Sonata Op. 109/iii/4–8, from bottom to top: (a) the
autograph; and the slurring in (b) Rampel's "überprüfte Abschrift,"
(c) Schlesinger's original edition, and (d) Schenker/KLAVIERSONATENm
IV 565)

a.

(Gesangvoll mit innigster Empfindung
Andante molto cantabile ed espressivo) 47

should be exactly as they are now. It is not all the same whether it is like this 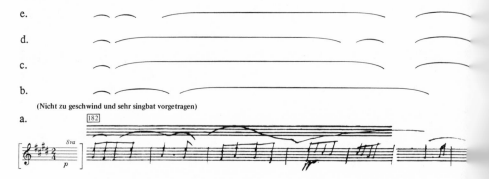 or like this "[6] And much of the time he did locate his slurs precisely and intelligibly enough to leave little doubt about either his intentions or their accuracy. In his Sonata Op. 26/i/191–92, the texture displays three different, simultaneous slurrings, clearly intentional and clearly distinguished, in the original edition as well as the autograph. But he seldom made it that easy to determine his intentions for the copyists and engravers, whom he berated so often. For instance, over measure 5 in the third movement of the Sonata Op. 110, he put two long slurs in the autograph that are too faint and too uncertain in their boundaries to have made their way into any subsequent source.[7] Yet those slurs cannot be discarded with impunity if, as seems to be their purpose, they outline the overall rise and fall of the passage.

Sometimes the ambiguity results from slurs with multiple curves (including slurs that may or may not be meant to extend over the end of one staff to the start of the next). Such slurs could mean several separate slurs, or one continuous slur, or some combination of these. Thus, a use of multicurve slur(s) from measures 182–88 in the autograph of the Sonata in E Minor Op. 90, second movement, has been read in four different ways in four leading editions—the original edition published by Steiner of Vienna, the 19th-century *Gesamtausgabe,* and two current editions (Ex. 5/4). These various readings illustrate why a categorical statement such as Czerny made has to be accepted with caution: "When, however,

6. Anderson, *Letters* III 1241–42.

7. Cf. BEETHOVEN OP. 110m I 30, II 36.

EXAMPLE 5/4 Sonata Op. 90/ii/182–88, from bottom to top:
(a) the autograph; and (b) the slurring from Steiner's original edition,
(c) BEETHOVEN GESAMTAUSGABEm, (d) Wallner/KLAVIERSONATEN, and
(e) Schenker/KLAVIERSONATEN

EXAMPLE 5/5   Sonata Op. 26/i/137–41 (from the autograph BEETHOVEN
OP. 26)

(Andante con Variazioni)

slurs are drawn over several notes, although the slurs are not continuous,
but are broken into several lines, they are considered as forming but one,
and no perceptible separation must take place."[8] Czerny illustrated this
statement with a six-measure passage that has one slur per measure,
barline to barline.

Less uncertainty results when a tie ends at the start of a slur, or vice-
versa. Then the slur is assumed to cover the tie, too, as at each occur-
rence in Variation 4 of the first movement in the Sonata in A♭ Op. 26 (Ex.
5/5).[9] That Beethoven still intended this 18th-century interpretation is
given some support by occasional instances when he did extend the slur
to cover the tie, anticipating modern practice. Indeed, he had already
extended the slur thus in the source for that same example, near the end
of the first system. On the other hand, the exception could have been
intentional, for Beethoven made it again in measures 148–49, at the corresponding place. Both Mies and Unverricht are among those who have
argued that when Beethoven separated the two signs, he did so deliberately, in order to point up the details of rhythm, melody, and harmony,
especially where the tied notes are suspensions.[10]

Another hazard in working with Beethoven's slurs is that of mistaking
for legato or syntactic slurs various similar markings that were intended
by him in other senses. Because of particularly obscure handwriting, his
autograph of Op. 110 provides more than its share of such problems. In
the last four measures of the second movement, three dashes that he
inserted to extend the inscription "poco ritardando" appeared as intended
in the *überprüfte Abschrift,* but were misread in the original and in the
early Clementi editions as a single, four-measure slur in the left hand.
Similar misreadings occur in the two leading modern editions.

Slurs intended to define triplets and other irregular groupings are
sometimes misread as legato slurs. For instance, in the second movement, measure 19, of the Sonata in G Op. 79, the autograph's indepen-

8. Czerny/SCHOOL I 187.

9. Cf., also, Ex. 10/24.

10. Mies/TEXTKRITISCHE 32 and 146–47; Unverricht/EIGENSCHRIFTEN 54–56.

dent slurs for the triplet and quintole were retained as such in the early editions, but are incorporated into one legato slur from the triplet to the barline in Wallner's and other modern editions. Wallner's slur could well signify the kind of touch Beethoven preferred, but as a legato slur it lacks any support in the primary sources.

The third difficulty is that of apparent inconsistencies in the use of slurs. This difficulty generally leaves one asking whether the inconsistency resulted from subtle premeditation or from haste and carelessness that could have crept in anywhere from the autograph to the most reputable edition now available. In the autograph of the first movement of Beethoven's "Farewell" Sonata Op. 81a, the slurring in measure 47 of the exposition differs from that in the corresponding measure 139 of the recapitulation, with the right hand slurred in the first instance and the left hand in the second (Ex. 5/6). As so often happened, the earliest editions, those of Breitkopf & Härtel and of Clementi, followed the autograph faithfully—indeed, blindly. Beethoven actually may have intended this supposed inconsistency, since he provided a comparably subtle difference in the notes themselves between measures 25–26 and 118–19. Or he merely may have intended the reading that Wallner arrived at in her modern edition, where the unsurprising compromise is to use the slurs in both hands both times.[11]

11. Wallner/KLAVIERSONATENm II 180 and 182.

EXAMPLE 5/6 Sonata Op. 81a/i, from the autograph: (a) m. 47, and (b) m. 139

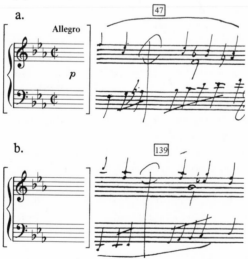

Often such apparent inconsistencies crept in after Beethoven had completed his manuscript. The autograph of his Sonata Op. 57 was one of his autographs that served as the original engraver's fair copy. In the finale he entered the same slurring every time he repeated the melody in the left hand of measures 76–83—that is, he slurred $2+2+4$ measures (employing a syntax that was to prevail in the music of Chopin and Brahms, among others). However, the original edition presented a different slurring each time this melody occurs, and subsequent early editions made the same and further changes. Fortunately, in this instance the modern editions of Schenker, Wallner, and Schmidt all return to Beethoven's original slurring.

Another frequent inconsistency is Beethoven's different slurring for the piano as compared to that for other instruments. However, rather than an inconsistency on Beethoven's part, this differentiation usually proves to be a deliberate accommodation of different instrumental idioms. Thus, it is typical that in the Concerto in C Minor, Op. 37, the piano's slurring of the theme in measures 340–43 of the first movement differs from the clarinet's and the violin's in measures 50–53. Contrary to Schenker's statement quoted earlier, this sort of distinction serves further to confirm Beethoven's conception of a slur's function as being much more specific than a general indication that legato prevails.

A fourth difficulty in trying to interpret Beethoven's slurs frequently proves to be their apparent illogic—their defiance of what one takes to be the sense of the music or of its technical means. We have already seen several ways in which Beethoven expected more from his slurs than the indication that legato prevails. And we know that he wanted his slurs copied exactly as he notated them. Therefore, as long as one can either make sense of them or attribute their apparent illogic to carelessness and inconsistency on his part (despite his constant pleas for more accuracy) the problem diminishes somewhat.

But what, then, is one to do with a series of apparently illogical slurs when that identical series reappears consistently with each repetition of the main theme? Such a series occurs in the opening eight measures of the "Adagio cantabile" in the *Sonate pathétique* Op. 13 (Ex. 5/7) and in each of their four complete repetitions. No autograph is extant for Op. 13, but all of eight early (lifetime) editions present the same series of slurs, repeated the same each time. So do the modern editions of Schenker, Wallner, and Schmidt, although in more than one instance Wallner later gave up on the problems of Beethoven's slurring in favor of more modern, uniform practices.[12]

12. Wallner/KLAVIERSONATENm II 131 and 132 (fns.).

Example 5/7 Sonata Op. 13/ii/1–8 (after the original Hoffmeister edition)

Attempts since the late 19th century to rationalize that slurring in Op. 13 have failed. In 1881 Franz Kullak protested remedial slurring that Rudolf Westphal had advocated a year earlier to regularize the antecedent-consequent relationships in the melody (including their upbeats). To Westphal's criticism of the original slurring, Kullak responded: "although we have not asserted that the hand *ought to be lifted at the end* of every slur, the opposite conclusion is not justifiable, that the hand may be lifted *under* a slur. That [conclusion] could be justified only by very peculiar conditions, like the assumption of an engraver's mistake. Perhaps the composer wished, in this very place, to prevent a 'lift'?"[13]

In 1966, the writers Grundmann and Mies proposed an ingenious rationale for those same slurs. They said the slurs "showed significantly how hard he [Beethoven] had tried to cover up the [overly] regular caesuras and grouping of the structure and accents."[14] They pointed, among other things, to the melodic bridges made by the slurring from measures 4 to 5 and 6 to 7, and to the further irregularity achieved by different, conflicting slurs in the bass. In short, they were saying that Beethoven used his slurs to mask the squareness of four-measure phrases and eight-measure, balanced periods, or what he reportedly protested as "the tyranny of the barline."

To be sure, this slurring in Op. 13 is not the only example Grundmann and Mies could have cited to support that rationale. There are occasional further examples, including the initial themes of the second movements in the sonatas for piano and violin Opp. 47 and 96. But the bulk of the evidence—early, middle, and late—contradicts the suggestion that Beethoven used slurs to mask square syntax, for his slurs more often do coincide with the straightforward syntax that prevails in his themes at slow and moderate tempos.

13. Kullak/beethoven 39–41, referring to Westphal/rhythmik.
14. Grundmann & Mies 77–78.

EXAMPLE 5/8 Sonata Op. 2/3/iii/110–111 (after the original, Artaria edition)

(Scherzo Allegro) [111]

p

Sometimes the slurring raises technical problems that make it illogical. Thus, the slurs that separate measures 110 and 111 in the "Scherzo" of the Sonata Op. 2/3 make a literal release and attack impractical both technically and musically because of the fast tempo (Ex. 5/8). But, of course, those slurs still can permit an attack by means of an accent and they still can suggest both the rhythmic grouping and dynamic direction of the notes.

Occasionally Beethoven writes slurs whose very lengths seem illogical, because the lengths may exceed one's technical or musical limits. The pianist does not face the impracticalities of Beethoven's slurs that are too long for the string player to include all the notes in one bow (as in measures 175–77 and 179–181 in the autograph of the Cello Sonata Op. 69/i) or for the wind player or singer to include them in one breath. But the pianist faces a kind of technical, even physiological, challenge when the slur exceeds one's typical mind-set for slur limits. Such is the case in the original edition of the Sonata Op. 109/i, where one slur lasts fifteen measures, or twenty-eight in all if the "sempre legato" that follows means the slur's extension, as performers usually assume (Ex. 5/9). Such an exceptional length has to be taken as a further example of psychological notation on the composer's part (as discussed in Chapter 2). Beethoven wanted to press on by extending the "breathing span" and disregarding the slight caesuras that otherwise might have occurred between phrases mostly of four measures. One recalls how Chopin seems to be pressing on similarly when he puts measures 3 to 28 of his Nocturne in F♯ Minor Op. 48/2 all under one unbroken slur (according to the Oxford edition).

Our final problem with Beethoven's slurs is their absence where their use seems essential. One's tendency would be to blame apparent omissions on carelessness and haste, if, indeed, the expected slurs were not left out deliberately. There can be no question that Beethoven simply forgot about the slurring right in the midst of his autograph of the Sonata Op. 57 when he started a new page during the second theme of the first movement (at m. 40). However, there could be some question in the autograph of the finale in the Sonata Op. 27/2 where he left out the slur at the ends of measures 23 and 24 that he had used in measure 22 but was to replace with staccatos an octave higher in measures 26–28

EXAMPLE 5/9 Sonata Op. 109/i/22–48 (after the original, Schlesinger edition)

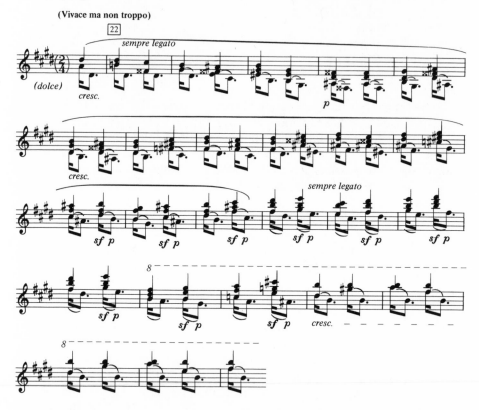

(Ex. 5/10). Did he intend to continue the same slurring through measures 22–24, as editors have assumed ever since, probably rightly, or could he have intended to anticipate those staccatos in measures 26–28?

Some of Beethoven's apparent omissions of slurs may have resulted from his habit of revising or adding editorial markings, especially articulation signs, after he had completed writing in the notes. In measure 41 of the first movement of his Sonata Op. 53, he apparently had to leave out the last measure of the three-measure slur expected in the left hand, because he had allowed no space for it over the page turn, between the staffs, when he came back to do the editing.

If Beethoven used slurs mainly to indicate that legato prevails, then why did he, himself a paragon of legato playing, omit slurs so often where the legato is most expected—that is, in songful slow movements? (These omissions are not merely the kind where the term *simile* might be under-

EXAMPLE 5/10   Sonata Op. 27/2/iii/21–27 (from the autograph)

stood from previous slurring.) The answer usually seems to be that in such places he already was indicating legato, and sometimes even the demarcation of ideas, by other means. For example, at the start of the "Largo appassionato" in Op. 2/2, the "tenuto sempre" insures that the right hand will play legato above the bass notes marked "staccato sempre." In that extra-long slur near the start of Op. 109, the words "sempre legato" in measure 36 clearly extend a use of legato that had been implied by the foregoing slur (recall Ex. 5/9). At the end of Op. 110, pedal indications produce the legato that slurs would have suggested. In smaller regions there are sometimes divisions and compoundings of the normal beams that indicate both legato and rhythmic groupings in place of slurs, as in Variation III of the Sonata Op. 26/i (Ex. 5/11; beams are discussed further below).

EXAMPLE 5/11   Sonata Op. 26/i/124–27 (from the autograph BEET-HOVEN OP. 26m)

(Andante con Variazioni)   124

Seven Tentative Explanations for Beethoven's Slurring

Although Beethoven's slurring does not reveal the consistency or precision of subsequent slurring, like that of Brahms and Hindemith, it does reveal at least an imperfect rationale. This rationale is summarized here, combining conclusions of past writers with some added ones of my own. These may be noted under seven, often overlapping categories—psychological, legato, harmonic, minimal, infraphrasal, phrasal, and supraphrasal.

1) There are several ways in which a Beethoven slur may suggest a psychological function, often a function that seems contrary to the practicalities of performance. For one, it may require the performer to reach beyond the usual musical horizons. We have seen how that extra-long slur cited in Op. 109 seems illogical, not only in a physiological sense, but in a psychological sense as well. In the first movement of the Sonata Op. 101 there is a slur that extends over a rest (mm. 19–20), psychologically implying continuity even while the physical continuity is interrupted.

Furthermore, some pianists undoubtedly wonder whether Beethoven was challenging their physical or their psychological talents when he put slurs over the so-called glissando octaves in the finale of his Sonata Op. 53 (at measures 465–70). It is likely that he did want those slurs to signal the glissando technique, as Czerny asserted some forty years later.[15] But Beethoven used neither the word glissando nor any equivalent in this passage. Perhaps he thought of the slurs rather as suggesting the glissando's effect psychologically, at the same time deliberately fingering each right- and left-hand octave with a 1 and a 5 so as to recommend the separate wrist actions needed for the "Prestissimo" tempo of the coda. (See further in Chapter 9.)

2) The legato function of Beethoven's slurs is the one most readily documented and illustrated. It is the one function that was recognized whenever the treatise writers from Marpurg to Hummel explained the slur. Furthermore, the slur for piano could hardly have meant anything else or more when it served no clear function of attack, release, or local grouping, as in those slurs over the main theme of Op. 13/ii (recall Ex. 5/7).

3) Occasionally Beethoven seems to have used a slur to enclose a harmonic function, either a chord or pedal point, or both, sustained over several measures. Two such slurs may be seen in the first movement of the Sonata Op. 28, whose popular title, "Pastoral" Sonata, may have derived partly from its generally slow harmonic rhythm. One is the long multi-

15. Badura-Skoda/CZERNY 51.

EXAMPLE 5/12 Sonata Op. 28/i/239–56 (after the original, Bureau d'Industrie edition)

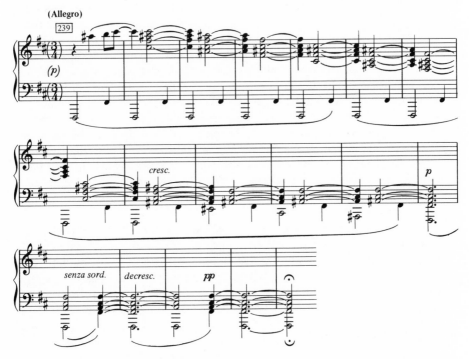

curve slur in the left hand, measures 239–56, during the unwinding of the development section on the F♯ major chord (Ex. 5/12). All of this slur covers an F♯ pedal, too. In Beethoven's autograph that multicurve slur seems to be intended as a single slur, since the breaks in it occur during ties in the right hand and where there would be no more vertical space for a continuous curve. But the principal modern editions interpret it as several slurs.

The other harmonic slur from Op. 28 is a ten-measure, left-hand slur during the pedal point that accompanies the first recurrence of the opening, main theme. This time the pedal point remains constant, but the harmony changes and shorter slurs divide the theme in the right hand.

4) As with the slurs of Bach, Haydn, and Mozart, the slurs of Beethoven function most consistently and most tangibly in modern terms when they identify with local (or minimal) rhythmic groupings. In Beethoven's earlier works, slurs of this sort often stop short of the final note in the grouping, adhering to the tradition of not crossing barlines or other metric divisions. But in his later works, the slurs usually cover the complete grouping. Thus, in Variation XII of the "Diabelli" Variations, the slurs

(which are the same in all primary sources including the autograph) cross the barlines in order to embrace the complete groupings.

When those local slurs define incises (subphrases or poetic feet), as they generally do, they help the performer to determine the dynamic direction (discussed in Chapter 6). For example, the practice of slurring an ornament—chiefly a trill or an appoggiatura—to its resolution in both Baroque and Classic music helps us to think of that ornament as a poetic foot (or "tone" foot) moving from strong to weak (often from dissonance to consonance), as in measures 55–56 from the middle movement of Beethoven's Sonata Op. 47 for piano and violin. A local rhythmic grouping often recurs as a pattern in the ongoing figuration, as happens in Variation XII of the "Diabelli Variations." Hence, the slur that exactly covers that grouping must define the pattern. Such a slur can also be a good clue to an appropriate keyboard technique—for instance, a shift of the full arm, pivoted at the shoulder, with each new grouping in that same Variation.

5) Beethoven used the infraphrasal slur to mark off any musically intelligible portion of a phrase, whether that portion is a single subphrase or a compound of several tone feet that are not marked off individually. Two infraphrasal slurs divide each subphrase in the four measures evenly that constitute the first phrase, measures 1–4, of the "Rondo" refrain in the Sonata Op. 22 (Ex. 5/13). Occasionally, Beethoven's infraphrasal slurs actually seem to define attacks and releases, as in the first movement, measures 80–84, of the Sonata Op. 53, where each slur ends with a staccato dot that confirms its ending. Indeed, in much of the third movement of Op. 53 the slurs seem to function in this way.

6) A limited number of Beethoven's slurs happen to mark off complete phrases. I use "happen" because they usually seem to do so coincidentally rather than by plan. As with the slurs used by the other great masters of the 18th and 19th centuries, Beethoven's slurs seem meant more often to define local and infraphrasal groupings. One infrequent, unequi-

EXAMPLE 5/13   Sonata Op. 22/iv/1–4 (after the original, Hoffmeister edition)

vocal exception is the slur that covers the piano's first, eight-measure response to the orchestral tutti in the middle movement of the fourth Concerto. But that slur also retains a slur's basic meaning of legato, as one realizes when comparing it with the shorter slurs and indications for detached notes over the piano's subsequent responses to the orchestral tutti.

7) Finally, the supraphrasal slur was illustrated earlier as one kind of illogical slur, extending beyond one's typical mind-set for slur limits. The example quoted was the cumulative, legato line in the first movement of the Sonata in E Op. 109 (recall Ex. 5/9).

Pauses as Further Demarcators and Characterizers

The foregoing rationale for Beethoven's slurs attaches considerable importance to their frequent, apparent uses as demarcators of ideas, despite certain ambiguities and a general disregard of such uses by treatise writers of the time. On occasion Beethoven also employed one or more of three other, less ambiguous, means to demarcate his ideas. One was to align his beams with the ideas themselves rather than with regular metric groupings. A second was to insert rests to separate the ideas. And a third was to conclude the ideas with *fermate,* presumably to emphasize their separations. Sometimes Beethoven employed one or more of those means to assert his ideas more rhetorically, implying a degree of elasticity in the tempo (refer to "flexibility" in Chapter 4). Then he employed them not only to demarcate his ideas but to help intensify their internal content.[16]

Typical uses of irregular beams to help point up an idea's shape occur in the second movement of the Sonata in D Op. 28, as in measure 14 (see m. 5 of Ex. 6/12, p. 181).[17] Those beams, which overlap the regular beats

16. The primary emphasis is on the rhetorical significance in Schwarz/PAUSEN, a helpful article that is directly relevant to the present discussion.

17. Cf. Unverricht/EIGENSCHRIFTEN 63–64.

EXAMPLE 5/14 Sonata Op. 28/ii/82–83 (after Beethoven/WERKEm VII/3/II 43; HV*)

(Andante)

EXAMPLE 5/15   Sonata in D Op. 10/3/iv/1–4 (after Beethoven/WERKEM VII/2/I 136; HV*)

EXAMPLE 5/16   Sonata in A♭ Op. 110/iii: (a) mm. 9–12 and (b) mm. 116–19 (after Wallner/KLAVIERSONATENm II 300–301 and 304–305; HV*)

of $\frac{2}{4}$ meter, highlight minimal masculine groupings within the current idea.[18] In the same movement a use of irregular beams to help separate the ideas—that is, to separate the end of one idea from the upbeat of the next—may be seen in the bass staff of measure 82 (though, for no evident reason, not in the treble staff; Ex. 5/14). In both of those examples the beams are coterminous with slurs, resulting in mutual reinforcement.

In the "Rondo" finale of the Sonata in D Op. 10/3, rests punctuate the main thematic elements rhetorically, helping to create two of those unanswered questions so characteristic of Beethoven's themes.[19] The two *fermate* that conclude the ensuing answer allow extra time to absorb the whole theme (Ex. 5/15). It is especially instructive to compare the *parlando* "Arioso dolente" in the finale of the Sonata in Ab Op. 110 with its heart-rending intensification some one hundred measures later (Ex. 5/ 16). The elaborated rhythms created by the hesitant figures and short rests bear out the correspondingly intensified inscription, "Perdendo le forze, dolente."

Problems in Distinguishing and Interpreting Beethoven's Staccato Signs

The three standard signs for staccato—dots, strokes, and wedges—all refer to relative degrees of staccato, or disconnection (disregarding occasional other meanings such as accents or styles of bowing and blowing). Telling one sign from another in the manuscripts depends, of course, on the clarity of the composer's handwriting. But it does not depend, as is sometimes argued, on the nature of quill pens, which were then in use. When properly shaped and sharpened, quill pens were well suited to making fine distinctions.[20] However, with any writing tool, insuring that the dot, stroke, and wedge are clearly distinguishable requires extra patience. In Beethoven's handwriting their imprecision seems to reflect his impetuosity during the heat and drive of creating (Ex. 5/17).[21]

Haydn's staccato markings are more clearly distinguished, whereas Mozart's and Beethoven's are so often indistinguishable that even our most faithful modern editors have generally given up and chosen to use only one of the three signs to represent all three. In practice these editors

18. Cf., also, both feminine and masculine groupings implemented by irregular beams in both the autograph and in the original, Steiner edition of the Sonata for Piano and Violin Op. 96/iv/34–80.

19. Cf., also, the openings of Opp. 10/1, 10/2, 22, and 31/3.

20. Cf. Winternitz/AUTOGRAPHS I 23–25.

21. Cf. Mies/TEXTKRITISCHE 26–31.

EXAMPLE 5/17   Sonata Op. 57/iii/168–173, from the autograph

have had only two of the three signs to contend with, anyway, since they have usually equated the stroke and the wedge, preferring ordinarily to retain the stroke as the easier of the two not only to draw but to engrave.

Thus, in their editions of Mozart's keyboard sonatas for Presser and Henle, respectively, both Nathan Broder and Ernst Herttrich decided to use dots to represent both signs after finding no secure basis for distinguishing between them. Paul Mies had recommended the same expediency for Beethoven.[22] In their editions of Beethoven's piano sonatas, Wallner and Schmidt similarly chose dots only, while Schenker chose strokes only (except in the sonatas up through Op. 13, where he had wavered between dots and strokes). Numerous inconsistencies and differences within and between the earliest editions show that the problem of distinguishing dots from strokes in Beethoven's manuscripts must have troubled the early copyists and engravers quite as much as it has current editors and engravers. Moreover, that problem had even less chance of a resolution then, when the prerogative of editorial reasoning scarcely existed. Hence, as far as the staccato markings are concerned, today's editors do better to start in afresh with the manuscript sources when these (or at least good facsimiles of them) are still accessible.

In any case, before one can engage in interpretive reasoning, one must determine what distinctions of meaning were intended between the signs for disconnection. Did Haydn, Mozart, and Beethoven actually intend for

22. Mies/TEXTKRITISCHE 86–91.

their dots and strokes to mean different degrees of staccato, and if so, how different? Their music suggests they did, but no sooner or more precisely than the differences were defined in the performance treatises of their times. In 1753 Emanuel Bach had recognized both the dot and the stroke in his *Versuch,* yet only to equate them and prefer the use of the dot because the stroke might be taken for a fingering indication[23] (which, indeed, may be true of some of the supposed fingerings in Beethoven's keyboard manuscripts[24]). To be sure, a year earlier, in his generally more retrospective *Versuch,* Quantz had already identified strokes with sharper attacks than dots, with quicker releases, and with predominantly faster tempos.[25] But, as in Leopold Mozart's *Versuch* four years later,[26] Quantz made that distinction only with regard to strokes and dots that occur under violin bowing slurs.

As late as 1789, in his *Klavierschule,* Daniel Gottlob Türk still preferred only to equate the dot and stroke.[27] Although he acknowledged that others by then were distinguishing between the signs, he argued, reasonably enough, that any distinctions in the degree of sharpness and crispness had to depend more on the character, intensity, and tempo of the composition in which the signs occurred. In 1801, however, Clementi left no doubt in his widely circulated *Introduction* that, depending "on the CHARACTER, and PASSION of the piece, . . . when composers are EXACT in their writing" there is a palpable transition from strokes to dots to slurred dots to slurs alone—that is, from the crispest staccato through less and less disconnection to total legato.[28]

That much information can be generalized safely regarding the distinctions between staccato signs in Beethoven's time. But no mechanically exact distinction can be assumed such as the one made in 1819 by Friedrich Starke of Vienna and by not a few other pedagogues of the time. Starke wrote that over a quarter-note a stroke meant that the note was to be held only through the first quarter of its value, a dot only the first half, and a slurred dot three-quarters of its value.[29]

Finally, two pianists, teachers, composers, and writers who figured among Beethoven's closest and most explicit compatriots disappoint us because the important piano methods they left after Beethoven died add

23. Bach/VERSUCH I 125.

24. Cf. Newman/FINGERINGS 175–76.

25. Quantz/VERSUCH 193–94.

26. Mozart/VIOLINSCHULE 43–44.

27. Türk/KLAVIERSCHULE 353.

28. Clementi/INTRODUCTION 8.

29. Starke/PIANOFORTE I 13. Among others who had arrived at this neat distinction between the three degrees of detachment was Louis Adam in 1804 (Adam/MÉTHODE 154–56).

little or nothing that helps to distinguish between the dot and stroke. Hummel illustrated these signs as though they were still no more than synonymous.[30] Czerny did not even mention strokes or wedges, although he did refine the meanings of dots in connection with portato and related styles.[31]

Most of the so-called *Richtlinien* prepared by the editors of the Classic *Denkmäler* and *Gesamtausgabe* have included basic suggestions for distinguishing between dots and strokes.[32] Moreover, several modern studies explore the confusion of dots and strokes more in detail, including five prize-winning studies on Mozart edited by Hans Albrecht in 1957 and an important study of Beethoven's autographs and original editions by Hubert Unverricht published in 1960.[33] The consensus among the authors of these studies is that editors should no longer be giving up, but instead be trying harder to distinguish between the dots and strokes. The authors find evidence that both Mozart and Beethoven did intend distinctions, whatever these may have been. (It is worth adding that the edition by Wolfgang Rehm and Wolfgang Plath of Mozart's piano sonatas has now appeared (1986) in Bärenreiter's *Neue Mozart Ausgabe* with clear distinctions between dots and strokes.)

In Beethoven's case, one finds handwritten passages from as early as 1791 that reveal unmistakable efforts to distinguish between strokes over unslurred notes and dots over slurred notes, as in his four-hand *Variationen über ein Thema des Grafen von Waldstein*, WoO 67.[34] More familiar illustrations, from 1801, occur in the finale of his Sonata Op. 27/2 (Ex. 5/18). (About the same time Beethoven was showing a new fascination with detached notes in general, as is manifest in the second movements of his sonatas Opp. 28, 31/1, and 31/3.)

From 1812 there are the copyist's orchestra parts for the "Allegretto" of his Seventh Symphony, in which Beethoven himself corrected dots and portato dots over its familiar main theme to strokes and portato dots.[35] From 1825 one finds similar corrections made in parts copied for his String Quartet Op. 132. And in the letter to the violinist Holz quoted earlier, he stipulated specifically, "where a dot occurs above a note no stroke should

30. Hummel/ANWEISUNG 54.

31. Czerny/SCHOOL I 186–88.

32. A number of these editorial guides, including those for editions of Bach, Haydn, Mozart, and Beethoven, have been collected in Dadelsen/EDITIONSRICHTLINIEN.

33. Albrecht/KEIL; Unverricht/EIGENSCHRIFTEN.

34. Cf. the last four measures (mm. 59–62 in the coda) of the autograph excerpt shown in facsimile as the frontispiece in BEETHOVEN WERKEM VII/1.

35. Nottebohm/BEETHOVENIANA 107–109.

EXAMPLE 5/18 Sonata Op. 27/2/iii/91–97 (from the autograph)

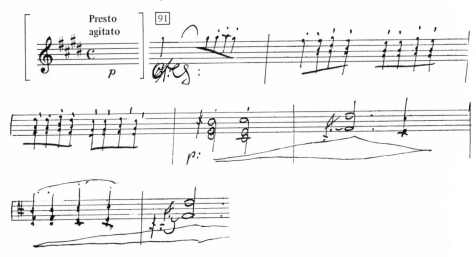

replace it, and vice-versa . . . ." On the other hand, by the time of that letter Beethoven had neither illustrated nor mentioned any slurs with the dots, and even in the letter's autograph he still was not executing very clear distinctions when he drew those strokes and dots.[36]Apparently, Beethoven began to apply distinctions between the dot and the stroke from the start of his career. But, unfortunately, he never did spell out just what distinctions he had in mind. Still, with this much confirmation of his intentions, the proficient editor can infer the nature of Beethoven's distinctions from certain frequent consistencies in his uses of the signs. For one, Beethoven almost always used dots, not strokes, under slurs to indicate the slightly disconnected notes in portato passages (or what Emanuel Bach had called *Tragen der Töne;*[37] recall Ex. 5/18). An example may be seen in the autograph of the second movement's main theme in the Sonata Op. 90 (mm. 6–8 and elsewhere; Ex. 5/19). Two unequivocal dots under a slur occur shortly before two unequivocal wedges over distinctly separate octaves (which exceptionally are marked *p* for *piano*).

Another frequent consistency is Beethoven's association of unequivocal dots with his lighter, softer, gentler music, as at cadential ritards and diminuendos. On the other hand, despite cases like Ex. 5/19, Beethoven

36. The whole letter is quoted in German in Unverricht/EIGENSCHRIFTEN 56–57 and in English in Anderson/BEETHOVEN III 1241–42; a facsimile of the most pertinent page (3) is given in Rothschild/MOZART opp. p. 100.

37. Bach/VERSUCH I 8–9.

EXAMPLE 5/19 Sonata Op. 90/ii/5–8 (from the autograph)

tended to associate his strokes with single, brighter, more accented sounds, including the reiterations in hammerstroke cadences (as in the autograph of his Sonata in F♯ Major, at the final cadence of the first movement [Ex. 5/20]).

EXAMPLE 5/20 Sonata Op. 78/i/104–105 (from the autograph)

In one important respect Beethoven tended to break down the distinctions that evolving practices and the treatises were establishing between dots and strokes. Not infrequently he drew his staccato signs in a graduated transition rather than an abrupt shift from one sign to the other, apparently to accompany a corresponding transition in the dynamics, pitch, and harmony. In other words, he seemed to be bridging the signs in his notation as he drew dots, then small strokes, then gradually larger strokes, progressing from gentler to stronger tensions—or vice-versa. (In this way he was surpassing that "palpable transition" between signs, implied above by Clementi.) Others have observed this process uncertainly in Mozart's and more tangibly in Beethoven's handwriting.[38] In Beethoven it may be

38. Cf. Dadelsen/EDITIONSRICHTLINIEN 122–23; Mies/TEXTKRITISCHE 85–87.

EXAMPLE 5/21 Sonata Op. 26/i/77–81 (from the autograph BEETHOVEN op. 26m)

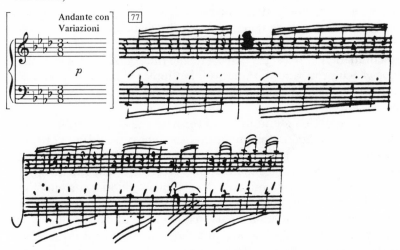

seen as early as the autograph of the Sonata Op. 26 (Ex. 5/21) (but, naturally, not in any printed edition of that work, early or modern). The process enhances not only that rise in Op. 26, but a subsequent fall (mm. 84–85) that is similarly implied by concurrent harmonic and pitch transitions, though not by any dynamic markings in this instance. In Ex. 5/18, above, the transition from dots to dashes associates unequivocally with a crescendo. In the Sonata Op. 90/i/100–108, even the change from quarter notes to eighth notes with eighth rests suggests increased crispness during the crescendo, and less during the diminuendo that ends in a short slur. The sole dot, in measure 100 (confirmed as a dot in the autograph), presumably was intended to establish the quarter notes as half staccato (or quasi-portato). Sometimes this bridging process appears to have been very subtle, consisting of several dynamic waves. An example may be found in the autograph of the Sonata Op. 53/i/31–35. There are enough such instances to suggest that (supposedly unconscious) psychological influences controlled Beethoven's notation at such times.[39]

Can Editors Help to Resolve the Ambiguity of Beethoven's Staccato Signs?

Whether sharply defined or almost imperceptibly graduated, any distinction that can be established between the dot and the stroke must

39. Cf. Mies/TEXTKRITISCHE 28–31 and 86.

contribute to those remarkably few means of expressive performance available to the pianist. Editorial merging of the two signs into either the dot or the stroke alone only attenuates the distinction by virtually eliminating it. What more can be done to clarify the distinctions for the performer? Even if awareness of Beethoven's psychological notation and careful examination of his signs can overcome the legibility problem, the difficulties of acquiring and working with facsimiles of Beethoven's autographs surely would discourage all but the most resolute and experienced performers.

The answer must be found in whatever help the editor can incorporate in the printed edition. Assuming that the editor would be drawing from that minority of Beethoven's piano works whose autographs (or clear facsimiles) remain accessible, there is one procedure that might bring about at least some improvement over the complete editorial surrender to the problem of ambiguous staccato signs that still exists even in our most respected editions. That would be to use a dot for the unequivocal dots, a stroke for the unequivocal strokes, and a different, specified symbol for all the uncertain staccato signs. The symbol probably should be not simply a dot or stroke that is singled out by boldface type, parentheses, or a question mark, because it would favor one sign over the other and because such standard devices would clutter the score instead of serving better in other editorial ways. But the symbol could be something as simple as a hollow square no larger than present staccato signs. It could at least encourage the performer to regulate the degree and intensity of the staccato in keeping with the direction of the prevailing harmony, melody, and dynamics.

Beethoven's Signs and Uses for Accents

Accents in music may be implied and they may be specified. They may be implied by focal points in the syntax or in technical figures and fingerings that contradict the metric accents (as discussed in Chapters 6 and 10); and they may be specified by a variety of signs. Both kinds of accents are discussed here. But neither kind should be assumed to exclude the other, for Beethoven's implied and his specified accents often coincide. As with his other interpretive aids, the signs that specify accents are hardly haphazard. And as with those that imply accents, the signs prove to be functional in ways that extend beyond the single accented note. Applied with remarkable imagination as well as consistency, they help appreciably to project the prevailing structures, moods, expressive goals, and technical styles of the music. Since Beethoven's accenting is relatively clear in both its indications and its purposes, the objective in this section is more to promote an increased awareness of it than to reveal any hidden or elusive practices.

Schindler is often quoted regarding the nature and extent of Beethoven's "particular style of accentuation" in his performance and teaching:

It was above all the rhythmic accent that he stressed most energetically [*kräftig*] and that he wanted others to stress. On the other hand, he treated the melodic accent (or grammatic, as it was generally called [see below]) mostly according to the internal requirements. He would emphasize all suspensions, especially those of the diminished second in *cantabile* sections, more than other pianists. His playing thus acquired a highly personal character, very different from the even, flat performances that never rise to tonal eloquence. In *cantilena* sections he adopted the methods of cultivated singers, doing neither too much nor too little. Sometimes he recommended putting appropriate words to a perplexing passage and singing it, or listening to a good violinist or wind player play it.[40]

Schindler's statement is creditable enough this time. Not only is accenting revealed almost everywhere in Beethoven's scores, but it was singled out by others who had heard Beethoven play, though not necessarily with approval. Furthermore, the rich accenting is quite what would be expected of such a dynamic creator. On the other hand, Schindler's statement stops short of the broader functional significance of Beethoven's accenting. And it betrays a certain confusion in his own musical understanding when Schindler identifies the "grammatic" with the melodic rather than the rhythmic (metric) accent.[41]

Of course, there is no reason to relate Beethoven's strategically located accenting to the indiscriminate pounding at the keyboard by which, at least in his later years, he is supposed to have compensated for his growing deafness and inadequately resonant pianos. Such a relationship would confuse internal musical function and purpose with external, unrelated, and unmusical circumstances. Naturally, accenting must be understood as relative emphasis and not necessarily absolute loudness. Also, the somewhat greater frequency of accenting found in Beethoven's earlier scores (as against somewhat less in his later, more judiciously edited scores) may well reflect the ebullience of youth and his healthy dose of animal spirits when he burst upon the musical world. But the musical intent of his accenting seems to have remained relatively constant throughout his creative career.

In the later 18th century, influenced by speech accents, musical accents were grouped mainly into three categories. One category was "gram-

40. Schindler & MacArdle/BEETHOVEN 416 (with slight revisions in the present translation).

41. Cf. the *Oxford English Dictionary* under "grammatical."

matic" accents, defined by Sulzer and Kirnberger in 1773 as those of "the long and strong notes which are the principal notes in each harmony (Accord) . . . . These notes coincide with the strong pulse in the bar . . . and are distinguished from the others, the passing notes, by their duration, weight and prominence."[42] The other two categories, the authors added, were the "rhetorical" and the "pathetic" accents, differing more in degree than in kind and applying to the most important thoughts and the less important thoughts.

The same categories held to the end of Beethoven's life, as in treatises by Türk (1789), Albrechtsberger (1790), Koch (1802), and Hummel (1828). Primarily, those high-Classic treatises added more specifics, largely elementary to us today, about the strong and weak notes in simple and compound meters.[43] But they also provided certain qualifications of interest, such as Koch's statement that rhetorical (or oratorical) accents and the more intensive pathetic accents differ from grammatic accents in being not only more pronounced but in being disassociated from the meter or any fixed beat of the measure; they "are created by the composer's fantasy, which he conveys by notes, and they must be discovered by the sensibility of the performer."[44]

Today, musical accents are usually classified more pragmatically, under three, more tangible but not wholly separate categories and under a variety of terms. Two of these categories relate directly to the meter: (1) metric accents, supporting the organization of the measure into strong and weak beats, and (2) contrametric accents, conflicting with the meter by means of syncopation, emphasis of weak (or off-) beats, hemiola, and the peaks of many incises (subphrases). (3) The remaining category is independent of the meter, with which it conflicts as often as it coincides. It is that of the expressive (or rhetorical, or pathetic) accent, applied to a tone or vertical group of tones that stands apart in pitch (tonic accent), harmony, texture (as in a polyphonic entry), intensity (dynamic accent), agogics (emphasis through hesitation or hurrying, shortening or lengthening of a tone), or even timbre. As will be apparent, the metric and contrametric accents are mutually exclusive, but the expressive accent may coincide with either, since it is a legitimate third category, free to satisfy any of the three functions just described.

Within these means of Beethoven's accenting, a performer can do nothing about the pitch, harmony, texture, or meter, which all have been predetermined by the composer. But much can be done about the dynamics and agogics. Indeed, one may tend to forget that abrupt contrast can be

42. Sulzer/ALLGEMEINE I 13–14, but with the sentences reordered here for greater clarity.

43. Cf. Rothschild/MOZART 20–24.

44. As quoted in Rothschild/MOZART 27.

EXAMPLE 5/22 Sonata Op. 26/i/13–17 (after BEETHOVEN WERKEM VII 2/I 212; HV*)

(Andante con Variazioni)

achieved by less as well as more of something. Thus, a dynamic accent may be achieved as readily by an abruptly soft as by an abruptly loud tone, as illustrated in Ex. 5/22 from the Sonata in A♭ Op. 26, with first a so-called Beethoven *piano* and then a *sforzando* (in the 3d and 4th measures, respectively). Of course, during this accenting the degree of the dynamic or agogic contrast may vary in the actual performance, from slight to very pronounced. An accent applies to a single note or chord. The variety of signs for accents is considerable in Beethoven's music.

EXAMPLE 5/23 (a) Sonata Opp. 2/2/iv/129–30 (after the original, Artaria ed. of Op. 2, p. 30); and (b) Sonata Op. 109/iii/107 (from the autograph)

a.   (Rondo Grazioso)

b.

Much the most frequent sign is *sf* or *sfz* for *sforzando*.[45] Other frequent signs are *f* or *ff* during a *piano* or *pianissimo* passage, *fp* or *ffp*, the horizontal or vertical wedge (>, <, or ^), and *rf* or *rfz* for *rinforzando*. No consistent distinctions can be made between any of those signs as Beethoven used them—for example, between *sf* and > in Op. 2/2/iv/129 and 130, or between > and *sfz* in Op. 109/iii/107 (Ex. 5/23).

Often Beethoven's accents are not marked as such, but only implied by other signs or by circumstances in the music. Thus, a tone will be accented if it initiates a group of notes abruptly marked loud or soft (as in Op. 31/1/i/11). So, of course, will a note marked *fp* if it occurs during a soft passage (as in Op. 10/3/i/278). Moreover, a tone will be accented, almost unavoidably, when it initiates an arm drop in a passage that is too fast to allow an alternative technique, as in each group of three eighth notes that begins on a *Schneller* in Op. 7/i/109–110, or in each slurred two-note group that occurs in Op. 31/2/i/182–84.

Metric Accents

Recognition of the metric accent as the basic (though not necessarily the overruling) accent and of its association with long and short notes was the norm in treatises after the mid-18th century, including those by Marpurg, Hiller, Sulzer, and Kirnberger.[46] In Beethoven especially, the

45. Graudan/SFORZATO briefly discusses *sf* as an accent sign, but mainly concerns the series of *sf* signs used by Beethoven to define a crescendo (as discussed in Ch. 8).

46. Cf. the quotations and examples in Rothschild/MOZART 16–19.

EXAMPLE 5/24 Sonata Op. 101/iv/29–34 (after Wallner/KLAVIER-SONATENm II 218; HV*)

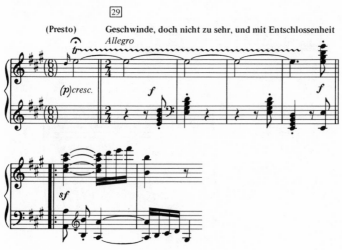

EXAMPLE 5/25 Sonata Op. 53/i/10–13 (after BEETHOVEN WERKEm VII 3/II 88; HV*)

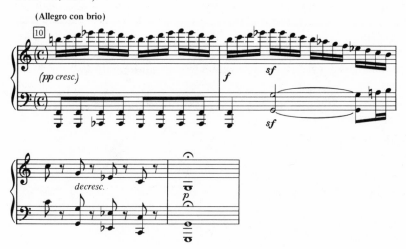

metric accent adds further significance by helping to outline the structure. For example, a *sf* marks the arrival at the tonic harmony and the start of a new section in the finale of Op. 101 (Ex. 5/24). It helps to prolong and intensify the climax of the development section in the opening movement of the "Sonate Pastorale," first occurring once in each measure, then twice (Op. 28/i/209–226). It tops the prolonged climax of the initial phrase grouping, a period of thirteen measures, in the "Waldstein" Sonata Op. 53 (Ex. 5/25). It points up the rhythmic organization of a tuneful, subordinate melody in the finale of that same sonata (mm. 71–92). It suggests a peak or climax in the "Arietta" and in ensuing variations of the final Sonata in C Minor (Op. 111/ii/16, 32, 48, etc.). And it hammers persistently at a main motive in the first movement of Op. 90 (Ex. 5/26).

Beethoven's metric accents also contribute to structural organization

EXAMPLE 5/26 Sonata Op. 90/i/93–97, after Wallner/KLAVIERSONATENm II 198; HV*

by enhancing the drive to a cadence. In the first movement of the little Sonata in C Minor Op. 10/1, an accent tops the main motive on each downbeat (while bass afterbeats expand stepwise), leading to a peak on a tonic six-four chord in the relative major key before a final cadence in that key (Ex. 5/27; also, recall the cadence on the new dominant in Op. 53/i/25–30). In the Sonata Op. 31/3/i in E♭, the f on four successive quarter-notes of measures 44–45 establishes a "hammerstroke" cadence.

EXAMPLE 5/27 Sonata Op. 10/1/i/87–90 (after BEETHOVEN WERKEM VII 2/I 93; HV*)

In numerous ways metric accents help define Beethoven's phrase and period structures. The syntax of two shorts and a long, mentioned earlier as being cultivated so generally from Beethoven to Brahms, is defined— in this instance as 2 + 2 + 4 measures—by sf signs in the finale of the "Appassionata" Sonata (Op. 57/iii/29–48). Thanks to six >signs and a sf, a kind of Schenkerian *Urlinie* is highlighted above the entire first variation in the finale of the Sonata in E Op. 109. A ffp determines the peak and hence the direction of a phrase in the finale of the Sonata in C Minor Op. 10/1 (Ex. 5/28). Abrupt shifts from p to ff announce alternate phrase members in Op.2/1/iv/13–17. And in the finale of the "Tempest" Sonata (Op. 31/2/iii/181–215), a series of accents clarifies and punctuates a phrase grouping that describes a dynamic and melodic curve.

EXAMPLE 5/28 Sonata Op. 10/1/iii/21–24 (after BEETHOVEN WERKEM VII 2/I 102; HV*)

This grouping starts with three four-measure phrases that peak characteristically on their penultimate measures and lead with cumulative effect
into three two-measure subphrases. It climaxes in four additional two-
measure subphrases, then unwinds with two four-measure phrases again.
In that phrase grouping all the accents are *sf* signs except for a *f* on
the peak note, which not only has brought the dynamic level up from *p*
but seems to call for a slight agogic delay as well.

Apart from clarifying the syntax of phrases and phrase groupings,
Beethoven's metric accents can exercise other organizing influences. In
particular, they can disclose a basic, slower-moving framework that outlines and supports ongoing figuration. Thus, three *sforzando* signs in Op.
27/1/iv/56–61 reveal a simple ascending triad that underlies the much
more rapid chordal figuration. Other *sforzando* signs call attention amidst
the fast passagework to an extended pedal point in Op. 28/iv/101–111
and to a broad descending bass line in Op. 54/ii/37–44. Even in the slow
movements the accents can disclose a broader, underlying framework, as
in the "Adagio con molta espressione" of Op. 22, where the one accent
per measure makes the majestically slow harmonic rhythm more apparent.(Ex. 5/29). When outlining accents occur on every beat they can
even have a slowing effect on the tempo, as in the "Fuga" of the "Hammerklavier" Sonata Op. 106, where a *sf* occurs every quarter note for
nine measures of $\frac{3}{4}$ (Ex. 5/30).

EXAMPLE 5/29 Sonata Op. 22/ii/34–36 (after BEETHOVEN WERKEM VII
2/I 199; HV*)

(Adagio con molto espressione)

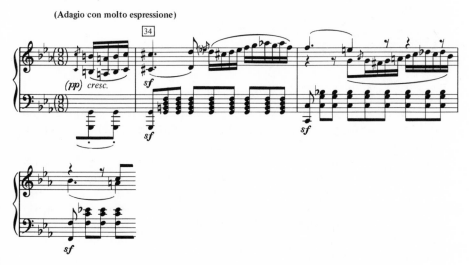

EXAMPLE 5/30 Sonata Op. 106/iv/102–105 (after Wallner/KLAVIER-
SONATENm II 261; HV*)

Beethoven's metric accents serve more immediate syntactic ends as
well. We have already seen how a Beethoven *piano* disappoints a projected climax by abruptly reversing its dynamic ascent (as in Ex. 5/22
above). Beethoven's accents may also identify poetic feet[47]—for instance,
the dactyls in the finale of the Sonata in C Op. 2/3 (Ex. 5/31); they may
determine the directions of incises, as in Op. 78/i/20–23, where offbeat
rather than downbeat accents might otherwise have been assumed; they
may cause alternative notes to stand out in a recurring figure (as in Op.
31/2/iii/87–90); and they may project modulatory signposts (as in Op.
13/iii/18 and 22).

EXAMPLE 5/31 Sonata Op. 2/3/iv/30–31 (after BEETHOVEN WERKEM
VII 2/I 58; HV*)

Contrametric Accents

Contrametric accents abound in Beethoven's music, adding tension
and excitement by conflicting with the prevailing meter. One fact about
them should be self-evident, yet is not always realized in practice. They
only have a "contra" effect as long as the barline accent (metric organization) remains clear, whether deliberately emphasized in the playing or
simply felt in the musical consciousness. In other words, the performance must expose the opposition of two kinds of accents, the contrametric versus the metric. On the principle that tension requires more
strength than relaxation (as in dissonance versus consonance), the contrametric accents are likely to be proportionally stronger than the metric

47. Cf. Steglich/AKZENTUATION 190–91.

EXAMPLE 5/32 Sonata Op. 26/ii/21–24 (after BEETHOVEN WERKEm VII 2/1 220; HV*)

ones. However, which should be the stronger is sometimes open to question. In Ex. 5/32, from the "Scherzo" of Beethoven's Sonata in A♭ Op. 26, the performer has to decide between letting the bass downbeat on B♮ predominate, or the syncopated (contrametric) minor-third, marked *sf*. The answer depends partly on how much importance the performer gives to the bass line, which has been rising chromatically from the A♭ in measure 17 (with the focal points in that line being the A♮ and the B♮.) Perhaps a more general answer lies in Newton's third law which states that to every action there is an equal and opposite reaction.

As with metric accents, contrametric accents can illuminate structural functions, though in different ways. For instance, a *sf* in the "Andante" of the *Sonatine* Op. 79 suggests that the division between phrases comes at the start of the third beat (Ex. 5/33), not anywhere in the second. Similarly, the *ff* in Op. 10/1/ii/45 marks an upbeat to a new phrase rather than a cadence extension of the previous phrase. By contrast, the two accents per measure in Op. 106/i/76, 78, 82, and 84 stress dynamic peaks on the truncated endings of four two-measure phrases.

EXAMPLE 5/33 Sonata Op. 79/ii/21–22 (after Wallner/KLAVIERSONA-TENm II 175; HV*)

An important and frequent structural use of the contrametric accent is to alter the meter by shifting to a *de facto* barline temporarily, at the end of which one more accent often announces the restoration of both meter and barline. In Ex. 5/34 the prevailing meter has been altered

EXAMPLE 5/34 Sonata Op. 54/i/47–49 (after BEETHOVEN WERKEm
VII/3/II 169; HV*)

from $\frac{3}{4}$ to $\frac{2}{4}$. Illustrated are the final three measures in *de facto* $\frac{2}{4}$ meter of
a longer passage from the first movement of Op. 54 in F. A similar pro-
cedure occurs in the finale of the "Tempest" Sonata (mm. 43–49), with
the accents being created by the starting notes of a recurring *Schneller*,
without the aid of accent signs. In Op. 106/iv/369–72, accents bring out
cumulative, *de facto* metric shifts from $\frac{3}{4}$ to $\frac{2}{4}$ to $\frac{1}{4}$.

The contrametric accent, like the metric accent, can serve to bring
out unifying motives. For twelve measures during the "Fuga" of the
"Hammerklavier" Sonata Op. 106 (mm. 140–51), it serves to bring out a
three-note motive by topping each recurrence as the motive roves through
the polyphony (Ex. 5/35). And like the metric, the contrametric accent
can call attention to a pedal point, as in the opening "Allegro assai" of the
"Appassionata" Sonata (Op. 57/i/249–53, in this instance an inverted
pedal point; cf., also, Op. 2/2/i/202–209).

More frequent are the contrametric accents that serve to emphasize
Beethoven's syncopations. A syncopation is best thought of not simply as
an offbeat accent, but as a displacement, by anticipation, of the next strong
beat in the prevailing meter (as in Op. 110/ii/114–17, in the bass). It
often figures in a dissonant suspension, where it is the consonant prepa-

EXAMPLE 5/35 Sonata Op. 106/iv/143–45 (after Wallner/KLAVIER-
SONATENm II 262; HV*)

ration on the weak beat that becomes the suspended dissonance on the strong beat before it resolves. (Recall Ex. 5/32 and see Op. 90/i/71–73, with an accent on the strong beat, too.) Syncopations can implement the dynamic direction of incises, as in Op. 2/1/i/15 (where the peak of the crescendo signs is equivalent to an accent sign). They can generate textural interest while enlivening the meter, as in the tenor line of Op. 2/3/ iv/119–25. They can make even more passionate the impassioned line of a slow movement, as in the Sonata in D Op. 10/3 (Ex. 5/36). They can give a rhetorical quality to the most conspicuous portion of a phrase, as in Op.26/i/187 and 189. And they can create a dramatic interruption in the flow, as in the "Marcia funèbre" of that same work (Op. 26/iii/18 and 20).

EXAMPLE 5/36 Sonata Op. 10/3/ii/23 (after BEETHOVEN WERKEm VII/2/I/130; HV*)

EXAMPLE 5/37 Sonata Op. 106/i/92–96 (after Wallner/KLAVIER-SONATENm II/230; HV*)

Beethoven's offbeat accents can strengthen a drive to a cadence and confirm it with even more energy than the downbeat accents can. A convincing instance is Ex. 5/37 from the first movement of the 'Hammerklavier" Sonata.[48] Closely related is Beethoven's intensification of the metric

48. Cf., also, Opp. 2/3/i/73–76, 7/iii/79–86, and 10/1/iii/14–16.

EXAMPLE 5/38 Sonata Op. 90/i/120–21 (after Wallner/KLAVIERSONA-
TENm II 199; HV*)

drive through offbeat accents,[49] as in Ex. 5/38 from Op. 90/i, which
shows two of ten measures of dynamic, quantitative thrusts on each second beat in the triple meter.[50] This example suggests that triple meter,
with its longs and shorts, seems to generate a stronger metric accent than
duple or quadruple meter in equivalent contexts, making all the more
striking any contrametric accents in triple meter.[51] By comparison, in Op.
109/i/33–41 the offbeat accents in nine measures of $\frac{2}{4}$ meter produce a
similar melodic surge but without quite the compelling sense of metric
drive.

Accenting the third beat in triple meter seems to have especially
appealed to Beethoven. Not infrequently, it becomes almost a hiccup, as
in Ex. 5/39, from the "Scherzo" of the Sonata in G Op. 14/2. A final jerk
at the end of a measure often occurs in duple or quadruple meter, too,
sometimes with a witty effect. Opp. 27/1/iv/76–80 and 31/3/ii/1–2 afford
choice examples.

49. This aspect of accenting is emphasized in Steglich/AKZENTUATION.

50. Cf., also, Opp. 2/2/iv/165–69, 13/i/27–28, 13/iii/113–17, 14/1/iii/42–45, 14/2/ii/
46–48, and 14/2/iii/219–24.

51. Cf., also, Opp. 10/2/ii/9–16, 26/i/57–59, and 28/i/100–103.

EXAMPLE 5/39 Sonata Op. 14/2/iii/97–99 (after BEETHOVEN WERKEm
VII/2/I/185; HV*)

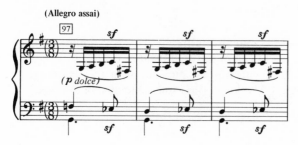

EXAMPLE 5/40 Sonata Op. 10/3/i/263–65 (after BEETHOVEN WERKEM VII/2/I 127; HV*)

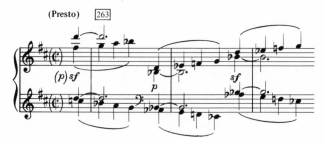

Like both metric and syncopation accents, offbeat accents can help clarify the direction, even the make-up, of Beethoven's incises. In Ex. 5/40 from the first movement of Op. 10/3, the *sf* or *p* signs give the impetus to three four-beat, feminine incises (in a whole series of such). A *sf* stamps the thematically vital, masculine grouping that announces numerous entries of the subject in the "Fuga" of the "Hammerklavier" Sonata Op. 106 (as in m. 26).

Expressive Accents

Earlier in this final section, expressive accents were defined as applying independently of the meter to tones that stand apart in pitch, harmony, texture, intensity, length, agogics, or timbre. They often inform us significantly about Beethoven's intentions. Furthermore, they provide essential clues to where other accents might be inserted by analogy. In other words, we can assume that Beethoven would have added similar accents had he been still more thorough in his editing. If that assumption has its dangers, as for performers inadequately grounded in his stylistic proprieties, it also has its justifications. Despite Beethoven's remonstrance to Czerny in 1816 stating that he wanted his music performed "exactly as it was written,"[52] there is evidence from his contemporaries suggesting that on occasion he himself departed in his own playing from what he had marked in the score.[53] To be sure, he could hardly be faulted for making changes in his own music. Yet, he set a precedent, which means for us that even Beethoven did not treat his own editing as inviolable.

52. Anderson/BEETHOVEN II 560; the pertinent passage was quoted near the end of Chapter 3 above.

53. E.g., cf. Badura-Skoda/CZERNY 22 on Beethoven's much greater use of the pedal than indicated, and p. 26 (par. 7) on his constantly different moods during performance; or WEGELER & RIES 106–107 on his infrequent liberties in playing; or Cramer (as quoted in Schindler & MacArdle/BEETHOVEN 413) on his inconsistencies during performance.

EXAMPLE 5/41 Sonata Op. 111/i/114–16 (after Wallner/KLAVIERSO-
NATENm II 314–15; HV*)

Expressive accents on or off the beat spotlight the extremes of pitch
range in the first movement of the Sonata in C Minor Op. 111 (Ex. 5/
41). They help to project pathetic, disconnected tones, quasi recitative,
in Op. 53/ii/10 and 12. They create bell-like tones in Op. 81a/iii/37–40
where the seven disconnected octaves appear (and surely are meant by
analogy to be echoed in the sequential repetition that follows).

With regard to its harmonic effect, an accent is expressive when it
focuses on a dissonance—for instance, the minor (rather than the major)
7th and 9th during the dominant pedal in Ex. 5/42, from the slow movement of the "Sonate" Pastorale, or the accented passing tones at measures 111–13 in the slow movement of Op. 31/1. With regard to its dynamic

EXAMPLE 5/42 Sonata Op. 28/ii/13–16 (after BEETHOVEN WERKEM
VII/3/II 40; HV*)

EXAMPLE 5/43 Sonata Op. 81a/iii/174–77 (after Wallner/KLAVIER-
SONATENm II 195; HV*)

effect, the expressive accent is seldom more telling than in Ex. 5/43,
from the finale of the "Farewell" Sonata Op. 81a in E♭. There it starkly
emphasizes the abrupt drop from the breathless, brilliant "Vivacissima-
mente" to a reflective pause, "Poco Andante," before the final outburst.
Somewhat similar accents, but in retrospective passages, occur in Opp.
7/ii/88–89 and 28/ii/94. Dynamic accents that signal imitative entries
in a polyphonic texture occur, among numerous other places, in the
marchlike movement of the Sonata in A Op. 101 (Ex. 5/44).

As for quantitative accents, an extreme instance is the three-beat tone,

EXAMPLE 5/44 Sonata Op. 101/ii/40–42 (after Wallner/KLAVIER-
SONATENm II 215; HV*)

EXAMPLE 5/45 Sonata Op. 2/2/ii/16–18 (after BEETHOVEN WERKEm
VII/2/I 27; HV*)

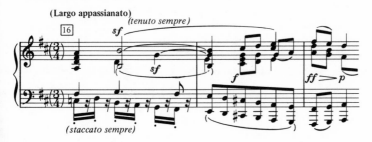

EXAMPLE 5/46 Sonata Op. 31/2/iii/25–29 (after BEETHOVEN WERKEm VII/3/II 88; HV*)

also marked with an *sf*, in an early slow movement (Op. 2/2/ii/16–17 and 47–48). The *sf* may have been inserted by Beethoven partly to insure that the tone survives, so as to keep the line flowing to its *ff* climax, for in his piano writing this tone's lasting power is challenged exceptionally (Ex. 5/45).

Finally, it will help to recall an earlier statement that an expressive accent may serve several functions at once. As must have already become apparent, that statement applies to most expressive accents. One further illustration should make it still clearer. The *sf* in Ex. 5/46, from the finale of the "Tempest" Sonata, empasizes at once not only a landmark in the phrase syntax, but the highest pitch in a phrase group, the moment of greatest intensity in that group, the longest-held note in that group, the peak of a feminine grouping, and a syncopation.[54] Beethoven expected a great deal of musical understanding from his performers!

54. Cf. Opp. 7/ii/12 and 101/iv/80.

CHAPTER *6*

THE INCISE AND PHRASE AS GUIDES TO RHYTHMIC GROUPING AND DYNAMIC DIRECTION

The Meaning of Incise

BOTH THE INCISE and the phrase got much attention from 18th- and early 19th-century theorists and composers as basic building blocks and expressive guides in music. But though the incise got even more attention than the phrase, it has largely disappeared from view today. In this chapter our first need is to re-examine what the term meant, what the theorists wrote about it, how it relates to the phrase, and how it can apply to the interpretation of Beethoven. Although Beethoven's treatment of the incise is exceptionally imaginative and varied, our focus could as well have been on the incise's expressive influence in the music of any or all of his great contemporaries, since the incise proves to have served as an almost universal building block of Classic and much Romantic music.

Even in the largest English dictionaries incise appears only as the verb "to cut." The use of it here as a noun in English simply adopts the French *incise*, the Italian and the Spanish *inciso*, and two German nouns that are entangled confusingly as musical terms, *Einschnitt* and *Abschnitt*.[1] In music these terms all share the double, interrelated meanings of

1. Cf. Raymond Haggh's valued effort to disentangle *Abschnitt*, *Einschnitt*, and related terms in Türk/SCHOOL 506–512.

a segment, or clause, in one sense, and of a caesura, or cadence, that demarcates that segment, in the other.

Eighteenth-century music theorists adopted incise from literary terminology when they began to indulge in detailed analogies between music and poetry. On the one hand, using incise to mean a segment, they described it as one level in a hierarchy of structural levels. More specifically, they described it as a clause, or subphrase, which ranked above one or more poetic feet at the minimal level (such as iambs or trochees), but below a verse, sentence, or phrase at the next higher level (or a period, a stanza, a paragraph, or a section, at yet higher levels). On the other hand, using incise to mean a caesura, the theorists described it as an incomplete cadence on a par with the comma. For they also perceived a hierarchy of cadences in music, from barely perceptible to complete and final, that was analogous to the progressive levels of punctuation in poetry, from the comma to the semicolon to the period.

Essential to this concept of a structural hierarchy, whether in poetry or music, was the inherence of an arsis and thesis, a rise and fall, at every level, not least at the incise level. In other words, in the hierarchy the sublevels functioned as wheels within wheels, revealing a separate arsis-thesis pairing within every arsis and within every thesis at each next higher level. And essential to that concept of the arsis-thesis pairing, especially in music, was not only a complementary but a causative relationship. The arsis caused the thesis. That is, it attained its peak, or release at some point during the thesis. The exact peak in an incise or phrase often depended on whether its thesis provided a masculine or feminine cadence. This peak overrode the prevailing metric accent when the peak and accent conflicted, but could itself be overridden by a broader peak at a higher structural level.

In Beethoven's piano music the foregoing might be illustrated by the regular four-measure phrase in measures 9–12 of the Bagatelle in E♭ Op. 33/1 (Ex. 6/1). Measures 9–10 (marked with a solid horizontal bracket) constitute the first, two-measure incise, or arsis, which leads into (or causes) the second, two-measure incise, or thesis (mm. 11–12), of that phrase. At the next lower hierarchic level—the minimal level in this phrase—measures 9–10 divide in turn into two one-measure sub-incises (marked with dotted horizontal brackets), or a sub-arsis and thesis, each consisting of an amphibrach (short-long-short), or "feminine" tone foot (Mattheson's musical equivalent of a poetic foot).[2] At the next higher level, this complete phrase becomes a supra-incise, or the supra-arsis, of its complementary phrase (or supra-thesis) into which it leads. (That particular supra-thesis is a near repetition an octave higher of its supra-arsis.)

2. Mattheson-Harriss/CAPELLMEISTER 344.

Example 6/1   Bagatelle Op. 33/1/9–12 (after Brendel/klavierstückem 32; HV*on)

To return to the arsis in measures 9–10, its own peak would be on the second *sforzando* chord (the peak of the sub-thesis), but that peak is overridden at the next higher level by the peak of the thesis in measures 11–12, which is marked by the third (and most dissonant) of the *sforzandi* chords.

Such fussy detail is typical of the more developed discussions by writers at the turn of the 19th century. These writers gave more attention to the incise and the phrase than to any of the other units, above or below, in the structural hierarchy. They needed to write that much in order to cover not only the regular or square sort (like the Bagatelle phrase just quoted), but especially the irregular sort, which might vary widely in its length, proportions, groupings, and dynamic directions. Presumably they also wrote that much because they found the incise and the phrase to be the most fruitful units to explore—the most manageable as building blocks, the most pliant and productive, the most receptive to expressive subtleties. Though continuing to approach the hierarchy through analogies with poetry, these theorists eventually paid most of their attention to the music. Within that attention they eventually concentrated mainly on expressive aspects, in particular on the rhythmic grouping and dynamic direction of the incise and the phrase.

The Evolution of the Incise in Theoretical Writings

To get a further idea of the prevalent thinking about musical syntax in Beethoven's day and to look closer at the incise and phrase in his music requires first a review of the evolution of these units as related concepts. Those concepts trace directly to the analogies between music and poetry mentioned earlier. Although such analogies turn up in 18th-century writings of other European nations, too,[3] they flourished above all in the

3. E.g., they underlie the distinctive treatise by the Spanish Jesuit exiled to Rome, Antonio Eximeno, *Dell' origine e delle regole della musica* (Rome, 1774), especially pp. 136–38.

important German and subsequent French writings to be recalled here. First to be mentioned is the outstanding German writer and theorist of Bach's day, Johann Mattheson, who discussed the incise (and its related structural units) most fully in four detailed chapters (6–9) of his *Vollkommene Capellmeister* (1739). Mattheson already recognized the theory of incises as being "the most essential in the whole art of melody," yet as being grossly neglected.[4]

Under the headings of "Rhythmopöia" and "Rhythmus" Mattheson explored prosody, or the scanning of longs, shorts, and accents, equating tone feet with poetic feet. In seven examples he illustrated how church songs might be changed to instrumental dances, not necessarily by altering their melodic pitch lines, but simply by rhythmicizing those lines with appropriate tone feet. Thus, in Ex. 6/2 (mm. 3, 6, and 7), he introduced the short-long pattern of iambic tone feet (among other patterns) to help derive a "Menuet" from the chorale "Wenn wir in höchsten Nöthen sein." He went on to illustrate how no fewer than twenty-six different poetic feet might be variously utilized as equivalent tone feet, especially in further dance types and in settings of the affections. Although prosody originated in verbalized song, it is significant that Mattheson applied his analogous tone feet as much to instrumental as to vocal music.

EXAMPLE 6/2 A "Menuet" from a chorale (after Mattheson/CAPELL-MEISTER 161)

Next Mattheson explored meter and flow in groups of tone feet, saying that without a sense of both beat and flow, melody cannot move its listeners. Basic to any metric relationships among tone feet, he stressed, is that complementation of arsis and thesis. It exists in all measured music, whether the meter is even (that is, two-part or a multiple of two) or uneven (always three-part). Basic to the flow of tone feet is what Mattheson says Rousseau called their "mouvement," a term for the psychological as well as the physical feel of tempo.[5] By stressing the psychological feel of tempo in relation to the incise, Mattheson was providing one foundation for modern approaches (like Hermann Beck's) to the determination of tempo in Beethoven's music.

Mattheson reached the acme of his discussion in the last of these four chapters, "Von den Ab- und Einschnitten der Klang-Rede," which might

4. Mattheson-Harriss/CAPELLMEISTER 380, echoed notably in MOZART/VIOLINSCHULE 108–109.

5. Mattheson-Harriss/CAPELLMEISTER 365.

be translated, in this instance, as "On the segments and [their] demarcations in musical rhetoric." Here, although he gave more attention to speech rhetoric, perhaps because of its better established terminology, he contributed much to the concept of a structural hierarchy in music. He described paragraphs as consisting of two or more complete sentences, sentences as two or more clauses, and clauses as two or more poetic feet. Units consisting of only one subunit would be incomplete, said Mattheson. For instance, a paragraph consisting of only one sentence—that is, only a rise or only a fall—would produce only an arioso in music.[6] He devoted special attention to the subphrase, or incise, and to the phrase levels of the hierarchy, already relating the phrase to breathing, and its internal rise and fall to systolic and diastolic forces.

Mattheson related the demarcations of his hierarchic units to corresponding levels of punctuation. Moving up the structural hierarchy, he thought of the comma as a demarcation for either poetic feet or incises, the semicolon for larger clauses, and the period for sentences. He also discussed colons, question marks, exclamation points, and parentheses as special, expressive demarcations, with significance in musical rhetoric analogous to demarcations in poetic rhetoric.[7] One is reminded of editors earlier in this century who indicated their recommended articulation of Baroque and Classic music, especially of the Beethoven piano sonatas, by literally inserting all those punctuation signs and more in their editions (see note 20 below).

Mattheson's musical analogy for a punctuation mark was, of course, the cadence. For him the cadence was a function of melody and not of the thorough-bass. He equated the conclusiveness of the cadence with the hierarchic level of the punctuation—finding, for example, only a tenuous cadence as the demarcator of a tone foot; a quarter-cadence (analogous to the comma) of an incise; a half-cadence (semicolon) of a phrase; and a full cadence (period) of a musical period.

Soon after Mattheson, Joseph Riepel explored further certain aspects of the musical incise, in both volumes (chapters) of his *Anfangsgründe zur musicalischen Setzkunst* (1752 and '55).[8] Starting with the same encompassing term "Rhythmopöia" and acknowledging confusion with the terms *Abschnitt* and *Einschnitt,* he insisted (even in his treatise's subtitle) that his conclusions were based on musical intuition and actual practice rather than abstract scientific laws. But his bases for those conclusions proved to be highly methodical, anyway—for instance, his preferences for symmetry and thematic consistency in his phrase members,

6. Mattheson-Harriss/CAPELLMEISTER 381–83.

7. Mattheson-Harriss/CAPELLMEISTER 396–404.

8. Riepel/ANFANGSGRÜNDE.

EXAMPLE 6/3 Symmetrical incises in a phrase (after Riepel/
ANFANGSGRÜNDE I 17)

phrases, and periods; and for neat balance within each arsis-thesis pairing and its supporting tonal harmony (as in Ex. 6/3).

Riepel's goal of an empirical rather than an eclectic approach to the
incise was to be realized some forty years later in the more extensive
writings of Koch, on whom Riepel exercised considerable influence.[9]

Referring once more to the term "Rhythmopöia" and to analogies
between poetry and music, Johann Philipp Kirnberger made his most
pertinent remarks on the incise in articles on "Abschnit" (*sic*) and
"Einschnitt" in Sulzer's *Allgemeine Theorie der schönen Künste* (1773).[10]
Although he too had to acknowledge the confusion of those terms, he
seemed generally to have regarded the *Abschnitt* as a phrase, meaning
either the antecedent phrase (arsis) in a period or the half-cadence that
ends that antecedent phrase and creates expectancy for the consequent
phrase (thesis). And he regarded the *Einschnitt* as we have defined the
incise in its sense of a segment—that is, as any of two or more subphrases
(whether in an antecedent or consequent position) within any phrase.
He said that the *Abschnitt* and *Einschnitt* are marked off, as it were, by
the semicolon and the comma, respectively.

Kirnberger advanced the concept of the incise in two ways. He distinguished between masculine and feminine cadences in both the phrase
and the incise, and he outlined the components of a structural hierarchy
in an actual composition—in this instance, a symmetrical song form.[11]
Also, he gave further evidence of his interest in the expressive aspect of
the incise when he said that his article on the "Einschnitt" was concerned mainly with its "soul" or underlying idea rather than its "body" or
(mere) prosodic elements. In emphasizing the expressive he was perhaps
extending his observation (somewhat as Mattheson was) to the effect that
the incise is a function of melody and not of harmony or polyphony.

9. Cf. Baker/MELODY, especially 3–8; Baker/KOCH, especially xviii–xix.

10. Sulzer/ALLGEMEINE I/1 6–9 and I/2 409–413.

11. Sulzer/ALLGEMEINE I/1 7–9.

Heinrich Christoph Koch

Heinrich Christoph Koch's *Versuch einer Anleitung zur Composition,* which appeared in 1787 during the peak of Haydn's and Mozart's output and the start of Beethoven's, provided the fullest, most detailed, and most tangible exploration of both the incise and the phrase thus far.[12] Only recently has his treatise been getting the recognition it deserves for its keen penetration into the musical structures of the Classic Era.

To be sure, Koch neither altered nor added to the incise concept in any fundamental way. Nor, in his primary concern with analysis and structure rather than interpretation, did he get to the immediate topic here—that is, to the incise as a guide to rhythmic grouping and dynamic direction. He had little to say about the rise and fall implicit in the arsis and thesis, which he treated mainly as antecedent and consequent in the structure. But in patient, perceptive detail he probed, clarified, and classified the traits of the incise and the phrase. Although he started by referring to the now venerable analogy between poetic and musical rhetoric, he soon summarily—and evidently gladly—dismissed that analogy as being beyond the comprehension of "beginning musicians." After all, his prime and steadfast goal was "to help the beginning musician learn how to compose."[13]

The point of departure for Koch, as for Riepel and Kirnberger before him, remained symmetrical and square construction. And, of course, the point of departure for the syntax in high-Classic music proves to be symmetry and squareness. But Koch also showed himself to be unusually receptive to the irregularities of asymmetric and unsquare construction. Indeed, much of his discussion involved almost countless ingenious ways to expand or contract the "basic" phrase and the two or more incises it normally contained. This discussion emphasized—again, in fine detail—the levels and types of punctuation, or cadence, that demarcated the incise and phrase.

Koch classified and explained phrases largely as Immanuel Faisst was to explain them in the mid-19th century and as the American theorist Percy Goetschius was still to explain them around the turn of this century—that is, by putting them in three categories. There were the basic (usually four-measure) phrase; the phrase extended by internal or cadential changes; and the compound phrase, made up of two or more phrases in apposition (often in sequence). Thus, as one example of a phrase

12. Koch/ANLEITUNG II. In Nancy K. Baker's excellent, annotated translation of Sections 3 and 4, it is Section 3 (Baker/KOCH 3–59) on the "nature of melodic sections" that pertains most directly here.

13. Koch/ANLEITUNG 356 fn.

EXAMPLE 6/4 A phrase extended by an internal change (after Koch/
ANLEITUNG II 378 Figs. 10 and 11)

extended by an internal change, Koch provided an expansion of a four-
into a five-measure phrase, with the initial, two-measure incise being
extended into three measures by a simple sequence (Ex. 6/4).

As would be expected, Koch said an antecedent phrase differed from
a consequent phrase in the conclusiveness of their cadences. He said that
the barline in a melody must be placed so that the melody closes on a
strong beat of the measure, which normally would mean on an appoggia-

EXAMPLE 6/5 The effect of a barline shift on the rhythmic gender of
a melody and its cadence (after Koch/ANLEITUNG II 388)

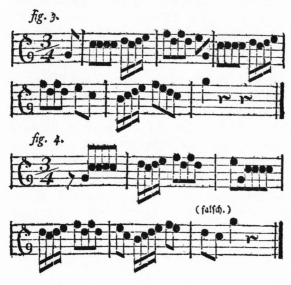

tura in a feminine ending.[14] And he illustrated how a shifting of the bar-line can alter the rhythmic gender of a melody and its cadence (from masculine to feminine in Ex.6/5). Also, he devoted much attention to the possibilities for embellishing the thesis of a feminine cadence—in part, it seems, to help clarify just when an incise is an incise. Unlike his predecessors, he no longer included a minimal rhythm (Matteson's tone foot) within the meaning of incise.[15]

Jérôme-Joseph de Momigny

Last and most important to our interests here, the Frenchman Jérôme-Joseph de Momigny discussed the incise and phrase especially in the second of the three volumes in his *Cours complet d'harmonie et de composition, d'après une théorie neuve et générale de la musique,* but also in four other publications that appeared between 1803 and 1834.[16] The *Cours* appeared in Paris in 1806, at the midpoint in Beethoven's career. It caused Koch to write a comparison of harmonic approaches, still in progress when he died in 1816 but apparently no longer extant.[17]

It was Momigny who took the giant step that remained, beyond the detailed classification and description of syntax and structure. It was he who penetrated the expressive factors of rhythmic grouping and dynamic direction, to which we now need to turn our attention.[18] Like his predecessors, Momigny started with the familiar analogy between poetry and music, but he reversed their priority by finding the rhythm of music to be the source for that of prose and verse, not vice versa. He believed that a horizontal approach to music, especially to the phrase and its syntax, needed to be restored after having been subordinated to a vertical approach. In this restoration he looked to rhythm as a synthesis—the synthesis of melody and harmony as well as of rhythm itself in its more limited sense.

Momigny's nucleus, or minimal building block, was the cadence, meaning essentially what Matteson had called a tone foot. But in the Frenchman's use, cadence included a rise as well as its original meaning of a fall, or both an arsis and a thesis. Momigny declared the cadence to be his "proposition musicale," in analogy with the French "proposition grammaticale" (or subject-predicate relationship in grammar), and he

---

14. Koch/ANLEITUNG II 384–90.

15. Koch/ANLEITUNG II 364–65.

16. Momigny/COURS; the 3d volume contains the music examples. A valuable, well-organized companion to the study of Momigny is Palm/MOMIGNY, which contains a biography, a detailed digest, and an analysis, and covers the four other most pertinent writings by Momigny, too.

17. Cf. Baker/KOCH xv.

18. The review of Momigny's ideas that follows comes largely from Momigny/COURS II 403–482 and Palm/MOMIGNY 153–98.

proceeded to examine its nature and behavior in great detail before advancing to larger units in the structural hierarchy. Only the high points in that detail can be summarized here.

In all music, even unmeasured music, said Momigny, the cadence inheres in each and every succession of two or three tones (Ex. 6/6). Its rise-fall (arsis-thesis) relationship needs to be regarded not merely as a sequence of events but as a cause-effect relationship. Moreover, when that relationship occurs over a barline, as it often does in measured music, the barline needs to be regarded not as a prison barrier that separates the rise from the fall, but as a link that unites them.

EXAMPLE 6/6 A cadence in every succession of two tones (after Momigny/cours III 158)

Although the rise and fall comprise just two parts physically, they comprise either two or three parts with regard to their intensity, or dynamic direction. In a dynamic sense, they comprise two parts when they describe a masculine rhythm, from strong to weak; and three parts when they describe a feminine rhythm, from strong on the rise or arsis to strong-to-weak on the fall or thesis. The masculine cadence is binary or even, the feminine cadence is ternary or uneven. Especially in the thesis of a feminine ending, the strong peak is often achieved by agogics, or dwelling on a tone, rather than dynamic stress.

Momigny got to one of his most basic principles when he emphasized repeatedly that the strong-to-weak directions of the cadence, whether masculine or feminine, sometimes reinforce, but sometimes oppose the strong and weak impulses of the meter. Moreover, he argued, when they do conflict, the cadence directions override the regular metric directions. If again we take a typically symmetrical phrase, this time from the start of the "Menuet" in Beethoven's Sonata in E♭ Op.31, No. 3, we can observe three instances of overriding, superimposed at three progressively higher levels of the "Menuet's" structural hierarchy (Ex. 6/7). The normal dynamic direction of the two two-note cadences, across the first and third barlines, would be from strong to weak, overriding the downbeat accents of the $\frac{3}{4}$ meter. But that direction is overridden in turn by the peaks, after the second and fourth barlines, of the feminine cadences at the next higher, level, the incise. And those peaks are overridden once again by the onset of the phrase's second incise—that is, its thesis—at the start of measure 3. As is often true, it is the masculine cadence that opposes and the fem-

EXAMPLE 6/7 Sonata Op. 31/3/iii/1–4 (after the original Nägeli edition of 1804)

Menuetto
Moderato e Grazioso

inine cadence that reinforces the dynamic directions of the underlying meter.

(I should insert here that it is in these aspects of dynamic direction that music goes significantly beyond poetry and that the earlier analogies between poetry and music break down. Any attempt to continue those analogies, especially to liken poetic feet to masculine and feminine rhythms in music, only contradicts the important conclusions that were being reached by Momigny and his successors. In terms of dynamic direction, an iamb in poetry moves from weak to strong. Unless it is overridden at a higher level, a masculine rhythm is a two-unit group that moves from strong to weak regardless of its metric position. In my opinion, this diametric difference explains much of the confusion between the ancient Greek and the 18th-century meanings of arsis and thesis.)

Momigny then proceeded to establish the link still needed between a cadence and its superior units in the total structural hierarchy. He graduated to the larger structural units by viewing especially the incise and the phrase[19] as successively larger macrorhythms of the minimal rhythmic grouping, or microrhythm, that formed his cadence. Consequently he also viewed the incise and phrase as each containing its own pairing of antecedent and consequent, or arsis and thesis, and its own causative rather than purely additive relationship. Momigny did not go as far as some later theorists since by regarding A–B and A–B–A designs (even sonata-allegro form) as macro applications of masculine and feminine rhythms.

Furthermore—and of chief concern here—Momigny maintained that the incise and the phrase derived their rhythmic grouping and dynamic direction from whichever cadence demarcates each, masculine or feminine. The incise compounds the two or more cadences that comprise *its* antecedent and consequent, as in the Beethoven "Menuet" just quoted.

19. Momigny's terms are usually "incise" and "hemistiche," respectively, although he sometimes used hemistiche to mean subphrase (incise) rather than phrase.

Like his predecessors, Momigny discussed and sometimes actually employed the punctuation signs of written speech to clarify the different levels of demarcation in the structural hierarchy.[20]

Subsequent Writings

Momigny carried the concept of the incise about as far as the theorists were to take it. Other contemporaries of Beethoven reached similar conclusions, if in different terms—notably the Berlin mathematician and musician August Leopold Crelle, in a piano method of 1823 that shows exceptional awareness of rhythmic grouping, dynamic direction, and agogic emphasis in the incise and phrase.[21] But if less interest in the incise and no further advances of significance have occurred since Beethoven's time, certain new interpretations, conclusions, and applications have appeared that deserve at least to be mentioned.

One landmark was the influential, impressively heralded *Traité de l'expression musicale* by the Swiss-French writer and piano pedagog Mathis Lussy, first published in Paris in 1873. Writing in full cognizance of Momigny's treatise and quoting abundantly from the Classic and early Romantic masters, Lussy further codified the nature and behavior, both regular and irregular, of the incise and the phrase within the total structural hierarchy. A highly sensitive and perceptive musician, he concentrated primarily on the rhythmic grouping, accenting, and dynamic directions of these units.[22]

Hugo Riemann, who acknowledged variously the precedence and importance of Koch, Momigny, and Lussy, made his own contribution to the understanding of phrase syntax and expression in his *System der musikalischen Rhythm und Metrik,* published in Leipzig in 1903.[23] Unfortunately, he made this contribution largely unacceptable by rigidifying the remarkably flexible principles of his predecessors into his uncompromising theory of universal *Vierhebigkeit* or four-bar squareness.

By that same year of 1903 the first volume of Vincent d'Indy's *Cours de composition musicale* was published, in Paris. It reflects Lussy's influence. D'Indy's emphasis also was on the rhythmic grouping, accenting,

20. Punctuation marks as articulation demarcators appeared in occasional editions throughout the 19th and early 20th centuries, as they still did in a collected edition of 1926 by one Jacob Fischer that included some Beethoven pieces (Berlin: Schlesinger, 1926; cf. CAT NYPL XV 541).

21. Crelle/AUSDRUCK (mentioned further under agogics in Chapter 8 below).

22. Lussy/EXPRESSION, especially Chaps. 5 and 6; also, Baker/MELODY 41–42, though without mention of Lussy's derivations from Momigny.

23. Cf. pp. 199–200. Also, cf. *Hugo Riemanns Musik-Lexikon,* 11th ed. (1929) 1197; Lussy/ EXPRESSION opp. p. 179; Baker/MELODY 42.

and dynamic direction of the incise and the phrase.[24] More recently, in Chicago in 1960, appeared *The Rhythmic Structure of Music* by Grosvenor Cooper and Leonard B. Meyer.[25] Without referring to any of the past writers cited here, Cooper and Meyer go over the same ground, starting with the literary analogy, the poetic feet, and the minimal rhythms, and gradually build similar rhythmic groupings and dynamic directions, and a similar structural hierarchy (as their book's title implies). Mainly their terminology differs. Along still other lines, it is worth recalling that somewhat similar groupings, directions, and even structural hierarchies have served the Benedictine monks of Solesmes for their expressive interpretations of the incise and other structural units of Gregorian chant.[26]

Even Alfred Lorenz's efforts in the 1920s and '30s to establish "Bogen-" and "Barform" as "the secret of Wagner's form" relate to incises, phrases, and structural hierarchies.[27] But at that point, if Wagner's operas, notably *Tristan,* marked a crisis in harmony and tonality, so they did in musical syntax and rhetoric. In much music from Wagner on—in that of Delius, Poulenc, Puccini, Falla, and Schoenberg, for example—the incise and phrase begin to function not only more subtly but more ambiguously.

These, in brief, have been some predominant concepts of the incise and phrase as well as of the syntax and structural hierarchy that have governed them. Those concepts should help us understand the theoretical ambience in which Beethoven composed. What remains is to sample Beethoven's own, most pertinent remarks and, especially, the evidence in his music to see how far he subscribed to such concepts. Learning that he did subscribe to them would throw considerable light on his intentions for the rhythmic grouping and dynamic direction in many of his incises and phrases.

Beethoven's Supposed Annotations in Twenty-One Cramer Etudes

Although it seems likely that Beethoven would have read discussions of the incise and phrase in contemporary or earlier treatises, I have found no documentary evidence to that effect. Moreover, his remarks that seem to pertain most closely to those structural units are admittedly suspect,

24. Cf. d'Indy/cours I, especially 23–46.

25. COOPER & MEYER.

26. Cf. pp. xiii–xiv in the preface to their edition of the *Liber usualis* (Paris, 1946).

27. Alfred Lorenz, *Das Geheimnis der Form bei Richard Wagner,* 4 vols. (Leipzig, 1924–33).

because they figure among the annotations that Schindler attributed to
Beethoven in twenty-one Cramer Etudes, but could well have forged.[28]
Yet, as suggested in our first chapter and illustrated presently, those
annotations could still be true to, and derived from, Beethoven's own performance practices and intentions. Though Schindler's jealous, conniv-
ing disposition does not encourage the speculation, it is even possible that
in his later years Schindler simply recalled the essentials of authentic
Beethoven advices and decided to insert them to complete the record, so
to speak.

Schindler implied that the annotations suggest what Beethoven would
have included in a piano method that, we learn from more than one source,
Beethoven hoped but never managed to write.[29] Moreover, Schindler said,
in the third edition of his Beethoven biography, that Beethoven planned
mainly to use examples from Cramer's Etudes in the method, because
the Etudes "contained all the fundamentals of good piano playing" and,
with their polyphonic interest, provided "the best preparation for the play-

28. Recall the brief discussion in our first chapter, with further details in Newman/SCHIN-
DLER.

29. Cf. Schindler & MacArdle/BEETHOVEN 379 and 397; also, Shedlock/CRAMERM ii and
fn. Also, recall note 2 for Ch. 1, above.

EXAMPLE 6/8 Cramer's Etude 16/1–4 with an annotation attributed
to Beethoven (after MS 35, 88 in the Deutschen Staatsbibliothek of East
Berlin)

ing of his own works." The final sentence in Beethoven's supposed annotation over Etude 16 reads, "These Etudes offer counsel and help for all situations."[30]

What is the gist of those annotations? They touch on several of the problems dealt with in this book.[31] But because their wording is often laconic, even obscure and awkward at times, they require some clarification and interpretation. First, it should be noted that they exclusively concern local relationships within the passagework and not any broad or independent melodic outlines that the passagework sometimes accompanies. Thus, in Etude 16 the annotation concerns only the accenting in the left-hand passagework, not the melodic line in the right hand (Ex. 6/8).

Second, the annotations reveal a constant alertness to polyphonic strands implicit in the passagework. For instance, the words "trochaic—4-part style" appear beside Etude 5 (Ex. 6/9).[32] Third, the annotations emphasize four aspects of performance—correct prosody (including the recognition and scanning of specific poetic feet), proper accenting, maximum legato [*Bindung*], and alertness to pseudopolyphony in the passagework. And last, they include occasional suggestions about keyboard technique. The annotation over Etude 5 is typical in touching on several of the foregoing topics: "The style is four-part throughout. The melody lies in the top voice, as the notation suggests [with its separate stems]. But even if the notation were thus [reduced to one set of stems and beams,

30. Two editions of the 21 Etudes, with the annotations and prefaces, are Shedlock/CRAMERm (marred by somewhat inadequate translations) and Kann/CRAMERm (marred by errors in the accompanying information).

31. For more detail, cf. Newman/CRAMER; Goldschmidt/CRAMER.

32. Cf. Goldschmidt/ERSCHEINUNG 232 fn. 118.

EXAMPLE 6/9 Cramer's Etude 5/1–4, with an annotation attributed to Beethoven (after MS 35,88 in the Deutschen Staatsbibliothek of East Berlin)

as in our Ex. 6/9], the first note of each group would have to be accented and sustained. The middle voice, *ec, fc, gc* etc., ought not be struck with the same force as the top voice. The poetic foot is trochaic."

More specifically, how do the annotations relate to the concepts of the incise and the phrase that we have been reviewing? They relate mainly at the level of the minimal rhythmic grouping in the structural hierarchy, or at the grouping that Mattheson had called a tone-foot and that Momigny dealt with under the term cadence—in other words, at that microcosm of the incise, phrase, and higher levels. The annotations tally with an interest in prosody and scanning on Beethoven's part that is corroborated by other evidence in a variety of sources.[33] As a sample, the annotation in Etude 4 brings to mind Momigny's assertion that "the cadence inheres in each and every succession of two or three tones" (as illustrated in Ex. 6/6 above). Beethoven supposedly wrote,

Here longs and shorts [for which read, strongs and weaks] are to be performed throughout—that is, the first note long (–), the second short (‿), the third long again, the fourth short again [etc.]. The same method [applies] as in scanning trochaic meter. At first[,] lengthen the first and third notes deliberately so as to distinguish the longs clearly from the shorts, yet not to the extent of making the first and third notes [as if] dotted. Only later speed up the flow, thereby gently rounding off the sharp edges. The student's gradually height-

33. Cf. Newman/SCHINDLER 407, 415–16; Goldschmidt/VERS 25–28; Solomon/TAGEBUCH 219 and 232; Anderson/BEETHOVEN III 1222 and 1314 (uncertain, hostile references). References to prosody had already occurred in Sulzer/ALLGEMEINE IV (1775), especially under "VERS," pp. 857–62 (kindly called to my attention by Richard Kramer). A further study of Beethoven and prosody was read by the late Harry Goldschmidt at a Beethoven Symposium (March 21–23, 1986)in Victoria, British Columbia; to be published in a conference report by Oxford University Press.

EXAMPLE 6/10   Cramer's Etude 4/1–2 (after Shedlock/CRAMERm 8)

ened perception [of the successive tone feet] will contribute and legato will result . . . .[34] [Ex. 6/10].

Sometimes the annotator's accents inserted in the Cramer scores encompass not just single tone feet but whole measures (as in Etude 15/ 21–24). The emphasis on a correct *Bindung,* or legato, throughout the annotations can only be understood as implementing the projection of incises and phrases (as in the annotation just quoted and in further references under "legato" in Chapter 8).

Rhythmic Grouping and Dynamic Direction as Revealed in Beethoven's Incises and Phrases

The following examples from Beethoven's piano music variously illustrate regular and irregular incises, arses and theses within these structural units, cadences that differ in conclusiveness, interrelations within the over-all structural hierarchy, multiple interpretations, rhythmic groupings, and dynamic directions. But it is well to remember that Beethoven's phrase syntax, like the structural means of any great art, is often capable of multiple interpretations—most of which, in any case, do agree with the expressive tendencies and limits that we have observed in the incise and the phrase.

Regularity and Irregularity

If Beethoven actually complained about the "tyranny of the bar-line,"—that is, the inevitability of square phrases—as he reportedly did,[35] then his complaint is not hard to justify. Performers tend both to sense and to seek square construction in his music. It is on that account, for instance, that they characteristically experience difficulties with the syntax in the surprisingly tricky middle section of the "Allegro molto" in the Sonata Op. 110. And it is on that account that an error was finally sensed and corrected in the second ending (m. 117) of the Sonata Op. 2/2/i. The "2" in the original edition had long been read as meaning a two- rather than a one-measure rest. Evidently, however, discomfort over the

---

34. I am indebted to Harry Goldschmidt for sending me (in a letter of Feb. 18, 1986) the complete text of Schindler's original pencil versions of Beethoven's supposed annotations, uncovered by "elektroanalytisch" means; these original versions prove not to have been altered materially in Schindler's pen versions (cf. Newman/SCHINDLER 410 for more details).

35. I can no longer recall either my source for this familiar phrase, which was perhaps one of the publications of Donald Tovey or Paul Bekker, or *its* source, if any was cited.

unsquare, extended cadential phrase that resulted has now caused the "2" to be reread correctly to mean nothing more than "2d ending."[36]

   With regard to irregularity, an oversize incise characteristic of late-Beethoven syntax, one that he stretched and stretched some more to fifteen measures, appears in Ex. 6/11, which comes from Beethoven's "Hammerklavier" Sonata just after the first movement's recapitulation begins. This incise is an elaboration of a sequential, regular, thetic incise within a consequent phrase. But as one level of a structural hierarchy, this elaborated incise proves to comprise its own complex of sub incises. Indeed, it shows once more how wheels can turn within wheels in the

36. As in BEETHOVEN WERKEM VII/2 p. 20, mm. 114–121, but not yet in Wallner/KLAVIER-SONATENm I p. 24, mm. 114–122. Warm thanks are owing to Paul Badura-Skoda for originally calling this information to my attention. Cf. Newman/SCHMIDT.

EXAMPLE 6/11 Sonata Op. 106/i/235–49 (after the original Artaria edition of 1819, uncorrected [with horizontal brackets added])

musical syntax of the masters. It starts with two of the sub incises ascending in stepwise sequence, continues to two more that are halved in length, then expands into an exalted, florid modulation to the lowered submediant key. In Ex. 6/11, the internal arses and theses within these sub incises (as I hear them) are marked by horizontal brackets. As we have seen (Chapter 5), they would not necessarily tally with Beethoven's original slurring.

Another kind of irregularity occurs when the incise that is elaborated is an arsis that leads to no thesis at all, producing only an incipient, or incomplete phrase. Such an incise occurs in measures 9–16 of the "Andante" in Beethoven's "Pastorale" Sonata Op. 28, where measures 12–16, continuing the pedal on *a*, are more likely to suggest an extension of the three-measure group in 9–11 than an independent, consequent unit (Ex. 6/12).

EXAMPLE 6/12   Sonata Op. 28/ii/9–16 (after the autograph)

Sometimes the incise is regular in length, usually two or four measures, but remains irregular as an incise because it lacks any clear internal arsis and thesis of its own. It may also lack any recognizable caesura in the sense of a rhythmic break, or any recognizable cadence in the sense of a harmonic resting point. The four-measure thesis (mm. 14–17) in Ex. 6/13, from the slow movement of Beethoven's Sonata in E♭ Op. 27/1, qualifies as an irregular incise on both these counts. If the performer does introduce a subtle, yet perceptible, caesura, just before the third beat of measure 15, it jeopardizes the integrity of the long line in that incise.

EXAMPLE 6/13   Sonata Op. 27/1/iii/9–17 (after the original Cappi edition of 1802)

Rhythmic Ambiguities

Ambiguities like those in the last two examples help explain why the music of Beethoven (and other great masters) is capable of multiple interpretations. Other explanations may be rhythmic in nature. For instance, in the opening, eight-measure phrase of Beethoven's Sonata in D Op. 10/3, the question has been raised as to whether the main metric accents should occur on the odd- or even-numbered measures (Ex. 6/14). Our approach to that question is one of determining the main cadences within the phrase's incises and thus the underlying dynamic directions. To take only the first sub incise (mm. 1–2) of the phrase's initial incise, if its main cadence is heard as the feminine cadence that overlaps the second barline, then the dynamic direction of the subincise tends to be that indicated by dotted lines in Ex. 6/14. If, instead, its main cadence is heard as the feminine cadence that overlaps the first barline, then the dynamic direction tends to be that indicated by dashed lines. The cadence over the second barline "rhymes," so to speak, with the masculine cadence over the fourth barline and with the culmination of the whole incise on a *sfor-*

EXAMPLE 6/14 Sonata Op. 10/3/i/1–4, after the original Eder edition
of 1798

zando. making a compelling argument for that interpretation. However,
the question must remain moot because of other arguments that could
outweigh these in turn, but then would take us too high in the structural
hierarchy, beyond the range of our topic.[37]

Another kind of rhythmic ambiguity that leads to multiple interpretations results from contrapuntal writing. It presumably illustrates why
theorists preferred to discuss the incise under melody rather than harmony or counterpoint. Both harmony and counterpoint could complicate
excessively the problem of locating expressive peaks. Ex. 6/15, from the

EXAMPLE 6/15 Sonata Op. 101/iv/150–55 (after the original Steiner
edition of 1817)

fugal finale in Beethoven's Sonata in A Op. 101, is a patent illustration.
In this episode the feminine cadence of each incise peaks clearly enough
after a barline, but the imitation of each soprano incise by the alto and
tenor two beats later naturally diffuses any singleness of rhythmic grouping or dynamic direction in the total texture.

Dynamic Directions and Peaks

Although the potency of their grouping and direction depends on
emotional range, the actual shaping of the incise and the phrase must

37. Cf. Imbrie/AMBIGUITY.

depend on the locations and types of their internal cadences. Momigny explored these expressive, interactive forces fully for their effect not only on the incises and phrases, but ultimately on the structural hierarchy. Yet he never quite reduced his conclusions to the clear pedagogic principles later expounded by Lussy. Near the middle of his treatise Lussy offered five rules for rhythmic peaks (accentuation). The rule that concerns the incise in particular states that, "The first note of an *incise* is strong, the last weak, regardless of where these notes fall in the measure and the meter."[38] This rule recalls anticipations and approximations of it in numerous 18th-century treatises, as at several places in Leopold Mozart's treatise of 1756 on violin playing:

> Now in a musical composition, if two, three, four, and even more notes be bound together by the [bowing] slur, so that one recognizes therefrom that the composer wishes the notes not to be separated but played singingly in one bow, the first of such united notes must be somewhat more strongly stressed, but the remainder slurred on to it quite smoothly and more and more quietly .... It will be seen that the [resulting] stress falls now on the first, now on the second, or third quarter-note [of the measure], yes, frequently even on the second half of the first, second, or third quarter-note. Now this [location of the stress] indisputably changes the whole style of performance ....[39]

However, neither Mozart's mid-18th-century statement nor Lussy's quoted rule includes the significant influence of the internal arsis and thesis, or rise and fall, on the incise's or phrase's over-all dynamic direction. This influence is discussed fully by Momigny, and by Lussy in the later portions of his treatise that deal more directly with expressive factors. But in the present discussion it should be possible to propose a single rule, almost a "unified-field theory" of musical expression, that comprehends both the conclusions and the implications of Momigny and Lussy. That rule—or, at least, that rule-of-thumb—would hold that *an*

38. Lussy/EXPRESSION 85–89.

39. MOZART VIOLINSCHULE 135, using most of the translation in MOZART VIOLIN 123–24; cf. Newman/SCHINDLER 406 (where most of this quote also appears) and fn. 26.

EXAMPLE 6/16 Sonata in F Op. 10/2/ii/1–8 (after the original Eder edition of 1798)

incise or a phrase reaches the peak of its rise and fall on its last strong beat before its final note. As a straightforward illustration, Ex. 6/16 from the middle movement of Beethoven's Sonata in F Op. 10/2 may be quoted. The peak on the penultimate strong beat in this example (marked by an asterisk) is supported further by the six-four chord of the feminine cadence at that point, by the near peak of the melodic rise and fall, and perhaps by the start of the new slur.

Of course, that proposed rule is oversimplified, being subject to several considerations raised by both Momigny and Lussy. First, it is based axiomatically on the assumption that both the incise and the phrase embody an arsis and a thesis. For inherent in the causative relationship of the arsis and thesis is the principle that the peak of their rise and fall normally will be the peak of the thesis. It will be the onset of the denouement, so to speak. In other words, it will tend to come near the end, as in Ex. 6/16 just quoted and, for that matter, as in any Western art form that occurs primarily in time rather than space.[40]

Second, to hold that the peak occurs on the penultimate strong beat requires some latitude in locating that strong beat. Locating it is less of an option in $\frac{2}{4}$ and $\frac{3}{4}$ meter at moderate tempos, as in Ex. 6/16 again. But locating it becomes more of an option—that is, more of an invitation to multiple interpretations—in $\frac{4}{4}$ meter and at tempos slow enough to be subdivided or fast enough to be compounded (Beethoven's "ritmo di tre battute"). Thus, in the opening phrase of the "Adagio cantabile" from Beethoven's *Grande Sonate pathétique,* Op. 13, the peak occurs optionally on the first or third eighth note of the third measure, as marked by asterisks in Ex. 6/17.

Third, the normal peak of an incise or a phrase may be outweighed by some special peak—an extra high, low, loud, soft, or long tone; a strong syncopation; or a conspicuously dissonant or chromatic tone.[41] In Ex. 6/18, from the "Adagio sostenuto" of Beethoven's "Hammerklavier" Sonata, Op. 106, the normal peak of the phrase would be the fourth beat of the third measure or even the first beat of the fourth measure. But the e♮ in the second measure qualifies as a special peak that outweighs either of

40. Cf. Newman/CLIMAX.

41. Cf., especially, Chapter VI on "l'accentuation pathétique" in Lussy/EXPRESSION.

EXAMPLE 6/17 Sonata in C Minor Op. 13/ii/1–4 (after the original Hoffmeister edition of 1799)

EXAMPLE 6/18 Sonata Op. 106/iii/28–31 (after the original Artaria edition of 1819)

those peaks not only by reaching the highest pitch but by causing the most biting dissonance, against the *e♯* in the harmony.

And fourth, as we have seen, the normal peak of an incise or a phrase may be overridden by a peak at a higher level in the structural hierarchy,

EXAMPLE 6/19 Sonata Op. 27/2/i/24–28 (after the original Cappi edition of 1802)

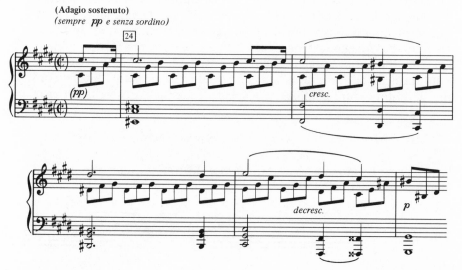

with its broader grouping and direction and its ever more comprehensive conditions and qualifications. Thus, consider the five-measure phrase in Ex. 6/19, from the opening "Adagio sostenuto" of Beethoven's Sonata in C♯ Minor Op.27/2. In the three-measure incise that is the arsis of this phrase, the peak, according to our rule and its qualifications, would occur on the b♮ in the second measure. But in the whole phrase, that peak is likely to be overridden by the last strong beat of the thesis—that is, the *e* in measure 4. From this *e* to the b♯, it is worth noting that the only marking in the autograph is a *p* under the *e* itself. In other words, originally Beethoven signalled that peak with the understatement of a Beethoven *piano* (recall Ex. 5/22, p. 149)! The foregoing interpretation is borne out in the original edition by the "cresc." and "decresc." that Beethoven entered in the second and fourth measures.

We have seen that Beethoven's original slurs are no safe clue to the grouping or direction of his incises and phrases. But it soon becomes evident that other of his editorial markings often do have a bearing, although sometimes these markings seem to occur in deliberate contrast to, rather than because of, the grouping and direction. We have noted that Beethoven may or may not have read discussions of the incise and phrase in contemporary or earlier treatises. But of course he did subscribe broadly to the musical laws of his times in his own music—to the behavior of melody and harmony, to the treatment of dissonance, to the organizational influence of meter—meaning that he stood quite as aware of and subject to the rules of the incise and phrase as any of his Classic contemporaries.

By way of closing this discussion, two questions may be raised. First, if the principles of rhythmic grouping and dynamic direction figured so importantly in Beethoven's time, why have they received so relatively little attention from 20th-century writers and theorists, and even from performers? My answer is that the reason they developed at all has been misinterpreted by the moderns. The moderns have tended to assume that the whole idea of the structural hierarchy was developed to fortify the beginning student with an elegant and convenient literary analogy rather than to provide an actual working approach to the composition and performance techniques of the day. They have revealed this misinterpretation when they have wondered, as I had,[42] at the apparent absence of such working approaches (other than of treatises on outmoded thoroughbass). Though many present-day musicians may be conservative in their tastes, present-day composers and apprentice composers tend to live in the present when they seek their practical approaches, quite as 18th-century musicians did. They seek these approaches not in Koch or Mom-

42. Cf. Newman/SCE 26–35.

igny but in Schenker or Hindemith or some more recent theorist. However, when it comes to the understanding of past music, should not the first approach be through the influential theorists who were writing at the time of that music and not ours?

Second, why does a rediscovery of the principles of the incise and phrase seem so important today? As the ideal building blocks in size and weight, as it were, and the ones that the Classic masters themselves seem to have found most workable, they remain the best guides to the expressive interpretation as well as to the structure of their music. Certainly they provide, for example, more realistic guides to the thematic material and the rhythmic organization of their great sonatas than does our 19th-century, formalistic concept of sonata-form, which is still the concept most widely expounded in textbooks today. It is pertinent that this latter concept rarely received any attention in the treatises written during the period of its own most heralded creations.[43]

The treatment of the incise and phrase account better than any other single factors for the vitality of Beethoven's music—its spontaneity, flexibility, fluency, and *joie de vivre*. One might suppose that their prevailing dynamic directions, from strong to weak according to the rule arrived at earlier, would open them to a charge of too little variety. Does not that near sameness of direction violate the aesthetic requisite of all art forms— a balance of variety within unity? Far from it! The variety occurs, again, in the location, type, conclusiveness, and elaboration of their internal cadences; in their unregimented conformity or conflict with the prevailing meter; and in their ever-changing relations to the lower and higher units in their structural hierarchy. Indeed, so varied is the treatment of the incise and the phrase in the hands of the masters that modern performers, like modern listeners, find themselves hard-pressed to keep up with their nearly constant subtleties.

A better understanding of the incise and phrase strikes me as the single most rewarding guide to more meaningful performance in Beethoven's music. In most Western music, every musical idea, large or small, must have a beginning, middle, and end. Put differently, every idea must come from and go to somewhere. Sensitive performers come to realize that principle keenly. But a better understanding of the incise and phrase can guide the less advanced and even the less sensitive performers to locate that "somewhere" with more intelligence and purpose. Indeed, it can prove to be their surest guide to convincing rhythmic grouping and compelling dynamic direction.

43. Cf. Newman/SSB 29–36.

CHAPTER 7

REALIZING BEETHOVEN'S
ORNAMENTATION

Types, Evidence, and Studies

A
S IT IS MOST OFTEN classified,[1] ornamentation falls into
three types: One type is indicated by the composer with
more or less conventional signs, another is written out
by the composer, and a third may be improvised during
performance. Ex. 7/1 provides samples by Beethoven of a turn indicated
by a sign, a trill written out, and a freer embellishment written out but
suggesting how it might have been improvised elsewhere. All three types
occur often in Beethoven's piano music, though how often the improvised type occurred in it when he himself played, or supervised the playing of, that music, can only be guessed. By its very nature, improvisation
left infrequent clues in the notation. Otherwise one must depend on
occasional contemporary documents or related practices that pertain to
it. The written-out ornaments, being the most explicit, raise the fewest
problems of realization and interpretation. Thanks to analogous contexts,
this type sometimes helps with the realization of a sign or the improvisation of an equivalent ornament.

Beethoven's chief ornaments, starting with the most frequent, are trills,
turns, freer groupings of (grace) notes, and short and long appoggiaturas.
As we consider their realizations from musical, practical, and historical
standpoints, we shall be amplifying an observation made earlier (Chapter
2), to the effect that those realizations are made more problematic by the
broad transition in performance practices during Beethoven's career.

1. E.g., Putnam Aldrich's article on "Ornamentation" in the *Harvard Dictionary of Music*,
2d ed. (Cambridge: Harvard University Press, 1969) 629–33.

EXAMPLE 7/1 (a) Sonata for Piano and Violin Op. 12/1/iii/1–3 (after
BEETHOVEN WERKEM V/1 18); (b) Trio for Piano, Violin, and Cello Op.
70/1/ii/31–33 (after Raphael & Klugmann/TRIOSM II 18); and (c) the
"Righini Variations" WoO 65/xiv/15–16 (after BEETHOVEN WERKEM
VII/V 18; HV*)

a. Allegro

b. (Largo assai ed espressivo)

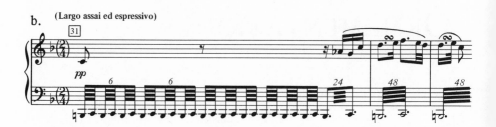

c. (Adagio)

What evidence do we have for the way Beethoven intended his ornaments to be played? From him we have occasional hard evidence of three
kinds—original fingerings, ornaments written out in full or in part, and a
very few specific explanations or comments. Each kind will be brought
up in this chapter where it applies. Most of this evidence concerns the
trills. In fact, of thirteen different, original fingerings for Beethoven's
ornaments that have turned up in all of his instrumental music (exclud-
ing recurrences in the same movements or pieces), [all] apply to trills.[2]
In addition, we have presumptive evidence from Beethoven in the musical context of his ornaments.

     The notated ornaments include all of Beethoven's main ornament types.
They would make ideal bases for analogous realizations of his signs if it
were not for one main question. Why did he write out just those and not

2. Cf. Newman/FINGERINGS 192–94.

other ornaments? Was he, in effect, confirming typical realizations or was he introducing exceptional realizations? Since we can seldom answer that question with certainty and usually must rely only on contextual (circumstantial) evidence, we can accept his written-out ornaments only as possible, not proven, realizations for his signs. (The most plausible reason for writing them out is suggested below, under "The Body of the Trill.")

The kinds of ornaments that Beethoven may have improvised or expected others to improvise can only be inferred from whatever freer embellishments he wrote out, whether the short kind illustrated in Ex. 7/1 above and later in this chapter, or the longer kind, including cadenzas (deferred until Chapter 9 on textural and structural considerations).

The presumptive evidence that derives from the musical contexts of Beethoven's ornaments often can help to determine their realizations. Thus, one ornament realization may prove to be better than another because it flows more convincingly in its rhythm, or creates a needed harmonic dissonance, or avoids a gauche voice-leading or parallelism, or relates to a main melodic idea, or facilitates an otherwise awkward keyboard passage. For instance, in Ex. 7/2, from the first movement of the "Emperor Concerto" in E♭, it is safe to assume that all four trills in the piano part were meant to begin on their main, consonant notes, because of the stepwise ascending line they define, the thematic reference contained in those notes, and the melodic precedent set by the first clarinet in the woodwind passage of the preceding two measures. Also, it is safe to assume that all four trills were meant to exit by way of suffixes from the half- or whole-step below their main notes, because only with a suffix can each trill approach the next, higher note gracefully, without that higher note having to be repeated.

Besides Beethoven's own few explanations of his ornament realizations or comments on them, there are others from members of his professional circle. There are fingerings and other suggestions from Czerny and Moscheles,[3] although as Kullak reports,[4] Czerny sometimes contradicted himself from one edition to the next. And there are remarks about

3. Especially as in Czerny/BEETHOVENm and Moscheles/BEETHOVENm.

4. Kullak/BEETHOVEN 71–76 and 83–92.

EXAMPLE 7/2 Concerto Op. 73/i/379–82 (after Altmann/CONCERTOS V 69)

improvised embellishments from Ries. Schindler had almost nothing to say about specific ornaments, in spite of his concern with Beethoven's other performance intentions.

Relatively little that throws special light on Beethoven's ornaments can be found in the treatises prior to and during his lifetime. There will be occasions here to cite several treatises for specific precepts, though one concludes, from Beethoven's treatment not only of ornaments but of other performance practices as well, that the one main authority he looked to for such practices was Emanuel Bach, probably initially through Neefe and subsequently by direct access to Bach's *Versuch*.[5] However, Beethoven seems to have maintained this allegiance to Emanuel Bach's precepts only through what he himself may have called his "first period"[6]— that is, through about Op. 22 in his piano music. Exceptional are his more lasting uses of two special applications, the trilled turn (*prallender Doppelschlag*) and a short trill that will be identified here with the *Schneller*. Otherwise, as in all else, Beethoven soon became very much his own person, so that by the time young Ferdinand Ries questioned parallel fifths in the C-minor String Quartet Op. 18, Beethoven could respond, in effect, "Who makes the rules!"[7]

Furthermore, Beethoven could not have derived much on ornaments that was new from later 18th-century writers, if only because he would have found that any he might have consulted had themselves all drawn heavily on Emanuel Bach's widely-known treatise. Among successful treatises published after 1800, Clementi's *Introduction to the Art of Playing on the Piano Forte* did win Beethoven's endorsement, though not soon enough to affect his own use of ornaments.[8] In any case, Clementi wrote relatively little on ornaments and only a little of that was innovative, all concerning the trill. Cramer, directly influenced by Clementi and likewise respected by Beethoven, offered still less.

Subsequent treatises, coming too late to be possible sources for Beethoven's treatment of ornaments, can serve us only as possible reflections of his practices. Unfortunately, the Viennese teacher and writer Friederich Starke, who proudly announced contributions from Beethoven to his

---

5. Recall that Beethoven's first assignment to his 10-year-old pupil Czerny was to read Bach's *Versuch* (cf. Badura-Skoda/CZERNY 11). Recall, too, his indirect acknowledgement of Bach's influence, in his letter of July 26, 1809, to Breitkopf & Härtel (Anderson/BEETHOVEN I 235).

6. Cf. Newman/SCE 505 and fn. 22a, p. 834.

7. WEGELER & RIES 87.

8. Cf. KONVERSATIONSHEFTE I 111. According to Sandra Rosenblum (Clementi/INTRODUCTION xxxv), a German translation appeared in Vienna from Hoffmeister in 1802. Beethoven bought 2 copies of a German translation by late 1826, one of them for Gerhard von Breuning (cf. Anderson/BEETHOVEN III letters 1432, 1525, 1532, and 1543).

three-volume *Wiener Piano-Forte Schule* of 1819–21, still revealed little about ornaments beyond what had already appeared in Emanuel Bach's *Versuch*.[9] Hummel and Czerny, who shows Hummel's clear influence, both provided significant remarks on ornaments. These remarks, which did not appear in print until Beethoven had died, suggest an awareness of his ornament practices and generally summarize the trends during the change-over mentioned earlier.

No major study has been done to date on the performance of Beethoven's ornaments in general. Even shorter studies have been remarkably few and those (as cited presently) have concentrated, again, almost exclusively on his trills. A useful chapter on the playing of Beethoven's various ornaments was included in Kenneth Drake's book of 1972 on *The Sonatas of Beethoven as He Played and Taught Them*.[10] A helpful list and capsule review of his ornament types and uses was presented by Shin Augustinus Kojima at the 1977 "Beethoven Kolloquium" in Vienna and published in its report.[11] Some interesting observations on ornaments appear in Eva Badura-Skoda's discussion of certain "Performance Conventions in Beethoven's Early Works" at the "Detroit Congress" that same year, published in its report.[12]

About Beethoven's Trills

The ornament that Beethoven used most in his scores, generally with a sign but often by writing it out, is the trill. Next to the choice and flexibility of tempo, the proper realization of his trills still seems to be the practice that pianists discuss most in his music. Yet even that aspect of his ornamentation has enjoyed remarkably few studies in any depth. From the late 19th century we may single out the latter portion of an enterprising essay on Beethoven's piano playing by the German pianist and teacher Franz Kullak. This essay was first published in 1881 as an introduction to Kullak's pathbreaking, critical edition for Steingräber of Beethoven's five Piano Concertos; it was translated and printed separately in 1901.[13] Reading like a detective story, it progresses step-by-step through imaginative deductions. Regrettably, it remains indecisive in its conclusions, although that indecisiveness becomes more understandable when one

9. Starke/PIANOFORTE I 17.

10. Drake/BEETHOVEN Ch. VI.

11. Kojima/VERZIERUNGEN.

12. Badura-Skoda/PERFORMANCE. Considerable information is included in Rosenblum/ PERFORMANCE, according to an advance copy kindly provided by the author.

13. Kullak/BEETHOVEN.

remembers how Beethoven flourished during a conspicuous change-over between older and newer performance practices. Also, it omits certain problems in Beethoven's uses of trills and it gives what now seems like too much weight to the contemporary treatises, especially Czerny's, which, as mentioned, are sometimes contradictory.

In 1976 appeared my own study on "The Performance of Beethoven's Trills," followed four years later by another that concentrated on "The Opening Trill in Beethoven's Sonata for Piano and Violin Op. 96."[14] The first of these was challenged by Robert Winter in 1977 and 1979, sandwiching a response from me in 1978.[15]

Beethoven's piano music makes an ideal field in which to study his treatment of trills. In his vocal writing the trill's use is negligible, without a single instance, for example, throughout the vocal parts of *Fidelio, Missa solemnis,* or the Ninth Symphony. In his writing for wind instruments, its use is greater, of course, and in the string writing it is still greater. But in no other works is the trill exploited so extensively or so resourcefully as in his most advanced works for piano. Clearly in them he was exploiting the instrument on which he himself excelled, or had excelled, and therefore was the most inclined to explore new expressive and technical possibilities. No later than 1791 or '92 (at age twenty-one or twenty-two), Beethoven experimented in a miscellaneous sketch with two astonishing double-note trills (Ex. 7/3).[16] The very fact that he would even consider these possibilities, with the second finger crossing over the thumb, says a lot for his youthful technical skills as well as his ingenious fingerings and the reach and flexible web of his hand. (However, this one among many such keyboard experiments can hardly be taken as the basis, as it has been, for assuming that a similar intention, including the inverted fingering, underlay the right hand's double-trill during the celebrated triple-trill in the Sonata Op.111/ii/112–114.[17])

14. Newman/TRILLS; Newman/OPUS 96. I am grateful to the American Musicological Society, to the Beethoven-Archiv in Bonn, and to G. Henle Verlag in Munich for permission to use some of the subject matter and occasional wording from these articles.

15. Winter/TRILLS; Newman/TRILLS.

16. Information about the correct identification and dating of this sketch has reached me through the kindness of Douglas Johnson.

17. Cf. Newman/TRILLS 101.

EXAMPLE 7/3 Sketch 705 in Schmidt/BEETHOVENHANDSCHRIFTEN 704–705 (as printed in Nottebohm/ZWEITE 359)

Discussions of the performance of a trill usually distinguish between its three obvious components—its start, its continuation, and its exit; or more specifically, which note to start it on, how fast and how much of its written value to keep trilling, and how to exit from it (with or without a suffix) into what follows. In that order, the performance of Beethoven's trills is discussed here, followed by special cases that include his use of the *Schneller* and the so-called "Beethoven trill."

The Starting Note

As still is true of Bach's trills, the starting note remains the most controversial component in the performance of Beethoven's trills. In Bach's trills the starting note is often, though by no means invariably, determined by whichever note is dissonant with the underlying harmony. This principle relates to the common explanation that the trill originated as a series of reiterated appoggiaturas.[18] It is no wonder, then, that the starting note was long said to be not the main, consonant note but its upper auxiliary with which the main note was trilled, or occasionally its lower auxiliary. In fact, despite frequent exceptions in Bach's time that prove necessary or advisable in practice,[19] the start on the upper note is both proclaimed and illustrated as the rule in nearly all main keyboard treatises of the 18th century and, indeed, of the early 19th century until Johann Nepomuk Hummel expressed contrary views in his *Ausführliche theoretisch-practische Anweisung zum Piano-Forte-Spiel* (1828).

To be sure, one should remember that although a trill's main note is normally consonant and its upper (or lower) note dissonant, either or both notes may be consonant or dissonant on occasion. For example, in Beethoven's Sonata Op. 27/1/iii/25–26 (Ex. 7/4), the starting note is evidently the main note (a) by analogy with the previous, notated trill;

18. E.g., cf. Marpurg/ANLEITUNG 53.

19. Cf. Neumann/ORNAMENTATION 244–58, 268–9. 272–80, chapters 27 and 28, 319–27, 352–55, 355–64, *et passim*.

EXAMPLE 7/4 Sonata Op. 27/1/iii/25–26 (after BEETHOVEN WERKEm VII/3/II/8; HV*)

(b) because Beethoven never used a sign for trilling with the note below; and (c) because the main note has a needed downward pull that is lacking in the upper note. But that main note is dissonant (as the 7th of the dominant harmony) and the upper note is consonant (as the root of the dominant). On the other hand, in the coda of his Twelve Variations on Wranitzky's Russian dance tune (WoO 71/102–107), the notated trill starts on its main note, a consonance, and trills with its lower note, a dissonance.

In those 18th- and 19th-century treatises the starting note is given unequivocally as the upper note up to about 1775. But from then on it is qualified more and more by main-note exceptions and other contradictions in the accompanying examples,[20] until the only credit that actually can be allowed to Hummel is for the arguments of melodic integrity and technical convenience on which he based his preference for the main-note starts:

> My chief reason for offering the rule that every trill ought to start on its main rather than its auxiliary note (unless specially marked) is that the trilled [or main] note, which usually is followed by some sort of cadential note, means more to the ear than the auxiliary [or upper] note, wherefore the emphasis needs to be on the main—that is, the trilled—of the two notes . . . . [Furthermore, the starting note justifies its own rule on the piano], since the piano, like every other instrument, has its individual manner of playing, fingering, and hand position.[21]

About eleven years after Hummel's treatise (1839?), Czerny helped consolidate this change-over to a main-note start. He formulated three rules for determining the starting note when it is not otherwise clarified by the composer. These might be reduced still further: Start on the main note unless (a) the trill is approached by that note, making an upper-note start technically more convenient; or unless (b) a striking effect is sought to enhance a long trill, making a lower-note start worth considering.[22] Of course, Hummel's and Czerny's sometime associations with Beethoven in Vienna add significance to their performance preferences.

In any case, dissonance, which seems to have been a main basis for determining the trill's starting note in Bach's time, became only one relatively incidental basis in Beethoven's music. It probably influenced

20. Cf. Newman/TRILLS 361, fn. 32.

21. Hummel/ANWEISUNG 394. My translation, which reverses the order of Hummel's arguments and reduces their wordiness a bit, is free, but less so than in the contemporary translation published the same year (1828) in London (cf. the verbatim excerpt in Edward Dannreuther's *Musical Ornamentation*, 2 vols. [London, 1893–95] II 145). Kalkbrenner added another argument in 1832, that of harmonic consonance (cf. Kullak/BEETHOVEN 68–69).

22. Czerny/SCHOOL I 172.

EXAMPLE 7/5 Ten Variations on Salieri's theme "La stessa, la stessissima" WoO 73/ix/14–15 (after BEETHOVEN WERKEM VII/5 99; HV*)

Beethoven's realizations of trills, especially short cadential trills, most during that first period while he was still an indirect disciple of Emanuel Bach. Thus, in Ex. 7/5, from the ninth of his Variations on a Salieri theme, the two cadential trills (like the other trills in this variation) can be assumed to start on their dissonant upper notes, an assumption that is supported by their allusions to the short appoggiatura on the second beat of the theme. But in Beethoven's subsequent music, too many other considerations militate too often against a dissonant, upper-note start—too many and too often, that is, to permit of any safe generalization about dissonance as an overruling justification for an upper-note start. These are based on both positive and presumptive evidence.

One consideration is the thirteen original fingerings for trills left by Beethoven. Although they represent but a small fraction of his trills, the high proportion of the thirteen that indicates main-note starts—nine, or nearly seventy percent—is worth noting. The reader who would like to see the main-note trill fingerings in context will find (1) "4–3" marked in an early fragment for "left hand";[23] (2) 3–4–3–2–1 for the right hand in the Piano Trio Op. 1/1/ii/69 (Ex. 7/6), if that potentially noteworthy fingering is actually authentic;[24] (3) an implication of 3–4, not 4–3, in

23. KAFKA SKETCHBOOK II 252, folio 132v–7/2.

24. According to Mies/TEXTKRITISCHE 163, this fingering appears only in the original Artaria edition; but according to information kindly sent by Elfrieda Hiebert it actually appears only in pencil and only in Anthony van Hoboken's copy of the original edition, meaning it might or might not trace back to Beethoven himself. Cf., also, Hiebert/WoO 39 fn. 18.

EXAMPLE 7/6 Piano Trio Op. 1/1/ii/69–70 (after the original Artaria edition, with the fingering added as in Mies/TEXTKRITISCHE 163)

EXAMPLE 7/7 Piano Trio Op. 1/3/i/308–309 (after Raphael & Klug-
mann/TRIOSM I 101; HV*)

(Allegro con brio)

the right hand of Piano Trio Op. 1/3/i/309 because of the fingering and
stepwise ascent in the approach (Ex. 7/7); (4) & (5) two fingerings in
sequence for the cello in the String Trio Op.3/ii/41–42, each marked
only 2 but played 2–3 or 2–4, not 2–1, to judge by the assumed suffix
from below, by the portato slur, and by the shift to 2 a 3d higher that
follows each; (6) 2–3 for a right-hand "Beethoven trill" (discussed below)
in the coda of the Variations for Piano and Violin WoO 40/7/74, a trill
that is acknowledged by the composer to be "somewhat difficult";[25] (7)
1–2 for the lower trill in the right hand, of the Sonata Op. 111/ii/112,
where the triple-trill begins (as mentioned above); and finally, (8) & (9)
1–2 and 3–4 for the two, successive, right-hand "Beethoven trills" that
occur first on top and then below in the opening two measures of the
Bagatelle Op. 119/7 (Ex. 7/8).[26]

Another kind of positive evidence is the grace note by which Beethoven began a fair number of his trills. He used this means most often to
call for lower-note, less often for upper-note, but apparently never for
main-note starts. In other words, since he resorted to no sign or other
means to indicate a lower-note start, he seems to have used the grace
note largely to indicate what to him were nonstandard realizations, the
main-note start having become more and more the standard rather than

25. WEGELER & RIES 57.

26. This fingering is found only in the original edition of this Bagatelle, in Starke/PIANO-
FORTE III 71. The 4 of the 13 fingered trills that indicate upper-note starts are in WoO 39/
8, WoO 40/59 (a double-note trill), WoO 40/60, and Op. 111/ii/112–14 (top note of the
triple-note trill).

EXAMPLE 7/8 Bagatelle Op. 119/7/1–2 (after Starke/PIANOFORTE III 71)

Allegro ma non troppo

EXAMPLE 7/9 Concerto for Piano, Violin, Cello, and Orchestra Op. 56/iii/116–19 (cello part) (after BEETHOVEN WERKEM III/1 155–56; HV*)

(Rondo alla Polaoca)

the exception. One grace note that does fall on the trill's main note is the second of two grace notes leading to a trill in the finale (cello part) of Beethoven's Triple Concerto Op. 56; but its effect is to cause the trill to be started on its upper note, both by analogy with the preceding, written-out trill and as an aid to technical fluency (Ex. 7/9). In Ex. 7/10, from the first movement of the "Appassionata Sonata," one sees first a lower-, then an upper-note approach. Earlier in that movement, after three grace-note approaches from below (mm. 3, 7, and 9), similar approaches may be assumed in two analogous trills that follow without grace-notes (mm. 11, 21, and elsewhere).[27]

A third kind of evidence for the starting note is provided by notated trills. That evidence is unassailable, of course, as far as the trill itself is concerned. But, as mentioned earlier, it is only conjectural when applied analogously to trills that were *not* notated. Even so, the preponderance of main-note starts revealed by the written-out trills is worth noting, as are some other aspects to be mentioned under the trill's other components. Frequently the written-out trill turns into a freer trill indicated only by a sign, as happens in both hands in the first movement of the Concerto in C Op. 15 (Ex. 7/11). In Ex. 7/12, a double-trill alternates 7ths and 9ths by starting on the main note in the right hand and the upper note in the left. Our discussion below of the special "Beethoven

27. For a few other grace-note approaches of interest, see, from below, Opp. 2/3/iv/285, 10/2/i/58, 54/i/133–5, WoO 68/coda/77; from above, Opp. 2/3/i/91–96, 53/iii/51.

EXAMPLE 7/10 Sonata Op. 57/i/44–45 (after BEETHOVEN WERKEM VII/3/II 180; HV*)

(Allegro assai)

Example 7/11 Concerto Op. 15/i/233–37 (after beethoven werkem III/2/I 21; HV*)

trill" cites Beethoven's writing out of a particular example by way of explanation.

Fingerings, grace notes, and notation have been considered here as reliable clues to the starting notes in Beethoven's trills. Both melodic and technical considerations can provide presumptive evidence that is almost as reliable, unlike dissonance, which was viewed as a more debatable and incidental consideration. A good example is the trill start that identifies with a thematic figure. In the fugal finale of the "Hammerklavier Sonata," the rising half-step that constitutes the oft-repeated *tête du sujet* begins on a trill that obviously must start on its main note in order to establish that half-step's identity (Ex. 7/13).[28] Similarly, the descending

28. Cf. mm. 48–52 *et passim*; also, Opp. 47/i/217–26; 97/i/7–8 etc., 27/iii/30 and 32.

Example 7/12 Sonata Op. 90/ii/49–50 (after Wallner/klaviersona-tenm II 203; HV*)

EXAMPLE 7/13 Sonata Op. 106/iv/16–17 (after Wallner/KLAVIERSO-NATENm II 257; HV*)

three-note figure in the Sonata Op. 101/iv/128 (*et passim*) includes a trill that must start on its main note in order to retain the subject's identity in that fugal finale. (Cf., also, the trills' obvious starting notes in the 6th of the "Diabelli" Variations.)

Other melodic considerations, especially the integrity of stepwise lines, can serve as significant clues to the starting notes, too. Beethoven's many stepwise chains of trills, both ascending and descending and both diatonic and chromatic, afford excellent examples of trills that almost invariably need to be started on their main notes. Thus, in the middle movement of the "Kreutzer" Sonata for Piano and Violin Op. 47 there is an ascending, diatonic chain of trills in which the suffix of each trill leads right into the main note of the next, thus producing a decorative line analogous to the one without trills in the previous two measures (Ex. 7/14). In the first movement of the Third Concerto is a descending, chromatic chain of trills that again need to be started on their main notes (Ex. 7/15). And earlier in the movement (mm. 93–97) there is another descending, but diatonic and embellished chain.[29] An extraordinary chain of trills provides a linear ascent during the apotheosis of the finale in the Sonata Op. 111, where the emphasis on each main note, rather than upper note, is essential in order to avoid a premature arrival at the $e\flat$ in measure 117. Stressing that $e\flat$ too soon would simply annul what for many is the most stunning moment in this sonata, the emergence of the transfigured leading tone into the new tonic tone and harmony of the key of $E\flat$

29. For other, different trill chains, cf. Opp. 101/iv/28; 111/ii/113–15; 73/ii/39–44; and 110/i/25–27.

EXAMPLE 7/14 Sonata for Piano and Violin Op. 47/ii/22–25 (after BEETHOVEN WERKEm V/2 102–103; HV*)

EXAMPLE 7/15 Third Concerto Op. 37/i/336–40 (after BEETHOVEN WERKEM III/2/I 191; HV*)

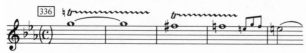

(Ex. 7/16).[30] In plainer terms, here is a reminder of the familiar rule: don't anticipate a resolution.

Even without the trill chain, a single trill in the course of a stepwise, descending or ascending line was the one exception to the upper-note rule likely to be made in most 18th- and early 19th-century treatises.[31] A partially notated example, from the first movement of the Second Concerto, tends to confirm Beethoven's acceptance of that practice (Ex. 7/17). A slur also tends to confirm it, especially in descending lines, as in the Six Variations in F Op. 34/VI/12–13. The main-note start applies quite as appropriately when the ascending or descending line is obscured

30. Cf. Newman/TRILLS 99–101.

31. E.g., cf. Clementi/INTRODUCTION 11.

EXAMPLE 7/16 Sonata Op. 111/ii/112–16 (from the autograph)

EXAMPLE 7/17 Second Concerto Op. 19/i/241–43 (after BEETHOVEN WERKEM III/2/I 114–15; HV*)

EXAMPLE 7/18 Sonata Op. 10/1/ii/8–9 (after BEETHOVEN WERKEM VII/2/I 98; HV*)

by a *fioratura* (Ex. 7/18). In the "Moonlight" Sonata finale (mm. 185–87), the melodic determinant for a main-note start is the peak of the line on the highest *a*. Melodic, stepwise progressions suggest that two successive trills on lower neighboring notes were intended to start differently, in the second movement of the Sonata Op. 2/2 (Ex. 7/19). The right-hand trill starts, presumably, on its main note, whereas the left-hand trill, with its ornamental approach, suggests an upper-note start if the tenuto sempre of that movement is to be maintained.

Whether one considers the composer's intention or the performer's physical capabilities, technical convenience and fluency become a rather frequent practical factor in determining a trill's starting note. That factor matters chiefly when a short trill or an even shorter *Schneller* occurs at a tempo fast enough to limit the number of notes that can be played (as discussed in the next section).

EXAMPLE 7/19 Sonata Op. 2/2/ii/9–11 (after BEETHOVEN WERKEM VII/2/I 9–11; HV*)

The Body of the Trill

The body of the trill—that is, everything between the trill's starting note and exit—raises questions about the speed and the freedom of the trilling itself. But the performer rarely has to decide how long to keep trilling during the value of the main note, as he often does in Bach's trills. In Beethoven's trills the extension of the sign or a notated suffix usually indicates that the trilling continues throughout the main note's value.

As to the speed of trilling, several clues suggest that Beethoven did not always want or expect maximum speed. One possible clue lies in Beethoven's notated trills, in which the speed usually relates to the context. In Ex. 7/20, from the "Rondo" in his first Sonata for Piano and Cello, the trill is (necessarily) very fast because the $\frac{6}{8}$ meter is marked "Allegro vivace." But in Ex. 7/12, above, it is slower because the tempo is marked "Not too fast . . .." Another clue is the option of a slower speed that Beethoven offers in his explanation of a "Beethoven trill" in Op. 53 (quoted below). Also, there is Starke's advice in 1819 that trills in the deep bass need to be played more slowly than usual, to insure clarity,[32] advice that is supported by the long notated trill near the end of Beethoven's Sonata Op. 101 (Ex. 7/21).

32. Cf. Starke/PIANOFORTE I 19; also, Türk/KLAVIERSCHULE 254.

EXAMPLE 7/20 Sonata for Piano and Cello Op. 5/1/ii/58–60 (after BEETHOVEN WERKEM V/3 25; HV*)

(Allegro vivace)

EXAMPLE 7/21 Sonata Op. 101/iii/352–54 (after Wallner/KLAVIER-SONATENm II 226; HV*)

(Allegro)

(Geschwinde doch nicht zu sehr und mit Entschlossenheit)

As for the freedom of the trilling, we have the implications or actual assurances of writers from Türk to Czerny that, in spite of the evenly measured realizations illustrated in their treatises, the literal number of notes played in trills was left to the performer's discretion.[33] That freedom would seem to invalidate Kullak's efforts to determine a starting note by counting back an exact number of oscillations from the final note.[34] Nor is there any justification for assuming because Beethoven started a trill

33. E.g., cf. Türk/KLAVIERSCHULE 253–54, Milchmeyer/WAHRE 42, Czerny/SCHOOL I 171.

34. Kullak/BEETHOVEN 69–76.

EXAMPLE 7/22 Sonata Op. 109/iii/153–68 (after Wallner/KLAVIER-SONATENm II 288; HV*)

Example 7/23 Sonata for Piano and Violin Op. 47/ii/IV/4–6 (after
Beethoven werkem V/2/II 110; HV*)

(Andante con Variazioni)

(dolce)

from the note below its main note (as in Op. 111/ii/106) that every odd-numbered note—that is, every upper note thereafter in the body of the trill—must be emphasized, too.

Indeed, Beethoven seems to have done the treatise authors one better by writing out the initial measures of certain trills so that those trills ease into their ultimate speed.[35] The most remarkable instance is the culminating trill near the end of Op. 109, which successively introduces quarter notes, eighth notes, and triplet-eighth notes on a single pitch, then starts trilling first in sixteenth and then in thirty-second notes before breaking into unregulated trilling at the sign (Ex. 7/22). Not shown in Ex. 7/22, the left hand joins in this progressive trill two octaves lower, beginning in measure 161. A more typical instance may be quoted from Variation IV of the middle movement in the "Kreutzer" Sonata (Ex. 7/23). Trills like those in Exx. 7/22 and 7/23 suggest to me Beethoven's most plausible reason for writing out part or all of some, but not other trills. He wanted better control over the speed and freedom of those particular trills, not only at the start and exit, but during the body of the trill.

The Trill's Exit—With a Suffix?

The treatises of Beethoven's time are in general agreement that a trill may be rounded off, or tailored, with a suffix whether one is indicated or not.[36] They often mention, too, the desirability of adapting the speed of a suffix to the trilling just completed. Czerny is a little more exacting:

The two little concluding notes [or suffix] must be played with the same celerity as those which form the shake [trill], and the lower of them must always

---

35. Czerny/school I 173 happens to mention ritarding during a trill, but not accelerating.

36. Eg., cf. Hüllmandel/principles 16, Viguerie/l'art 29, Clementi/introduction 11, Hummel/anweisung 394.

Example 7/24 Second Concerto Op. 19/i/145–48 (after Beethoven werkem III/2/I 105; HV*)

precede [that is, lead to] the principal [main] note [of the trill], and never the auxiliary note. /Though the concluding notes are generally written, yet when this happens not to be the case, they must be added by the player. /It is only when several shakes immediately follow each other, which is called a *chain of shakes*, that the two concluding notes are omitted. A chain of shakes in ascending [order], may, however, be played with the concluding notes.[37]

Beethoven raises less of a problem with his suffix than his starting note, simply because he writes out the suffix in more than half of his trills, either as regular notes or grace notes (Exx. 7/24 and 7/25, respectively). But one main question does arise. When he supplies no suffix in a trill, does he omit it intentionally or inadvertently? The performer must try to resolve that question each time by deciding whether a suffix would implement or impede the trill's exit into its context. As with the choice of the starting note, melodic and technical considerations are uppermost, along with a few others to be noted below.

Establishing analogies with similar passages that are more fully edited or marked continues to be a main help. In the opening movement of the Sonata Op. 31/3, a suffix may be taken for granted in the first trill of a descending trill chain because it appears in each of six succeeding trills (Ex. 7/26). In Ex. 7/27, the richly ornamental context and a likely analogy with the first written-out quintuplet in the next measure suggest suffixes on the second and third trills (and starts on their main notes).

37. Czerny/school I 171–72.

Example 7/25 Sonata Op. 27/1/iv/82–83 (after Beethoven werkem VII/3/II; HV*)

EXAMPLE 7/26 Sonata Op. 31/3/i/67–69 (after BEETHOVEN WERKEM VII/3/II 100; HV*)

EXAMPLE 7/27 Six Variations Op. 34/I/15–16 (after BEETHOVEN WERKEM VII/5 135; HV*)

The tempo is too fast to allow for suffixes in most of the difficult, veritable orgies of trills that mark the fugal finale of the "Hammerklavier" Sonata (Ex. 7/28). But from the standpoints of both technical and melodic fluency, a suffix proves to be advantageous when a trill resolves up a step rather than down, as in the opening movement of the first Piano Trio Op. 1 (Ex. 7/29). Support for that particular suffix may be found in a similar passage, with a notated suffix, in Op. 22/iv/19.

In his later works Beethoven sometimes precludes the use of a suffix by inserting a rest, apparently deliberately, where the suffix would have gone, as in the last two measures of Ex. 7/30, from the first movement of the "Archduke" Trio Op. 97. There the trills have to end abruptly in

EXAMPLE 7/28 Sonata Op. 106/iv/243–46 (after Wallner/KLAVIER-SONATENm II 267; HV*)

EXAMPLE 7/29 Trio for Piano, Violin, and Cello Op. 1/1/i/55–56 (after Raphael & Klugmann/TRIOsm I 7; HV*)

thin air, as it were, rather than resolving on their main notes, as in the previous three measures. Because Beethoven seems to have inserted suffixes so conscientiously throughout that whole section, his omission of them in the first two trills in Ex. 7/30 could have been intentional in spite of the analogy suggested with the suffix in the next measure.[38] This suffix has a momentary cadential effect, as though closing off the group of trills immediately preceding it. The same suffix is also interesting for requiring that the main note needs to be repeated when it becomes the note of resolution. By contrast, a resolution on the main note in the first movement of the Fourth Concerto (m. 169–70) does not require an anal-

38. The trills and suffixes in this section are identical in the neat, newly recovered autograph of Op. 97.

EXAMPLE 7/30 Trio for Piano, Violin, and Cello Op. 97/i/153–57 (after Raphael & Klugmann/TRIOsm II 90; HV*)

EXAMPLE 7/31 Sonata Op. 106/iv/11–15 (after Wallner/KLAVIERSONA-TENm II 257; HV*)

ogous repetition, for it indicates only a one-note suffix (not mentioned by Czerny). In the three trills that anticipate the finale fugue subject of the "Hammerklavier" Sonata" Op. 106 no suffixes are indicated, but a one-note suffix (without repetition) seems necessary on the third trill if the performer is to climax successfully and *forte* on its main-note resolution (Ex. 7/31).

Special Trills

Two kinds of trills in Beethoven's piano music are different enough to justify individual discussions—first, short trills, including cadential trills and *Schneller;* and second, so-called Beethoven trills. His short trills are defined here as trills of three to six notes. The three-note kind starts on its main note and omits a suffix; it is always identified by a short, wavy, horizontal line, and it is called a *Schneller* here. The four-note kind starts on its upper note and includes a suffix in the four notes; it is the same in shape if not necessarily in rhythmic details as Beethoven's four-note turn. By way of an example, it was probably intended during the final cadential measures of the "Adagio" in the "Tempest" Sonata Op. 31/2, to judge by the slowly paced, decorative environment (Ex. 7/32).

The five-note short trill, starting on the main note and including a suffix, has already been illustrated in the second and third trills of Ex. 7/27 above; it evidently equates with the ornament indicated by a turn sign in that variation's first measure (Ex. 7/33). And lastly, the six-note kind, with two oscillations (starting on the dissonant upper note) and a suffix,

EXAMPLE 7/32 Sonata Op. 31/2/ii/101–102 (after BEETHOVEN WERKEm VII/3/II 87; HV*)

EXAMPLE 7/33 Six Variations Op. 34/i/1 (after BEETHOVEN WERKEm VII/5 134; HV*)

EXAMPLE 7/34   Sonata Op. 31/3/iv/62–64 (after BEETHOVEN WERKEM
VII/3/II 115; HV*)

often seems appropriate in traditional cadence formulas, as in Ex. 7/34
and when more than four notes are desired (tempo permitting), as may
have been intended in the first movement of that same Sonata (Ex. 7/
35).

Because the three-note *Schneller* is the most restricted of Beethoven's
trill types, it poses the fewest interpretive problems for the performer. But
those problems, as well as its genesis and its prominence in his piano
writing, call for a number of observations and illustrations. The Beethoven *Schneller* derived from both the *Pralltriller* and the *Schneller,* as
taken up separately by Emanuel Bach (Ex. 7/36) and interrelatedly by
Marpurg (and succeeding writers).[39] During the next half century the
two terms retained approximately the meanings Bach had given them,
all the while undergoing a certain amount of confusion. For instance,
Bach, claiming priority in 1753 for naming and describing the *Schneller,*
defined it in 1787 as "the opposite of the mordent," but Marpurg, object-
ing soon after, apparently to any such alien association, preferred the
distinction of the original term, *Schneller.*[40] As late as Beethoven's time it
must have been such continuing confusions and objections that delayed
the use of "inverted mordent" as a synonym and eventual successor to
the term *Schneller.* They even seem to have led to quite contrary desig-

39. Bach/VERSUCH I 81–84 and 111–12; Marpurg/ANLEITUNG 57–58.

40. Bach/VERSUCH I 111 and Bach/ESSAY 142–43 (cf. fn 1 on p. 142); Marpurg/ANLEI-
TUNG 57.

EXAMPLE 7/35   Sonata Op. 31/3/i/22–23 (after BEETHOVEN WERKEM
VII/3/II 98; HV*)

EXAMPLE 7/36 A *Pralltriller* and a *Schneller* as illustrated by Emanuel Bach in Bach/VERSUCH Tables IV/45 and VI/94

nations like "mordent" itself in an influential treatise of 1802 by Louis Adam and like the sign ⚹ rather than ⚹ in Hummel's treatise of 1828.[41]

Beethoven himself seems to have been the first composer of renown to employ the *Schneller* in one, unequivocal sense and with almost total consistency. His familiar use of it in recurring passages during the first movement's second theme in his "Sonate pathétique" Op. 13 is typical (Ex. 7/37). And typical is his reservation of a single sign to designate the *Schneller*'s use in his music. This sign is the same wavy line without a slant through it (⚹) that had been equated generally with *tr* for trill throughout 18th-century practice, in spite of occasional distinctions in treatises, including fewer or more waves in the wavy line.[42]

Beethoven approaches the *Schneller* freely—legato or staccato, by leap or stepwise, from the same note or a rest; yet he almost always exits from it in the same manner, by a descending step and connecting slur, as in the middle movement of the "Kreutzer" Sonata (Ex. 7/38). That connecting slur relates to another consistency about Beethoven's *Schneller*, one that concerns its dynamic direction. His *Schneller* and the slurred note to which it leads usually comprise a masculine tone foot which moves from strong to weak.[43] By contrast, his other trills occur both on weak and strong components of tone feet.

41. Adam/MÉTHODE 54; Hummel/ANWEISUNG 398.

42. Clementi/INTRODUCTION 11 distinguishes between 3 and 2 waves, possibly echoing Adam/PRINCIPE 142, although neither author applied this distinction in any of his piano music found here.

43. For an exception see Op. 2/3/i/58–59.

EXAMPLE 7/37 Sonata Op. 13/i/57–59 (after BEETHOVEN WERKEM VII/2/I 144; HV*)

EXAMPLE 7/38 Sonata for Piano and Violin Op. 47/ii/I/25–26 (after
BEETHOVEN WERKEM V/2 105; HV*)

The idea of a snap, from which the *Schneller* had acquired its name
in Emanuel Bach's *Versuch*, proves to be another constant in Beethoven's
use of this ornament. The *Schneller* must be played rapidly, since the
tempo itself will either be fast (as in Ex. 7/37 above) or slower with shorter
note values (Ex. 7/38 above). This rapidity causes, if not compels, one to
conclude that Beethoven's *Schneller* divides evenly into a triplet covering
its full value, and not unevenly as illustrated in most treatises of his time
including Clementi's *Introduction* (Ex. 7/39). Czerny's astonishing pre-
scription for Beethoven's *Schneller*, with not the first but the final note
getting the accent, is ruled out by the many instances where the rapidity
of the approach prevents the *Schneller* from starting before the beat,[44] as
in the first movement of the Sonata Op. 7 (Ex. 7/40). Moreover, when
Kullak objected to Czerny's realization in the finale of Beethoven's "Tem-

44. Czerny/SCHOOL I 163. But several treatises do mention that the *Schneller* begins "on
the beat"—that is, when its written note begins—including Hummel/ANWEISUNG 398.

EXAMPLE 7/39 The *Schneller* as illustrated in Clementi/INTRODUCTION 11

EXAMPLE 7/40 Sonata Op. 7/i/108–110 (after BEETHOVEN WERKEM
VII/2/I 69–70 ; HV*)

EXAMPLE 7/41 Czerny's recommended realization of the *Schneller* in the Sonata Op. 3l/2/iii/43–45 (as reproduced in Badura-Skoda/CZERNY 48; EA*)

pest" Sonata Op. 31/2 (Ex. 7/41),[45] his alternative proposals only took him from the frying pan into the fire. It is worth noting that on all recordings of that finale that could be heard for this study, performers have chosen to play even triplets starting on the first f.

In summary, the *Schneller* differs from many short trills not only in its single designation by the wavy line, but in its invariable progression from strong to weak, in its lack of a suffix, in its start on and at (not before) its main note, and in the consonance or dissonance of that main note, without restriction (recall the main notes in Exx. 7/37, 7/38, and 7/40 above).[46]

Regarding the so-called Beethoven trill, it may be defined as the combination of a trill and a separate melodic line in one hand. It may be realized either simultaneously, as written out in the finale of the "Lebewohl" Sonata Op. 81a (Ex. 7/42), or by substitution, letting each melody note substitute for one note of the trill, as written out in the middle movement of the "Sonata Appassionata" Op. 57 (Ex. 7/43). Beethoven offered his own explanation of the simultaneous realization, at the end of the

45. Kullak/BEETHOVEN 77–78.

46. Cf., further, in Newman/TRILLS 359–61.

EXAMPLE 7/42 Sonata Op. 81a/iii/53–54 (after Wallner/KLAVIERSO-NATENm II 190; HV*)

EXAMPLE 7/43 From Sonata Op. 57/ii/73–75 (after BEETHOVEN WERKEM VII/3/II 196; HV*)

(Andante con moto dolce)

autograph of his "Waldstein" Sonata Op. 53, referring to measures such as 485–86 in the finale. His explanation provides two trill speeds, triplet quarter notes and "twice as fast, if ability permits" (Ex. 7/44; cf., also, Ex. 2/5, above).

Among Beethoven's earliest uses of the "Beethoven trill" are those in his Variations of 1792–93 on Mozart's "Se vuol ballare," for piano and violin (WoO 40, Coda). That Beethoven regarded these as innovational uses is revealed in his amusingly human note of June, 1794, to the dedicatee, Eleanore von Breuning:

> The variations will be rather difficult to play, and particularly the trills in the coda. But this must not intimidate and discourage you. For the composition is so arranged that you need only play the trill and can leave out the other notes, since these appear in the violin part as well. I should never have written down this kind of piece, had I not already noticed fairly often how some people in

EXAMPLE 7/44 Beethoven's own explanation of the Beethoven trill at the end of the autograph of the Sonata Op. 53 (as translated and transcribed in Kullak/BEETHOVEN 93)

or taken twice as fast, if ability permits:

Vienna after hearing me extemporize of an evening would note down on the following day several peculiarities of my style and palm them off with pride as their own. Well, as I foresaw that their pieces would soon be published, I resolved to forestall those people. But there was yet another reason, namely, my desire to embarrass those Viennese pianists, some of whom are my sworn enemies. I wanted to revenge myself on them in this way, because I knew beforehand that my variations would here and there be put before the said gentlemen and that they would cut a sorry figure with them.[47]

Beethoven's fingering for the Beethoven trills in WoO 40 implies a simultaneous realization, if only because a substitute realization would not make for that much difficulty. There had been occasional precedents for each sort of realization. Thus, measure 111 in the "Fuga" of J. S. Bach's *Chromatic Fantasy and Fugue* reveals the simultaneous sort and the twenty-eighth of his "Goldberg" Variations the substitution sort (written out). The simultaneous sort is illustrated in Louis Adam's first treatise (1798) as each hand might play it.[48] In both Hummel's and Czerny's treatises the substitution sort is actually introduced as the way to facilitate the simultaneous sort.[49] Beethoven did not mention realization by substitution in any explanation. Nor did he write out any other explanation of the simultaneous type like that in Ex. 7/44 above. On the other hand, he did compose several Beethoven trills—admittedly some of his most difficult trills—in which the busyness of the melodic line makes a realization by substitution impractical, as in Ex. 3/12 (p. 75; from Op. 106/iv/112–14).

One can only wonder, then, how out of touch with the exigencies of piano technique Beethoven, who reportedly could scarcely reach a 10th,[50] had become in his later works. Even if one assumes that he had a wide and flexible web between his fingers (as certainly is suggested by his early experiment in trilling 6ths, Ex. 7/3 above), could he have stretched the major 7th between his second and fifth fingers when the *a* of the trill in Ex. 7/44 above is later flatted (m. 493)? The evidence is clear enough that Beethoven had the simultaneous realization in mind, but it is equally clear that from his own day to this, the large majority of performers need and prefer a realization by substitution.

Trills Whose Performance Remains Uncertain

It is hoped that the foregoing discussion of Beethoven's trills will illuminate main clues to their performance and relieve undue apprehensions

47. Anderson/BEETHOVEN I 14–15; cf. WEGELER & RIES 57–59 (including fn. 6).

48. Adam/PRINCIPE 149.

49. Hummel/ANWEISUNG 397; Czerny/SCHOOL I 175–77.

50. Badura-Skoda/CZERNY 22.

EXAMPLE 7/45 Sonata for Piano and Violin Op. 96/i/1–2 (after
BEETHOVEN WERKEM V/2 133; HV*)

about their components, especially about the question of dissonant or
upper starting notes. But it must be acknowledged after this discussion
that a fair number of Beethoven's trills contain no obvious clues. A few
years ago I did a little study of such a trill partly to discover what tentative
performance clues might be revealed.[51] The trill in question is the one
that opens Beethoven's lovely, last Sonata for Piano and Violin Op. 96
in G (Ex. 7/45). Its performance has often been debated because in its
first appearance it occurs without an approach, or harmonization, or texture, or technical consideration, or hint in the notation, and without
an exit one note up—any or all of which could limit and help to pin
down its realization. In particular, what were Beethoven's presumed
intentions regarding this trill's starting note and its incorporation of a
suffix?

A tentative answer—the only possible kind in this instance—must
depend first on internal analysis, then on analogies with similar but better defined trills in other Beethoven works, on the very spirit and import
of the music, and finally on the respected though changing tastes of
experienced performers since his time. The study's findings may be summarized briefly to the effect that thematic, stylistic, and technical considerations in the many later recurrences of the trill in Op. 96 all point
persuasively, though not conclusively, to a start on its main note and the
omission of a suffix. Fingerings and other editorial inserts show that performers have always preferred the main-note start, but that up to about
World War I they preferred to include rather than omit the suffix. All
available recordings made since then reveal main-note starts and no suffixes.

51. Newman/OPUS 96.

Beethoven's Turns and Freer Short Embellishments

Beethoven's turns and short embellishments often have much in common in their shape, function, and uncertain rhythmic details. For our purposes they differ chiefly in that about half of the turns are indicated by the turn sign, the others being written out in grace notes or in regular notes incorporated into the melodic line, whereas all of the freer embellishments are written out in grace or regular notes. Also, as will be explained, Beethoven's turns indicated by signs differ from his written-out turns with regard to starting on or before the beat.

The sign for a turn (*Doppelschlag*), like that for a *Schneller*, occurs most often in Beethoven's early and middle works. (In Ex. 10/25, p. 294, from an early sketch, Beethoven illustrates what appears to be a four-note turn from above.) Earlier in this chapter we related his turns to short, four- or five-note trills in shape though not necessarily in their rhythmic details (see Exx. 7/6, 7/27, and 7/33). Deciding on those rhythmic details raises the chief problems in the turns (and in the freer embellishments written as grace notes), though the starting notes and the pitch inflections of the upper and lower neighboring notes can be problems as well. However, the starting notes do not need more than incidental consideration now, because they pose only the same questions that came up in the trills. And the pitch inflections present only infrequent questions, since Beethoven generally was careful to insert any needed accidentals. When he failed to do so, one still can find help in the treatises of his time, according to which a turn's neighboring notes will adhere to the pitch inflections of the diatonic (or unaltered) notes in the currently operative key.[52]

In Ex. 7/46 I have proposed realizations of the two turns. The starting note of the first turn is assumed to be its main note, because that note

52. E.g., cf. Türk/KLAVIERSCHULE 263–64 and 283.

EXAMPLE 7/46 "Thema" of the Six Variations Op. 34/11–15 (after BEETHOVEN WERKEM VII/5 133; HV*). The proposed rhythmic realizations are added here.

figures in a conspicuous, recurring thematic element. The starting note of the second turn was probably intended to be the upper note, chiefly because starting on the main note would inject one too many consecutive *g*'s. Both lower neighboring notes are inflected by the accidentals Beethoven wrote in, becoming chromatic rather than diatonic.

About the rhythmic details in Ex. 7/46, there is a rule-of-thumb that usually applies effectively and musically, although it is more often implied than spelled out in the treatises.[53] It stipulates that a turn exits directly to the next written note unless its sign appears over or right after a note with a dot or tie. In the latter case, the turn exits to its main note for all or part of the dot's or tied note's value. Thus, the first turn in Ex. 7/46 would exit directly to the *d″* that follows and the second one to a thirty-second note on *g′*.

But as with Beethoven's other ornaments, further considerations still may affect the performer's decisions. The turn after the dotted *g♯′* near the start of the "Tempest" Sonata Op. 31/2 presumably is to be understood not as belonging to the first, dotted beat, but as appearing over the start of the (undotted) second beat and therefore as exiting directly to the *b′♮* (as proposed in Ex. 7/47). And the turn on the note in the second theme of the Sonata Op. 10/1/i probably was meant—to judge by the resulting rhythm—not to start until the second half of that first beat (as proposed in Ex. 7/48). A similar, but differently notated, error occurs in the Sonata Op. 2/3/i/45–46 (Ex. 7/49) and 179–80, where the turns were placed—probably because of the psychological appeal of the curving line—over main notes that are surely one note too low to be used for the intended turns. Those last turns could have been written as they are at the start of the second theme (mm. 27 [Ex. 7/50] and 161),[54] except that

53. E.g., cf. Clementi/INTRODUCTION 10 and Hummel/ANWEISUNG 398–99.

54. Milchmeyer/WAHRE 41 illustrated m. 27 and its realization (without giving the source) in 1797, one year after Beethoven's Op. 2 first appeared.

EXAMPLE 7/47 Sonata Op. 31/2/i/5–6 (after BEETHOVEN WERKEm VII/3/II 77; HV*). The rhythmic realization is added here.

EXAMPLE 7/48 Sonata Op. 10/1/i/60–63 (after BEETHOVEN WERKEm VII/2/I 93; HV*). The rhythmic realization is added here.

EXAMPLE 7/49 Sonata Op. 2/3/i/45–46 (after BEETHOVEN WERKEm VII/2/I 42; HV*)

EXAMPLE 7/50 Sonata Op. 2/3/i/27 (after BEETHOVEN WERKEm VII/2/I 42; HV*)

they would exit to their main note rather than to the next higher note.

A hybrid ornament related to the turn, the "trilled turn" (*prallende Doppelschlag*) was another self-proclaimed creation of Emanuel Bach.[55] It appears several times in the first movement of the Sonata Op. 54 (Ex. 7/51), but otherwise only seldom in Beethoven's piano music. Another instance occurs in the Sonata Op. 78/i/17. In view of the trilled turn's origin, there is no reason to doubt that its realization as illustrated by Emanuel Bach would still apply in Beethoven's music.

Both Hummel and Czerny break with Milchmeyer, Clementi, Starke, and previous treatise writers when they illustrate the turn with its sign

55. Bach/VERSUCH I 92–93. It is not mentioned in the treatises of Milchmeyer, Hummel, or Czerny.

EXAMPLE 7/51 Sonata Op. 54/i/19–20 (after BEETHOVEN WERKEM
VII/3/II 168; HV*)

above a note as starting before that note.[56] All internal evidence—rhythmic, melodic, harmonic, and technical—suggests that Beethoven still
intended a turn to start where its main note appears as long as he indicated it with a sign. When he wanted a turn to start before its main note,
he evidently preferred to write it out in grace notes as one of his freer
short embellishments. Ex. 7/52, from the "Adagio cantabile" of the *Sonate pathétique*, illustrates this difference with a turn indicated by its sign
and then a turn written out.

In Ex. 7/53 are illustrated two such notated turns from the middle

56. Hummel/ANWEISUNG 398–99; Czerny/SCHOOL I 164–65.

EXAMPLE 7/52 Sonata Op. 13/ii/22 (after BEETHOVEN WERKEM
VII/2/I 150; HV*)

EXAMPLE 7/53 Sonata Op. 81a/ii/4 and 9 (after Wallner/KLAVIER-
SONATENM II 186; HV*)

EXAMPLE 7/54 Sonata Op. 7/iv/55 (after BEETHOVEN WERKEM VII/2/I 86; HV*)

movement of the "Lebewohl" Sonata, the first starting with its upper note and the second with its main note. Beethoven never inverts his turn signs to indicate starts from below (as in the treatises), but he frequently writes out his turns to start in that way, as in Ex. 7/54 from the finale of the Sonata Op. 7. A more familiar instance of the same kind, but at a more challenging speed, occurs in the subordinate theme of the finale in the "Moonlight" Sonata Op. 27/2 (m. 22 etc.). In the autograph of the Sonata Op. 109/iv/7 (see Ex. 5/3, p. 125), the rhythmic subdivision of the turn is notated carefully, although performers frequently fail to take the rhythm literally, thereby finding it difficult to make that free embellishment fit convincingly into the flow.

Another free embellishment that begins before the beat suggests what might otherwise have been called a written-out *Schneller*. It is a less common two-note ornament, known best in the theme of the finale in the "Archduke" Trio Op. 97 (Ex. 7/55). Beethoven's uses of the arpeggio, or roll, also qualify as written-out ornaments that precede the beat, according to the treatises of the time as well as the melodic and technical demands of the music. In the coda of the "Moonlight" Sonata's finale the arpeggios are written as regular note values (mm. 163–66) and at the opening and

EXAMPLE 7/55 Trio for Piano, Violin, and Cello Op.97/iv/1–2 (after Raphael & Klugmann/TRIOsm II 122; HV*)

EXAMPLE 7/56 Variations on J. Haibel's "Menuett à la Vigano" WoO
68/VI/12 (after BEETHOVEN WERKEM VII/V 48; HV*)

the return in the first movement of the Sonata Op. 110 they are written as grace notes (mm. 9 and 58). Generally these freer short embellishments scarcely reduce to codifiable performance practices, as in
several of the Variations on J. Haibel's "Menuett à la Vigano" WoO 68
(Ex. 7/56).

Short and Long Appoggiaturas

By short appoggiaturas I mean the kind that sound just before—that
is, all but simultaneously with—the beat. Long appoggiaturas refer to the
kind that occur on the beat and borrow a certain part of its value. The
long kind occurs only rarely in Beethoven's piano music, not nearly so
often as in Mozart's. Beethoven's most familiar use of it is in the second
theme of the opening movement in his Sonata Op. 10/3 (Ex. 7/57). For
that use we have Czerny's specific remark that the grace note is "a long
appoggiatura and hence must be played as an eighth note," which he
then illustrates as the first of four even eighth notes.[57] Without that sin-

57. Badura-Skoda/CZERNY 36; but I have been unable to find a source for the statement in
Badura-Skoda/PERFORMANCE 65 that "Czerny reports that Beethoven always played these
long appoggiaturas as equal eighth notes."

EXAMPLE 7/57 Sonata Op. 10/3/i/54 (after BEETHOVEN WERKEM
VII/2/I 121; HV*)

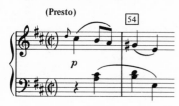

EXAMPLE 7/58 Second Concerto Op. 19/ii/1–7 (after BEETHOVEN
WERKEm III/2 142; HV*)

gle mention by Czerny of the long appoggiatura in Beethoven we might
have more difficulty distinguishing long from short.[58] Beethoven certainly gives no help in his notation, for he uses the eighth or sixteenth
note quite indiscriminately, with or without a stroke across the stem, leaving
editors even more nonplussed than with his dots and strokes for staccato
(as discussed in Chapter 5). However, nearly all his short appoggiaturas
may be confirmed as such by their contexts—that is, by their tempo,
thematic relationships, technical requirements, and harmonic considerations, as with the other ornaments. In the Rondo refrain of the Second
Concerto Op. 19, short appoggiaturas relate the antecedent phrase better
than sixteenth-note pairs would, to the falling seconds in the consequent
phrase (Ex. 7/58). In the twenty-fifth of the *Thirty-Two Variations in C
Minor* WoO 80, short appoggiaturas are made obligatory by the speed
(Ex. 7/59).

Some doubt does exist as to whether certain appoggiaturas should be
treated as short or long, although the conclusions here have generally
pointed toward the short variety. In the development section of the Son-

58. Czerny's only reference to Beethoven's short appoggiaturas that was found here, in
Badura-Skoda/CZERNY 98–99, suggests that the initial two sixteenth notes in the rondo
refrain of the First Concerto would sound better as a short appoggiatura and an eighth note,
which, indeed, is how both the orchestra and the piano statements of the refrain are notated
in mm. 277–87.

EXAMPLE 7/59 Thirty-Two Variations WoO 80/XXV/1–2 (after
BEETHOVEN WERKEM VII/5 190; HV*)

EXAMPLE 7/60 Sonata Op. 31/3/i/101–102 (after BEETHOVEN WERKEM VII/3/II 101; HV*)

ata Op. 31/3/i a syncopated rhythm of a sixteenth, eighth, and sixteenth note may have been intended, in keeping with the rhythm that follows (Ex. 7/60). And in the opening theme of the "Waldstein" Sonata Op. 53, a syncopation, or Scotch snap, may have been intended, with a sixteenth note and a dotted-eighth note tied to the next beat. But as these two themes are developed, the emphasis still seems better placed on the notes to which these appoggiaturas lead.

EXAMPLE 7/61 Sonata Op. 31/1/ii/5–6 (after BEETHOVEN WERKEM VII/3/II 60; HV*)

EXAMPLE 7/62 Sonata Op. 109/iii/17–19 (after the autograph at the Library of Congress)

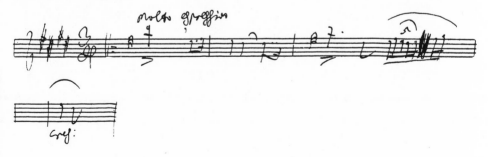

The same conclusion applies to a number of short appoggiaturas that resolve by leap, as in the middle movement of the Sonata Op. 31/1 (Ex. 7/61). It is pertinent to observe in his autograph of Op. 109, during the finale, that Beethoven clearly notated his leaping appoggiaturas before the beat (Ex. 7/62). In both Exx. 7/61 and 7/62 the importance of the top line clearly outweighs that of any line described by the appoggiaturas.

CHAPTER 8

FURTHER EXPRESSIVE
FACTORS

Legato and Tone Production

A T THIS POINT we need to explore several additional expressive factors. But these differ in being a kind whose only clue for the performer is likely to be no more than a feeling for Beethoven's unwritten intentions. Among them are legato and tone production, pedalling, dynamics, and agogics (or rhythmic inflections). As with his pianos, tempos, editorial refinements, and ornamentation, those expressive factors all shared in the important style transition that went on during his career.

At about the turn of the century, legato became valid as an expressive keyboard means with several unequivocal declarations that it had replaced nonlegato as the "normal" touch. Thus, in 1801, Clementi's *Introduction* stated, "When the composer leaves the LEGATO, and STACCATO to the performer's taste; the best rule is, to adhere chiefly to the LEGATO; reserving the STACCATO [only] to give spirit occasionally to certain passages, and to set off the HIGHER BEAUTIES of the legato."[1] Comparable statements were made by Hüllmandel in 1796, Milchmeyer in 1797, and Adam (echoing Clementi?) in 1802;[2] also, in 1804 by the editor of an updated, fourth edition of Leopold Mozart's *Violinschule*, where one reads, "Everything cantabile needs slurred, bound and sustained notes; this is even more imperative in an Adagio than in an Allegro."[3]

1. Clementi/INTRODUCTION 9; cf., also, Sandra Rosenblum's comments on pp. x–xi. Jenkins/LEGATO is a full study (though with relatively little attention to Beethoven) of the transition from the "ordinary touch" that prevailed in the 18th century to the legato touch.

2. Cf. Rosenblum/PERFORMANCE Ch. 5, where similar statements are found in Italian treatises from as early as 1757 and 1775.

3. As in Badura-Skoda/PERFORMANCE 70–71.

    In subsequent treatises, as by W. S. Stevens in 1811 and August Crelle in 1823 (both pioneer works on musical expression in piano music), legato became an important focus of attention.[4] Thus, Stevens said at the outset of his treatise, " . . . all music in such passages that are capable of it, that has not a sign for other expression, should be played in the manner here directed for legato . . . from the commencement of a piece of music *the finger or fingers should never quit the keys but by necessity, for expression, by the operation of rests or at the end.*"[5] Crelle said, "The usual consequence of an indifferent touch is that loudness dominates, all keys are played staccato, and both *portamento* and legato, even the harmony itself, are sacrificed more or less."[6] Crelle takes as his illustration of an ideal vehicle for legato and melodic projection the main theme of the "Adagio cantabile" in the *Sonate pathétique* Op. 13.[7]

    Stevens also discussed *tenuto* (his word is *tenute*), which he defined as "holding any note the whole of its time."[8] "Tenuto"—defined further and somewhat paradoxically by Unverricht as "a legato on a single tone"[9]—was a term that Beethoven linked closely with legato. He used it especially for sustained, connected chords (and in opposition to nonlegato or staccato), as at the start of the slow movement in the Sonata Op. 2/2 (Ex. 8/1; cf., also, Op. 110/iii/5). "Cantabile" was a term that he linked much more frequently with legato, but with a somewhat different connotation. He applied it especially to songful, connected melodic lines,

4. Stevens/EXPRESSION; Crelle/AUSDRUCK.

5. Stevens/EXPRESSION 2 *et passim.*

6. Crelle/AUSDRUCK 78–79.

7. Crelle/AUSDRUCK 90–91 and Ex. 32.

8. Stevens/EXPRESSION 14.

9. Unverricht/EIGENSCHRIFTEN 62; cf. pp. 62–63.

EXAMPLE 8/1   Sonata Op. 2/2/ii/1–2 (after BEETHOVEN WERKEm VII/2/I 26; HV*)

EXAMPLE 8/2   Fourth Concerto Op. 58/ii/6–13 (after Altmann/CONCER-
TOSM IV 69)

as at the solo piano's first entry in the middle movement of the Fourth
Concerto Op. 58 (Ex. 8/2).[10]

The transition from nonlegato to legato as the "usual touch" took place
rather quickly, largely in conjunction with the supplanting of the harpsichord by the piano.[11] As late as 1789 Türk still recognized nonlegato as
the usual touch, though with reservations.[12] It is more surprising to learn
that, according to Czerny, Beethoven described Mozart, whom he had
heard "several times," as still playing in the "chopped, crisply disconnected style" associated with the harpsichord ("Flügel, in this instance"),
and that thus far Beethoven was the unique, consummate master of legato
on the fortepiano.[13] (Here, incidentally, was one of numerous confirma-
tions that Beethoven proved to be a leader in the performance practices
of his time.)

It will be recalled that legato was one of the traits most praised in
Beethoven's own playing. Reichardt, who heard him in 1808 as soloist in
his Fourth Concerto, wrote of the middle movement, "The Adagio [sic],
a masterpiece of lovely drawn-out melody, he truly sang on his instrument with deep, melancholy feeling that moved me to the core."[14] Czerny
called Beethoven's playing "particularly remarkable for the strict Legato
of the full chords, and which therefore formed a new kind of melody
. . . ."[15] Schindler wrote in the first, 1840 edition of his Beethoven biog-

10. Cf. pp. 91–92 in the closely related article Kleindienst/CANTABILE.

11. Recall Clementi's partial crediting in 1806 of his reformed, songful, legato style to the
newer English pianos (reported in *Caecelia* X [1829] 239).

12. Türk/KLAVIERSCHULE 356.

13. Badura-Skoda/CZERNY 11. Mozart, in turn, had implied in 1783 that Clementi's playing
had "an atrocious choppy effect" (Anderson/MOZART II 850).

14. Reichardt/BRIEFE I 207.

15. As quoted near the end of Chapter 3 above, among other contemporary descriptions.
Cf., also, the important, frequently relevant recollections that Czerny related to Nottebohm,
in Nottebohm/ZWEITE 356–58.

raphy (where he was more wildly careless than in his third, 1860 edition, but not yet so maliciously inventive),

Beethoven always inculcated the following rule:—"Place the hands over the key-board in such a position that the fingers need not be raised more than is necessary. This is the only method by which the player can learn to *generate tone*, and, as it were, to make the instrument sing." He abjured the *staccato* style, especially in the performance of phrases, and he derisively termed it "finger-dancing," or "manual air-sawing." There are many passages in Beethoven's works which, though not marked with slurs, require to be played *legato* . . . .[16]

Beethoven's well-known letter of 1796 to Streicher (quoted in Chapter 3, above) about the piano's potential for singing and for being something other (if not more) than a harp is an early plea for legato treatment.[17] His emphasis on legato in his teaching is another evidence of his dedication to this style.[18] So is his emphasis on it in the early exercises he left and in the annotations he inserted in them, such as "The hands must keep together as much as possible, [and] with the strictest legato" (Ex. 8/3).[19] And so is his recurring call for a correct "Bindung" throughout his supposed annotations in the Cramer Etudes (as reported in Chapter 6, above).

Mainly, it becomes apparent that this evidence of Beethoven's emphasis on legato playing and a singing effect link closely with tone projection, the drawing out of a melodic line, and the shaping of incises and phrases. One can observe the co-ordination of all four elements in a phrase like that from the slow movement of the Sonata Op. 2/2/ii/14–19 (see Ex.

16. Schindler/BEETHOVEN II 129 fn. For corroborating views cf. Gerhard von Breuning and Friedrich Wieck as quoted in Leitzmann/BEETHOVEN I 329 and 339, respectively.

17. Anderson/BEETHOVEN I 25–26.

18. Badura-Skoda/CZERNY 11.

19. Nottebohm/ZWEITE 357–63.

EXAMPLE 8/3 An early Beethoven exercise (as quoted in Nottebohm/ ZWEITEM 362, mm. 1–7)

5/45, p. 161), in which each of them depends on each of the others for a realization of the musical ideal set by Beethoven.

Beethoven's Use of the Pedals

Pedalling holds a central position among the additional expressive factors discussed in this chapter. Beethoven was described in Chapter 3 as using two main kinds of pedals on his pianos—that is, the damper-raising and the action-shifting (or *una corda*) pedals that continue to control our pedalling today. He was identified as the first front-rank composer to call for pedals to any appreciable extent. Haydn had made isolated requests for the "open [damper] pedal" late in his pianistic career (in his Sonata in C, H. XVI/50/i, as in mm. 72–73) and while he was intrigued by English instruments. And Mozart in his letter of October 17–18, 1777, had revealed his admiration for the knee-lever damper controls on the early Stein pianos that he sampled. Indeed, Mozart may well have used damper controls in his own masterly playing, even though he is not known to have ever specified their use in his scores. But with Beethoven it was different. He left little doubt as to the extent, the nature, or the practical application of his use of the pedals.

There are two reasons why we might have expected Beethoven to pioneer an increased use of the pedals. Both yield questions of the chicken-or-the-egg sort: One generation after Haydn and Mozart, did the evolving construction of the piano's pedals finally lead the way to Beethoven's uses or did Beethoven's more expressive music finally lead the way to their contruction? As for the construction (the first question), the control of the dampers by a true pedal—that is, not by a knee lever but by a foot pedal that had been introduced a quarter-century earlier[20]—did not come into general use until just after 1800. Nor did action-shifting devices enabling the hammer to strike only one string (*una corda*) or two strings (*due corde*) rather than three strings (*tre corde*) become more widely used until about 1800. (Yet, devices for both damper control and action-shifting had existed for nearly a century, from the time of Cristifori's pioneer pianos.[21])

As for Beethoven's more complexly expressive music, it was the increasingly sensitive tonal requirements of that music that brought about the more extensive cultivation of the pedals. Much as Beethoven was

20. Hirt/KLAVIERBAUS 124 credits Adam Beyer in England with the first use of the foot damper pedal, in 1777.

21. Cf. Harding/PIANO-FORTE 31, 28–29.

EXAMPLE 8/4 The opening of "Für Elise" (WoO 59) (at the start of
the sketch in Unger/HANDSCHRIFT Tafel VII)

finding it necessary to qualify his tempos more precisely, so he was finding it necessary to qualify the sounds and textures that he was creating,
with respect to both timbres and enrichments. How much the pedalling
entered into his composing can be surmised from the care he seems to
have given it in his manuscripts. For instance, in an abbreviated sketch
(dating from 1810) of the popular little piece "Für Elise," Beethoven did
not trouble to insert markings for dynamics or slurs, but did mark the
pedalling, which he "evidently regarded as essential to the sonority"[22]
(Ex. 8/4, with the signs "ped" and "O" between the staffs).

Just how much use did Beethoven make of the pedals? Considerably
more than those performers may suppose who have been disregarding
his original pedal indications in the Urtexts except to question the more
puzzling ones. Of course, they cannot be aware of his indications at all if
they have been using an edition that replaces them with alternatives preferred by some later editor.[23]

Beethoven's original pedal indications are scattered throughout much
of his piano music, not only the solo works but chamber and orchestral
music as well. In all, nearly 800 such indications have turned up in a
tabulation of authentic sources done here. Each of those indications calls
for an application of either the damper or the action-shifting pedal, followed most of the time, but not always, by its release. Not surprisingly,
98 percent call for the damper pedal, with only about 2 percent calling
for the *una corda* control (mostly in the later works).

Furthermore, nearly 60 percent of all the indications occur in the solo
piano music (three-fourths are in the sonatas), about 15 percent occur in
the chamber music, and the remaining fourth in the concertos (including
the "Triple Concerto," Op. 56). Beethoven probably used damper controls
from the start of his professional piano playing in Bonn in the mid 1780s,

EXAMPLE 8/5 Early indication of damper control (from a diplomatic transcription in KAFKA SKETCHBOOK II 132; cf. p. 287; BL*)

mit dem knie

or about as soon as they became available to him on the early Stein pianos that he played (discussed in Chapter 3). But aside from one still earlier indication, he did not begin to call for the damper controls in his scores until about 1795 (in the manuscripts of his first two piano concertos, Opp. 19 and 15), continuing thereafter right up to his last year of composing, 1826. The earlier indication, in a sketch dating from 1790–92, is simply that inscription "with the knee" mentioned in Chapter 3 as being in a series of repeated chords (Ex. 8/5). It does happen to be the earliest known indication for a damper control in a score (that of Haydn, mentioned above, does not date until 1794 or even later).

It will be recalled further from Chapter 3 that while Beethoven was still using knee levers for those damper controls—that is, up to about 1802 and the final completion of the Concerto No. 3 in C minor—he used the terms *senza* and *con sordino* (*sic*), meaning without and with the dampers.[24] Thereafter, he used the more modern signs for pedal and release. Also, we saw that by 1802 he already knew about and presumably was using the *una corda* control, although he did not start to indicate it in his scores until later. He indicated it first in his Piano Concerto No. 4, Op. 58, composed about 1805–06, but not again until some twenty further uses in his last five piano sonatas, composed from about 1816 to 1822. And by about 1803, he revealed that he knew about the split damper pedal in his annotation that appears at the start of his "Waldstein" Sonata Op. 53 in the autograph.

None of this information should suggest that once he started inserting them, Beethoven spread his pedal indications evenly throughout his

24. Cf. Badura-Skoda/CZERNY 51. But Czerny was wrong if he was implying that the change did not begin until Op. 53; it began with the "Kreutzer Sonata" Op. 47, one indication in a sketch for the Piano Variations Op. 35, and the start of the "Tempest Sonata" Op. 31/2, completed in 1802 (the year before Beethoven received his Érard piano), although Beethoven reverted to "senza sordino," etc., in his Piano Concerto Op. 37. For more details on the foot pedal's first uses by Beethoven and others, cf. Kramer/DATING.

works. On the contrary, he seems to have confined those indications largely to places where he wanted to make a particular point of their effect. He grouped them in certain movements, as in the finale of the "Waldstein" Sonata, and left them out entirely in others, as in the first movement of the Sonata in A♭ Op. 110, where he could even have assumed their need would be obvious to the performer!

In any case, we have two kinds of reports from Czerny that suggest Beethoven made considerably more use of the pedal in his playing, especially the damper pedal, than he indicated in his markings. The first report is indirect, telling of an unfavorable comparison of Beethoven's playing with Hummel's: "Hummel's partisans charged that Beethoven maltreated the fortepiano, lacked all purity and distinctness, brought only confusing noise through the use of the pedal, and that his compositions were affected, unnatural, melodyless, and, what is more, without proportion."[25] Presumably Hummel's "partisans" meant that Beethoven pedalled too much of the time and too long without changing the pedal. Czerny's second report is his own comment that Beethoven used the pedal much more than he indicated in the scores,[26] this time presumably meaning more often and in more (different) places.

The two statements juxtapose conservative and progressive attitudes toward the relatively innovative use of the pedal. Hummel, a pupil of Mozart, still showed a wary attitude toward it in his treatise.[27] Czerny, himself a pupil of Beethoven, proved more than ready to accept, even promote, it.[28] If Beethoven actually did let his "animal spirits" drive him to play loudly and frenetically in excited passages, as some of his observers reported, then he could very well have compounded the whole effect with the "confusion" of the pedal.[29] On the other hand, if he was as intrigued by the pedals' effects as his indications for them suggest, then he could well have cultivated much use of the pedal in his own playing.

As in almost all other aspects of Beethoven performance, the question arises as to how much his deafness may have affected his intentions. Did it distort his reactions to the piano's sound and therefore influence his judgment as to the effects of the pedals? Of course, subjective factors must qualify any answer. But considering some circumstantial evidence as well as the more patent success with which Beethoven showed he could hear new melodic, harmonic, and rhythmic combinations, I have

25. Czerny/ERINNERUNGEN 19.

26. Badura-Skoda/CZERNY 22.

27. Cf. Hummel/ANWEISUNG 452.

28. Czerny/SCHOOL III 57–58.

29. Frimmel/BEETHOVEN II 240–49, 254–57.

concluded that he did understand, hear, and want essentially the pedal effects that he indicated.

The question also arises as to how accurately Beethoven's pedal indications themselves are being understood (after which one should be able to ask with more confidence how accurately they are being interpreted in relation to his music). Is it possible, for example, that Beethoven used "senza sordino" to mean "without the dampening strip (or mute) [with which many pianos were equipped then]"[30] and not "without the dampers resting on the strings"? No, it may have been possible in earlier uses, but not in Beethoven's contexts. Besides which, Czerny's several mentions of *senza* and *con sordino* in Beethoven's music include no reference

30. As argued in Melville/PIANOS 50–53 at first, but cf. MT CXII (1971) 1171 and CXIII (1972) 361–62.

EXAMPLE 8/6 Sonata in A♭ Op. 26/iii/35, after (a) the autograph; (b) the original edition of Cappi in 1802; and (c) the modern BEETHOVEN WERKEM VII/2/I 223 (HV*)

to a dampening possibility. And in that connection, Beethoven's use of "sordino" in the singular to mean "dampers" in the plural needs only to be recognized as one of the countless linguistic laxities of the times. Of more concern can be the uncertainty as to exactly where Beethoven wanted the pedal to be raised or lowered when he spread out the terms *senza sordino* or *con sordino* too diffusely in his manuscripts, resulting, for instance, in three different versions of a passage in the "Marcia funèbre" of the Sonata in A♭ Op. 26 (Ex. 8/6).

Beethoven's Use of the Damper Pedal

Beethoven seems to have had seven uses of the damper pedal particularly in mind. These include sustaining the bass, improving the legato, creating a collective or composite sound, implementing dynamic contrasts, interconnecting sections or movements, blurring the sound through harmonic clashes, and even contributing to the thematic structure. Among

EXAMPLE 8/7   An annotated sketch from about 1793 (after a diplomatic transcription in Nottebohm/ZWEITEM 361)

EXAMPLE 8/8 Piano Concerto Op. 37/ii/11–12 (after the original Bureau
d'Industrie edition of 1804)

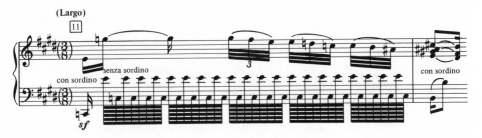

those uses, we shall come presently to the one that has proved most controversial: the blurring of the sound through harmonic clashes, whether
deliberate or unwitting.

The most obvious use was to sustain the bass, providing harmonic
support while the hands remain free to play elsewhere on the keyboard.
In Ex. 8/7, which is a fragment of a sketch from about 1793, we have
early evidence of Beethoven's concern with the lasting power of the bass.
Although Beethoven does not yet indicate the pedal here, he does include
the pertinent annotation, "The sustained notes in the bass produce a good
effect, since with such notes the bass lasts longer than the high [notes]."
A clear example of Beethoven's use of the pedal to sustain the bass might
be quoted from the Piano Concerto No. 3 in C Minor (Ex. 8/8). In this
example, the pedal sustains c throughout the broken, 128th-note 10ths
and until it resolves to B.

Two of Beethoven's close associates in Vienna, Friedrich Starke and
Carl Czerny, emphasized the sustaining of the bass in their discussions
of the damper pedal, though for different reasons. Said Starke, "Generally
one may use this pedal for *forte* only in [passages] that maintain the
same harmony and [only] if a bass or melody note is to be sustained
throughout several measures."[31] Said Czerny, "With pedal we are enabled
to make the bass-notes vibrate as long as if we had a third hand at our
disposal, while two hands are engaged in playing the melody, and the
distant accompaniment."[32] Starke seems to have been troubled by the
problem of blurring the sound, to be discussed shortly. Czerny was concerned more with ways to facilitate certain passages. Beethoven confirmed his own concern with prolonging the bass when he ordinarily scored
it so that the ten fingers could manage to hold it and still play the other
strands of the texture, as in Ex. 8/9, from the "Andante favori" (originally
the middle movement of the "Waldstein" Sonata Op. 53).

31. Starke/PIANOFORTE I 16.

32. Czerny/SCHOOL III 58–61.

EXAMPLE 8/9 "Andante favori" WoO 57/121–123 (after Brendel/
KLAVIERSTÜCKEM 55; EA*)

That Beethoven expected the treble to survive much less long than
the bass is suggested by the well-known, two-note slurs in the Sonata in
A♭, Op. 110/iii/5. Their separations while the dampers are kept raised
may actually have been audible in his day, but must be acknowledged as
largely if not entirely visual on today's pianos, with their longer-lasting
tones (Ex. 8/10). Another hint that Beethoven expected less survival of
the treble than the bass may be found in the first three measures of Ex.
8/11, from the slow third movement of the Sonata in A Op. 101. There is
at least an apparent contradiction created by a rest during each pedal
application. That rest is partly psychological, in a syntactic sense (rounding off each one-measure incise) and partly actual, in that the register an
octave higher than the tenor would die away more quickly on Beethoven's instruments, especially during the application of the *una corda* pedal
throughout this movement.

On the other hand, what are we to make of the pedalling in the first
four measures in the left hand of that same Ex. 8/11? Here pedalling and
(presumed) fingering are each contributing to implement legato. Beethoven seems to have intended the fifth finger to hold each lowest, down-
stem bass note until the pedal has to take over, so that the rising tenor
line can be encompassed in the left hand. It will be observed that the

EXAMPLE 8/10 Sonata in A♭ (Op. 110/iii/5, after Wallner/KLAVIER-
SONATENm II 300; HV*)

EXAMPLE 8/11 Sonata in A Op. 101/iii/14–20 (after the original Steiner edition of 1817)

down-stem bass notes in the third- and second-last measures before the end of Ex. 8/11 have no pedal indications at all. The heavy action and greater distance from the floor made the pedals clumsier to manipulate then, even at the "Adagio" tempo, and would have proved generally impractical with the faster changes that would have to have been made.[33]

An interesting question is whether Beethoven ever achieved legato by using "syncopated pedalling"—that is, by raising rather than lowering the damper pedal exactly as each tone or chord is played, so as to clear out previous sounds, then promptly lowering it so as to sustain that new tone or chord until the next one is played. Because many sensitive pianists arrive at syncopated pedalling intuitively (since it is easier to do than not to do, and easier to do than to describe), one can scarcely believe that such an enterprising, inquiring experimenter as Beethoven would not have stumbled on the procedure and called attention to it, whether in his own scores and documents or by way of the contemporary treatises. Yet, Czerny's detailed and precise description of the damper pedal's use would seem to rule out the possibility of syncopated pedalling.[34] And Czerny told Gustav Nottebohm specifically that "Beethoven understood remarkably well how to connect full chords to each other *without the use of the pedal* [italics mine]."[35] It is hard to realize that no writer is known to have mentioned this procedure before Louis Köhler in 1862[36] and that no master composer is known to have recognized it before Liszt greeted it late in his own career as "an ingenious idea . . . especially in slow *tempi*."[37]

33. Cf. Grundmann & Mies 23.

34. Czerny/SCHOOL III 58–61.

35. Nottebohm/ZWEITE 356.

36. Köhler/CLAVIERFINGERSATZ 104–106 (information kindly supplied by Ms. Yona Knorr).

37. LISZT LETTERS II 278 (information kindly supplied by Ms. Geraldine Keeling).

Perhaps it had been precluded at least in Beethoven's day by that same clumsiness of the early pedals.

Thanks to the sympathetic vibrations made by the partials of other strings, the damper pedal offered one further way of implementing legato, for it increased the duration of a tone. It could sometimes help a melodic tone last into and connect with the next. The writers of Beethoven's day appreciated this possibility—for example, Starke, who, however, stretched his point when he said that a tone that would scarcely survive one measure without the damper pedal in an adagio tempo could last "several measures" with it.[38] Generally, Beethoven did not write melodic tones that exceeded the likely duration of keyboard sounds. An exception occurs with the treble octave on b at the peak of the lovely line in the second movement of the Piano Sonata Op. 2/2 (see Ex. 5/45, p. 161). Given the more distinct registers of Beethoven's pianos, that b octave would have been more likely to survive into the $c'\sharp$ octave if it had been marked with one pedal through its three beats, than it would be on today's pianos. Even the staccato bass notes would have been heard better then than now if they had been marked with pedal. In other words, the same octave today, with our pianos' greater carrying power, is more likely to get lost in the blur of the passing tones, unless our hypothetical single pedal application is replaced by several, more fleeting, pedal applications.

There is no doubt about Beethoven's important use of the damper pedal to create a collective, composite sound. Ex. 8/5, above, suggests that Beethoven had this use in mind from the start. And Ex. 8/12, from the Bagatelle Op. 126 (completed in 1824), suggests that he still had it in mind in some of his last keyboard writing. Any experienced keyboardist will sense the desirability of the full sound in these examples that the release of the dampers will produce.

Collective sound through pedalling, especially the elaboration of a single harmony, is what Czerny intended by "harmonioso," a term that he

38. Starke/PIANOFORTE I 16.

EXAMPLE 8/12 Bagatelle in E♭ Op. 126/3/24 (after Brendel/KLAVIER-STÜCKEM 102; EA*)

(Andante Cantabile e grazioso)

used frequently. In his brief remarks about how to perform Beethoven's works, he applied this term almost from the start of the sonatas, as in the statement about the Sonata in C, Op. 2/3/i/218–223 (at a six-measure, arpeggiated passage on an A♭ harmony).[39] Here we have another hint that Beethoven was likely to have started using the pedals well before he started specifying them in his scores. Collective sound was the one value of the damper pedal recognized by Daniel Gottlieb Steibelt in an explanation of pedal signs that prefaces his accompanied Sonata in C Minor Op. 35 (1799).[40]

When Beethoven seems to be building collective sound through pedalling, either graduated or sharply contrasted dynamic change is often in progress. Thus, in the slow movement of the "Archduke" Trio, Op. 97, which suggests many opportunities for "harmonioso" pedalling, four dominant, cadential measures go through both a crescendo and a diminuendo (Ex. 8/13). An example during sharply contrasted dynamics occurs at the first movement's close in the "Hammerklavier" Sonata, Op. 106 (Ex. 8/14). As mentioned below, the absence of a release in this pedal indication and in the final one in the next example may or may not have been intentional.

Curiously, Beethoven seldom puts the damper pedal mark right at a *forte* or *fortissimo*, an exception being the cadence in Ex. 8/15, from the very end of the finale in Op. 106—curiously because Starke retained the

39. Badura-Skoda/CZERNY 30.

40. Cf. Newman/PEDALS 154, including a facsimile of Steibelt's explanation.

EXAMPLE 8/13 Trio Op. 97/iii/170–174 (after Raphael/TRIOsm II 121; HV*)

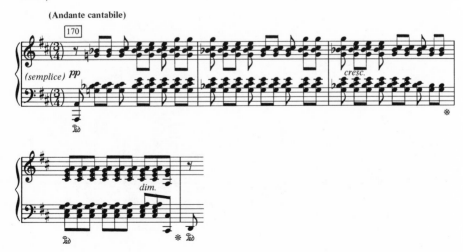

EXAMPLE 8/14 Sonata Op. 106/i/402–405 (after Wallner/KLAVIER-SONATENm II 239; HV*)

long established term "Fortezug" (loud pedal) as his term for the damper pedal and Czerny ackowledged the prevalence of that term.[41] But both men cautioned against any identification of the damper pedal itself with a particular dynamic level, which may be soft quite as readily as loud. (And both men already warned against the use of this pedal to hide a multitude of sins!) Probably the term loud pedal originated simply in the sense of main pedal, or "grande" pedal as the Frenchman Louis Adam called it.[42] If it had any other meaning of loud, it was rather in the sense of bigness produced by collective sound. Yet, it clearly associates with collective sound in both *fortissimo* passages, as in Ex. 8/16 from Sonata Op. 81a/iii, and in *pianissimo* passages, as in Ex. 8/17 from Sonata for Piano and Violin Op. 96/ii. The absence of a release mark in the pedal indication of Ex. 8/17 is characteristic of Beethoven's *attacca* connections between movements. The pedalling through rests in both

41. Starke/PIANOFORTE I 16; Czerny/SCHOOL III 57 and 63.

42. Adam/MÉTHODE 218–26.

EXAMPLE 8/15 Sonata Op. 106/iv/398–400 (after Wallner/KLAVIER-SONATENm II 272; HV*)

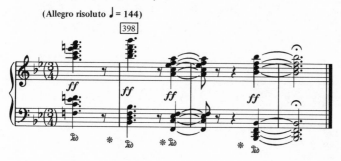

EXAMPLE 8/16 Sonata Op. 81a/iii/130–133 (after Wallner/KLAVIER-
SONATENm II 193; HV*)

(Viracissimamente)

Exx. 8/16 and 8/17 is characteristic of the echo and reverberation in
"collective sound," especially on the pianos of Beethoven's time.

   Before we get to Beethoven's most controversial use of the damper
pedal, at least brief mention should be made of two further aspects of its
treatment. One of these is the damper pedal's occasional correlations with
thematic and even structural aspects of his composition. The other is the
rather frequent lack of a release sign after a pedal application is indicated.
As for the correlations, we have already seen how the mature Beethoven
came to appropriate virtually all his musical resources to his structural
processes—for example, not only a trill pattern but a pedalling. Thus, he
exploited the damper pedal so as to include both the enunciatory bass
note and the tonic-dominant succession (or vice-versa) in the rondo refrain
of the "Waldstein" Sonata Op. 53 (Ex. 8/18). Used in this way at each
restatement, the pedal contributes to both theme and structure by qualifying the refrain's character and identity significantly. Czerny even said,
"without the pedal [this movement] would lose its effect altogether."[43]

43. Czerny/SCHOOL III 64.

EXAMPLE 8/17 Sonata for Piano and Violin Op. 96/ii/65–67 (after
BEETHOVEN WERKEM V/2 147; HV*)

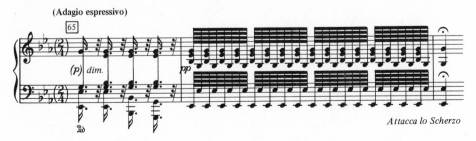

(Adagio espressivo)

Attacca lo Scherzo

EXAMPLE 8/18 Sonata Op. 53/iii/1–8 (after BEETHOVEN WERKEM
VII/3/II 151; HV*)

As for absent release signs after the pedal is indicated, occasionally
such an omission is an obvious error, as after the pedal mark immediately preceding Ex. 8/14, above. There a release is required by the middle
of the measure because a new pedal application is indicated at that point.
But more often the omission seems to mean that the sound is left to die
away, whether at the end of a movement or whole work, as with the
gentle, final chord of the Sonata in E, Op. 109, or at the end of a section
that passes into another section (see Ex. 8/24, below). Sometimes the
release is present but ends on a rest. That such an indication was likely
to be deliberate is suggested by a place in the finale of the "Waldstein"
Sonata where "Beethoven used a red crayon to replace a quarter rest
[in his autograph] with two eighth rests in order [, apparently,] to show

EXAMPLE 8/19 Sonata Op. 53/iii/113 (after the autograph BEETHOVEN
OP. 53m)

that the pedal was to be released with the second eighth rest."[44] (Ex. 8/19).

Harmonic Blur Caused by Beethoven's Pedal Marks

Now, how does one account for Beethoven's relatively infrequent yet "most controversial" uses of the damper pedal—that is, those that cause blur by providing no change during conflicting harmonies? And should one conclude that Beethoven used the pedal this way in spite of the resulting clashes, because of them, or with no awareness of them at all? For one of the most frequently cited instances of this problem, recall Ex. 8/18, above, from the "Rondo" refrain in the "Waldstein" Sonata. In that example, the pedal's continuation through two alternations of the tonic and dominant harmonies can hardly be dismissed as an oversight, since it recurs either that way or similarly throughout the movement. The conclusion reached here, for both musical and historical reasons, is that Beethoven deliberately cultivated the resulting, gently confused sounds in certain passages and that what he got is what he wanted, at least in terms of the instruments of his time.

My first reason for that conclusion is that Beethoven had significant precedents for his harmonic blur. Thus, Emanuel Bach had written in 1762 that the "undampened [undampered] register of the forte piano is the most pleasing, and the most appealing for fantasizing [improvising] if one can exercise the necessary precautions against the reverberations [that is, if one can avoid letting the harmonic clash be too pronounced]."[45] And Haydn, after trying the newest English instruments during his second London trip (1794–1795), had devoted his one venture with pedal indications to just such pedalling. His "open pedal," which he requested twice in his late Sonata in C (H. XVI/50/i/73–74 and 120–23), causes the changing harmonies to blur enchantingly during a single, protracted raising of the dampers.[46]

The second reason is that among his contemporaries Beethoven had ample company in the use of the pedal to create a gentle blur. Contrary to the assumptions of piano methodologists like Rudolf Breithaupt, who believed the great master was merely being careless and unaware,[47] Beethoven was sharing in a taste that was generally in the air, not only

44. Drake/BEETHOVEN 151.

45. Bach/VERSUCH II 327.

46. "Open pedal" is wrongly identified with a muting device in Landon/HAYDN III 444–45; cf. Wm. S. Newman in PQ No. 100 (Winter 1977–78) 46.

47. Cf. Friege/INTERPRTETATIONS 60.

in Haydn's music, but in Clementi's and many others', too.[48] In theory one can find an opposing school of thought about the harmonic blur. Pianist/writers who accepted pedalling more cautiously, like Milchmeyer, Adam, Starke, Crelle, and Hummel, expressed clear preferences for a change of the damper pedal with every change of harmony.[49] Yet even they included illustrations that reveal occasional preferences for pedal blur.[50]

There is a curious sort of documentation that supports Beethoven's taste for harmonic blur on the pianos (and other chordal instruments) of his time. If the reader will bear with what surely must be the epitome of indirect citations, there is a statement that goes back to Beethoven himself, but six times removed! According to the Beethoven specialist Paul Mies, the editor Carl Krebs learned from Franz Kullak that Kullak's father Theodor had been told by Czerny what Beethoven had in mind when he indicated the celebrated damper release throughout each of the first movement's recitative passages in the Sonata in D Minor, Op. 31/2/143–48 and 153–59. Beethoven reportedly wanted the effect to suggest someone speaking from a cavernous vault, where the sounds, reverberations, and tones would blur confusingly.[51]

Another comment comes from the contemporary Bohemian composer Anton Koželuch, who likened such effects of the damper pedal to the sound of the then popular (glass) harmonica.[52] Around 1832 the critic Ludwig Rellstab compared them in Beethoven to the sound of the Aeolian harp[53] (or of wind chimes, one might add). Of particular relevance may be Berlioz's reaction to a performance by Liszt in 1837 of the first movement of the "Moonlight" Sonata. He noted how "the left hand spreads out gently over wide-spaced chords, whose character is solemn and sad, and whose duration permits the piano vibrations gradually to die away into one another."[54] One implication in these comments—that the blur was regarded as most successful in its effect when the music was both slow and soft—is supported clearly by the treatise authors, especially Starke and Czerny.[55]

The mention of the first movement of the "Moonlight" Sonata brings

---

48. E.g., cf. Ex. 20, by Clementi, in Newman/PEDALS.

49. Milchmeyer/WAHRE 58–59, Adam/MÉTHODE 218, Starke/PIANOFORTE I 16, Crelle/AUSDRUCK 83–86, Hummel/ANWEISUNG 452.

50. E.g., Hummel/ANWEISUNG 453.

51. Mies/TEXTKRITISCHE 189.

52. Cf. Kramer/REVIEW 28.

53. Lenz/BEETHOVEN 199.

54. As cited in Newman/PIANOS 496.

55. Starke/PIANOFORTE I 16; Czerny/SCHOOL III 61.

EXAMPLE 8/20 Sonata Op. 27/2/i/12–15 (after BEETHOVEN WERKEM VII/3/II 17; HV*)

up the most puzzling of Beethoven's harmonic blurs. Although the first and last pages of the autograph of that sonata are missing, there is no reason to doubt the fact of two inscriptions at the very beginning as they appear in all the earliest editions: "This whole movement should be played delicately and without damper(s) [that is, with the damper pedal depressed]"; and again, more briefly, "constantly *pianissimo* and without damper(s)." It has to be granted that in most of Beethoven's harmonic clashes created by the damper pedal the bass does not change, only the harmony changes above it. But, of course, if the pedal is to be depressed for a whole movement, there will be many bass changes to consider. In the "Moonlight" first movement the bass changes at least once a measure in most measures (Ex. 8/20), greatly increasing the blur problem, even on the early pianos and even if the playing is both very slow and very soft.

To Czerny we owe the most authoritative clarification of the problem that we have—one that is plausible, simple if not obvious, and workable.[56] By about 1840 he had to recommend that performers forsake Beethoven's marking in that movement and throughout the slow movement's opening theme in the Concerto in C Minor, Op. 37. As he explained regarding the latter,

Beethoven (who played the concerto publicly in 1803) depressed the pedal throughout this whole theme, which worked very well on the weak-sounding pianos of that time, especially if the action-shifting [*una corda*] pedal was used

56. Badura-Skoda/CZERNY 43 and 101–102.

at the same time. But now, with a much stronger tone [on the newer pianos], we must advise that the damper pedal be reapplied with each significant change of harmony, yet so that no break in the tone [continuity] be noticed. For the whole theme must sound like a distant, holy, unearthly harmony.

The only hitch in that clarification is the extent of the blur in the "Moonlight" first movement that still results even on the earlier pianos and is still hard to keep within tolerable limits. But other explanations and alternatives that have been suggested have fared less well. One such explanation lies in the possibility that the initial inscription in Op. 27/2/i merely means "keep using the damper pedal throughout," somewhat as we understand the French instruction, "Gardez les pédales." However, both Beethoven's reworded repetition of the instruction and the consistent mood of the movement make that interpretation less likely. Another explanation assumes the use of the divided damper pedal that is visible on pictures of Beethoven's Broadwood piano and that Beethoven prohibited in his annotation at the start of the "Waldstein" Sonata Op. 53 (see p. 66–67). The idea is that the bass dampers might have been lowered and raised with each new harmonic bass in the "Moonlight" first movement, leaving the treble dampers unchanged. (Or in other passages the treble dampers might have been lowered, leaving the bass unchanged, as in the Sonata for Piano and Violin Op. 47/ii/192–93.) However, there is no actual support for this explanation. And the Erard piano, at which Beethoven is supposed by some to have composed both the "Waldstein" and the "Appassionata" sonatas, had no divided damper pedal.

Finally, the more distinct octave registers of the early pianos (as against today's uniform scale throughout the piano's range) have been given as yet another reason why the harmonic blur was more acceptable then.[57] To those who have lived with the early instruments the point seems well

57. Grundmann & Mies 40–41.

EXAMPLE 8/21 Sonata Op. 106/iii/165 (after the original edition of Artaria in 1819)

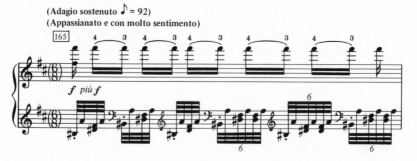

EXAMPLE 8/22   Sonata in E Op. 109/iii/184 (after Wallner/KLAVIER-
SONATENm II 290; HV*)

taken. In a bass passage like that in Ex. 8/21, from the slow movement
of the "Hammerklavier" Sonata, Beethoven would hardly have supposed
that the staccatos would have come through the pedalling if he had not
regarded the bass register as sufficiently distinct in its own right. Yet in
Ex. 8/22, from the last page of the Sonata in E, Op. 109, one must recognize that Beethoven was either too optimistic when he kept repeating
five tones within the range of a 7th for four measures during one pedal
application, or (quite possibly) that he really wanted the low quiet rumble
that results.

While the gist of the foregoing discussion is a belief that Beethoven
deliberately cultivated the harmonic blur where his pedalling produces
it, it should be obvious, as the treatise writers cautioned, that the one
consequential proviso had to be a careful handling of that blur in actual
practice. As the instruments grew in size and carrying power, increasing
adjustments of the pedalling had to be made, until today the solutions—
more pedal changes, holding some keys down (as in the recitatives of Op.
31/2/i), using the sostenuto pedal, and so on—can be quite sophisticated.[58]

Distantly related to the blur question is Beethoven's rather frequent
request for the damper pedal right through a rest.[59] This procedure, which
seems paradoxical in itself, is an understandable, further manifestation
of his psychological notation (as described in Chapter 2). A certain punctuation of the syntax is achieved in sight and feel without any disconti-
nuity in the sound.

The Uses of the Una Corda Pedal

We have already seen that by 1802 Beethoven knew and wanted an
action-shifting pedal, that he used this pedal by 1803 in performing the

58. Cf. Jarecki in ÖMZ PEDAL 197–200; Banowetz/PEDALING Chapter 8.

59. E.g., Opp. 31/2/i/148, 53/iii/98 et passim, 78/ii/74, 81a/iii/37–44, 106/iii/187, and
106/iv/1–3.

Third Concerto (according to Czerny), and that he first specified it in 1805–06, in the Fourth Concerto. Furthermore, Czerny recommended its use in a still earlier work, Beethoven's Sonata in E♭, Op. 7 (completed by 1797), noting the abrupt "modulation" in the finale (at m. 155) to E from E♭ major and to *pianissimo* from *fortissimo*.[60] At the start of the Fourth Concerto Beethoven wrote this note (in French): "Through all of this Andante one should apply the pedal that sounds but one string [*una corda*]; otherwise, at the 'Ped.' sign, one should raise the dampers." Even so, during the swell that starts the cadenza with the long trill (m. 56), the pianist is asked to release the action-shifting pedal (gradually) from *una* through "due e poi tre corde" (two and then three strings) and then to reverse that graduated shift before the end of the cadenza (m. 60).[61]

Although neither the graduated shift nor the reduction to "one string" is possible on today's pianos, Czerny was still advocating such pedalling around 1840.[62] Otherwise, his concern with the *una corda* pedal was limited to very specialized uses—as, indeed, was Beethoven's, to judge by his infrequent requests for it. Quoting Czerny once more, dynamic control is best achieved by the fingers, for "it is only in a few passages, very rich in melody, that it is desirable to use this pedal to produce another species of tone."[63] (Czerny showed at least equal interest in the soft pedal that depended on a shortening of the hammer stroke, without causing any alteration of the timbre.[64] However, Beethoven did not.)

Beethoven's most extensive and (to me) sensitive use of *una corda*

60. Badura-Skoda/CZERNY 33.

61. Cf. Jander/ORPHEUS 204–206 and fn. Those graduated shifts will be cited again in our next chapter, in the discussion of possible programmatic influences.

62. Czerny/SCHOOL III 64–65.

63. Czerny/SCHOOL III 65.

64. Harding/PIANO-FORTE 124.

EXAMPLE 8/23 Sonata Op. 106/iii/82–84 (after Wallner/KLAVIER-SONATENm II 248; HV*)

EXAMPLE 8/24 Sonata Op. 106/iii/85–88 (after Wallner/KLAVIER-SONATENm II 248; HV*)

and its graduated shifting back to *tutte le corde* occurs in that longest and most profound of his slow movements for piano, the "Adagio sostenuto" of the "Hammerklavier" Sonata Op. 106. One can imagine in Ex. 8/23, for instance, that he used the *una corda* pedal to achieve not only an echo but for the reason Czerny was to give—that is, for a contrast of color, as if created by a different instrumental timbre. In Ex. 8/24, starting three measures later, the *una corda* indicated in Ex. 8/23 graduates to "tre corde." The combined application of the damper and *una corda* pedals was often recommended in Beethoven's day, as by Starke.[65] (In that same Ex. 8/24 it should be noted that the absence of a release sign for the damper pedal where the bass changes was surely an oversight on Beethoven's part.)

Certain modern authors have wanted to equate *pianissimo* with the *una corda* pedal in Beethoven's day,[66] but no primary evidence has turned up here to support their contentions. There is circumstantial evidence both pro and con. On the one hand, Czerny advised using the *una corda* pedal wherever *pianissimo* appears in the finale of the "Waldstein" Sonata,[67] quite possibly following Beethoven's own example. But on the other hand, why then would *una corda* and *pianissimo* occur together a fair

65. Starke/PIANOFORTE I 16.

66. E.g., Hirt/KLAVIERBAUS 334; Harding/PIANO-FORTE 127.

67. Badura-Skoda/CZERNY 51.

number of times? Furthermore, why then would Beethoven go directly from *pp* to *ppp* at the end of the slow movement of the "Hammerklavier" Sonata as he also goes from *una corda* to *tutte le corde?*

Summary of Beethoven's Use of Dynamics and Agogics

The remaining two topics in this chapter, dynamics and agogics, are actually explored in comments and examples throughout the book. Hence, we need here only to recall and take note of those comments and examples in one place. Among numerous references to Beethoven's use of dynamics, emphasis has been put on them as they help in the shaping and peaking of the incise and phrase (Chapter 6). Fortunately, his editing of the dynamic levels and contrasts is fuller and more consistent in his scores than that of his chief Viennese predecessors and contemporaries. In his later years, his use of dynamic signs increased in both variety and relative quantity.[68] And Beethoven wanted them observed precisely.[69] Furthermore, he seems generally to have introduced even more dynamic inflections in his playing than can be found in his editing. Such is implied, for example, by the many interpretive suggestions not to be found in his scores but made by Czerny,[70] who apparently had derived them from his prolonged, close contact with Beethoven.[71]

In any case, the performer should bear in mind that Beethoven used his dynamic signs judiciously and in moderation. He did not exceed a *ff* or a *ppp* in his scores (avoiding the extremes of the late 19th-century composers—for instance, Tchaikovsky's gradual drop to *pppppp* early in the *Symphonie pathétique* and sudden return to a neck-jerking *ff*). But the *ppp* (used first at the end of Op. 57/i) did appear already to be needed, to judge by the pleas of Beethoven's contemporaries for more sensitive dynamics and, quite as today, for more use of *pianissimo* in performance.[72]

---

68. In Rothschild/MOZART 34–35 are comparative charts listing Beethoven's uses before and after 1812. Further support appears in the comparative charts in Ravnan/STATISTICAL, showing the extent of qualitative as well as quantitative use both within and between the sonatas of Haydn, Mozart, and Beethoven.

69. As he reminded Holz in that same letter of August 1825 in which he also begged for a distinction between dots and strokes (cited in Chapter 5, above, from Anderson/BEETHOVEN III 1241).

70. Badura-Skoda/CZERNY *passim*, beginning from p. 26.

71. Badura-Skoda/CZERNY 24 fn.

72. E.g., cf. Crelle/AUSDRUCK 41–45.

EXAMPLE 8/25 Sonata Op. 106/i/32–36 (after Wallner/KLAVIERSONA-TENm II 228; HV*)

To be sure, Beethoven provided many dynamic surprises in his own way—perhaps still more effectively, as in the abrupt shift from *ritardando* and [pianissimo] to *a tempo* and *forte* at the first return of the opening theme in the "Hammerklavier" Sonata Op. 106 (Ex. 8/25). He also shifted abruptly in the opposite direction, as in the breath-catching drop from *fortissimo* to *piano* in the finale of the "Farewell" Sonata Op. 81a (mm. 174–78, illustrated in Ex. 5/43, p. 161). Similar is his frequent, characteristic use of the so-called Beethoven piano—a crescendo that comes to a peak not on its loudest note but on an unexpectedly soft note (see Ex. 5/22, p. 149). However, only in his late music and rarely did he seem to employ psychological notation to implement his graduated dynamics. Thus, as illustrated in Op. 106/iii (Ex. 2/4, p. 36), he seems to use pairs of tied sixteenth-notes in place of single eighth-notes to point up the graduated steps in a crescendo.[73] (Related comments on Beethoven's structural use of dynamics and his so-called "Bebung" fingerings will be found in Chapters 9 and 10, below.)

Agogics concern the subtle lengthening or shortening of individual tones as a means of expression. With regard to Beethoven's use, the only sure evidence is that provided by his notated examples. Those examples relate directly to 18th-century rubato as defined by Mozart (and cited in Chapter 4, p. 112)—that is, rhythmic flexibility in the melody while the accompaniment continues in strict time. Two notable instances were quoted earlier, from the slow movements of the sonatas Op. 106 and 110 (Exx. 4/17 and 5/16, pp. 116 and 138). Such freedom is characteristic especially of Beethoven's late works.

As for Beethoven's use of agogics in the more modern sense of local rubato or an actual flexibility of pulses, the possibility was discussed in Chapter 4. The conclusion here is that he did favor such agogic inflec-

---

73. This procedure is the focus of Platen/NOTIERUNGSPROBLEM, but with regard to Beethoven's late string quartets and other works (in which tone intensity can be controlled) rather than his piano music.

tions, especially a lingering on the most expressive tones, in his later
works, but he also favored Classic restraint. That conclusion was based
on his own editorial markings, such as a *fermata* at the end of a phrase
(as in Op. 101/i/5; Ex. 4/14, p. 110), and on contemporary reports. But
for every pro there is a con in this question. One again recalls Beethoven's
annotation early in the finale of his Ninth Symphony, "In the manner of
a recitative, but in tempo"; or Ries's remark that Beethoven "himself played
his compositions very impetuously, yet for the most part stayed strictly in
time . . . ."[74]

This chapter on "further expressive factors" might well end with a
further mention of the Berlin writer August Crelle, not to add anything
specific about Beethoven interpretation, but to suggest the nature of some
of the most influential German thought on musical interpretation during
Beethoven's last creative period. Crelle, who was Beethoven's junior by
ten years, devoted the large part of his penetrating and illuminating treatise of 1823 "on musical expression in fortepiano playing" to two aspects
that have received special emphasis in this book.[75] One is the character
and dynamic direction of the incise and the other is a painstaking consideration, case by case, of many circumstances that favor agogic liberties.

Although Crelle used neither term, "incise" nor "agogic," and although
he did not discuss the incise in the specific ways that Koch and Momigny
did, he revealed a full, thoroughly musical, and flexible understanding of
these basic Classic means of musical expression. For his starting point
he returned once more to relationships between speech and music (para-
phrased here):

> Speech does not submit fully to measure and tone, but falls rather into spon-
> taneous interactions between both time and pitch. Consequently, in both respects
> speech proves less exact in its expression of emotions than music, whereas music
> is capable of arousing only general emotions but submits fully to the predictable
> control of measure and tone. The further music draws away from speech and
> recitative and the more it changes from fantasy and the verbalized toward har-
> mony or any other of its idiomatic means, the more apparent becomes this dis-
> tinction between speech and music.[76]

After exploring that principle and arriving at his equivalent of the
arsis-thesis relationship, both complementary and dynamic, Crelle reaches
his springboard for the expressive deviations and liberties that occupy
him throughout the remainder of his treatise. This springboard is a sim-

74. WEGELER & RIES 106.

75. Crelle/AUSDRUCK; also cited in the present book near the ends of Chapters 4 and 6, and
earlier in the present chapter (with his only reference to Beethoven, over his only illustration by a named composer [Ex. 32, Op. 13/ii/i–viii]).

76. Crelle/AUSDRUCK 15–16.

ple acknowledgment: Quite as in speech, there must be many exceptions to the foregoing principles, depending on the immediate "meaning" of the music.[77] And he arrives at a particular rule for agogics, restated repeatedly, that one must not hurry—in other words, must dwell on—the significant and the weighty.[78] His detailed exploration of these principles gives further support to our explanations of expressive accents in Chapter 5 and of the expressive peaks of incises and phrases, in Chapter 6, above.

77. Crelle/AUSDRUCK 27–34.

78. Crelle/AUSDRUCK 46 *et passim.*

CHAPTER *9*

SOME BROAD, STRUCTURAL CONSIDERATIONS

Taking Larger Views Within a Movement

*E*ARLY IN THIS BOOK the observation was offered that performance practice studies have concentrated generally on the local, or micro, rather than the over-all, or the macro, aspects of interpretation. At the same time the ultimate purpose of interpretation as expressed by many aestheticians was acknowledged to be an ideal projection of the music's total form. In this chapter the aim is to relate the total form of the music to certain interpretive aspects of Beethoven's performance that were previously considered only at their local levels. First come aspects that apply chiefly to a single movement or piece, including dynamics, textural enrichments, cadenzas and other free passages, repeats, structural rhythm, and programmatic influences. Then come those that apply to the interrelationship and cycle of two or more movements, including thematic relationships, proportions, interconnections, and options regarding the cycle itself.

However, the object of this chapter is not to widen the scope of this book by adding structural analysis and all of its attendant problems. Rather it is to hint at some broader aspects of interpretation insofar as Beethoven's intentions can be fathomed. Because of this broader view, it becomes all the more necessary to follow these discussions with the scores at hand. Music examples are impractical in this chapter except to illustrate a few specifics.

A Macro View of Dynamics?

The topic of dynamics makes a good starting point here, since its micro, or local, aspects were just reviewed in the previous chapter. From a macro,

EXAMPLE 9/1 Sonata for Piano and Violin Op. 30/2/i—a dynamic schema

Exposition   **Development**

Measures	1–12	13–28	29–46	46–74	75–99	100–112	113–124
Dynamics	p ----	< ff	p -----	< ff	p -----	f -------	p
Themes	Main		Second	Closing			
Keys	c		E♭		→		

Recapitulation   **Coda**

Measures	125–128	129–142	143–161	162–178	179–194	195–207	208–220	221–236	236–254
Dynamics	ff -------	p --------	< ff	p -------	< ff	< ff	< ff	< ff	< ff
Themes	Main			Second	Closing				
Keys	c			C			C	c	

or over-all viewpoint, a schema of the dynamic markings in a well-integrated musical work can reveal its directions and structural goals in new ways. It can bring to the fore the form's broadest changes in intensity, whether these occur abruptly or gradually—that is, in terraces of intensity or in one or more "climax cycles."[1] For instance, Ex. 9/1 offers a schema of the over-all dynamic changes in the opening movement, "Allegro con brio," of Beethoven's Sonata in C Minor Op. 30/2 for Piano and Violin. (The intensity terraces are indicated by dotted lines, crescendos and decrescendos by their corresponding hairpin signs, modulatory passages by horizontal arrows, and other structural components by their most standard terms.) Granted that a form viewed from that distance may easily reduce to a standardized type, a Procrustean bed to which the components must be fitted by stretching or truncation, this chart can still reveal a dynamic pattern of levels and climaxes that simply alternate, followed by a series of climax cycles in the coda. Alerting performers to such patterns can strengthen their perspective of a work's totality. It can help them to keep in focus not only the details of the trees but the outlines and directions of the forest.

To be sure, some of Beethoven's larger works do not seem to reveal underlying dynamic patterns. Surprisingly, the "Diabelli" Variations, for all its broadly conceived architecture, figures among such works. Other considerations evidently determined the order of those variations, along with the element of chance in some instances.[2] In any case, it would be hard to argue that a dynamic pattern was ever a generative factor in that work (as it was, for example, in Ravel's *Bolero* or in a programmatic work like *Les Djinns* by Franck) rather than a consequence. One should recall that dynamics were among the editorial markings that Beethoven tended to put in last, after he had written his sketches and even his autographs (Chapter 1). Indeed, the dynamic plan is regarded by Martin Staehelin as having played only a subordinate role in the master's creative process.[3] But enough writers have commented on the existence of those underlying patterns in particular works by Beethoven to suggest that performers might well be on the watch for them as they explore his interpretive intentions.[4]

1. Cf. Newman/CLIMAX.

2. The order and grouping of the variations gets new, important attention in Kinderman/ DIABELLI.

3. Staehelin/DYNAMIK, based primarily on a rediscovered copy of Mozart's Quartet K. 387 that Beethoven made in preparation for his work on Op. 18. In that copy Beethoven disregarded all but one of Mozart's original dynamic signs.

4. Cf. Luoma/DYNAMICS.

Textural Enrichments

Textural options and enrichments concern the macro as well as the micro aspects of musical form, since they can influence its whole character as well as its details. However, they must be regarded as only peripheral to this study, which concentrates on problems of the pianist as a soloist or ensemble participant. There is little reason to believe and good reason to doubt that Beethoven endorsed the sorts of textural fillers in his solo piano parts, not to mention other elaborations, that Czerny both played and edited in published editions on occasion. Thus, he would not have been likely to have approved the unacknowledged additions made in his early Rondo for Piano and Orchestra WoO 6 as Czerny edited it for publication in 1829, only two years after Beethoven's death (Ex. 9/2).[5] His oft-cited letter of 1816 to Czerny explicitly objected to such changes.[6]

5. Cf. Schindler & MacArdle/BEETHOVEN 447.

6. Anderson/BEETHOVEN II 560; cf. Schindler & MacArdle/BEETHOVEN 415–16.

EXAMPLE 9/2 Rondo in B♭ for Piano and Orchestra WoO 6, mm. 346–58, (a) in its original version (after BEETHOVEN GESAMTAUSGABE Suppl III/1 31; Breitkopf & Härtel in Wiesbaden); (b) in Czerny's edition of 1829 (after BEETHOVEN GESAMTAUSGABE Series 9/II/72 25)

b.

We also have Ries's recollection of "only two places in which Beethoven authorized him to fill in a few notes, once in the Rondo of the *Sonate pathétique* (Opus 13) and once in the theme of the Rondo in his First Concerto, where he suggested a few double-notes to make it more brilliant."[7]

Another kind of textural filler is the realization of the continuo part that Beethoven still supplied in the orchestral tutti of every concerto except the middle movement of his Fourth Concerto. It will surprise many concerto soloists to learn that not only did Beethoven expect them to assume this responsibility, but that he treated the continuo part more fully than either Haydn or Mozart had, especially in the autograph of his "Emperor" Concerto. Yet since his day these continuo parts have been discarded, overlooked, or deliberately rejected. Only in recent years, partly because of increased interest in authentic practices and instruments and partly in response to controversies on the subject, the continuo has come into use again in an increasing number of concerto performances. Every potential soloist in a Beethoven concerto will want to pay special attention to this problem.[8]

7. WEGELER & RIES 106.

8. Paying this attention will be easier when certain studies and editions become available that are still in progress or awaiting publication. I am indebted to Tibor Szász for a preview of his helpful article SZÁZS/CONTINUO, which summarizes the problems, arguments pro and

Cadenzas and Shorter Free Passages

The autographs of original cadenzas by Beethoven are extant for all of his concertos with opus numbers, even for his piano transcription of his Violin Concerto Op. 61, though not for his "Triple Concerto" Op. 56. A splendid facsimile collection of these autographs was published by Willy Hess in 1979, but without the cadenzas for the "Emperor" Concerto, Op. 73.[9] The cadenzas reveal the evolution in Beethoven's concept, from an emphasis on the virtuosity that had become fashionable to an increasing exploitation of the concerto's content.[10] In the finale of the Fourth Concerto Beethoven challenged the performer's time-honored prerogative (and too-frequent prolixity) by dictating that "the cadenza will be short." And with the first movement of the "Emperor" Concerto he denied that prerogative entirely by inserting his own integrated cadenza, preceded by his well-known introductory note, "Do not make a [that is, your own] cadenza, but go right into the following" (m. 497).

A distinction is made between a full-fledged cadenza, in which, typically, the ideas in a movement are developed harmonically as well as melodically, and a shorter passage called an *Eingang* (lead-in), in which, typically, a single scale or chordal figure is elaborated over a single har-

---

con, primary and secondary sources, and suggestions for treatment on the modern piano. An edition of continuo realizations for the concertos of Haydn, Mozart, and Beethoven is planned by Szász.

9. Beethoven/CADENZASm.

10. This changing concept is discussed in Kross/IMPROVISATION; cf. an equivalent evolution in Mozart's cadenzas, as discussed in Badura-Skoda/MOZART Chapter 11.

EXAMPLE 9/3 "Diabelli" Variation Op. 120/0/32/160–61 (after BEET-HOVEN WERKEM VII/5 235; HV*)

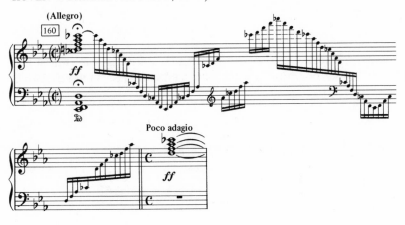

mony. Both types are signalled by a *fermata* in the score, the cadenza
being introduced by a six-four chord on the tonic harmony and the *Eingang* by a half cadence on the dominant.[11] True to the strongly penultimate character of those *fermata* harmonies, the cadenza and the *Eingang*
function as strategic landmarks, whether in the whole structure or in a
section of it. After all, the cadenza is literally a cadence, but one that is
prolonged and elaborated.

Eingänge occur rather frequently not only in Beethoven's concertos,
but in other piano works, as in the "Diabelli" Variations just before the
"Tempo di Menuetto moderato" (Ex. 9/3). Especially in his earlier works,
he often did not write out these *Eingänge* but left them for the performer
to improvise. The only clue to do so was the *fermata* on a dominant harmony. Such a clue appears around the two-thirds point in the theme and
each of the Thirteen Variations on "Es war einmal ein alter Mann" WoO
66 (Ex. 9/4). Then, of course, the performer's best recourse is to model
his improvisations after the *Eingänge* Beethoven did write out.[12]

When editors have been left to supply the *Eingänge* themselves, they
often have done so in a manner that seems stylistically inconsistent today.
In the 19th century performers usually created their own *Eingänge* (or
their own cadenzas) to display their special virtuosic accomplishments,
with stylistic consequences that could well prove joltingly incongruous.
Today, they create their own for a different reason—to achieve the stylistic consistency they may miss in some editor's realization. A further reason is suggested by Edward T. Cone, who submits his own cadenza for
the opening movement of the First Concerto Op. 15 along with a brief
explication.[13] His main reason is that writing a cadenza leads to a fuller

11. Cf. Badura-Skoda/MOZART 214.

12. E.g., cf. Sonatas Opp. 31/1/ii/26 and 90, 47/i/36, 101/iii/20, 106/ii/112; Variations
Op. 34/vi/60 (on $\frac{6}{4}$ chord), Op. 35/ii/12; Concertos Opp. 15/iii/457 (on $\frac{6}{4}$ chord), 37/iii/
152 and 407.

13. Cone/CADENZA.

EXAMPLE 9/4 "Thema" of the "13 Variationen über 'Es war einmal ein
alter Mann" WoO 66, mm. 19–23 (after BEETHOVEN WERKEM VII 5
28; HV*)

understanding of how a cadenza may exploit a concerto's ideas. In other words, one learns by doing.

Repeats—Their Observance and Effect

The chief question about Beethoven's indications for repeating sections is not *how* or in what order to repeat them (often asked about earlier music), but *whether* to repeat them and why. Yet, there is good evidence that Beethoven did not regard his repeat signs as optional and that he inserted them advisedly, not merely perfunctorily. Thus, in a letter of February 12, 1805, his brother Carl explained in the following significant note why a first ending was being added to the "Eroica" Symphony already sent to the publisher Breitkopf & Härtel: "My brother thought at first, before he had heard the Symphony, that a repeat of the first part of the first movement might be too long; but after repeated performances it was found that it was even detrimental if the first part remained unrepeated."[14]

It is true that composers themselves were beginning to do away with repeat signs by Beethoven's time, particularly in sonata forms. Certain minor composers seemed to make a point of leaving them out entirely in these forms.[15] Beethoven did so most noticeably in the five most intimate of his first movements, Opp. 27/2, 90, 101, 109, and 110 (all of which have been analyzed as sonata forms by one writer or another). In the piano sonatas all but eight of the sonata forms that do have repeat signs still enclose only the exposition in them. Undoubtedly, one reason why he did not enclose the rest of the movement in a second set of repeat signs, from the development to the end, was his expansion of the coda. Thus, he did use the second set in a movement that has no coda (Op. 10/2/i), in one with only a short coda (Op. 78/i), and in one where the closing repeat sign precedes the coda (Op. 79/i). Possibly he omitted repeat signs altogether in the first movement of the "Appassionata" Sonata to counterbalance the physically exhausting repeat of the longer second half (only) of the finale, as well as the independent repeats within the "Presto" coda. But the absence of a repeat sign at Op. 53/i/3 in most extant copies of its first edition cannot be charged to Beethoven; the sign had been present in his autograph and was quickly restored in reprintings of that edition.

It must be clear enough by now that Beethoven took all of his editorial markings seriously and tolerated no failures to observe them (as revealed in that oft-cited protest to Holz of August 1825[16] and in numerous similar

14. As cited and translated by Boris Schwarz in notes XXV (1968–69) 41.

15. Cf. Newman/sce 144–45 and 667; also, Newman/ssb 150–51.

16. Anderson/beethoven III 1241–42.

letters). If we apply this generalization to his repeat signs and grant that he used them deliberately, and not merely as casual concessions to a declining tradition, then we must seriously question almost any argument for disregarding those signs, even arguments based on "improved" balance and proportions or reduced length. However, when doubt does exist about the fact of the signs themselves, then balance, proportion, and length become our chief kinds of evidence.

The best-known case in point is the long-argued question in the first movement of the *Sonate pathétique* Op. 13 as to whether the repeat of the exposition returns to the "Grave" in measure 1 or to the "Allegro di molto con brio" in measure 11. Recently the evidence and arguments regarding Op. 13 have been well summarized and documented by Elfrieda Hiebert.[17] In my opinion, her conclusions in favor of the return to the "Allegro" are thoroughly convincing. Of the original and sixteen other early editions of Op. 13 that she could examine, only two, both foreign, return to the "Grave" rather than the "Allegro." Those editions constitute the only contemporary evidence.

The notion that the repeat returned to the "Grave" almost certainly originated with two posthumous editions—one from Haslinger in Vienna about 1828, endorsed by a certificate of authenticity that in fact did not apply; and the other in the BEETHOVEN GESAMTAUSGABEm, published in the 1860s, although its sign was changed back to the "Allegro" in the revision of 1888. Arguments that the balance and proportions are improved by including the "Grave" in the repeat seem weak and far-fetched to me. The most obvious response is that Beethoven did not include any return to the "Grave" in his recapitulation, and this at a time when he was still being consistent about making his recapitulation run parallel to his exposition. In the total form of Op. 13/i, the function of the "Grave" seems to be straightforward—that is, to introduce each of three main structural high points, the beginning, middle, and end.

In recent years pianists have begun to observe the repeats of expositions in sonata forms more faithfully. However, most pianists, like most conductors and chamber-musicians, apparently have yet to alter their treatment of the repeats in minuets and scherzos. To Max Rudolf goes much of the credit for correcting a "tradition" that cannot be traced back to Beethoven or the Classic Era.[18] Traditionally, repeats have been observed up to the *da capo*, but not in the *da capo* itself. Again, there is reason to believe that the repeat signs were not simply "casual concessions to a declining tradition." Balance and proportion were evidently Beethoven's determinants, as before. For instance, when the main section's second

17. Hiebert/OPUS 13.

18. Rudolf/REPEATS.

half was extra long in the "Menuetto" of his Sonata Op. 10/3, Beethoven specified "senza replica" for its *da capo*. (Not concerned with the same structural position, but pertinent, was his reminder that the second half of the "trio" is not to be repeated in the "Trio" in the "Scherzo" of his Sonata Op. 28.)

Moreover, Rudolf has found strong support in a statement of 1802 by Türk that taking the repeats during the *da capo* was normally expected, not opposed; and he has located statements almost as unequivocal by three others—Koch, Hummel and Czerny—in keeping with Türk's statement. Türk wrote, "A Sort of repeat is also the *da capo* . . . After the trio of a minuet we usually find the words *Minuetto da capo* . . . . This indicates that the minuet is to be played from the beginning—that is, with the prescribed repeats—consequently, like the first time, unless *ma senza replica* (but without repeat) is explicitly added." [19]

Frequently only the first of the two sections in each variation of a set is repeated, presumably not only to reduce the length but to interrupt the unbroken succession of sectional repeats. (Bach's "Goldberg Variations" are performed in this way more often than not.) Of course, the second section of a variation theme is often longer than the first. But if it has its own repeat signs that are disregarded on that account, the variation will be out of kilter with one kind of "double variation" in which no omission of repeats is possible—that is, the kind in which the repeat of each section is written out and often changed internally (as in the tenth of the "Diabelli" Variations).

Structural Rhythm

Structural rhythm, a term whose connotations have varied, is used here to mean a macro version of a micro structural unit. More specifically, it is used to mean a structure whose outline is defined and given dynamic direction by strategically located accents, or by peaks in complementary arses and theses (whether incises or phrases), or by the downbeats of strong measures in a series of strong and weak measures.

In Chapter 5 a number of examples were cited to illustrate Beethoven's use of accents to outline incises and phrases or harmonic and tonal progressions. In his own playing, Beethoven is reported to have brought out melodic elements in that manner, especially elements in the accompaniment or passagework. Czerny mentions this practice in connection with the recurring, staccato octave leap in the accompaniment of the finale in the Sonata in A♭ Op. 26 (Ex. 9/5).[20] He also cites a recurring

---

19. Türk's statement is in the 1802 edition of his *Klavierschule*, p. 143 (as translated here by Max Rudolf). As Rudolf observes, Türk seems to have gone out of his way to strengthen and clarify his statement in his original, 1789 edition.

20. Badura-Skoda/CZERNY 42.

EXAMPLE 9/5 Sonata in A♭ Op. 26/iv/5–6 (after BEETHOVEN WERKEM VII/2/I 225; HV*)

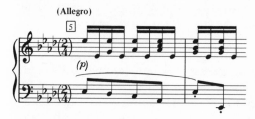

EXAMPLE 9/6 Sonata in E♭ Op. 7/iv/11–12 (after BEETHOVEN WERKEM VII/2/I 84; HV*)

figure in the finale of the Sonata in E♭ Op. 7, which Beethoven points up with separate stems (Ex. 9/6).[21]

Actually, more extended figures abound similarly in Beethoven's fresh accompaniments, as throughout the region of his subordinate theme in the Sonata Op. 10/1/i/56–105, or the corresponding region in the Sonata Op. 90/i/55–81. Several of his supposed annotations to twenty-one Cramer Etudes (already discussed in Chapter 6) call attention to melodic lines hidden more or less widely in the passagework, as in Etude 3: "The melody lies almost always in the third note of each [rhythmic] grouping" (Ex. 9/7). The annotation to Etude 8 reads in part, "The melody lies in the high upstem notes. The rhythmic accents divide unevenly—in the first measure they occur on the first and third beats, but in the second measure on the first note of each group [of 4 sixteenths]. The right hand should rest broadly and firmly on the accented beats . . . ."

Often it helps to achieve a better structural perspective if the player can view a form as a macro version of an incise or phrase, much as Momigny viewed the incise and phrase as macro versions of his basic "cad-

21. Badura-Skoda/CZERNY 33, but with hairpin accents added by Czerny to his illustration from mm. 150–55.

Example 9/7 Cramer's Etude 3/1–4 (after Shedlock/cramerm 6)

ence" (see pp. 173–174). Thus, the A–B–A design in the "Menuetto" of the Sonata Op. 22 might be viewed at its top hierarchic level as a feminine complementation of arsis and thesis (as charted below, down to its third level). And its peak might be viewed as the feminine close of its "Minore" trio (Ex. 9/8). Since the feminine grouping is a ternary grouping, the thesis in this design consists of the B section plus the *da capo* shortened (senza replica).

The alternation of strong and weak measures was introduced (and illustrated in Ex. 6/14, p. 183) under possible "rhythmic ambiguities" because the question often arises as to which measure was intended to be the strong one. It is referred to here only to emphasize again that determining the answers to such questions can significantly affect one's understanding of the underlying structure.[22]

22. Cf. Imbrie/ambiguity.

Example 9/8 The arsis-thesis syntax at the top three hierarchic levels in the "Menuetto" of the Sonata Op. 22

A			B					A*
a	: ‖ : b		: ‖ : a		: ‖ : b		:	A*
a'	b'	a'	b'	a'	b'	a'	b'	A*
(1–4) + (5–8) ‖	(9–16) + (17–30) ‖	(31–34) + (35–38) ‖	(39–42) + (43–46) ‖	A* ‖

*"da capo senza replicata"

Programmatic Influences on Character and Structure[23]

About the finale of the "Appassionata" Sonata Op. 57 Czerny wrote,

If Beethoven, who was so fond of portraying scenes from nature, was perhaps thinking of ocean waves on a stormy night when from the distance a cry for help is heard, then such a picture will give the pianist a guide to the correct playing of this great tonal painting. There is no doubt that in many of his most beautiful works Beethoven was inspired by similar visions or pictures from his reading or from his own lively imagination. It is equally certain that if it were always possible to know the idea behind the composition, we would have the key to the music and its performance.[24]

However, in a footnote Czerny added, "But he [Beethoven] knew that the music would not always be felt so freely by its listeners if a specific object were to predetermine their imaginations." And even Schindler voiced a similar caveat,[25] although previously he had attributed more unlikely programmes to Beethoven himself, such as the marital dispute and reconciliation that supposedly goes on throughout the innocent Sonata Op. 14/2.[26] Referring to a letter from the composer not otherwise known, Schindler said that Beethoven protested the efforts by those who insisted on ascribing programmatic meanings to his or any other composer's music.

In those remarks, Czerny and Schindler pinpointed at once the potential values and risks of programmatic interpretations. Beethoven inserted no programmatic inscriptions in his piano music comparable to those in his "Pastoral" Symphony. The closest he came were the occasional descriptive titles assumed or known to be authentic. The sometimes picturesque titles of variation sets, like "Es war einmal ein alter Mann" (WoO 66), do not go beyond identifying and perhaps characterizing the subjects of their borrowed themes. The title of Op. 13, *Sonate pathétique*, rightly associates with pathos and the nobler emotions, but hardly with the extreme fantasies that it and Beethoven's other most popular works have spawned across the arts during subsequent generations.[27] The title of the Sonata Op. 81a, *Das Lebewohl* (or *Les Adieux*), is a little more specific, with its three movements referring to the "Farewell," "Absence," and "Return" of Beethoven's longtime pupil, friend, and chief patron, the Archduke Rudolph, during the French threat of 1809–10. But again, it provides no specific interpretive clues to the performer—hardly such details

---

23. Parts of this section derive from Chapter 8 on Programmatic Content in Newman/PERFORMANCE; cf., also, Newman/PROGRAMME.

24. Badura-Skoda/CZERNY 54, as translated in Schindler & MacArdle/BEETHOVEN 406.

25. Schindler & MacArdle/BEETHOVEN 399–400 and 446 (fn. 321).

26. Cf. Schindler & MacArdle/BEETHOVEN 406–407; Newman/SCE 513–14.

27. Cf. Newman/MYSTIQUE, as on p. 383; Comini/BEETHOVEN, *passim*.

EXAMPLE 9/9 Sonata Op. 81a/iii/5–6 (after Bülow & Lebert/BEET-HOVENm II 514).

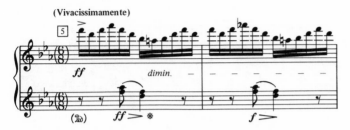

as Bülow unabashedly footnoted in his widely circulated edition of 1871: "Even a player with the most deeply rooted antipathy to programs cannot help seeing, that in the falling pairs of thirds for the left hand the gesture of beckoning with a handkerchief—the tone-picture of a sign—is illustrated, a sign apprising the coming one of the waiting one's presence [see Ex. 9/9]."[28]

There is no reason to believe that Beethoven authorized or even knew any of the titles that his other piano works soon acquired, including "Moonlight" Sonata for Op. 27/2 or "Appassionata" Sonata for Op. 57, although there is no reason to assume that he would have objected to any particular title, either. Evidently, most performers have been more than satisfied to retain these nicknames, finding them not inappropriate for the music's character (if, indeed, the character can be considered apart from the nicknames). In any case, some performers are not disposed to be absolutists about their music and must *feel* something to perform at all, granted that the nicknames may even have the effect of delimiting the range of feeling. The one nickname that conceivably might stem from Beethoven is "The Tempest" for the Sonata Op. 31/2 (and Op. 57, as well), if Schindler's attribution of it to Beethoven can still be believed.[29]

In the 19th and early 20th centuries a literature developed that expounds similar though largely undocumented interpretations. These interpretations originated in associations that did spring from Beethoven himself, according to Czerny, such as the association of a horse and rider galloping by, with the prevailing rhythm of Op. 31/2/iii.[30] (As in Ex. 9/10, would not that association have been more likely to inspire the rhythm of Op. 31/3/iv?) Of course, the authors themselves were responsible for associations like Adolph Bernhard Marx's reading of a funeral procession into the Sonata Op. 111/ii, or Tolstoy's introduction of *The Kreutzer Son-*

28. Bülow & Lebert/BEETHOVENm II 514; cf. Newman/CHECKLIST 516.

29. Cf. Schindler & MacArdle/BEETHOVEN 406.

30. Badura-Skoda/CZERNY 48 fn.

EXAMPLE 9/10 Sonatas (a) Op. 31/2/iii/1–4, and (b) 31/3/iv/1–4 (after
BEETHOVEN WERKEM VII/3/II 88 and 114; HV*)

EXAMPLE 9/11 Sonata Op. 81a/i/1–2 (after Wallner/KLAVIERSONATENm
II 179; HV*)

ata Op. 47 as the catalytic agent leading to murder (in his minor novel of
that title), or Arnold Schering's ties between some of the world's greatest
poetic and dramatic masterworks and nearly all of Beethoven's piano sonatas (not to mention numerous other masterpieces). Schering went so far
as to fit sample prosodic settings from those literary masterworks to Beethoven's "related" works, taking his cue partly from Beethoven's own setting of "Le-be-wohl" in the first two measures of his Sonata Op. 81a/i
(Ex. 9/11).[31]

To me, one of the programmatic interpretations most deserving of
serious consideration is that in a recent article by Owen Jander, which
relates the middle movement, "Andante con moto," of the Fourth Concerto, Op. 58, to the familiar Orpheus legend.[32] Briefly, Jander credits not

31. Cf. Schindler & MacArdle/BEETHOVEN 232; Newman/MYSTIQUE 380–81; Newman/
SCE 504–505.

32. Jander/ORPHEUS (anticipated in its programmatic leanings by Jander's article on
"Romantic Form and Content in the Slow Movement of Beethoven's Violin Concerto," in

Liszt (as has been claimed) but the early Beethoven specialist Marx with "discovering" this frequently suggested association, especially the impassioned plea of Orpheus against the harsh, but gradually fading, rejections by the austere chorus of furies. But Jander finds Beethoven's most likely source among several possible sources for that association to be a successful opera called *Orpheus* by Beethoven's warm friend Friedrich August Kanne, rather than Gluck's *Orpheus*. Indeed, Kanne's *Orpheus* was introduced in Vienna in the same year as the Fourth Concerto, 1807. Jander includes a "program" that details the associations he finds between episodes in Kanne's opera and passages in Beethoven's "Andante con moto."

Although Jander has turned up no hard evidence that proves Beethoven had the Orpheus legend in mind when he composed that particular movement, he does succeed in bringing out closer and more frequent circumstances and relationships than can be readily dismissed as coincidental. These add meaning, for example, to Beethoven's rich pedalling in the movement, including his first indication of the progression from *una* through *due* to *tre corde*. In a response to Jander's article that is quite as interesting in its own way, Edward T. Cone says that he is prepared to accept Jander's circumstantial evidence, which he regards as impressive. But he himself still prefers to hear Beethoven's music as absolute music— that is, as a valid language in its own right, a language of time, pitch, and harmony in which the music serves as its own best ambassador, free of any confining associations with a particular story or verbalized idea.[33]

Interrelationships Among Movements of a Cycle

Thematic Relationships

Beethoven must have attached some importance to thematic relationships among movements (sometimes called cyclical relationships). The best-known evidence is a letter of 1819 in which he instructed Ries to add one simple introductory measure to the London publication of his "Hammerklavier Sonata" Op. 106.[34] This measure consisted of the portentous rising third that serves as an incipit to the slow, third movement, relating it to the incipits of the first two movements and to the tenth that announces the fugue subject of the finale (Ex. 9/12). A fair number of Beethoven's cyclic works reveal similarly unequivocal relationships—for

---

MQ LXIX [1983] 159–79). Jander believes that all of Op. 58 actually associates with the Orpheus legend.

33. Listed in our Bibliography under Jander/ORPHEUS.

34. Cf. Anderson/BEETHOVEN II 806; Ries's reaction is quoted near the middle of Chapter 2.

EXAMPLE 9/12 Sonata Op. 106: The incipits of the first three movements and of the fugue subject in the fourth movement

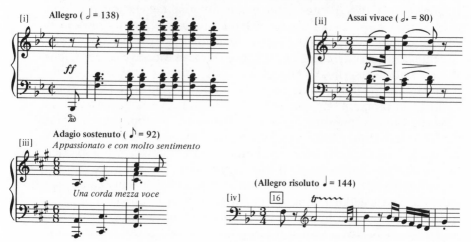

instance, his Sonata Op. 2/3, in which the main theme of each movement and certain subordinate themes begin by describing a melodic turn, or his Sonata Op. 22, in which each movement starts with or soon peaks on a rising third, whether the third is open or filled in stepwise (as it is in movements ii and iii, and in iv at the peak of the first period, mm. 6–8).

The "thematic" relationships may be as much a similarity of style as of melody. In Op. 2/2, the chordal character of the main themes interrelates the fast movements even more than the emphasis on the first and fifth steps of the key. Certainly the interpretation of the whole work can benefit from at least an intellectual awareness of such relationships.

Proportional Tempos?

One gets another macro view of Beethoven's cyclic works by considering the relationships of the tempos in the several movements. These relationships raise problems that were barely hinted at in Chapter 4 and that only can be introduced here. Some writers have argued that the proportional relationships arbitrarily established by Quantz and others still applied to Beethoven, so that an andante might be taken, for example, at twice the speed of an adagio and an allegro at twice the speed of an andante. Others (I, among them) have concluded that the relationships are less arbitrarily chosen, more subtle, and more dependent on each movement's individual rhythmic character (see pp. 91 et passim).

Since Beethoven was not mathematically disposed (as numerous errors in his more complex time signatures and other rhythmic details bear witness), he is not likely to have involved himself consciously in the details of proportions. In any case, supporting evidence about proportional relationships of any sort is hard to find, especially concerning his piano music; the whole problem of tempo relationships between movements needs much further study; and decisions regarding that problem obviously matter vitally to the performer's concept of a Beethoven work as a whole. The most substantial study of the subject is one by the writer on "rhythmic character," Hermann Beck (discussed in Chapter 4).[35] Beck goes back to Beethoven's metronome markings and to that universal heartbeat pulse between 60 and 80 beats per minute to argue for a balanced whole in each cycle. That is, he relates all the movements of a cycle approximately to a single tempo by establishing a ratio between them of 2 or 3 to 1.

To take the "Hammerklavier" Sonata Op. 106 once more, as the only cyclic (or other) work for piano with original metronome markings, I believe that the observer can perceive proportional relationships between the movements only by making unacceptable allowances. Superficially, one might say that the markings in the successive movements are proportional to the extent that the first movement is roughly similar to or twice that in the other movements. That is, the 138 for a half note in the first movement is roughly similar to the 144 for a quarter note in the last movement, while it is very roughly twice that of the 80 for a dotted-half note and the 92 for an eighth note in the two inner movements. But those proportions are virtually meaningless, anyway. It is not only the prevailing beat or its mathematical quotient or product that gives meaning to a proportional relationship. Rather, it is the compound rhythmic character—the note-values, meter, inscription, and more subjective aspects. And in this respect, whatever cyclic relationships there are in Op. 106 do not seem to be implemented by proportional tempos. If anything, Beethoven supports the latter view in his letter to the publisher Schott in 1826 (quoted on p. 84), for the letter suggests that he welcomed the freedom from rigid tempo relationships and potential monotony when the opportunity arose to escape from the standard tempo beats of the past.

Interconnections that Help to Bind the Cycle

Beethoven showed his concern for binding certain of his cycles more closely by running together some or all of the movements in two possible ways. One way was by using the term *attacca* or, more often, *attacca subito,* to lead from one movement right into the next. The *subito* (suddenly) usually implies a dramatic approach. The other way was to end

---

35. Beck/PROPORTIONEN. Among other pertinent studies are Saslav/HAYDN, Zaslaw/TEMPO, Malloch/MINUET, and Brown/SCHUBERT; but only Beck's study concentrates on Beethoven.

one movement in harmonic suspense, on the dominant or other related chord of the next movement. Beethoven had already used both means within the first movement of his *Sonate pathétique* Op. 13 as he led back and forth between its introductory "Grave" and its driving "Allegro di molto e con brio." In his Sonata Op. 27/1 he not only used *attacca* similarly in the coda of its finale, but he used both means to interconnect all of its adjacent movements.

Furthermore, Beethoven led *attacca* into the "Allegretto" of his "Moonlight" Sonata Op. 27/2 (and performers often seem to assume the same approach to its finale, "Presto agitato," with justification only by analogy). And in the Sonata Op. 81a he used both means to lead from the "Adagio" to the "Allegro" of its first movement, and a suspensive cadence to lead into its finale. As in the other macro views that are being taken in this chapter, the performer's main interpretive role is to become aware of Beethoven's intentions and to understand their function in the cycle as a whole.

When Beethoven used a suspensive harmony as a connecting link, he often delayed it with a *fermata* sign, as at the end of Op. 57/ii. But the use of a *fermata* alone should be noted at the end of a majority of his cyclic movements. When neither the *attacca* instruction nor a suspensive harmony leads to the next movement, then the function of the *fermata* seems to be quite the opposite. It provides a necessary breathing space either at the close of the cycle, to let the whole effect sink in, or between movements in order to let the mood of one movement be digested while that of the next is awaited.

The Optional Choice and Order of Movements

Finally, one more kind of macro view is introduced here, more for its interest and for the record than for any likely application of it by today's performers. As recently as early in this century it was not uncommon for pianists to program only a single movement from a sonata or other cyclic work, much as conductors would program a single movement of a symphony. Today, most performers and listeners, being more sophisticated, would regard this practice as a shocking violation of the cycle as a whole. Perhaps these same persons would be surprised to learn that Beethoven himself acceded to and even proposed options in the choice and order of the movements in one or more of his cyclic works, not once but on several occasions.

In more than one early letter he extended a virtual *carte blanche* to the publisher to do as he saw fit with a work in press. For instance, in a letter of 1802 to Breitkopf & Härtel he added at the end, "Should you consider it necessary to alter or correct anything, you have my full permission to do so."[36] That sentence could have referred only to an introductory statement that he asked (in vain) to have included with his *Six Variations* Op. 34. But in a letter of 1819 to Ries about the imminent publication in London of the "Hammerklavier" Sonata Op. 106, Beethoven granted this incredibly free license:

> Should the sonata not be suitable for London, I could send another one; or you could also omit the Largo and begin straight away with the Fugue . . . , which is the last movement; or you could use the first movement and then the Adagio, and then for the third movement the Scherzo—and omit entirely no. 4 with the Largo and Allegro risoluto. Or you could take just the first movement and the Scherzo and let them form the whole sonata. I leave it to you to do as you think best.[37]

Sometimes the proffered option was the substitution or deletion of a movement. It was a friend who persuaded Beethoven that the original middle movement in the "Waldstein" Sonata Op. 53 made the work too long. Consequently Beethoven substituted the present "Introduzione" and, according to Ries, eventually decided the change was for the better, publishing the "Andante" separately ('Andante favori," WoO 57).[38] Richard Wagner was never happy about that substitution.[39] And according to Schindler, Beethoven considered omitting the inner movements—the scherzos, minuets, and allegros—from his earlier sonatas in the definitive edition of his complete works that he kept projecting but never saw in his lifetime.[40] Furthermore, said Schindler, Beethoven came to feel that three movements could achieve greater unity, especially in the highly emotional Sonata for Piano and Violin Op. 30/2 (and in spite of his late solo sonatas in four movements).

Maybe prospective income figured more than art in what today seem like epochal options and decisions. But such flexibility does remind all of us that along with Beethoven's (well-justified) fussiness about details in his dealings with publishers, he also revealed a heartening freedom in his makeup when the occasion demanded.

36. Anderson/BEETHOVEN I 84.

37. Anderson/BEETHOVEN II 804–805.

38. WEGELER & RIES 101–102.

39. Cf. Badura-Skoda/CZERNY 19; Schmidt/EDITION 109.

40. Schindler & MacArdle/BEETHOVEN 402–403; reportedly, the deleted movements would have been published separately in the projected edition.

CHAPTER *10*

KEYBOARD TECHNIQUES AS BOTH CLUES AND CONSEQUENCES

I N CHAPTER 3 we summarized Beethoven's technical exploitations by comparing his pianism, or writing for piano, with that of the three masters who were his near contemporaries in Vienna—Haydn, Mozart, and Schubert. In this final chapter we explore his technical idioms and innovations both as clues to and consequences of his interpretive intentions. After reviewing what is known about his own technical equipment and approach to the keyboard, we will concentrate on his original fingerings, because they generally furnish the most tangible of those clues.

Beethoven's Own Technical Endowments and Attributes

His Finger and Hand Physiology

Czerny provides the most specific, and probably the most reliable, descriptions of Beethoven's own finger and hand physiology. He tells us that Beethoven's "fingers were very strong, not long, and broadened at the tips from so much playing. For he often said to me that in his youth he frequently had exercised endlessly [at the keyboard] until well past midnight."[1] Czerny also said that Beethoven could barely span a 10th on the keyboard.[2] But we have seen that Beethoven must have had an

---

1. Badura-Skoda/CZERNY 22.
2. Badura-Skoda/CZERNY 22.

exceptionally wide, flexible web between his fingers for him even to consider playing the trills in 6ths that were quoted previously from an early sketch (Ex. 7/3, p. 194).

His Approach to the Keyboard

Contemporary observers repeatedly singled out three aspects of Beethoven's approach to the keyboard.[3] These were his decidedly rounded fingers, their consistent placement on or close to the keys, and his quiet, unaffected manner. Therese Brunsvik recalled lessons in 1799 at which Beethoven "never grew weary of *holding down* and *bending* my fingers, which I had been taught to lift high and hold straight."[4] Gerhard von Breuning added that "he appeared to have the so-called older hand position, as opposed to that currently practiced [1874] with more flattened fingers."[5] Czerny said, "His bearing while performing was ideally restful, noble, and beautiful, without the slightest grimace, [and was altered] only [by his] leaning forward with increasing deafness."[6]

Whether Beethoven, who was relatively short in height, could or would have maintained this quiet bearing in his later life had he continued to perform actively, is less certain. Some of his later technical innovations—such as the wide-ranging scale, arpeggio, octave, and chordal passages throughout the fast outer movements of the "Emperor" Concerto—can hardly be managed without greater participation of the upper body. Czerny does say that Beethoven showed little concern for technical convenience or standardized fingerings, especially in his later works.[7]

His Use of the Basic Touches

The Finger Touch

Keyboard touches are commonly named according to either the body mechanism used or the joint (or hinge) from which that mechanism operates. Thus, the four main touches are most often referred to as (1) the finger or the knuckle, (2) the hand or the wrist, (3) the forearm or the elbow, and (4) the full (locked) arm or the shoulder touch.[8] When

3. Several of the references used in this and the next subsection were turned up by Ms. Geraldine Keeling in an unpublished paper on Beethoven's piano playing.

4. Quoted from Thayer & Forbes/BEETHOVEN 235.

5. Breuning/SCHWARZSPANIERHAUSE 106.

6. Badura-Skoda/CZERNY 22. Cf., also, Simrock as quoted from 1816 in Kann/CRAMERM vii; Schindler/BEETHOVEN II 129 fn.; and Schindler & MacArdle/BEETHOVEN 415.

7. Badura-Skoda/CZERNY 25.

8. Cf. Newman/PROBLEMS Chapter 2.

the touch intended in a particular passage by an experienced composer/ pianist can be determined, it becomes one clue to the interpretation of that passage.

For the most part, the finger touch must predominate. One concludes that it predominated in Beethoven's playing, because of his quiet bearing, nearly constant contact with the keys, and strong predilection for a legato style. Pertinent is "one circumstance [that] attracted . . . the particular notice" in 1803 of one of his chief portrait painters, Willibrord Joseph Mähler. Mähler recalled to Thayer in 1860 that "Beethoven played with his hands so very still; wonderful as his execution was, there was no tossing of them to and fro, up and down; they seemed to glide right and left over the keys, the fingers alone doing the work."[9]

Partial descriptions of Beethoven's playing like that one, sometimes including his great speed at the keyboard, are as much as the contemporary observers left us (for others, see Chapter 3). Further information about his use of the basic touches must be deduced from the technical demands of his scores. Many very fast passages in those scores leave no alternative, since only the finger touch permits such speeds. In the first movement, "Allegro molto e con brio," of the Sonata Op. 7, Czerny gives M. M. = 116 and Moscheles 126 (!) for a dotted-quarter note (see Chapter 4 regarding their metronome markings). For pianists who can manage them at all, those speeds are only possible in the sixteenth-note

9. Thayer & Forbes/BEETHOVEN 337 and 610.

EXAMPLE 10/1   Sonata Op. 7/i/285–95 (after BEETHOVEN WERKEM VII/2/I 74; HV*)

EXAMPLE 10/2 "Diabelli" Variations Op. 120/xxvi/29–32 (after BEET-HOVEN WERKEM VII/5 226; HV*)

passages because these remain within the span of the 10th that Czerny said Beethoven could reach, hence can be played conveniently by the fingers alone (Ex. 10/1). The same applies to numerous other high-speed passages, including those in Opp. 2/3/iv/8–18, 27/2/iii/33–42 (etc.), 53/iii/183–216, and even 81a/iii/23–36 (etc.). A maximum of independent finger action is required to play the double-notes legato in the 26th of the "Diabelli" Variations. There Beethoven's initial inscription "piacé-vole" (pleasing) has to be balanced against the climate of continuing high speed created by the surrounding variations (Ex. 10/2).

Other Touches

The other touches that Beethoven may have intended are not documented by contemporary descriptions, but can only be inferred from the passages in question and whatever editorial markings he may have inserted.

EXAMPLE 10/3 Sonata Op. 2/3/iv/73–79 (after BEETHOVEN WERKEM VII/2/I 60; HV*)

EXAMPLE 10/4 Sonata Op. 31/3/ii/39–43 (after BEETHOVEN WERKE m VII/3/II 107; HV*)

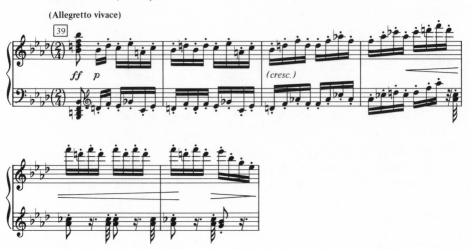

The series of staccato eighth-note chords and octaves in the Sonata Op. 2/3/iv cannot be played by the fingers alone, nor can they be played fast enough by the full arm, leaving a choice between a forearm or (more likely) a hand touch (Ex. 10/3). This choice is also the only possibility for the somewhat similar chords and octaves in the finale of the "Moonlight" Sonata Op. 27/2. But especially in the works from the "Moonlight" through Op. 31/3, where Beethoven revealed a decided new taste for staccato effects in both slow and rapid movements, he left numerous fast single-note passages that are more readily, though not necessarily, played by a finger staccato, as in much of the "Scherzo" of the Sonata Op. 31/3 (Ex. 10/4).

In Ex. 10/4 the thirty-second and eighth-note pattern of the bottom staff dictates a full-arm touch, if the pattern is to be played smartly enough and in one impulse. There are still other passages that virtually dictate the touches that will be used, mostly involving the full arm. In the middle section of the "Scherzo" in the "Hammerklavier" Sonata Op. 106, the very fast eighth-note triplets (according to Beethoven's own marking of a dotted-half note at 80) cannot be played by the fingers alone, but require some rotary motion of the full arm, at least wherever the span exceeds a 10th. Throughout the outer sections of the "Allegro molto e vivace" in the Sonata Op. 27/1//ii, the one-measure slurs suggest to me that the full arm will attack once per measure (Ex. 10/5) and not simply that legato prevails (as was probably intended by the similar slurs in Mozart's Sonata in B♭ K. 570). The full-arm attacks seem to be confirmed by Beethoven's

EXAMPLE 10/5 Sonata Op. 27/1/ii/1–4 (after BEETHOVEN WERKEM VII/3/II 5; HV*); cf., also, Ex. 3/9, above

Allegro molto e vivace

persistent continuation of the one-measure slurs during the syncopated return, as well as by his obviously deliberate discontinuation of them at the end, where an apparent relaxation of the tension and shift to a finger touch are strongly suggested by the single slur that extends over the last five measures. They could be confirmed in some degree, too, by Beethoven's supposed annotation over Cramer Etude 29, which treats of its two-note slurs: "The aim is to learn how to withdraw the hand [arm?] lightly; it [the aim] is achieved by placing it [the hand or arm?] firmly on the first note of each slurred pair and raising it almost vertically on the second note."[10] Such passages tend to refute any idea that Beethoven knew and intended only a finger touch. More importantly, they help to suggest what other touches he may well have had in mind for analogous passages that lack quite such clear touch clues. For those are the passages, it must be acknowledged, that predominate in Beethoven's piano writing.

His Exploitation of Idiomatic Techniques

The idiomatic techniques that soon became every pianist's stock-in-trade were cultivated especially in keyboard etudes. Although etudes had figured in keyboard literature much earlier and included such notable examples as Domenico Scarlatti's *Essercizi*, it was not until Beethoven's day that a first flowering of the genre occurred. Then the major landmarks were the etudes of Clementi, Cramer, and Czerny, characterized, as in the concurrent piano methods, by innovative technical idioms and virtuosity.[11]

Beethoven's scores show him to have been thoroughly conversant with these idioms. He used them as his music required, or even, in his earlier, more flamboyant sets of variations, for the sake of sheer virtuosity. In

10. Shedlock/CRAMERM 38–39.

11. Cf. the difficult drills in 6ths and 8ves that already appeared in 1797 in Milchmeyer/WAHRE 27–30, and in 3ds, 4ths, 6ths, and 8ves in 1802 in Adam/MÉTHODE 56–57.

EXAMPLE 10/6 Sonata Op. 28/iv/17–18 (after BEETHOVEN WERKEM VII/3/II 45; HV*)

1824 he improvised for Friedrich Wieck for more than an hour, revealing among other things that he was "still skilled at crossing over of the left and right hands, sometimes in quick succession, while inserting the most clear, charming melodies that poured from him effortlessly, with eyes gazing upward and tightly rounded fingers."[12] A well-known example of hand-crossing occurs during a kind of drinking song in the "Trio" of his "Menuetto" in the Sonata Op. 10/3.

Beethoven made frequent use of the "dog-paddle" technique, as in the finale of the "Pastoral" Sonata Op. 28 (Ex. 10/6). This technique requires that the full arms will alternate in moving each hand to each new group, where the fingers then do the actual playing. The same technique is also mandatory in the finale of the "Tempest" Sonata Op. 31/2 (see the long passage starting in m. 95), and virtually mandatory in the finale of the Sonata Op 78, as in Ex. 10/7. But despite its advantages of strength and accuracy, Beethoven generally does not use the dog-paddle technique unless the hands actually overlap. Depending on their idiosyncrasies, some pianists choose to adapt it by dividing unbroken runs between the hands like those in the opening movement of the Sonata Op. 31/3 (Ex. 10/8). But in doing so they would find that Beethoven himself sel-

12. As quoted in Nohl/BEETHOVEN 49.

EXAMPLE 10/7 Sonata Op. 78/ii/134–35 (after Wallner/KLAVIER-SONATENmm II 168; HV*)

EXAMPLE 10/8 Sonata Op. 31/3/i/177–83 (after BEETHOVEN WERKEM VII/3/II 103–104; HV*)

dom indicates the same in his other, similarly unbroken runs (or *Eingänge*).[13] A rare, only tentative exception may be seen in Ex. 9/3 (p. 261) from the "Diabelli" Variations Op. 120/xxxii.[14]

Beethoven's presumed use of the glissando technique was brought up earlier, in connection with some legato slurs (p. 134). We know the use of that technique from the finale of the "Waldstein" Sonata, Op. 53 (Ex. 10/9). He had also made a similar use some eight years earlier in his First Concerto Op. 15/i/344–46. And Mozart had made one still earlier (1778?) in the concluding cadenza of his Variations on "Lison dormait" K. 264, among other early uses. These three examples all must be described as "presumed" uses because the word "glissando" does not accompany any of them. In spite of the difficulty of controlling octaves

13. E.g., cf. the variations Op. 34/vi/60 or Op. 35/ii/12.

14. Three similar exceptions may be found in the concertos Op. 37/iii/26 and 282–88, and Op. 73/i/2.

EXAMPLE 10/9 Sonata Op. 53/iii/465–69 (after BEETHOVEN WERKEM VII/3/II 166; HV*)

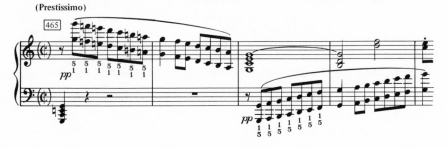

evenly (or rising 6ths, in the Mozart example) and of alternatives offered by editors or invented by performers,[15] there can be little doubt that a literal glissando technique was intended in Opp. 15 and 53. A mitigating consideration is the shallower and lighter action on the pianos of the time. Furthermore, the word "glissando" does appear in a rising (!) octave scale in G in a set of "Variations in G" by the Archduke Rudolph, composed about 1809 while he was studying composition with Beethoven.[16] But that term was still little known, appearing in no known treatise or method up to Czerny's time.[17]

Beethoven's Original Fingerings[18]

The Significance of His Fingerings

Every experienced teacher comes to realize the value of original fingerings in a composer's works, not only to facilitate technical problems but to reveal that composer's interpretive intentions. Remarks stressing the interpretive value of fingerings abound in the treatises of Beethoven's time—for example, in those by Türk, Milchmeyer, Clementi, Starke, Hummel, and Czerny. Thus, Clementi wrote, "To produce the BEST EFFECT [that is, style of playing], by the easiest means, is the great basis of the art of fingering. The EFFECT, being of the highest importance, is FIRST consulted; the way to accomplish it is then devised; and THAT MODE of fingering is PREFERRED which gives the BEST EFFECT, tho' not always the easiest to the performer . . . ."[19] And Czerny provided this "fundamental rule": "Every passage which may be taken in several ways, should be played in that manner which is the most suitable and natural to the case that occurs, and which is determined partly by adjacent notes, and partly by the style of execution."[20]

15. Referring only to "the slidden [or glided, or slurred; *geschliffenen*] octaves for 2 fingers" in Opp. 53 and 15, Czerny recommended single notes for little hands in both occurrences (Badura-Skoda/CZERNY 51 and 97).

16. Cf. Kagan/RUDOLPH 138.

17. Nearest to it is "glissicato," defined by nothing more than the two words "sanft, geschleift" (smooth, slidden) in Starke/PIANOFORTE I 19.

18. Some of the information and a little of the wording in this final section derive from Newman/FINGERINGS (by kind permission of the *Journal of Musicology*). Among the very few previous studies of Beethoven's fingering, two may be singled out here—Grundmann & Mies 113–32, which concentrates on about 2 dozen of the fingerings and their bearing on performance, and Bamberger/FINGERINGS, which probes deeper into about half as many and their interpretive significance. Cf., also, the 1986 article Hiebert/WoO 39 on the copious, mainly pedagogic fingerings in the one-movement Trio WoO 39.

19. Clementi/INTRODUCTION 14.

20. Czerny/SCHOOL II 4.

Those writers usually applied this sort of remark to a particular aspect of interpretation, such as articulation, rhythmic grouping, ornamentation, or tone production. Thus, Türk recommended re-using the same finger to implement desired separations between slurs; he also recommended irregular (disconnected) fingerings to implement fast clear mordents in the bass.[21] Starke saw suitable fingering as one prerequisite of good tone production.[22] Hummel advocated the consistent fingering of rhythmic groupings that are demarcated by short rests or hiatuses, in order to separate the groupings more clearly.[23]

Among several remarks that Beethoven himself made about fingering, the one most directly applicable to interpretation occurs in his letter of 1817 to Czerny about nephew Karl's instruction. In that letter he tells Czerny to concentrate on interpretation only after the fingering, notes, and time are learned correctly. But "in certain passages [Ex. 10/10] I'd like all the fingers to be used sometimes, so that one might slur such [passages better]. To be sure, with fewer fingers that sort of [passage] sounds, as they say, [as if] 'pearled,' or 'like a pearl'; yet occasionally one wants another [sort of] jewel . . . ."[24] The full intention of Beethoven's sentences is clear enough, although it seems not to have been recognized. His instruction was to use a fingering (such as I have added in brackets above the notes in Ex. 10/10) that would implement the newer legato style rather than a fingering (similarly added below) that would implement the detached playing more common in the past. However, it must be acknowledged parenthetically that by his criterion, Beethoven's

21. Türk/KLAVIERSCHULE 276, 343.

22. Starke/PIANOFORTE I 15.

23. Hummel/ANWEISUNG 323.

24. This letter was published first in August Schmidt's *Allgemeine Wiener Musik-Zeitung* V (1845) 450. Several of its reprintings have been marred by wrong notes in its music fragments and errors in its translated versions. It may be seen in its original German in Kastner & Kapp/BRIEFE letter 732.

EXAMPLE 10/10 Three illustrations taken from Beethoven's letter to Czerny of 1817, with implied fingering added by the present author.

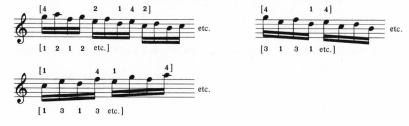

original fingerings actually favor the detached at least as often as the legato style of playing.

There is further evidence that Beethoven placed special emphasis on fingering in his teaching. For instance, there is the remark made by the Baron Kübeck von Kübau some time after studying with Beethoven in 1796: "The importance of fingering and the strict precision became clear to me for the first time . . . ."[25] There is also the copious fingering Beethoven supplied in three compositions dedicated to pedagogic use, the Sonatina in F WoO 50/i written for Wegeler about 1788–90, the Variations for piano and violin WoO 40 written for Eleanore von Breuning in 1792–93, and the one-movement Piano Trio in B♭ WoO 39 written for Maximiliane Brentano in 1812. Evidently at the level of learning represented by those three compositions, Beethoven attached more importance to fingering than to pedalling, for which he supplied no markings.

Beethoven supplied much more fingering in his scores, whether for keyboard or for bowed stringed instruments, than any of the other Classic masters. Like J. S. Bach's before him and Brahms's after, his keyboard fingerings reflected the master performer's typical absorption in the technical idioms and tonal possibilities of his instrument. Yet his near contemporaries Clementi and Mozart took a similar interest in their keyboard writing without inserting any fingering that can be confirmed as theirs (apart from profuse fingerings in Clementi's pedagogic publications[26]). Haydn inserted fingering in virtually none of his keyboard music[27] and Schubert inserted none at all that has been confirmed as his. But neither Haydn nor Schubert exhibited the pianistic skills or virtuosic flairs of Clementi, Mozart, and Beethoven.

According to a tabulation done for an earlier study,[28] Beethoven inserted about 300 fingerings (including recurrences in the same or similar passages) in his scores for piano and for the various stringed instruments. Some 120 of these appear in his piano scores. Understandably, the piano fingerings are the ones that reveal his most innovational techniques and interpretive effects. They turn up from the start to the end of his career in his sketches, autographs, supervised copies, earliest (presumably supervised) editions, and letters with revision lists. One of the early instances (1792 or earlier) is the experiment with two cross-over fingerings of trills in chromatic 6ths that was cited in Ex. 7/3 (p. 194), the first

25. According to Nohl/BEETHOVEN 74–75.

26. Tyson/CLEMENTI 125 says that Clementi only supervised Vol. VI of Breitkopf & Härtel's publication of the 17 vols. in his *Oeuvres complettes*. Warm thanks are owing to Sandra Rosenblum for further information about Clementi's fingering.

27. Cf. Christa Landon's preface to her 3-vol. ed. of Haydn's *Sämtliche Klaviersonaten* I xix.

28. Newman/FINGERINGS 172.

of which he labelled "difficult" and the second "not possible to do with the [indicated] fingering." And late instances occur in 1826 in his two-piano transcription Op. 134, of his "Grosse Fuge" for String Quartet, Op. 133 (as in Ex. 10/11, below).

Some Specific Technical and Interpretive Clues

Apparently, nearly half of Beethoven's fingerings are intended to alleviate technical difficulties, whether to suggest unusual solutions or simply to enable greater physical agility. But in Chapter 7 we also saw such fingerings disclosing his intended realizations of numerous trills, including both starting notes and suffixes. And in the present chapter we find them serving as good clues to intended legato. For a sample of a legato clue, a fingering from the left-hand staff of the *Primo* part in Op. 134 suggests a way to shift without a break between one hand coverage and the next (Ex. 10/11). To be sure, a fair number of Beethoven's technical fingerings seem obvious to the point of being gratuitous. These occur mostly in those pedagogic pieces, where every note throughout entire passages is likely to be fingered. But there are more difficult passages that justify this sort of fingering, as in the finale of the Fourth Concerto Op. 58 (Ex. 10/12). In these the fingering is needed to accommodate the different hand-and-finger positions that each four-note figure requires.

EXAMPLE 10/11 From the *Primo*, left hand, of the "Grosse Fuge," Op. 134/380–81 for four hands, two pianos (after BEETHOVEN WERKEM VII/1 67; HV*)

EXAMPLE 10/12 Fourth Concerto Op. 58/iii/45–48 (after a sketch among 5 pp. of "Fingersatzstudien und Skizzen" in GRASNICK 32m [cf. BEETHOVEN STAATSBIBLIOTHEK 111], as transcribed in MT XXXV [1894] 597)

N.B.–ist zu bemerken
dass der Daumen
oder erster Finger
sogleich untergesetzt wird

EXAMPLE 10/13 Variations for Cello and Piano on "See the Conqu'ring Hero Comes" WoO 45/iii/1–2 (after BEETHOVEN WERKEM V/3 140; HV*)

Insofar as practical, Beethoven seems to have favored consistent fingering for repeated or similar figures. In fact, in one brief sketch he adds this note to a diminished-7th arpeggio on *b* that he fingers 1–2–3–4 in each octave: "N.B.: in wide-ranged or extended passages [use] the same fingering as far as possible."[29] He did just that, for instance, in the Sonata Op. 101/iii/248–51. He alternated 1–4, 2–5 consistently, regardless of variations in the right hand's rising and falling successions of 4ths. Therefore, it is reasonable to assume that the pattern 3–2–4–1 over the first four-note group in Ex. 10/13 (from the right-hand piano part in the Variations for Cello and Piano WoO 45) is meant to serve each of the rising, sequential groups.

When Beethoven did use inconsistent fingering, he usually had a reason, either technical or interpretive. One such reason was a demonstrable indecision on his part as to the use of the thumb on a black key. Couperin, Emanuel Bach, Türk, and even Clementi had explicitly eschewed this use; Hummel and Czerny were among the first to accept it to any extent.[30] An example of Beethoven's indecision may be seen in Ex. 10/14 by comparing the similar passages from two early sketches. Later he seems to have preferred the thumb on a black key, as in the Sonata Op. 110/ii/71, where his use of 4 on the first right-hand note makes 1 almost imperative on the *a*♭. For that matter, in several places he provided a

29. Sketch 699 in Schmidt/BEETHOVENHANDSCHRIFTEN.

30. E.g., cf. Couperin/L'ART 63, Bach/VERSUCH I 22 and 33, Türk/KLAVIERSCHULE 131–32, Clementi/INTRODUCTION 49, Hummel/ANWEISUNG 310, Czerny/SCHOOL II 3.

EXAMPLE 10/14 Two early sketches, (a) after Johnson/FISCHHOFm II 63, folio 30r-11; and (b) after KAFKA SKETCHBOOK II 37 (BL*)

EXAMPLE 10/15 Sonata Op. 28/iv/205 and 208 (after Starke/PIANO-FORTE II 63)

choice of fingerings, as in Ex. 10/15 from the finale of the Sonata Op. 28,[31] where Beethoven probably wanted to allow for smaller hands, or in the Sonata Op. 90/ii/132, where he simply provided a choice between equals.

At other times Beethoven seems to have been inconsistent for interpretive reasons. Thus, as Jeanne Bamberger has argued persuasively,[32] he seems to have fingered the successive 4ths in the "Menuetto" of the Sonata Op. 2/1 not consistently as he did those cited above in Op. 101/iii, but irregularly in order to implement their irregular slurs and dynamic peak (Ex. 10/16).

31. The fingering in Ex. 10/15 appears only in the publication of Starke/PIANOFORTE II 63; a note by Starke on p. 56 says "The fingering is by himself [i.e., Beethoven]."

32. Bamberger/FINGERINGS 250–54.

EXAMPLE 10/16 Sonata Op. 2/1/iii/60–62 (after BEETHOVEN WERKEm VII/2/I 11; HV*)

EXAMPLE 10/17 Piano Trio Op. 70/2/iv/151–52 (after Raphael & Klugmann/TRIOsmm II 72; HV*)

Beethoven's fingering generally includes more notes in one span or grasp of the hand when large rather than small intervals predominate in a passage (as suggested, respectively, in Exx. 10/11 and 10/17). Ex. 10/17, from the finale of his Piano Trio Op. 70/2/iv, shows his marked inclination not only to finger in small segments but to emphasize the use of fingers 1, 2, and 3, with frequent, quick passing-under of the thumb, and rapid arm shifts to transfer the hand to each new hand position.[33]

Indeed, this practice ties in with the closed-hand position and tightly rounded fingers that were mentioned so often by his contemporaries. One recalls the pertinent advice about fingering in his letter of 1817 to Czerny about Karl's instruction. Passages like that in Ex. 10/17 require very quick shifting of the thumb when it alternates with any other fingers, if their indicated speed is to be attained smoothly. Below a similar passage (from a sketch for the finale of the Fourth Concerto) Beethoven wrote, "It should be noted that the thumb or, [that is,] first finger [must be] put under at once."[34]

Beethoven's fingerings of scales and arpeggios remind us that he was no slave to pedagogic rules. He used the standard fingerings on occasion, but he also mixed in other solutions—for instance, 1–2–1–2 or 1–2–3–4 1–2–3–4 in both diatonic and chromatic scales—evidently to tally with or even accent particular rhythmic groupings.[35] In such alternatives he came closer to the older, optional solutions offered by Emanuel Bach and Türk than to the single prescriptions that were to be offered by Hummel and Czerny.[36] However, he seems only infrequently to have crossed 3 over 4 on white keys, as Bach and Türk still had done.

33. Beethoven regarded the fingering in Ex. 10/17 as important enough to add it in a letter of 1809 to Breitkopf & Härtel (Anderson/BEETHOVEN I 232).

34. The sketch is found in the manuscript Grasnick 32m, which contains 5 pp. that have been labelled "Fingersatzstudien und Skizzen" (BEETHOVEN-JAHRBUCH VI item 58; BEETHOVEN STAATSBIBLIOTHEK 111); it is transcribed in MT XXXV (1894) 597 and used here as Ex. 10/12, above.

35. Samples of these alternatives occur in the "Fingersatzstudien" cited in the previous fn.

36. Cf. Bach/VERSUCH I 24–34, Türk/KLAVIERSCHULE 146–56, Hummel/ANWEISUNG 172–78, Czerny/SCHOOL II 1–28.

EXAMPLE 10/18 *Secondo* part of the Waldstein Variations for four hands at one piano WoO 67/vi/7 (after BEETHOVEN WERKEM VII/1 11; HV*)

(Andante con moto)

EXAMPLE 10/19 From the Variations on "Es war einmal ein alter Mann"
WoO 66/ix/8–9 (after BEETHOVEN WERKEM VII/5 37; HV*)

The two-note stepwise slide by the same finger occurs often enough
among his fingerings for it to qualify as another of his technical preferences. In order to achieve a legato over a wide left-hand stretch he called
for two successive slides in the sixth of the "Waldstein" Variations for
four hands, WoO 67 (Ex. 10/18).[37] Related to the slide is another ingenious means of achieving legato found among Beethoven's fingerings. In
the ninth of the Variations on "Es war einmal ein alter Mann" WoO 66,
he rounds off a short downward arpeggio in the left hand in a graceful
manner by crossing 4 over 5 (Ex. 10/19).[38] Also ingenious is his way of
insuring the opposite touch, staccato, when one hand must make way for
the immediate repetition of the same note by the other. This situation
occurs in the second of the Variations Op. 34 (Ex. 10/20), where Beethoven's use of 5 on *d'* forces a jump over what surely will be 1 on the
previous right-hand key. The jump insures that the first *f'* will make way
for the second.

As resourceful as they are, some of Beethoven's fingerings reveal less

37. Cf., also, Op. 96/iv/81–84 and 88–92.

38. Cf., also, Opp. 28/ii/31 as fingered in Starke/PIANOFORTE II 57 (4 over 3) and 106/i/
96–97 (5 over 1).

EXAMPLE 10/20 Variations Op. 34/ii/21, after BEETHOVEN WERKEM
VII/5 136 (by permission of G. Henle Verlag)

of a rationale than might be expected. Thus, his fingerings for the parallel scalewise passages in the Trio WoO 39/27–32 and 78–83 offer neither any consistency of pattern or uniformity between the hands (such as coinciding uses of the thumbs), nor any evident interpretive justification. But his intentions may simply escape us today. All pianists who have tried his detailed fingering for the right hand's alternating octaves in the Sonata Op. 2/2/i/84–85 (also 88–89, 303–304, and 307–308) must have wondered why he did not let the left hand take the first note of each triplet. As with the long runs mentioned earlier, the advantages of ease and strength to be gained by such divisions are obvious. If Beethoven did not reject them because he enjoyed the display of virtuosity that his present fingering encourages (cf. the similar but even more difficult passage in Ex. 10/28, below), then perhaps he believed he could control the passage more evenly by leaving it all in one hand (as with that long run in Ex. 10/8, above).

Beethoven left relatively few fingerings for repeated notes, partly, no doubt, because he wrote series of repeated notes so infrequently. In both slow and fast music, when he did finger them, his usual preference was for changing fingers, as between 1 and 2 on *a* in the Sonata Op. 28/ii/10 (until 5 is required in m. 11).[39]

Implementing Articulation of Touches and Ideas

The aspect of interpretation for which Beethoven's fingering provides clues most tangibly is the articulation of his musical ideas. That is, by suggesting, if not determining, legato or staccato touches at strategic points, the fingering also suggests the connections or separations of ideas. To illustrate the determination of touch, one remarkable, further indication of legato may be quoted, from another early sketch (Ex. 10/21). In that sketch the finger slides are the surest clues and the musical idea is simply one segment of a chromatic scale. The segment rises four times, each of the last three rises being covered by a slur and "the last [of them is played the] softest" (as an appended note by Beethoven reads). At the second rise, the slur and the two successive finger slides, replacing four

39. This fingering is found only in Starke/PIANOFORTE II 56.

EXAMPLE 10/21 An early sketch, folio 39v-15, in KAFKA SKETCHBOOK II 187 (by permission of the British Library)

EXAMPLE 10/22 Bagatelle Op. 126/1/36–37 (after Brendel/KLAVIER-
STÜCKEM 99; EA*)

individual fingers, create a super legato not unlike the velvety, slithering
sort identified later with the Chopin style.

Beethoven had still other ways of implementing legato through fingering. In Ex. 10/22, from the left hand of the Bagatelle Op. 126/1, he
ends the first measure not on 5 but by passing the thumb under, evidently so that the line can continue unbroken past the tie. In Ex. 10/23,
from the last of the "Diabelli" Variations, Op. 120, right hand, he chooses
the one fingering that leads legato and most conveniently into every tone
of the chord. And in Ex. 10/24, from the twenty-first of those same variations, left hand, he helps to confirm that the characteristic slur–tie–slur
of Classic editing (see p. 127) actually means one over-all legato slur,
when he implies a transfer from 4 to 1 on the tied note. Moreover, in the
sixth of those same variations, at m. 17, he changes fingers on the same
key (d″), presumably to make its two surrounding trills belong to the same
rising line. In another early sketch (which also implies his fingering 4–
3–2–3 for a four-note turn), he illustrates and explains the change on a

EXAMPLE 10/23 "Diabelli" Variations, Op. 120/xxxiii/24 (1.) (after
BEETHOVEN WERKEM VII/5 237; HV*)

EXAMPLE 10/24 "Diabelli" Variations Op. 120/xxi/6 (after BEETHOVEN
WERKEM VII/5 222; HV*)

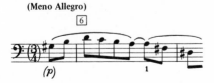

EXAMPLE 10/25 An early sketch, transcribed from folio 39v-1/3 in KAFKA SKETCHBOOK II 186 (BL*; also transcribed in Nottebohm/ZWEITE 363 staff 3)

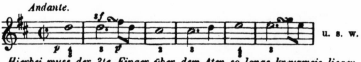

Hierbei muss der 3te Finger über dem 4ten so lange kreuzweis liegen, bis dieser wegzieht und alsdann der 3te an seine Stelle kömmt.

single key: "Here the third finger must lie across the fourth until the latter withdraws and the third takes its place" (Ex. 10/25).

Just as some of Beethoven's fingerings implement legato, others serve to disconnect notes in varying degrees. An intriguing instance is his request for successive thumbs to force partial detachments within several two-note slurs. This occurs during the close of his accompaniment to the song "Aus Goethes Faust" Op. 75/3/80 (Ex. 10/26). Another instance worth quoting occurs near the opening of the "Lebewohl" Sonata Op. 81a, where

EXAMPLE 10/26 "Aus Goethes Faust" Op. 75/3/80 (upper staff in the accompaniment); after BEETHOVEN GESAMTAUSGABEm XXIII/219 11

EXAMPLE 10/27 Sonata Op. 81a/i/5 (after Wallner/KLAVIERSONATENmm II 179; HV*)

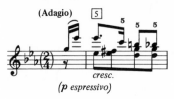

EXAMPLE 10/28 An early sketch (after KAFKA SKETCHBOOK II 230 folio 89v-7/4; BL*)

mit der Hand geworfen.

his use of 5 on three successive upstem notes distinctly changes the effect that the connected fingering 5–4–3 would have provided (Ex. 10/27). A crisp staccato is insured by his fingering of alternating octaves with 2–4 in a sketch cited above (Ex. 10/28). As Beethoven's annotation adds, "[It should be played] with the hand flung [*geworfen*]."

A Special Case—the Repeated-Note Slur Misnamed "Bebung"

A special case that involves two notes on the same pitch, sometimes with an exchange of fingers indicated, is the pair of slurred notes still often called by the familiar misnomer "Bebung." It is cited especially in the slow movements of the sonatas Op. 110 (see Ex. 8/10, p. 238) and Op. 106 (see Ex. 8/21, p. 248), and in the "Scherzo" of the Sonata for Piano and Cello Op. 69 (Ex. 10/29), all fingered 4–3 by Beethoven.[40] Among presumed examples without his fingerings are those in the "Pastoral" Sonata Op. 28/i (Ex. 10/30) and in the "Grosse Fuge," Op. 134 (Ex. 10/31).

The term preferred here for that phenomenon is "repeated-note slur," though with no intention of begging the chief question that the phenomenon has raised. That question is whether the second note is sounded

40. But in Op. 106/iii the same measure is fingered 1–2 in the first London edition, presumably based on a different source copy.

Example 10/29 Sonata for Piano and Cello Op. 69/ii/1–6 (after beethoven werkem V/3 82; HV*)

Example 10/30 Sonata Op. 28/i/136–42 (after beethoven werkem VII/3/II 33; HV*)

EXAMPLE 10/31 "Grosse Fuge" Op. 134/28–32 (after BEETHOVEN-WERKEm VII/1 49; HV*)

individually or is literally tied—in other words, whether the second note is to be heard as such or not. We have no statement from Beethoven. Nor do we know what he may have answered orally when Karl Holz asked him, in a Conversation book of early 1826, to explain this notation as it appears in Op. 133 (from which Beethoven transcribed Op. 134): "Why did you write two 8th-notes instead of 1/4 [quoting m. 26, which is m. 28 in Op. 134]?"[41] But we do know that Beethoven continued to retain those slurred pairs, even after Anton Halm also asked him about them, this time in reference to Op. 134.[42]

The question of whether the second note is to be sounded or not has often been discussed[43] and as often confused by the misidentification with "Bebung." But this supposed link with "Bebung," which continues to crop up in the 20th century along with related terms like "undulating tremolo,"[44] gets no support in any historical, theoretical, or practical document of past clavichord technology or performance. Nor for that matter does it find support in any document by Beethoven or his contemporaries that is known here. The term "Bebung" seems not to have been related to Beethoven's repeated-note slurs before 1871, and then not with any factual justification, but as a felt sensation.[45]. Schenker still subscribed to it when he came to Op. 110/iii/5.[46] In that work he asked that the effect of the clavichord's *Bebung* be approximated by not actually playing the second note, instead feeling the slurred pair of notes psychologically

41. KONVERSATIONSHEFTE VIII 243.

42. Platen/AUFFÜHRUNGSPRAXIS 104–105, from a Conversation Book not yet published in KONVERSATIONSHEFTE as of July, 1986. Only distantly related is the discussion in Platen/NOTIERUNGSPROBLEM of Beethoven's multiple slurred repeated notes that mark graduated dynamics (as mentioned in Chapter 8).

43. E.g., cf. Schenker/LETZTEN (110) 63–72, Grundman & Mies 126–31, Bamberger/FINGERINGS 246–49, Newman/FINGERINGS 186–88, all with further references.

44. Cf. the helpful D.M.A. study Beers/BEBUNG 41 and 48 (citing W. Apel!).

45. Tappert/KLAVIERSONATEN 339–40.

46. Schenker/ORNAMENTIK 72 and Schenker/LETZTEN(110) 63–72. The latter is a detailed, valuable discussion, in spite of Schenker's typically vituperative remarks in his disagreements with Bülow and Riemann. Bamberger/FINGERINGS 246–49 endorses Schenker's psychological interpretation.

as if sung, bowed, or blown. Because he viewed these pairs as syncopations, he was compelled to rationalize the last nine of them, which apparently are meant to start on rather than off the beat, as strokes of genius that contribute to the larger design of rise and fall in measure 5. (My "apparently" refers to Schenker's interpretation of Beethoven's faulty calculation of the note values in that measure.)

There can be no question about the larger rise and fall in measure 5, what with Beethoven's explicit markings and his notated *accelerando*. Otherwise, I believe that there is a much simpler, more characteristic, and more musical explanation for his repeated-note slurs. I believe that these represent no more nor less than the primordial, two-note, masculine groupings discussed in Chapter 6—that is, what Momigny called masculine cadences, or the lowest level in the hierarchic structure that includes the incise and the phrase. With this interpretation go the main traits of the masculine grouping, especially the flow from arsis to thesis, or strong to weak, regardless of the metric position. In the repeated-note slurs, that flow may be thought of as a process of initiation and release that occurs virtually in one motion, almost as if produced by one bow or one breath. That is, it may be thought of as holding the first of the two notes right into the second, and playing the second only as an audible, but barely audible, release. This flow happens to be the very one supposedly recommended by Beethoven for pairs of two different notes under single slurs (in the annotation over Cramer's Etude 29 that was quoted earlier in this chapter).

There are several further arguments that favor that interpretation of an initiation and release in virtually one motion. First is the change of fingers on the same key, which was not likely to have been made purely for psychological reasons, as has been argued. We have seen that Beethoven's notation does exhibit pronounced psychological associations, surely unconscious on his part. But they hardly apply to his conscious fingering of 4–3 over his three main uses of repeated-note slurs in his piano music. We have also seen that Beethoven was an eminently practical musician, not given to subtle psychological ruses to gain his ends. As any experienced pianist knows, there is a practical reason for the change of fingers on the same key in the repeated-note slur. It can come closer to that ideal single motion of initiation-release than a repetition by the same finger. A small but not irrelevant argument, concerned with the masculine cadence, is the hairpin diminish sign that Holz included when he illustrated his question to Beethoven about the repeated-note slur in Op. 133. That sign indicates a dynamic direction that is consistent with the strong-weak motion of the masculine cadence.

Further arguments include a brief but unequivocal instruction by Czerny concerning the "Scherzo" of Op. 69:

EXAMPLE 10/32 Sonata for Piano and Cello Op. 69/ii/1–6, as edited by Czerny (after Badura-Skoda/CZERNY 82; EA*)

The slurs in the right hand and the fingering over them mean something quite unusual. The second, or slurred, note is to be sounded again, by the third finger, so that the passage goes approximately as follows [Ex. 10/32]—that is, [play] the first note (with the fourth finger) very *tenuto* and the other (with the third finger) crisply staccato and less prominently. And so on. Thus, the fourth finger must play and then make way for the third.[47]

In that same movement another argument is that the repeated-note slurs relate directly to further two-note slurs in which the second notes must sound because they move to a different pitch (Ex. 10/33).

Lastly, Tovey offers what he calls "trustworthy evidence" that the second notes of Beethoven's unfingered, repeated-note slurs are to be sounded.[48] He gets it from an early edition by the Englishman Cipriani Potter, who had known Beethoven. In that edition a dot-under-dash appears over each second note in Op. 28/i so as to insure that that note is sounded. A tentative confirmation of Tovey's argument might be seen in the right-hand staccato in the last measure of Ex. 10/30 (though Tovey's edition does not have it). Belittling the *Bebung* analogy, Tovey did not hesitate to relate the unfingered slurs in Op. 28 to the fingered slurs in Opp. 69, 106, and 110.[49]

To all this hard evidence, ranging from respectable to tenuous, might be added a bit of circumstantial statistical evidence based not on documentation but on experienced musical judgments. Audible releases of

47. Badura-Skoda/CZERNY 82.

48. Tovey/BEETHOVENm II 68; cf. Grundmann & Mies 128–29.

49. Cf. Tovey/BEETHOVENm III 141 and 216.

EXAMPLE 10/33 Sonata for Piano and Cello Op. 69/ii/90–95 (after BEETHOVEN WERKEm; HV*)

the second notes in the repeated-note slurs are revealed in fourteen out of nineteen recently available recordings of Op. 106 and fourteen out of sixteen of Op. 110, though in only two out of ten in Op. 69.[50] Perhaps the high speed, with less opportunity for initiation-release motions, and the equivalent slurs without fingerings in the cello part, have worked against sounding the second notes in the repeated-note slurs of Op. 69.

Metric and Contrametric Fingerings

In our discussion in Chapter 5 of metric and contrametric accents, certain seemingly perverse fingerings were saved for the present broader discussion of Beethoven's fingerings. Two examples should suffice to illustrate, in opposite ways, how Beethoven seems deliberately to have reinforced or opposed the natural accenting of the prevailing meter through his fingerings. In Ex. 10/34, from the finale of the Sonata Op.2/3, the fingering opposes the normal metric subdivisions of three eighth notes in ⅜ meter, but reinforces the pitch groupings of two eighth notes. Had he preferred to reinforce the normal metric subdivisions, Beethoven could have realized this fingering at least as well in groups of three eighth notes (as by 5–2, 3–1, 4–2), although he would not have been able to continue as consistently. In Ex. 10/35, from the finale of the Sonata Op. 78, the circumstances are reversed. Beethoven's fingering reinforces the metric

50. Cf. Newman/FINGERINGS 188; also, Kaiser/INTERPRETEN 598–600.

EXAMPLE 10/34 Sonata Op. 2/3/iv/269 (after BEETHOVEN WERKEm VII/2/I 66; HV*)

EXAMPLE 10/35 Sonata Op. 78/ii/116–18 (after Wallner/KLAVIER-SONATENmm II 168; HV*)

subdivisions of two sixteenth-note pairs in $\frac{2}{4}$ meter, but opposes the pitch groupings of three sixteenth-note pairs in each octave. This time, he could have realized the fingering at least as well in threes according to the pitch groupings—for instance, by 1/3–2/4–3/5. In my opinion, Beethoven did intend both the reinforcements and the oppositions implemented by those fingerings.

A FEW AFTERTHOUGHTS

*T*HROUGHOUT THIS BOOK the objective has been to retrieve Beethoven's intentions regarding the performance of his piano music while exploring the main facets of that performance, including its background, sources, instruments, tempo, articulation, syntax of incise and phrase, ornamentation, legato and pedalling among further expressive factors, macro perspectives, and pertinent problems of technique. Obviously, it has been impossible to exhaust these facets in one volume; it would be impossible to do so even if our ten chapters were expanded into ten separate volumes.

One reason, as we have seen repeatedly, is that those searches for authenticity so seldom lead to final answers. More often they lead only to conjectures, or—as suggested at the outset—only to educated guesses. And even after the performer manages to come up with an educated guess, certain imponderables still remain to be considered, such as the influence of contemporary tastes, or the special circumstances of a particular performance, or even Beethoven's sparkling flashes of creative genius that cause unpredictable departures from norms previously postulated.

Several of the chief topics discussed in those ten chapters have received too little, if any, attention previously. Among these topics are the probable validity of many of Schindler's observations on performance, notwithstanding his dishonored attempts to dress up his failing image; the clues to Beethoven's performance intentions that lie in his psychological notation; the trend toward critical editions that include authoritative interpretive aids and advices (clearly distinguished as such); Beethoven's lifelong allegiance to Viennese pianos as it bore upon his performance styles; tempo analogies between Beethoven's music with and without metronome markings, based on extensions of Beck's "rhythmic character"; and the identification, meaning, and function of Beethoven's various slurs and staccatos.

Other topics that have received little, if any, previous attention are the rhythmic grouping and dynamic direction that inhere in the incise and phrase as well as in their micro and macro equivalents in Beethoven's total structural hierarchies; the ascendancy of melodic over harmonic considerations in the realization of his trills and other ornaments; his innovative handling of legato, pedalling, dynamics, and still other expressive factors; the broader relationships within and between the movements of Beethoven's cycles; and his idiomatic keyboard techniques (especially his original fingerings) as potential indicators of his expressive intentions.

Finally, it seems worth restating briefly what have seemed to me to be certain essential, over-all approaches to "authentic" interpretation and to the intelligent application of our findings in Beethoven performance practices. These approaches are suggested as general attitudes that have been adopted in the preparation of this book and, it is hoped, that may prove helpful in the interpretation of Beethoven's piano music.

Be flexible and tolerant in your interpretations. The "educated guess" implies an awareness of about how flexible and how tolerant you can be without exceeding the bounds of what you will come to recognize as good Beethovian taste. Avoid the rigidity of uncompromising rules, as Beethoven himself reportedly did when the young Ferdinand Ries questioned parallel fifths in his C Minor String Quartet Op. 18. From Chapter 7, above, you may recall what Beethoven replied, in effect: "Who makes the rules!"

Do not scoff at the interpretations of another era, such as those of the late Romantics as revealed by their editing and the early recordings of their performances that have survived. (Recall Xaver Scharwenka's recording of the Sonata Op. 90, cited on p. 119). They were as sincere about their editing and playing as we are about ours today. It is not only the attitudes toward the interpreter's role but the very understanding of the music that is different. We tend to deplore the histrionics of a Karg-Elert or a MacDowell much as MacDowell deplored the very different "pretensions" of a Mozart (cf. Newman/SSB 759–60).

Think of Beethoven as an eminently practical musician in whatever concerned his performance intentions, and not as an irrational visionary. That approach helped here most recently in deciding how to treat Beethoven's "repeated-note slurs."

And think of Beethoven primarily as an innovator rather than as a traditionalist in his performance practices. Do not expect to find precedents for all that he did, either in theory or practice. That response, "Who makes the rules!" is only one of numerous reminders that he became his own man comparatively early in his maturing process, and that he did so with a fierce pride.

But with all these afterthoughts on the side of tolerance and flexibility of approach and with all Beethoven's presagings of the imminent Romanticism, do bear in mind that this master was still a product of the Classic Era in music. He was still the musical offspring of Haydn and Mozart. He was still direct and honest in his musical speech, sometimes even austere in his slow movements and severe in his fast movements. Whoever is inclined to become too free in the interpretation of Beethoven needs to return to such curbing remarks by him as that significant reproach after a performance by Czerny (Chapter 3, above): " . . . you must forgive a composer who would rather have heard a work performed exactly as written, however beautifully you played it in other respects."

Above all, it should be self-evident, if not axiomatic, to restate that any interpretation can be valid only when it proves to be *musically* convincing to performer and hearer alike. Put differently, no performance of Beethoven's piano music can be successful until the pianist's musical sensibilities can be brought to terms with Beethoven's intentions. Only then can one really speak of "playing his piano music *his* way."

BIBLIOGRAPHY

NOTE: All sources cited by short titles in this book, music scores as well as literature, are included in this one bibliography. The bibliography does not include occasional citations that bear only incidentally on this book's topic. A lower-case "m" is added to short titles of publications that consist predominantly of music.

Adam/MÉTHODE—Louis Adam, *Méthode de piano* (Paris, 1805; originally 1802). Geneva: Minkoff, 1974, facsimile reprint.

Adam/PRINCIPE—Louis Adam, *Méthode ou principe général du doigté pour le forté-piano.* Paris: Sieber, [1798?].

Ahlgrimm/BAROCKE—Isolde Ahlgrimm, "Barocke Tradition bei Beethoven," in BEETHOVEN-ALMANACH 156–68.

Albrecht/KEIL—Hans Albrecht (ed.), *Die Bedeutung der Zeichen: Keil, Strich[,] und Punkt bei Mozart . . . fünf Lösungen einer Preisfrage*, by Hermann Keller, Hubert Unverricht, Oswald Jonas, Albert Kreutz, and Ewald Zimmermann. Kassel: Bärenreiter, 1957. Cf. Mies/ARTIKULATIONSZEICHEN.

Albrechtsberger/ANWEISUNG—Johann Georg Albrechtsberger, *Gründliche Anweisung zur Komposition.* Leipzig: J. G. I. Breitkopf, 1790.

Allanbrook/GESTURE—Wye Jamison Allanbrook, *Rhythmic Gesture in Mozart: Le Nozze di Figaro and Don Giovanni.* Chicago: University of Chicago Press, 1983. Cf. the review in the *Journal of Musicology* IV [1985–86] 535–38.

Altmann/CONCERTOSm—Wilhelm Altmann (ed.), *Five Piano Concertos by Ludwig van Beethoven,* with his own cadenzas; miniature scores, Edition Eulenberg. London: Soho Press, 1933–35.

Altmann/FEHLER—Gustav Altmann, "Ein Fehler in Beethoven erster Violin-Sonate," in *Die Musik* XI/13 (1912) 28–29.

AMZ—*Allgemeine musikalische Zeitung,* 3 series: 1798–1848, 1863–1865, 1866–1882.

Anderson/BEETHOVEN—Emily Anderson (ed. and trans.), *The Letters of Beethoven,* 3 vols. New York: W. W. Norton, 1985.

Anderson/MOZART—Emily Anderson (ed. and trans.), *The Letters of Mozart and His Family,* 2d ed., 2 vols. New York: St. Martin's Press, 1966.

Angermüller/METRONOMS—Rudolf Angermüller, "Aus der Frühgeschichte des Metronoms: Die Beziehungen zwischen Mälzel und Salieri," in ÖMZ XXVI (1971) 134–40.

Arnold & Fortune/BEETHOVEN—Denis Arnold and Nigel Fortune (eds.), *The Beethoven Reader.* New York: W. W. Norton, 1971.

Babitz/ERRORS—Sol Babitz, "Modern Errors in Beethoven Performance," in CONGRESS BONN 1970 pp. 327–31.

Bach/ESSAY—Carl Philipp Emanuel Bach, *Essay on the True Art of Playing Keyboard Instruments*, translated (from Bach/VERSUCH and its 1787 ed.) and edited by William J. Mitchell. New York: W. W. Norton, 1949.

Bach/VERSUCH—Carl Philipp Emanuel Bach, *Versuch über die wahre Art das Clavier zu Spielen*, 2 vols., facs. of the original editions of 1753 and 1762, ed. by Lothar Hoffmann Erbrecht. Leipzig: Breitkopf & Härtel, 1957.

Badura-Skoda/CZERNY—Paul Badura-Skoda (ed.), *Carl Czerny, Über den richtigen Vortrag der sämtlichen Beethoven'schen Klavierwerke*. Vienna: Universal, 1963.

Badura-Skoda/MOZART—Eva and Paul Badura-Skoda, *Interpreting Mozart on the Keyboard*. New York: St. Martin's Press, 1962.

Badura-Skoda/OP 106—Paul Badura-Skoda, "Noch einmal zur Frage Ais oder A in der Hammerklavier-Sonate Op. 106 von Beethoven," in HENLE GEDENKSCHRIFT 53–81; English translation prepared for PQ (1986?) by Frank E. Kirby.

Badura-Skoda/PERFORMANCE—"Performance Conventions in Beethoven's Early Works," in CONGRESS DETROIT 1977 52–76.

Badura-Skoda/QUELLE—Paul Badura-Skoda, "Eine wichtige Quelle zu Beethovens 4. Klavierkonzert," in ÖMZ XIII (1958) 418–27.

Badura-Skoda/TEXTPROBLEME—Paul Badura-Skoda, "Textprobleme in Beethovens Hammerklaviersonate Op. 106," in *Melos* III (1977) 11–14.

Badura-Skoda & Demus—Paul Badura-Skoda and Jörg Demus, *Die Klaviersonaten von Ludwig van Beethoven*. Wiesbaden: Brockhaus, 1970.

Baker/KOCH—Nancy K. Baker, *Heinrich Christoph Koch: Introductory Essay on Composition—The Mechanical Rules of Melody, Sections 3 and 4*, translated, with an introduction, by Nancy Kovaleff Baker. New Haven: Yale University Press, 1983.

Baker/MELODY—Nancy K. Baker, "Heinrich Koch and the Theory of Melody," in *Journal of Music Theory* XX (1976) 1–48.

Bamberger/FINGERINGS—Jeanne Bamberger, "The Musical Significance of Beethoven's Fingerings in the Piano Sonatas," in *Music Forum* IV (1976) 237–80.

Banowetz/PEDALING—Joseph Banowetz, *The Pianist's Guide to Pedaling*. Bloomington: Indiana University Press, 1985.

Basart/FORTEPIANO—Ann P. Basart, *The Sound of the Fortepiano—A Discography of Early Pianos*. Berkeley: Fallen Leaf Press, 1985.

Bauer & Deutsch/MOZART—W. A. Bauer & O. E. Deutsch (eds.), *Mozart: Briefe und Aufzeichnungen*, 7 vols. Kassel: Bärenreiter, 1962–75.

Beck/BEMERKUNGEN—Hermann Beck, "Bemerkungen zu Beethovens Tempi," in *Beethoven-Jahrbuch* (3d series) II (1955–56), pp. 24–54.

Beck/PROPORTIONEN—Hermann Beck, "Die Proportionen der Beethovenschen Tempi," in *Festschrift Walter Gerstenberg zum 60. Geburtstag* (Wolfenbüttel: Möseler, 1964) 6–16.

Beck/TEMPOPROBLEM—Hermann Beck, "Studien über das Tempoproblem bei Beethoven," unpub. diss., University of Erlangen, 1954.

Beck & Herre/CRAMER—Dagmar Beck and Grita Herre, "Anton Schindlers 'Nutzanwendung' der Cramer-Etüden," preliminary typed manuscript (kindly sent in 1985 by Professor Harry Goldschmidt) of article projected for pub. in full in Goldschmidt/BEETHOVEN III.

Beck & Herre/SCHINDLER—Dagmar Beck and Grita Herre, "Anton Schindlers fingierte Eintragungen in den Konversationsheften," in Goldschmidt/BEETHOVEN 11–89.

Beechey/RHYTHMIC—"Rhythmic Interpretation: Mozart, Beethoven, Schubert and Schumann," in MR XXXIII (1972) 233–48.

Beers/BEBUNG—Deborah Yardley Beers, *"Bebung* in Beethoven?" unpub. D.M.A. thesis, draft version, University of Colorado, 1982.

BEETHOVEN-ALMANACH—*Beethoven-Almanach 1970.* Vienna: Elisabeth Lafite, 1970.

BEETHOVEN CADENZASm—*Ludwig van Beethoven: The Complete Cadenzas,* facsimiles of the autographs, ed. by Willy Hess, with a preface (and a faulty translation). Zürich: Eulenburg, 1979.

BEETHOVEN GESAMTAUSGABEm—*L. van Beethoven's Werke,* 25 Series, including Supplement. Leipzig: Breitkopf & Härtel, 1864–67 and '87.

BEETHOVEN-JAHRBUCH—*Beethoven-Jahrbuch,* 3d series. Bonn: Beethovenhaus, 1953–54—.

BEETHOVEN-KOLLOQUIUM 1977—*Beethoven Kolloquium 1977 Dokumentation und Aufführungspraxis,* ed. by Rudolf Klein. Kassel: Bärenreiter, 1978.

BEETHOVEN OP. 26m—*As-dur Sonate, Op. 26, von Ludwig van Beethoven,* facsimile of the holograph of 1801, ed. by Erich Prieger. Bonn: Friedrich Cohen, 1895.

BEETHOVEN OP. 27/2m—*Sonata quasi una fantasia, "Mondschein," Op. 27, no. 2,* facsimile of the autograph, ed. by Keisei Sakka. Tokyo: Ongaku No Tomo Sha, 1970.

BEETHOVEN OP. 30/3m—*Ludwig van Beethoven, Violin Sonata in G Major, Op. 30, No. 3, Facsimile of the autograph manuscript in the British Library Add. MS 37767,* introduction by Alan Tyson. London: The British Library, 1980.

BEETHOVEN OP. 53m—*Ludwig van Beethoven, Klaviersonate in C-dur, Op. 53 (Waldsteinsonate),* facsimile of the autograph, ed. by Dagmar Weise. Bonn: Beethovenhaus, l954.

BEETHOVEN OP. 57m—*Ludwig van Beethoven/Klaviersonate F-moll Opus 57 im Faksimile der Urschrift.* Leipzig: Peters, [1970].

BEETHOVEN OP. 69m—*Ludwig van Beethoven, Sonata for Violoncello and Pianoforte, Opus 69, first movement only, facsimile of the autograph,* with introduction by Lewis Lockwood. New York: Columbia University Press, 1970.

BEETHOVEN OP. 78m—*Sonata, Op. 78, Ludwig van Beethoven,* facsimile of the autograph. Munich: Drei Masken Verlag, 1923.

BEETHOVEN OP. 79m—Ludwig van Beethoven, Sonata Op. 79, facsimile of the autograph at the Beethoven-Haus in Bonn.

BEETHOVEN OP. 81m—Ludwig van Beethoven, first movement of Sonata Op. 81a, facsimile of the autograph at the Gesellschaft der Musikfreunde in Vienna.

BEETHOVEN OP. 90m—Ludwig van Beethoven, Sonata Op. 90, facsimile of the autograph (privately held).

BEETHOVEN OP. 96m—*Ludwig van Beethoven: Sonate für Klavier und Violine G-Dur Opus 96,* facsimile of the autograph in the Pierpont Morgan Library, with "final note" by Martin Staehelin. Munich: G. Henle, 1977.

BEETHOVEN OP. 98m—*Ludwig van Beethoven: An die ferne Geliebte,* Op. 98, facsimile of the autograph. Munich: G. Henle Verlag, 1970.

BEETHOVEN OP. 101m—Ludwig van Beethoven, Sonata Op. 101, facsimile of the autograph (privately held).

BEETHOVEN OP. 109m—*Sonate für das Hammerklavier von L. v. Beethoven,* facsimile of autograph ed. by Oswald Jonas. New York: Robert Owen Lehmann Foundation, 1965.

BEETHOVEN OP. 110m—Karl Michael Komma (ed.), *Die Klaviersonate As-Dur Opus 110 von Ludwig van Beethoven,* Faksimile-Ausgabe [and Beihefte], 2 vols. Stuttgart: Ichthys Verlag, 1967.

BEETHOVEN OP. 111m—*Ludwig van Beethoven: Klaviersonate in C-moll, Op. 111*, facsimile of holograph. Leipzig: C. F. Peters, 1952.

BEETHOVEN OP. 120m—Ludwig van Beethoven, "Diabelli" Variations Op. 120, facsimile of the autograph (privately held).

BEETHOVEN SKETCHBOOKS—Douglas Johnson (ed.), Alan Tyson, and Robert Winter, *The Beethoven Sketchbooks, History—Reconstruction—Inventory.* Berkeley: University of California Press, 1985.

BEETHOVEN STAATSBIBLIOTHEK—*Die Beethoven-Sammlung in der Musikabteilung der Deutschen Staatsbibliothek,* ed. by Eveline Bartlitz. Berlin: Deutsche Staatsbibliothek, 1970.

BEETHOVEN STUDIES—*Beethoven Studies,* ed. by Alan Tyson, 3 vols. (to 1982). New York: W. W. Norton, 1973 (Vol. I); London: Oxford University Press, 1977 (Vol. II); Cambridge: Cambridge University Press, 1982 (Vol. III).

BEETHOVEN SUPPLEMENTEm—Willy Hess (ed.), *Beethoven: Supplemente zur Gesamtausgabe,* 14 vols. Wiesbaden: Breitkopf & Härtel, 1959–71.

BEETHOVEN-SYMPOSION—*Beethoven Symposion Wien 1970,* ed. by Erich Schenk. Vienna: Hermann Böhlaus, 1971.

BEETHOVEN WERKEm—Joseph Schmidt-Görg and others (eds.), *Beethoven Werke,* projected in 14 series; 20 vols. as of Jan. 1987. Munich: G. Henle Verlag, 1959–.

Berg/IDEEN—Conrad Berg, *Ideen zu einer rationellen Lehrmethode für Musiklehrer überhaupt mit besonderer Anwendung auf das Clavierspiel.* Mainz: B. Schott's Söhnen, 1826.

Beyschlag/ORNAMENTIK—Adolf Beyschlag, *Die Ornamentik der Musik.* Leipzig: Breitkopf & Härtel, 1908.

Bilson/BEETHOVEN—Malcolm Bilson, "Beethoven and the Piano," in *Clavier* XXII (Oct. 1983) 18–21.

Brandenburg/OP. 96m—Sieghard Brandenburg, "Bemerkungen zu Beethovens Op. 96," in BEETHOVEN-JAHRBUCH IX (1973–77) 7–25.

Brandenburg/TAKTVORSCHRIFTEN—Sieghard Brandenburg, "Über die Bedeutung der Änderungen von Taktvorschriften in einigen Werken Beethovens," in BEETHOVEN-KOLLOQUIUM 1977 37–51.

Braun/RECORDED—Joachim Braun, "Beethoven's Fourth Symphony: Comparative Analysis of Recorded Performances," in *Israel Studies in Musicology* I (1978) 54–76.

Brendel/KLAVIERSTÜCKEm—Alfred Brendel (ed.), *Beethoven: Klavierstücke.* Vienna: Universal, 1968.

Breuning/SCHWARZSPANIERHAUSE—Gerhard von Breuning, *Aus dem Schwarzspanierhause, Erinnerungen an Ludwig van Beethoven aus meiner Jugendzeit* (Vienna, 1874), with additions and annotations by Alfred Christlieb Kalischer (Berlin, 1907), facsimile reprint. Hildesheim: Georg Olms, 1970.

Brown/HAYDN'S—A. Peter Brown, *Joseph Haydn's Keyboard Music—Sources and Style.* Bloomington: Indiana University Press, 1986.

Brown/SCHUBERT—A. Peter Brown, "Performance Tradition, Proportional Tempo, and Schubert's Symphonies" (1984), scheduled in 1986 for pub., with revisions, in *Journal of Musicology.*

Bülow & Lebert/BEETHOVEN—Hans von Bülow & Sigmund Lebert (eds.), *Beethoven: [32] Sonatas for Pianoforte Solo,* with translations by Theodore Baker and biographical sketch by Philip Hale, 2 vols. New York: G. Schirmer, 1894.

CAT NYPL—*Dictionary Catalog of the Music Collection, the New York Public Library Reference Department,* 33 vols. Boston: G. K. Hall, 1964. *Cumulative Supplement,* 10 vols., 1964–71. Annual supplements since 1974.

Černý/OP. 106/i—Miroslav K. Cerny, "Zur heutigen Beethoven-Interpretation, ihrer Untersuchung und Auswertung (op. 106, erster Satz)," in CONGRESS BERLIN 1977 415–421.

Churgin/BEETHOVEN—Bathia Churgin, "A New Edition of Beethoven's Fourth Symphony," in Israel Studies in Musicology I (1978) 9–53.

Clemen/STREICHER—Otto Clemen, "Andreas Streicher in Wien," Neues Beethoven-Jahrbuch IV (1930) 107–117.

Clementi/INTRODUCTION—Muzio Clementi, Introduction to the Art of Playing on the Piano Forte, facsimile reprint of the 2d issue (1804?) of the original ed. (London, 1801), with an "Introduction" and a "List of Editions" by Sandra P. Rosenblum. New York: Da Capo Press, 1974.

Cone/CADENZA—Edward T. Cone, "A Cadenza for Op. 15," in Lockwood/FORBES 99–107.

CONGRESS BERLIN 1970—Bericht über den Internationalen Beethoven Kongress . . . 1970 in Berlin, ed. by H. A. Brockhaus and K. Niemann. Berlin: Verlag neue Musik, 1971, pp. 565–68.

CONGRESS BERLIN 1977—Bericht über den Internationalen Beethoven-Kongress 20. bis 23. März 1977 in Berlin, ed. by H. Goldschmidt, K.-H. Köhler, & K. Niemann. Leipzig: VEB Deutscher Verlag, 1978.

CONGRESS BONN 1970—Bericht über den internationalen musikwissenschaftlichen Kongress Bonn 1970 (Kassel: Bärenreiter, 1971).

CONGRESS COPENHAGEN 1972—International Musicological Society: Report of the Eleventh Congress Copenhagen 1972, 2 vols. (Copenhagen: Wilhelm Hansen, 1974).

CONGRESS DETROIT 1977—Robert Winter & Bruce Carr (eds.), Beethoven, Performers, and Critics, the International Beethoven Congress, Detroit, 1977. Detroit: Wayne State University Press, 1980. Cf. W. S. Newman in MQ LXVIII (1982) 133–38.

CONGRESS VIENNA 1927—Internationaler Musikhistorischer Kongress (Beethoven Zentenarfeier) Wien 1927. Vienna: Universal, 1927.

COOPER & MEYER—Grosvenor Cooper & Leonard B. Meyer, The Rhythmic Structure of Music. Chicago: University of Chicago Press, 1960.

Couperin/L'ART—François Couperin, L'Art de toucher le clavecin (1716–17), facs. of original ed., in Maurice Cauchie (general ed.), Oeuvres complètes de François Couperin (12 vols. Paris: L'Oiseau Lyre, 1932–33) I.

Cramer/INSTRUCTIONS—Johann Baptist Cramer, Instructions for the Piano Forte . . . , 5th ed., translated from the original Leipzig ed. of ca. 1813. Boston: John Ashton, ca. 1849.

Crelle/AUSDRUCK—August L. Crelle, Einiges über musikalischen Ausdruck und Vortrag für Fortepiano-spieler. Berlin: Maurerschen Buchhandlung, 1823.

Czerny/BEETHOVENm—BEETHOVEN[,] Sonates pour le Piano, édition revue, corrigée, métronomisée et doigtée par Ch. [Carl] Czerny, 2 vols. Bonn: Simrock, 1856–68. Cf. Newman/CHECKLIST 510–12.

Czerny/ERINNERUNGEN—Carl Czerny, Erinnerungen aus meinem Leben, ed. and annotated by Walter Kolneder. Strasbourg: P. H. Heitz, 1968.

Czerny/SCHOOL—Carl Czerny, Theoretical and Practical Piano Forte School . . . , Op. 500, 3 vols. (not including the supplementary Vol. IV that takes up Beethoven), translated from the original German by J. A. Hamilton. London: R. Cocks, [1839?–42?; cf. Newman/SSB 180, fn. 34].

Dadelsen/EDITIONSRICHTLINIEN—Georg von Dadelsen (ed.), Editionsrichtlinien musikalischer Denkmäler und Gesamtausgaben. Kassel: Bärenreiter, 1967.

Deas/ALLEGRO—Stewart Deas, "Beethoven's 'Allegro assai,' " in Music and Letters XXXI (1950) 333–36.

Debussy/CROCHE—Claude Debussy, *Monsieur Croche at autres écrits*, ed. by François Lesure. Paris: Gallimard, 1971.

Deutsch/AUSGABE—Otto Erich Deutsch, "Beethovens gesammelte Werke—des Meisters Plan und Haslingers Ausgabe," in *Zeitschrift für Musikwissenschaft* XIII (1930–31) 60–79; with the contents of "Haslingers Ausgabe" reprinted and revised by Alexander Weinmann in Dorfmüller/BEETHOVEN 269–79.

DMF—*Die Musikforschung.* 1948–.

Dorfmüller/BEETHOVEN—Kurt Dorfmüller (ed.), *Beiträge zur Beethoven-Bibliographie, Studien und Materialien zum Werkverzeichnis von Kinsky-Halm.* Munich: G. Henle Verlag, 1978.

Drabkin/BEETHOVEN—William Drabkin, "The Beethoven Sonatas," MT CXXVI (1985) 216–220.

Drabkin/OP III—William M. Drabkin, "The Sketches for Beethoven's Piano Sonata in C Minor Op. 111," 2 vols., unpub. Ph.D. diss., Princeton University, 1980.

Drake/BEETHOVEN—Kenneth Drake, *The Sonatas of Beethoven as He Played and Taught Them.* Cincinnati: Music Teachers National Association, 1972.

Dreyfus/EARLY—Laurence Dreyfus, "Early Music Defended Against Its Devotees: A Theory of Historical Performance in the Twentieth Century," in MQ LXIX (1983) 297–322.

EARLY MUSIC—*Early Music.* 1973–.

Eibner, Franz—see ÖMZ PEDAL.

Elvers/TEMPI—Rudolf Elvers, "Untersuchungen zu den Tempi in Mozarts Instrumentalmusik," unpub. diss., Berlin Freie Universität, 1953.

Fischer/OP 109—Johannes Fischer, "Eine neue Quelle von Beethovens Klaviersonate op. 109, E-dur," *Melos/Neue Zeitschrift für Musik* II (1976) 29.

Friege/INTERPRETATIONS—Bärbel Friege, "Beiträge zur Interpretationsgeschichte der Klaviersonaten Ludwig van Beethovens," unpublished Ph.D. diss. (University of Halle-Wittenberg, 1970).

Frimmel/BEETHOVEN—Theodor von Frimmel, *Beethoven-Studien*, 2 vols. Munich: G. Müller, 1905–06.

Frimmel/HANDBUCH—Theodor Frimmel, *Beethoven-Handbuch*, 2 vols. Leipzig: Breitkopf & Härtel, 1926.

Frimmel/KLAVIEREN—Theodor von Frimmel, "Von Beethovens Klavieren," *Die Musik* II/3 (1903, Heft 14) 83–91.

Frimmel/KLAVIERSPIELER—Theodor von Frimmel, "Der Klavierspieler Beethoven," in Frimmel/BEETHOVEN II 203–271.

Fuller/STREICHER—Richard A. Fuller, "Andrea Streicher's Notes on the Fortepiano," in EARLY MUSIC XII (1984) 461–70.

György Gábry/KLAVIER—"Das Klavier Beethovens und Liszts," *Studia Musicologica* VIII (1966) 379–90.

Gelfand/TEMPO—Yakov Gelfand, "Bach, Handel and Beethoven: On Tempo Indications Based on Beethoven's Music," in *College Music Symposium* XXV (1985) 92–129.

Gill/PIANO—Dominic Gill (ed.), *The Book of the Piano.* Ithaca: Cornell University Press, 1981.

Goldschmidt/BEETHOVEN—Harry Goldschmidt (ed.), *Zu Beethoven: Aufsätze und Annotationen,* 2 vols. up to 1984. Berlin: Verlag neue Musik, 1979.

Goldschmidt/CRAMER—Harry Goldschmidt, "Beethovens Anweisungen zum Spiel der Cramer-Etüden," revised (from CONGRESS BERLIN 1970 545–57), in Goldschmidt/ERSCHEINUNG 115–29.

Goldschmidt/ERSCHEINUNG—Harry Goldschmidt, *Die Erscheinung Beethoven.* Leipzig: VEB Deutscher Verlag für Musik, 1974.

Goldschmidt/VERS—Harry Goldschmidt, "Vers und Strophe in Beethovens Instrumentalmusik," revised from *Sitzungsberichte der Österreichischen Akademie der Wissenschaften Philosophisch-historischer Klasse* Vol. 271 (Vienna, 1971) 97–120, in Goldschmidt/ERSCHEINUNG 25–48.

Goldstein/OP. 111–Joanne Goldstein, "An Analysis of Interpretation in Selected Recorded Performances of Beethoven's *Sonata Op. 111*," unpub. Ph.D. diss., New York University, 1985.

Good/PIANOS—Edwin M. Good, *Giraffes, Black Dragons, and Other Pianos.* Stanford: Stanford University Press, 1982.

GRASNICK 32—'Fingersatzstudien und Skizzen," Grasnick 32, listed in BEETHOVEN STAATSBIBLIOTHEK 111.

Graudan/SFORZATO—Nikolai Graudan, "Das Sforzato bei Beethoven," in *Beethoven-Jahrbuch* VI (1965–68) 225–42.

GROVE—*The New Grove Dictionary of Music and Musicians.* ed. by Stanley Sadie, 20 vols. London: Macmillan, 1980.

GROVE BEETHOVEN—Joseph Kerman & Alan Tyson, *The New Grove Beethoven.* New York: W. W. Norton, 1983.

Grundmann/CLAVICEMBALO—Herbert Grundmann, "Per il Clavicembalo o Piano-Forte," in *Colloquium Amicorum—Joseph Schmidt-Görg zum 70. Geburtstag,* ed. by S. Kross and H. Schmidt (Bonn: Beethovenhaus, 1967) 100–117.

Grundmann & Mies—Herbert Grundmann and Paul Mies, *Studien zum Klavierspiel Beethovens und seiner Zeitgenossen.* Bonn: Bouvier, 1966.

Hackman/RHYTHMIC—Willis H. Hackman, "Rhythmic Analysis as a Clue to Articulation in the Arietta of Beethoven's Op. 111," in PQ No. 93 (Spring 1976) 26–37.

Harding/PIANO-FORTE—Rosamond E. M. Harding, *The Piano-forte, Its History Traced to the Great Exhibition of 1851,* 2d ed. (first published in 1933). Surrey: Gresham Press, 1978).

HENLE GEDENKSCHRIFT—Martin Bente (ed.), *Musik-Edition, Interpretation, Gedenkschrift Günter Henle.* Munich: G. Henle, 1980.

Henle/OP. 96—Günther Henle, "Ein Fehler in Beethovens letzter Violin-Sonate?" in *Die Musikforschung* V (1952) 53–54.

Hess/EDITIONSPROBLEME—Willy Hess, "Editionsprobleme bei Beethoven," in W. Hess, *Beethoven-Studien* (Bonn, 1972) 96–102.

Hess/ORIGINALKADENZEN—Willy Hess, "Die Originalkadenzen zu Beethovens Klavierkonzerten," in *Schweizerische Musikzeitung* CXII (1972) 270–75.

Hess/TEILWIEDERHOLUNG—Willy Hess, "Zur Frage der Teilwiederholung in Beethovens Symphoniesätzen," in *Festschrift Joseph Schmidt-Görg zum 60. Geburtstag* (Bonn, 1957) 142–55.

Hiebert/OPUS 13—Elfrieda Hiebert, "Beethoven's Pathétique Sonata, Op. 13: Should the Grave Be Repeated?" in PQ No. 133 (Spring 1986) 33–37.

Hiebert/WoO 40—Elfrieda Hiebert, "Beethoven's Fingerings in the Piano Trio in B Flat, WoO 39," in *Early Keyboard Journal* IV (1985–86) 5–27.

Hill/RIES—Cecil Hill (ed.), *Ferdinand Ries[,] Briefe und Dokumente.* Bonn: Ludwig Röhrscheid, 1982.

Hirt/KLAVIERBAUS—Franz Josef Hirt, *Meisterwerke des Klavierbaus.* Olten (Switzerland): Graf-Verlag, 1955.

Huber/BEETHOVEN—Anna Gertrud Huber, *Ludwig van Beethoven, seine Schüler und Interpreten.* Vienna: Walter Krieg, 1953.

Huber/CRAMER—Anna Gertrud Huber, *Beethovens Anmerkungen zu einer Auswahl von Cramer-Etuden (mitgeteilt von A. Schindler)—Beethoven-Studien, No. 1.* Zürich: Hug & Co., 1961.

Hüllmandel/PRINCIPLES—Nicolas Joseph Hüllmandel, *Principles of Music, Chiefly Calculated for the Piano Forte or Harpsichord . . .*, Op. 12. London, [1796?].

Hummel/ANWEISUNG—Johann Nepomuk Hummel, *Ausführliche theoretisch-practische
Anweisung zum Piano-Forte-Spiel . . .*, 2d ed. Vienna: Tobias Haslinger, 1828.

Imbrie/AMBIGUITY—Andrew Imbrie, "'Extra' Measures and Metrical Ambiguity in Beethoven," in BEETHOVEN STUDIES I 45–66.

d'Indy/COURS—Vincent d'Indy, *Cours de composition musicale*, with collaboration of A.
Sérieyx and De Lyoncourt, 3 vols. (2 parts in Vol. II). Paris: Durand, 1909–50.

JAMS—*Journal of the American Musicological Society*. 1948–.

Jander/ORPHEUS—Owen Jander, "Beethoven's 'Orpheus in Hades': The *Andante con moto*
of the Fourth Piano Concerto," in *19th Century Music* VIII (1985) 195–212 (with
response by Edward T. Cone, pp. 283–86).

Jarecki/CRAMER—Gerschon Jarecki, "Beethovens Anmerkungen zu Etuden von Cramer,"
in *Beethoven-Almanach* (Vienna, 1970) 169–71.

Jarecki, Gerschon—see ÖMZ PEDAL.

Jenkins/LEGATO—"The Legato Touch and the 'Ordinary' Manner of Keyboard Playing From
1750–1850," unpub. Ph.D. diss, St. Catharine's College (Cambridge), 1976.

Johansen/VIOLIN—Gail Nelson Johansen, "Beethoven's Sonatas for Piano and Violin Op.
12 No. 1 and Op. 96—a Performance Practice Study," D.M.A. thesis, Stanford University, 1981, unpub.

Johnson/FISCHHOFm—Douglas Porter Johnson, *Beethoven's Early Sketches in the "Fisch-
hof Miscellany," Berlin Autograph 28*, 2 vols. Ann Arbor: UMI Research Press,
1980.

Johnson/SKETCHES—Douglas Johnson, "Beethoven Scholars and Beethoven's Sketches,"
in *19th Century Music* II (1978–79) 3–17 (with 4 responses, pp. 270–79).

KAFKA SKETCHBOOK—Joseph Kerman (ed.), *"Kafka Sketchbook," Autograph Miscellany From
Circa 1786 to 1799: British Museum Additional Manuscript 29801*, facsimile and
transcription, 2 vols. London: British Museum, 1970.

Kagan/RUDOLPH—Susan Kagan, "The Music of Archduke Rudolph—Beethoven's Patron,
Pupil, and Friend," unpub. Ph.D. diss., the City University of New York, 1983.

Kaiser/INTERPRETEN—Joachim Kaiser, *Beethovens 32 Klaviersonaten und ihre Interpreten*. Frankfurt a/M: S. Fischer, 1975.

Kalischer/ZEITGENOSSEN—Alfred C. Kalischer, *Beethoven und seine Zeitgenossen*, 4 vols.
Berlin: Schuster & Loeffler, 1908–1910(?).

Kann/CRAMER—Hans Kann (ed.), *J. B. Cramer 21 Etüden für Klavier, nach dem Handex-
emplar Ludwig van Beethovens, nebst Fingerübungen von Beethoven*. Vienna: Universal Ed., 1974.

Kastner & Kapp/BRIEFE—Emerich Kastner, *Ludwig van Beethovens sämtliche Briefe*, revised
by Julius Kapp. Leipzig: Hesse & Becker, [1923].

Kerman/CONTEMPLATING—Joseph Kerman, *Contemplating Music, Challenges to Musicology*. Cambridge: Harvard University Press, 1985.

Kerst/BEETHOVEN—Friedrich Kerst, *Die Erinnerungen an Beethoven*, 2 vols. Stuttgart: Julius
Hoffmann, 1913.

KESSLERSCHES SKIZZENBUCH—Sieghard Brandenburg (ed.), *Kesslersches Skizzenbuch,
vollständiges Faksimile* [and transcription] *des Autographs, Ludwig van Beethoven*,
with "Nachwort" and index. Munich: E. Katzbichler, 1976.

Kinderman/DIABELLI—William Kinderman, *Beethoven's Diabelli Variations* (revision of Ph.D.
diss., 2 vols., University of California at Berkeley, 1980), Oxford: Clarendon Press,
1987.

Kinsky/HEYER—Georg Kinsky, *Musikhistorisches Museum von Wilhelm Heyer in Cöln-
Katalog* I (*Besaitete Tasteninstrumente*). Leipzig: Breitkopf & Härtel, 1910.

Kinsky & Halm/BEETHOVEN—Georg Kinsky, *Das Werk Beethovens, thematisch-bibliographisches Verzeichnis seiner sämtlichen vollendeten Kompositionen*, completed by Hans Halm. Munich: G. Henle Verlag, 1955. See the supplement under Dorfmüller/BEETHOVEN.

Kiraly/ÉRARD—William & Philippa Kiraly, "Sebastian Érard and the English Action Piano," in PQ No. 137 (Spring 1987) 49–53.

Kleindienst/CANTABILE—Sigrid Kleindienst, "Cantabile im sinfonischen Werk Beethovens," in *Musicologica Austriaca* IV (1984) 85–95.

Koch/ANLEITUNG—Heinrich Christoph Koch, *Versuch einer Anleitung zur Composition*, 3 vols. Leipzig: Adam Friedrich Böhme, 1782–93.

Koch/LEXIKON—Heinrich Christoph Koch, *Musikalisches Lexikon*. Frankfurt/M: August Hermann dem Jüngern, 1802.

Köhler/CLAVIERFINGERSATZ—Louis Köhler, *Der Clavierfingersatz*. Leipzig: Breitkopf & Härtel, 1862.

Kojima/VERZIERUNGEN—Shin Augustinus Kojima, "Über die Ausführung der Verzierungen in Beethovens Klaviermusik," in BEETHOVEN-KOLLOQUIUM 140–53.

Kolisch/TEMPO—Rudolf Kolisch, "Tempo and Character in Beethoven's Music," MQ XXIX (1943) 169–87 and 291–312.

KONVERSATIONSHEFTE—*Ludwig van Beethovens Konversationshefte*, 8 vols. (1–8) as of 1987, ed. by Karl-Heinz Köhler and others. Leipzig: VEB Deutscher Verlag für Musik, 1968–.

Kramer/DATING—Richard A. Kramer, "On the Dating of Two Aspects in Beethoven's Notation for Piano," in BEETHOVEN-KOLLOQUIUM 1977 160–73.

Kramer/EDUCATION—Richard A. Kramer, "Notes to Beethoven's Education," in JAMS XXVIII (1975) 72–101.

Kramer/REVIEW—Richard A. Kramer, review of *The Beethoven Reader* in NOTES XXIX (1972–73) 27–29.

Kramer/SKETCHES—Richard A. Kramer, "The Sketches for Beethoven's Violin Sonatas, Opus 30: History, Transcription, Analysis," 3 vols., unpub. Ph.D. diss., Princeton University, 1973–74.

Kravitt/TEMPO—Edward F. Kravitt, "Tempo as an Expressive Element in the Late Romantic Lied," in MQ LIX (1973) 497–518.

Kross/IMPROVISATION—Siegfried Kross, "Improvisation und Konzertform bei Beethoven," in BEETHOVEN-KOLLOQUIUM 1977 pp. 132–39.

Kullak/BEETHOVEN—Franz Kullak, *Beethoven's Piano Playing, With an Essay on the Execution of the Trill*, trans. by Theodore Baker (from the German preface to the Steingräber ed. of Beethoven's Piano Concertos pub. in 1881). New York: G. Schirmer, 1901.

Landon/BEETHOVEN—H. C. Robbins Landon, *Beethoven, a Documentary Study*, transl. by R. Wadleigh & E. Hartzell. London: Thames and Hudson, 1970.

Landon/HAYDN—H. L. Robbins Landon, *Haydn: Chronicle and Works*, 5 vols. Bloomington: Indiana University Press, 1976–1980.

Leicher-Olbrich/ORIGINALAUSGABEN—Anneliese Leicher-Olbrich, *Untersuchungen zu Originalausgaben Beethovenscher Klavierwerke*, 2 vols. in one. Wiesbaden: Breitkopf & Härtel, 1976.

Leitzmann/BEETHOVEN—Albert Leitzmann, *Ludwig van Beethoven: Berichte der Zeitgenossen, Briefe und persönliche Aufzeichnungen, gesammelt und erläutert von . . .*, 2 vols. Leipzig: Insel-Verlag, 1921.

Lenz/BEETHOVEN—Wilhelm von Lenz, *Beethoven et ses trois styles*, reprint of the original edition of 1852. Paris: Gustave Legouix, 1909.

Leux/NEEFE—Irmgard Leux, *Christian Gottlob Neefe (1748–1798)*. Leipzig: Fr. Kistner & C. F. W. Siegel, 1925.

LISZT LETTERS—*Letters of Franz Liszt*, ed. by La Mara (Marie Lipsius), translated by Constance Bache. London: H. Grevel, 1894.

Lockwood/FORBES—Lewis Lockwood & Phyllis Benjamin (eds.), *Beethoven Essays: Studies in Honor of Elliot Forbes*. Cambridge: Harvard University Press, 1984.

Lockwood/OP. 69—Lewis Lockwood, "The Autograph of the First Movement of Beethoven's Sonata for Violoncello and Pianoforte, Opus 69," in *Music Forum* II (1970) 1–109 (including Beethoven/OP. 69m in reduced size).

Lockwood/SKETCHES—Lewis Lockwood, "On Beethoven's Sketches and Autographs: Some Problems of Definition and Interpretation," in *Acta musicologica* XLII (1970) 32–47.

Löhlein/CLAVIER-SCHULE—Georg Simon Löhlein, *Clavier-Schule* . . . . Leipzig: Waisenhaus, 1779–81 and later eds. (including A. E. Müller's *Fortepiano-Schule*).

Loesser/PIANOS—Arthus Loesser, *Men, Women and Pianos*. New York: Simon and Schuster, 1954.

Lohmann/ARTIKULATIONSPROBLEMEN—Ludger Lohmann, *Studien zu Artikulationsproblemen bei den Tasteninstrumenten des 16–18. Jahrhunderts*. Regensburg: Gustav Bosse, 1982.

Lütge/STREICHER—Wilhelm Lütge, "Andreas und Nanette Streicher," *Der Bär* (Jahrbuch von Breitkopf & Härtel) IV (1927) 53–69.

Luoma/DYNAMICS—Robert Luoma, "The Function of Dynamics in the Music of Haydn, Mozart, and Beethoven: Some implications for the Performer," in *College Music Symposium* XVI (1976) 32–41.

Lussy/EXPRESSION—Mathis Lussy, *Traité de l'expression musicale*. Paris: Heugel, 1873.

MacArdle/SCHINDLER—Donald W. MacArdle, "Anton Felix Schindler, Friend of Beethoven," in *Music Review* XXIV (1963) 51–74.

Malloch/MINUET—William Malloch, "Toward a 'New' (Old) Minuet," in *Opus, The Magazine for Recorded Classics* I (Aug. 1985) 14–21 and 52.

Marpurg/ANLEITUNG—Friedrich Wilhelm Marpurg, *Anleitung zum Clavierspielen*, 2d ed. (originally 1755). Berlin, 1765.

Marschner/ZÄHLZEIT—Franz Marschner, "Zählzeit, Tempo und Ausdruck bei Beethoven," in CONGRESS VIENNA 1927 100–103.

Marx/ANLEITUNG—Adolf Bernhard Marx, *Anleitung zum Vortrag Beethovenscher Klavierwerke*, 3d ed. (originally Berlin, 1863). Berlin: Behncke, 1898.

Marx/BEETHOVEN—Adolf Bernhard Marx, *Ludwig van Beethoven, Leben und Schaffen*, 2 vols., reprint of original ed. of 1859. Leipzig: Adolph Schumann, 1902.

Massenkeil/CANTABILE—Günther Massenkeil, "*Cantabile* bei Beethoven," In BEETHOVEN-KOLLOQUIUM 1977 154–59.

Mattheson/CAPELLMEISTER—Johann Mattheson, *Der vollkommene Capellmeister*, (Hamburg, 1739), facs. ed. by Margarete Reimann. Kassel: Bärenreiter, 1954.

Mattheson-Harriss/CAPELLMEISTER—Johann Mattheson, *Der vollkommene Capellmeister* (Hamburg, 1739), revised translation by Ernest C. Harriss. Ann Arbor: UMI Research Press, 1981.

Meer/PIANOFORTE—J. H. van der Meer, "Beethoven et le Pianoforte," in *L'Interpretation de la musique classique de Haydn á Schubert* (Colloque international, Evry, 13–15 Oct. 77). Paris: Editions Minkoff, [1980].

Melville/PIANOS—Derek Melville, "Beethoven's Pianos," in Arnold & Fortune/BEETHOVEN 41–67; cf. further in the *Musical Times* for December 1971, p. 1171, and April 1972, pp. 361–62.

Mendelssohn/REISEBRIEFE—Paul Mendelssohn Bartholdy (ed.), *Reisebriefe von Felix Mendelssohn Bartholdy aus den Jahren 1830 bis 1832*, 2d ed. Leipzig: H. Mendelssohn, 1862.

Meredith/OPUS 109—William Rhea Meredith, "The Sources for Beethoven's Piano Sonata in E Major, Opus 109," 2 vols., unpub. Ph.D. diss., University of North Carolina at Chapel Hill, 1985.

Mertin/KLAVIERE—Josef Mertin, "Über die Klaviere Beethovens," in BEETHOVEN ALMANACH 91–100.

Meyer/AUFFÜHRUNG—Ernst Hermann Meyer, "Zur Frage der Aufführung alter Musik," in *Festschrift für Walter Wiora zum 30. Dezember 1966* (Munich, 1967) 57–61.

MGG—*Die Musik in Geschichte und Gegenwart*, 16 vols. (including 2 supplementary vols. and an Index vol.). Kassel: Bärenreiter-Verlag, 1949–79.

Mies/ARTIKULATIONSZEICHEN—Paul Mies, "Die Artikulationszeichen Strich und Punkt bei Wolfgang Amadeus Mozart," in DMF XI (1958) 428–55.

Mies/NOTATION—Paul Mies, "Einige allgemeine und spezielle Beispiele zu Beethovens Notation," *Beethoven-Jahrbuch* VI (1965–68) 215–24.

Mies/QUELLENBEWERTUNG—"Quellenbewertung bei den Werken Ludwig van Beethovens," in *Beethoven-Jahrbuch* IV (1959–60) 72–84.

Mies/SKETCHES—Paul Mies, *Beethoven's Sketches, An Analysis of His Style Based on a Study of His Sketch-Books*, translated (from the German of 1925) by Doris L. Mackinnon. New York: Dover, 1974 (unaltered reprint of the 1929 edition from Oxford University Press).

Mies/TEXTKRITISCHE—Paul Mies, *Textkritische Untersuchungen bei Beethoven*. Munich: G. Henle Verlag, 1957.

Milchmeyer/WAHRE—Johann Peter Milchmeyer, *Die wahre Art das Pianoforte zu spielen*. Dresden: C. H. Meinhold, 1797–98.

ML—*Music & Letters*. 1920–.

Momigny/COURS—Jérôme-Joseph de Momigny, *Cours complet d'harmonie et composition, d'après une théorie neuve et générale de la musique*, 3 vols. Paris: author, 1806.

MOSCHELES—Charlotte Moscheles, *Life of Moscheles, With Selections From His Diaries and Correspondence*, 2 vols., trans. (from the original German ed., Leipzig, 1872) by A. D. Coleridge. London: Hurst and Clackett, 1873.

Moscheles/BEETHOVENm—*Beethoven[,] Sämmtliche Sonaten für Pianoforte, neu herausgegeben mit Bezeichnung des Zeitmasses und Fingersatzes von J. Moscheles*, 4 vols. Stuttgart: Eduard Hallberger, [1858?–1867?]. Cf. Tyson/MOSCHELES.

MOZART VIOLIN—Leopold Mozart, *A Treatise on the Fundamental Principles of Violin Playing* (1756), translated by Editha Knocker. London: Oxford, 1948.

MOZART VIOLINSCHULE—Leopold Mozart, *Versuch einer gründlichen Violinschule*, facsimile of the original ed. of 1756, with preface by Bernhard Paumgartner. Vienna: Carl Stephenson, 1922.

MQ—*The Musical Quarterly*. 1915–.

MR—*The Music Review*. 1940–.

MT—*The Musical Times*. 1844–.

Münster/DIABELLI—Arnold Münster, *Studien zu Beethovens Diabelli-Variationen*. Munich: G. Henle Verlag, 1982.

MUSIK-KONZEPTE 8—*Musik-Konzepte 8, Beethoven, Das Problem der Interpretation*, ed. by H. K. Metzger & R. Riehn. Munich: Hans Pribil, 1979.

Neumann/ORNAMENTATION—Frederick Neumann, *Ornamentation in Baroque and Post-Baroque Music, With Special Emphasis on J. S. Bach*. Princeton: Princeton University Press, 1978.

Newman/ACCOMPANIED—William S. Newman, "Concerning the Accompanied Clavier Sonata," MQ XXXIII (1947) 327–49.

Newman/AMBIGUOUS—William S. Newman, "Ambiguous Staccatos and Slurs in Beethoven's Piano Music," a lecture delivered June 6, 1985, for an N. E. H. Humanities Institute at the University of Maryland on "Editing Music of the Classic Period"; scheduled for publication if a report appears from that Institute.

Newman/ARRAU—William S. Newman, review of C. Arrau and L. Hoffmann-Erbrecht (eds.), *Beethoven Sonaten für Klavier* I, in PQ No. 87 (fall 1974) 42–45.

Newman/ARTICULATION—William S. Newman, "Some Articulation Puzzles in Beethoven's Autographs and Earliest Editions," CONGRESS COPENHAGEN 1972 II 580–85.

Newman/AUTHORITATIVE—William S. Newman, "On the Problem of Determining Beethoven's Most Authoritative Lifetime Editions," in Dorfmüller/BEETHOVEN 128–36.

Newman/BACH—William S. Newman, "Is There a Rationale for the Articulation of J. S. Bach's String and Wind Music?" *Studies in Musicology, in Memory of Glen Haydon*, ed. by J. W. Pruett (Chapel Hill: Univ. of North Carolina Press, 1969) 229–44.

Newman/BAROQUE—William S. Newman, "Four Baroque Keyboard Practices and What Became of Them," in PQ No. 130 (Summer 1985) 19–26; originally read at Sweet Briar College 18 Apr 85 (as "Keynote Address" for Tercentenary Celebration).

Newman/CHECKLIST—William S. Newman, "A Chronological Checklist of Collected Editions of Beethoven's Solo Piano Sonatas Since His Own Day," NOTES XXXIII (1976–77) 503–530.

Newman/CLIMAX—William S. Newman, "The Climax of Music," in MR XIII (1952) 283–93.

Newman/CRAMER—William S.Newman, "On the Rhythmic Significance of Beethoven's Annotations in Cramer's Etudes," in CONGRESS BONN 1970 pp. 43–47.

Newman/ENIGMA—William S. Newman, "The Enigma of the Curved Line [slur]," *Piano Teacher* I/5 (May–June 1959) 7–13.

Newman/EXPRESSIVE—William S. Newman, "Expressive Subtleties in Beethoven's Late Piano Sonatas," scheduled for publication in a Festschrift yet to be announced.

Newman/FINGERINGS—William S. Newman, "Beethoven's Fingerings as Interpretive Clues," *Journal of Musicology* I (1982) 171–97.

Newman/GENERATIVE—William S. Newman, "Musical Form as a Generative Process," *Journal of Aesthetics and Art Criticism* XII (1953–54) 301–309.

Newman/HAYDN—William S. Newman, "Haydn as Ingenious Exploiter of the Keyboard," in *Internationaler Joseph Haydn Kongress, Wien, 5.–12. September 1982* (Munich: G. Henle Verlag, 1986; ed. by Eva Badura-Skoda) 43–53.

Newman/INCISE—William S. Newman, "The 'Incise' as an Expressive Guide in Beethoven's Piano Music," slightly Hispanicized summary read at International Conference ("España en la Música de Occidente") in Salamanca, Spain, Oct. 4 1985, with publication planned in the proceedings; full paper read in Classic Symposium at Ohio State University Oct. 26, 1985.

Newman/KUERTI—William S. Newman, review of Anton Kuerti's recordings for Aquitaine of Beethoven's [32] Sonatas and the "Diabelli Variations," 4 vols., in MQ LXIV (1978) 113–121.

Newman/LISZT—William S. Newman, "Liszt's Interpreting of Beethoven's Piano Sonatas," MQ LVIII (1972) 185–209.

Newman/MOZART—William S. Newman, "Styles and Touches in Mozart's Keyboard Music," in *Handbook for Piano Teachers*, ed. by Roberta Savler (Evanston, Ill.: Summy-Birchard, 1958) 65–73.

Newman/MYSTIQUE—William S. Newman, "The Beethoven Mystique in Romantic Art, Literature, and Music," MQ XLIX (1983) 354–87.

Newman/OPUS 96—William S. Newman, "The Opening Trill in Beethoven's Sonata for Piano and Violin Op. 96," in HENLE GEDENKSCHRIFT 384–93.

Newman/OPUS 106—William S. Newman,"Some 19th-Century Consequences of Beethoven's 'Hammerklavier' Sonata, Op. 106," PQ No. 67 (Spring 1969) 12–18 and No. 68 (Summer 1969) 12–17.

Newman/PEDALS—William S. Newman, "Beethoven's Uses of the Pedals," in Banowetz/ PEDALING 142–66 (Ch. 7; 1985).

Newman/PERFORMANCE—William S. Newman, Performance Practices in Beethoven's Piano Sonatas—An Introduction. New York: W. W. Norton, 1971.

Newman/PIANISM—William S. Newman, "The Pianism of Haydn, Mozart, Beethoven, and Schubert Compared," in PQ No. 105 (Spring 1979) 14–30.

Newman/PIANOS—William S. Newman, "Beethoven's Pianos Versus His Piano Ideals," in JAMS XXIII (1970) 484–504.

Newman/PROBLEMS—William S. Newman, The Pianist's Problems, 4th ed. (originally pub. in 1950). New York: Da Capo Press, 1984 (paperback 1986).

Newman/PROGRAMME—William S. Newman, "Programmists vs. Absolutists—Further Thoughts About an Overworked 'Dichotomy,'" scheduled for publication in a Festschrift to be announced.

Newman/RANGE—William S. Newman, "Range as a Structural Determinant in Beethoven's Piano Music," a paper read Oct. 1, 1975, at the Annual Meeting of the American Musicological Society (Los Angeles); revised for publication, in A Seventieth Birthday Tribute to Gwynn McPeek (C. P. Comberiati and M. C. Steel [eds.], London: Gordon & Breach, 1988?).

Newman/SCE—William S. Newman, The Sonata in the Classic Era (originally 1963), 3d ed. New York: W. W. Norton, 1983.

Newman/SCHINDLER—William S. Newman, "Yet Another Major Beethoven Forgery by Schindler?" in the Journal of Musicology III (1984) 397–422.

Newman/SCHMIDT—Review of Hans Schmidt (ed.), Beethoven Werke VII/2: Klaviersonaten I, in PQ No. 82 (Summer 1973) 37–39; with follow-ups in No. 85 (Spring 1974) 47–48 and No. 86 (Summer 1974) 1 and 41.

Newman/SCHUBERT—William S. Newman, "Freedom of Tempo in Schubert's Instrumental Music," in MQ LXI (1975) 528–45.

Newman/SSB—William S. Newman, The Sonata Since Beethoven (originally 1969), 3d ed. New York: W. W. Norton, 1983.

Newman/TEMPO—William S. Newman, "Tempo in Beethoven's Instrumental Music—Its Choice and Its Flexibility," in PQ No.116 (Winter 1981–82) 22–29 and No. 117 (Spring 1982) 22–31.

Newman/TRILLS—William S. Newman, "The Performance of Beethoven's Trills," Beethoven-Jahrbuch IX (1973–77) 347–76 (with slight revisions of the same article in JAMS XXIX [1976] 439–62); also, "Second and One-Half Thoughts on the Performance of Beethoven's Trills," MQ LXIV (1978) 98–103 (reply to Robert Winter in MQ LXIII [1977] 483–504).

Nohl/BEETHOVEN—Walther Nohl, Ludwig van Beethoven als Mensch und Musiker im täglichen Leben; Ein Gedenkbuch zu seinem 150. Geburtstag. Stuttgart: Carl Grüninger, [1920].

NOTES—Music Library Association Notes, Second Series. 1943.

Nottebohm/BEETHOVENIANA—Gustav Nottebohm, Beethoveniana: Aufsätze und Mittheilungen. Leipzig: Rieter-Biedermann, 1872.

Nottebohm/METRONOMISCHE—Gustav Nottebohm, "Metronomische Bezeichnungen," in Nottebohm/BEETHOVENIANA 126–37.

Nottebohm/PUNKTE—Gustav Nottebohm, "Punkte und Striche," in Nottebohm/BEETHOVENIANA 107–25.

Nottebohm/ZWEITE—Gustav Nottebohm, Zweite Beethoveniana; nachgelassene Aufsätze. Leipzig: Rieter-Biedermann, 1887.

Obelkevich/OP 96—Mary Rowen Obelkevich, "The Growth of a Musical Idea—Beethoven's Op. 96," in Current Musicology XI (1971) 91–114.

ÖMZ—Österreichische Musikzeitschrift. 1946–.

ÖMZ PEDAL—Three interrelated articles in ÖMZ XX (1965): Franz Eibner, "Registerpedalisierung bei Haydn und Beethoven" 189–96; Gerschon Jarecki, "Die Ausführung der Pedalvorschriften Beethovens auf dem modernen Klavier" 197–200; Kurt Wegerer, "Beethovens Hammerflügel und ihre Pedale" 201–211.

Palm/MOMIGNY—Albert Palm, Jérôme-Joseph de Momigny, Leben und Werk. Köln: Arno Volk, 1969.

Paolone/AUTOGRAFO—Ernesto Paolone, "L'originale autografo della lettera del 16 aprile 1819 di L. van Beethoven," in Nuova rivista musicale italiana II (1981) 181–196.

Paolone/OP 106—Ernesto Paolone, La grande sconosciuta "Grosse Sonate für das Hammerklavier Op. 106" di Ludwig van Beethoven. Cagiari: Il Solco, [1977].

Piersel/ORNAMENTATION—Thomas Piersel, "Ornamentation as Presented in Piano Method Books, ca. 1790–1850," unpub. Ph.D. thesis, University of Iowa, 1970.

Platen/AUFFÜHRUNGSPRAXIS—Emil Platen, "Zeitgenössische Hinweise zur Aufführungspraxis der letzten Streichquartette Beethovens," in BEETHOVEN-KOLLOQUIUM 1977 100–107.

Platen/NOTIERUNGSPROBLEM—Emil Platen, "Ein Notierungsproblem in Beethovens späten Streichquartetten," in BEETHOVEN-JAHRBUCH VIII (1971–72) 147–56.

Poniatowska/INTERPRETATION—Irena Poniatowska, "Zur Frage der Interpretation von Beethovens Klavierwerken," in CONGRESS BERLIN 1970 565–68.

Poniatowska/KLAVIEREN—Irena Poniatowska, "Der Klaviersatz Beethovens," unpub. diss., University of Warsaw (?), 1970. (Cf. DMF XXVI [1973] 518.)

Potter/BEETHOVEN—Cipriani Potter, "Recollections of Beethoven, With Remarks on His Style," in MT X (1861) 150–56 (reprinted from The Musical World I [1836]).

PQ—The Piano Quarterly (originally Piano Quarterly Newsletter). 1952–.

Prod'homme/BEETHOVEN—Jacques-Gabriel Prod'homme, Les Sonates pour piano de Beethoven. Paris: Delagrave, 1937.

Quantz/VERSUCH—Johann Joachim Quantz, Versuch einer Anweisung die Flöte traversiere zu spielen, facsimile of 3d ed. (1789). Kassel: Bärenreiter-Verlag, 1953.

Raphael & Klugmann/TRIOSM—Günter Raphael & Friedhelm Klugmann (eds.), Beethoven Trios für Klavier, Violine und Violoncello, nach den Originalausgaben, 3 vols. Munich: G.Henle Verlag, 1964, 1955, and 1968.

Reicha & Czerny/COMPOSITION—Anton Reicha, Vollständiges Lehrbuch der musikalischen Composition, translated (with both French and German texts) by Carl Czerny (from Reicha's publications between 1814 and 1826). Vienna: A. Diabelli, [1832].

Reichardt/BRIEFE—Johann Friedrich Reichardt, Vertraute Briefe geschrieben auf einer Reise nach Wien und den österreichischen Staaten . . . 1808–09, 2 vols., ed. (from original ed. of 1810) by Gustav Gugitz. Munich: Georg Müller, 1915.

Riehn/METRONOM—Rainer Riehn, "Beethovens Verhältnis zum Metronom," in MUSIK-KONZEPTE 8, pp. 70–84.

Riehn/ORIGINALE—Rainer Riehn, "Beethovens originale, Czernys und Moscheles' auf Erinnerung gegründete, Kolischs und Leibowitz' durch Vergleiche der Charaktere erschlossene Metronomisierungen," in MUSIK-KONZEPTE 8, pp. 85–96.

Riemann/CLAVIERPÄDAGOG—Hugo Riemann, "Beethoven als Clavierpädagog," in *Musikalisches Wochenblatt* XXIV (1893) 541–42, 553–54, 569–70, 581–82.

Riemann/RHYTHM—Hugo Riemann, *System der musikalischen Rhythm und Metrik*. Leipzig: Breitkopf & Härtel, 1903.

Riepel/ANFANGSGRÜNDE—Joseph Riepel, *Anfangsgründe zur musicalischen Setzkunst*, 2 vols. Regensburg: 1752 and 1755.

Rosenblum/CALANDO—Sandra P. Rosenblum, "Calando: The Life of a Musical Term," in PQ No. 139 (fall, 1987) 60–65.

Rosenblum/PERFORMANCE—Sandra P. Rosenblum, "Performance Practices in Classic Piano Music," typed, book-length manuscript (1984) of a forthcoming publication from the Indiana University Press (kindly supplied in advance by the author).

Rosenthal/AUFTAKT—Felix Rosenthal, "Auftakt und Abtakt in der Thematik Beethovens," in CONGRESS VIENNA 1970 97–99.

Rostal/BEETHOVEN—Max Rostal, *Ludwig van Beethoven: Die Sonaten für Klavier und Violine, Gedanken zu ihrer Interpretation, mit einem Nachtrag aus pianistischer Sicht von Günther Ludwig*. Munich: R. Piper & Co., 1981.

Rothschild/MOZART—Fritz Rothschild, *Musical Performance in the Times of Mozart and Beethoven*. New York: Oxford University Press, 1961 (see W. S. Newman in PQ No. 36 [Summer 1961] 25–26).

Rudolf/MINUETS—Max Rudolf, "On the Performance of Mozart's Minuets," in the *Newsletter of the Friends of Mozart*, 1984.

Rudolf/MOZART—Max Rudolf, "Ein Beitrag zur Geschichte der Tempoanahme bei Mozart," in *Mozart-Jahrbuch 1976/77*, pp. 204–224.

Rudolf/REPEATS—Max Rudolf, "Inner Repeats in the Da Capo of Classical Minuets and Scherzos," in *Journal of the Conductors' Guild*, III/4 (fall 1982) 145–50.

Sakka/KLAVIERE—Keisei Sakka, "Beethovens Klaviere—Der Klavierbau und Beethovens künstlerische Reaktion," in *Colloquium Amicorum—Joseph Schmidt-Görg zum 70. Geburtstag*, ed. by S. Kross and H. Schmidt (Bonn: Beethovenhaus, 1967) 327–37.

Saslav/HAYDN—Isidor Saslav, "Tempos in the String Quartets of Joseph Haydn," unpub. diss., Indiana University, 1969.

Sasse/KLANGES—Konrad Sasse, "Bemerkungen zur Berücksichtigung des Klanges historischer Hammerflügel für die Interpretation Beethovenscher Klavierwerke auf in modernen Instrumenten," in CONGRESS BERLIN 1970 559–64.

Schenker/KLAVIERSONATEN—Heinrich Schenker (ed.), *Beethoven: Klaviersonaten nach den Autographen und Erstdrucken*, revised by Erwin Ratz, 4 vols. Vienna: Universal, 1946–47.

Schenker/LETZTEN—Heinrich Schenker (ed.), *Die letzten [fünf] Sonaten von Beethoven: Kritische [Ausgabe mit] Einführung und Erläuterung*, new ed. by Oswald Jonas, 4 vols. (Op. 106 lacking). Vienna: Universal, 1972 (originally 1913–21).

Schenker/ORNAMENTIK—Heinrich Schenker, *Ein Beitrag zur Ornamentik als Einführung zu Ph. Em. Bachs Klavierwerken, mitumfassend auch die Ornamentik Haydns, Mozarts, Beethovens etc*. Vienna: Universal, [1908?].

Schenker/PHRASIERUNGSBOGEN—Heinrich Schenker, "Weg mit dem Phrasierungsbogen," in *Das Meisterwerk in der Musik I* (Munich: Drei Masken Verlag, 1925) 41–60.

Schiedermair/BEETHOVEN—Ludwig Schiedermair, *Der junge Beethoven*. Leipzig: Quelle & Meyer, 1925.

Schindler/BEETHOVEN—Anton Schindler, *The Life of Beethoven*, 2 vols., ed. [and trans.?] (from the original German ed. of 1840) by Ignaz Moscheles. London: Henry Colburn, 1841.

Schindler/1860—Anton Schindler, *Ludwig van Beethoven* (from 3d ed., 2 vols., 1860), 5th ed., ed. by Fritz Volbach. Münster: Aschendorff, 1927.

Schindler & MacArdle/BEETHOVEN—Anton Schindler, *Beethoven as I Knew Him*, 2 vols. in one, trans. by Constance S. Jolly and annotated by Donald W. MacArdle from the 3d ed. of 1860. Chapel Hill: The University of North Carolina Press, 1966.

Schlesinger/CRAMER—Thea Schlesinger, *Johann Baptist Cramer und seine Klaviersonaten*, (Ph.D. diss., Universität München). Munich: Knorr & Hirth, 1928.

Schmid-Lindner/KLAVIER—August Schmid-Lindner, "Beethoven am Klavier," in *Neues Beethoven-Jahrbuch* [2d series] X (1942) 40–58.

Schmidt/EDITION—Hans Schmidt, "Edition und Aufführungspraxis am Beispiel von Beethovens Waldsteinsonate," in BEETHOVEN-KOLLOQUIUM 1977 108–116.

Schmidt/BEETHOVENHANDSCHRIFTEN—Hans Schmidt, "Die Beethovenhandschriften des Beethovenhauses in Bonn," in BEETHOVEN-JAHRBUCH VII (1969–70) vii–xxiv, 1–443; with revisions in VIII (1971–72) 207–220.

Schmidt/KLAVIERSONATENm—Hans Schmidt (ed.), *Beethoven: Klaviersonaten*, 2 vols. (through Op. 57), in *Beethoven Werke* VII/2–3. Munich: G. Henle Verlag, 1971.

Schmidt-Görg & Schmidt/BEETHOVEN—Joseph Schmidt-Görg & Hans Schmidt (eds.), *Ludwig van Beethoven, Bicentennial Edition 1770–1970*, English translation by Deutsche Grammophon staff. Hamburg: Polydor International, 1972.

Schwarz/PAUSEN—Vera Schwarz, "Funktion und Interpretation der Pausen bei Beethoven," in BEETHOVEN-KOLLOQUIUM 1977 117–31.

Seifert/METRONOMISIERUNGEN—Herbert Seifert, "Beethoven Metronomisierungen und die Praxis," in BEETHOVEN KOLLOQUIUM 1977 183–89.

Shedlock/BEETHOVEN—John S. Shedlock, *Beethoven's pianoforte sonatas, the origins and respective values of various readings*. London: Augener [1918].

Shedlock/CRAMERm—John South Shedlock, *Selection of Studies by J. B. Cramer, with Comments by L. van Beethoven, and Preface, Translation, Explanatory Notes, and Fingering . . . .* London: Augener, [1893].

Smiles/ORNAMENTATION—Joan Ellen Smiles, "Improvised Ornamentation in Late Eighteenth-Century Music: An Examination of Contemporary Evidence," unpub. Ph.D. diss., Stanford University, 1976.

Solomon/BEETHOVEN—Maynard Solomon, *Beethoven*. New York: G. Schirmer, 1977.

Solomon/CREATIVE—'On Beethoven's Creative Process: A Two-Part Invention," in ML LXI (1980) 272–83.

Solomon/TAGEBUCH—Maynard Solomon, "Beethoven's Tagebuch of 1812–1818," in BEETHOVEN STUDIES III 193–288.

Sonneck/BEETHOVEN—O. G. Sonneck (ed.), *Beethoven: Impressions by His Contemporaries*, reprint of original G. Schirmer ed. of 1926. New York: Dover, 1967.

Spohr/LEBENSERINNERUNGEN—Louis [Ludwig] Spohr, *Lebenserinnerungen*, ed. by Folker Göthel. Tutzing: Hans Schneider, 1968.

Stadlen/FORGERIES—Peter Stadlen, "Schindler's Beethoven Forgeries," in MT CXVIII (1977) 549–552.

Stadlen/METRONOME I—Peter Stadlen, "Beethoven and the Metronome," in *Music and Letters* XLVIII (1967) 330–49.

Stadlen/METRONOME II—Peter Stadlen, "Beethoven and the Metronome," in *Soundings* IX (1982) 38–73.

Stadlen/SCHINDLER—Peter Stadlen, "Schindler and the Conversation Books," in *Soundings* VII (1978) 2–18.

Staehelin/DYNAMIK—Martin Staehelin, "Zur Stellung der Dynamik in Beethovens Schaffensprozess," in BEETHOVEN-JAHRBUCH X (1978–81) 319–24.

Starke/PIANOFORTE—Friedrich Starke. *Wiener Pianoforte-Schule*, 3 vols. Vienna, 1819–1821.

Steglich/AKZENTUATION—Rudolf Steglich, "Beethovens überaus merkwürdige Akzentuation," in *Kongressbericht International Gesellschaft für Musikwissenschaft, 4. Kongress* (Basel 1949) 190–94.

Steglich/TAKTQUALITÄT—Rudolf Steglich, "Über Dualismus der Taktqualität im Sonatatensatz," in CONGRESS VIENNA 1927 104–106.

Steglich/WIEDERHOLUNGSTAKTE—Rudolf Steglich, "Acht Wiederholungstakte zuviel in Drucken von Beethovens Op. 5 Nr. 2?" in *Die Musikforschung* XII (1959) 473–74.

Stevens/TREATISE—W. S. Stevens, *Treatise on Piano-forte expression* . . . . London: M. Jones, 1811.

Stockmann/INTERPRETATIONSAUSGABE—Bernhard Stockmann, "Die Interpretationsausgabe der Klaviersonaten Beethovens," in CONGRESS BONN 1970 pp. 590–92.

Streicher/BEMERKUNGEN—J. A. Streicher, *Kurze Bemerkungen über das Spielen, Stimmen, und Erhalten* . . . . Vienna: Geschwistern Stein, 1801.

Sulzer/ALLGEMEINE—Johann Georg Sulzer, *Allgemeine Theorie der schönen Künste*, 4 vols. Leipzig: Weidmann, 1773–75. (The music articles were written from A through "Modulation" by Sulzer and J. P. Kirnberger, from "Preludiren" through R by Kirnberger and J. A. P. Schulz, and from S to the end [except for "System"] by Schulz.)

Szász/CONTINUO—Tibor Szász, "Piano Concertos of Haydn, Mozart, and Beethoven Restored: Concerto Functions of the Soloist" (1985), projected for publication.

Talsma/ANLEITUNG—Willem Retze Talsma, *Anleitung zur Entmechanisierung der Musik*, Vol. I of *Wiedergeburt der Klassiker*. Innsbruck: Wort und Welt, 1980.

Tappert/KLAVIERSONATEN—Wilhelm Tappert, "Beethovens Klaviersonaten: Ein Beitrag zur Säkularfeier," in *Musikalisches Wochenblatt* II (1871) 339–40

Taruskin *et al.*/AUTHENTICITY—Richard Taruskin, Daniel Leech-Wilkinson, Nicholas Temperley, and Robert Winter, "The Limits of Authenticity [in performance practices]: A Discussion," in EARLY MUSIC XII (1984) 3–25.

Temperley/TEMPO—Nicholas Temperley, "Tempo and Repeats in the Early Ninetenth Century," ML XLVII (1966) 323.

Tenhaef/VORTRAGSBEZEICHNUNG—Peter Tenhaef, *Studien zur Vortragsbezeichnung in der Musik des 19. Jahrhunderts*. Kassel: Bärenreiter, 1983.

Thayer & Forbes/BEETHOVEN—[Alexander Wheelock] *Thayer's Life of Beethoven*, revised and ed. by Elliott Forbes, reprint of 1964 ed. Princeton: Princeton University Press, 1970.

Thayer & Riemann/BEETHOVEN—Alexander Wheelock Thayer, *Ludwig van Beethovens Leben*, 5 vols., trans. by H. Deiters, rev. by Hugo Riemann. Leipzig: Breitkopf & Härtel, 1917–23.

Timbrell/NOTES—Charles Timbrell, "Notes on the Sources of Beethoven's Op. 111," in ML LVIII (1977) 204–215.

Timbrell/OP 111—Charles Timbrell, "Beethoven's Opus 111: A Study of the Manuscript and Printed Sources," 2 vols. in one. Unpub. Ph.D. diss., University of Maryland, 1976.

Tomlinson/CULTURE—Gary A. Tomlinson, "The Web of Culture: A Context for Musicology," in *19th Century Music* VII (1984) 350–62.

Tovey/BEETHOVENm—Donald F. Tovey (ed., with Harold Craxton), *Beethoven Sonatas for Pianoforte*, 3 vols. London: Associated Board of the Royal Schools of Music, [1931].

Türk/KLAVIERSCHULE—Daniel Gottlob Türk, *Klavierschule*, facsimile of original, 1789 edition. Kassel: Bärenreiter, 1962.

Türk/SCHOOL—Daniel Gottlob Türk, *School of Clavier Playing*, translated, with introduction and notes, by Raymond H. Haggh. Lincoln: University of Nebraska Press, 1982.

Tyson/CLEMENTI—Alan Tyson, *Thematic Catalogue of the Works of Muzio Clementi*. Tutzing: Hans Schneider, 1967.

Tyson/ENGLISH—Alan Tyson, *The Authentic English Editions of Beethoven*. London: Faber and Faber, 1963.

Tyson/KANN—Alan Tyson, review of Kann/CRAMER in ML LVIII (1977) 247–49.

Tyson/MOSCHELES—Alan Tyson, "Moscheles and his 'Complete Edition of Beethoven,'" in MR XXV (1964) 136–41.

Tyson/RIES—Alan Tyson, "Ferdinand Ries (1784–1838): The History of His Contribution to Beethoven Biography," in *19th Century Music* VII (1984) 209–21.

Tyson/SCHLESINGER—Alan Tyson, "Maurice Schlesinger as a Publisher of Beethoven, 1822–1827," in *Acta Musicologica* XXXV (1963) 182–91.

Tyson/SKETCHES—'Sketches and Autographs" and "Steps to Publication and Beyond," Chapters 12 and 13 in Arnold & Fortune/BEETHOVEN.

Uhde/KLAVIERMUSIK—Jürgen Uhde, *Beethoven's Klaviermusik*, 3 vols. Stuttgart: Philipp Reclam, 1968–74.

Unger/HANDSCHRIFT—Max Unger, *Beethoven's Handschrift*. Leipzig: Quelle & Meyer (for the Beethovenhaus in Bonn), 1926.

Unger/URTEXTPROBLEME—Max Unger, "Urtextprobleme bei Beethoven," in *Musica* IX (1955) 111–115.

Unverricht/EIGENSCHRIFTEN—Hubert Unverricht, *Die Eigenschriften und die Originalausgaben von Werken Beethovens in ihrer Bedeutung für die moderne Textkritik*. Kassel: Bärenreiter, 1960.

Viguerie/L'ART—Bernard Viguerie, *L'Art de toucher le piano-forte*. Paris, [1798?].

Voss/ZEITMESSUNG—Johann Heinrich Voss, *Zeitmessung der deutschen Sprache, Beilage zu den Oden und Elegien*. Königsberg: Friedrich Nicolovius, 1802.

Wallner/KLAVIERSONATENm—Bertha A. Wallner (ed.), *Beethoven: Klaviersonaten nach Eigenschriften und Originalausgaben*, 2 vols. Munich: G. Henle Verlag, 1952–53 (with later, unacknowledged revisions).

Walter/HAYDN—Horst Walter, "Haydns Klaviere," in *Haydn-Studien* II (1969) 256–88.

WEGELER & RIES—Franz Gerhard Wegeler and Ferdinand Ries, *Biographische Notizen über Beethoven*, facsimile of original ed. (Koblenz, 1838) plus Wegeler's *Nachtrag* (Koblenz, 1845). Hildesheim: Georg Olms, 1972.

Wegerer, Kurt—see ÖMZ PEDAL.

Weise/OP 53—Dagmar Weise, "Zum Faksimiledruck von Beethovens Waldsteinsonate," in *Beethoven-Jahrbuch* II (1955–56) 102–111.

Westphal/RHYTHMIK—Rudolf Westphal, *Allgemeine Theorie der musikalischen Rhythmik seit Joh. Seb. Bach*. Leipzig: Breitkopf & Härtel, 1880.

Wehmeyer/INTERPRETATION—Grete Wehmeyer, "Interpretation im 'klassischen' Tempo," in ÖMZ XL (1985) 369–76.

WIELHORSKY SKETCHBOOKm—Nathan Fishman (ed.), "Wielhorsky Sketchbook" [Russian title], 1802–03, facsimile and transcription. Moscow, 1962.

Winter/TRILLS—Robert Winter, "Second Thoughts on the Performance of Beethoven's Trills" (commentary on Newman/TRILLS above), in MQ LXIII (1977) 483–504; followed by, "And Even More Thoughts on the Beethoven Trill . . . ," in MQ LXV (1979) 111–16.

Winternitz/AUTOGRAPHS—*Musical Autographs from Monteverdi to Hindemith*, revision of original ed. from Princeton University Press in 1955, 2 vols. New York: Dover, 1965.

Wolf/KLAVIERSPIELEN—Georg Friedrich Wolf, *Unterricht im Klavierspielen.* Halle: J. C. Hendel, 1799.

Wythe/GRAF—Deborah Wythe, "The Pianos of Conrad Graf," in EARLY MUSIC XII 447–60.

Young/BEETHOVEN—*Beethoven: A Victorian Tribute,* based on the papers of Sir George Smart. London: Dennis Dobson, 1976.

Zaslaw/TEMPO—Neal Zaslaw, "Mozart's Tempo Conventions," in CONGRESS COPENHAGEN 1972 720–33.

APPENDIX

Beethoven's Works for Piano

Key to the charts

B & H BEETHOVEN GESAMTAUSGABE
NGA BEETHOVEN WERKE
Hess BEETHOVEN SUPPLEMENTE

VF Very fast	Mi Minuet
F Fast	Ro Rondo
M Moderate	Sc Scherzo
S Slow	Va Variations

CHART 1. THIRTY-SEVEN SOLO SONATAS OR SONATINAS

Number	Title	Collected edition	Composed	Original edition	Sketches extant	Autograph extant	Facsimile published	Movements		
								Tempos or types	Keys	Measures
WoO 47/1	"Kurfürsten"	B & H 16/33	1782–83	Speyer: Bossler, 1783	no	no	no	F, M, Ro	E♭, B♭, E♭	75, 61, 108
WoO 47/2	"Kurfürsten"	B & H 16/34	1782–83	Speyer: Bossler, 1783	no	no	no	S/F, M, VF	f, A♭, f	83, 85, 126
WoO 47/3	"Kurfürsten"	B & H 16/35	1782–83	Speyer: Bossler, 1783	no	no	no	F, M, Sc	D, A, D	111, 119, 159
WoO 50		Hess IX/2	1788–90?	Berlin, 1909	no	yes	1909	F?, F	F, F	30, 26
WoO 51	"Eleonore"	B & H 16/36	1791–92	Frankfurt: Dunst, 1830	no	frag	no	F, S	C, F	93, 36
Op 2/1	"Haydn"	NGA VII/2	1795	Vienna: Artaria, 1796	yes	no	no	F, S, Mi, VF	f, F, F, f	152, 61, 73, 196
Op 2/2	"Haydn"	NGA VII/2	1795	Vienna: Artaria, 1796	no	no	no	VF, S, Sc, Ro	A, D, A, A	337, 80, 68, 187
Op 2/3	"Haydn"	NGA VII/2	1795	Vienna: Artaria, 1796	no	no	no	F, S, Sc, F	C, E, C, C	257, 82, 128, 312
Op 7	"Die Verliebte"	NGA VII/2	1796–97	Vienna: Artaria, 1797	yes	no	no	F, S, F, Ro	E♭, C, E♭, E♭	362, 90, 149, 183
Op 10/1	"Little Pathétique"	NGA VII/2	1796–98	Vienna: Eder, 1798	yes	no	no	VF, S, VF	c, A♭, c	284, 112, 122
Op 10/2		NGA VII/2	1796–98	Vienna: Eder, 1798	no	no	no	F, F, VF	F, f, F	202, 170, 150
Op 10/3		NGA VII/2	1796–98	Vienna: Eder, 1798	yes	no	no	VF, S, Mi, Ro	D, d, D, D	344, 87, 86, 113

| | | | | | | | | Movements | | |
Number	Title	Collected edition	Composed	Original edition	Sketches extant	Autograph extant	Facsimile published	Tempos or types	Keys	Measures
Op 13	*Pathétique*	NGA VII/2	1798–99	Vienna: Hoffmeister, 1799	yes	no	no	S/VF, S, Ro	c, A♭, c	310, 73, 210
Op 14/1		NGA VII/2	1798–99	Vienna: Mollo, 1799	yes	no	no	F, F, Ro	E, e, E	162, 116, 131
Op 14/2		NGA VII/2	1798–99	Vienna: Mollo, 1799	no	no	no	F, M, Sc	G, C, G	200, 90, 254
Op 22		NGA VII/2	1799–1800	Vienna: Hoffmeister, 1802	yes	no	no	F, S, Mi, Ro	B♭, E♭, B♭, B♭	199, 77, 46, 199
Op 26	"Funeral March"	NGA VII/2	1800–01	Vienna: Cappi, 1802	yes	yes	1894	Va, Sc, S, F	A♭, A♭, a♭, A♭	219, 95, 75, 169
Op 27/1	"quasi una fantasia"	NGA VII/3	1800–01	Vienna: Cappi, 1802	yes	no	no	M, VF, S, VF	E♭, E♭, A♭, E♭	86, 140, 76, 285
Op 27/2	"Moonlight"	NGA VII/3	1801	Vienna: Cappi, 1802	yes	yes	1971	S, F, VF	c♯, D♯, c♯	69, 60, 200
Op 28	"Pastoral"	NGA VII/3	1801	Vienna: Bureau, 1802	yes	yes	no	F, M, Sc, Ro	D, d, D, D	461, 99, 94, 210
Op 31/1		NGA VII/3	1801–02	Zurich: Naegeli, 1803	yes	no	no	F, S, Ro	G, C, G	325, 119, 275
Op 31/2	"Tempest"	NGA VII/3	1801–02	Zurich: Naegeli, 1803	yes	no	no	S/F, S, F	d, B♭, d	228, 103, 399
Op 31/3	"La Chasse"	NGA VII/3	1801–02	Zurich: Naegeli, 1804	yes	no	no	F, Sc, Mi, VF	E♭, A♭, E♭, E♭	253, 171, 62, 333
Op 49/1	"Easy Sonata"	NGA VII/3	1798	Vienna: Bureau, 1805	yes	no	no	M, Ro	g, G	110, 164
Op 49/2	"Easy Sonata"	NGA VII/3	1796	Vienna: Bureau, 1805	yes	no	no	F, Mi	G, G	122, 120
Op 53	"Waldstein"	NGA VII/3	1803–04	Vienna: Bureau, 1805	yes	yes	1954	F, S, Ro	C, F, C	302, 28, 543
Op 54		NGA VII/3	1804	Vienna: Bureau, 1806	yes	no	no	Mi, F	F, F	154, 188
Op 57	"Appassionata"	NGA VII/3	1804–05	Vienna: Bureau, 1807	yes	yes	1972	F, Va, F	f, D♭, f	262, 97, 361
Op 78	"Therese"	B & H 16/24	1809	Leipzig: B & H, 1810	no	yes	1923	S/F, VF	F♯, F♯	105, 183
Op 79	"Cuckoo"	B & H 16/25	1809	Leipzig: B & H, 1810	yes	yes	no	VF, M, F	G, g, G	201, 34, 117
Op 81a	"Das Lebewohl"	B & H 16/26	1809–10	Leipzig: B & H, 1811	yes	i only	no	S/F, M, VF	E♭, c, E♭	255, 42, 196
Op 90		B & H 16/27	1814	Vienna: Steiner, 1815	yes	yes	no	F, M	e, E	245, 290
Op 101	"Sensitive"	B & H 16/28	1813–16	Vienna: Steiner, 1817	yes	yes	no	M, F, S/F	A, F, a/A	102, 94, 361
Op 106	"Hammerklavier"	B & H 16/29	1817–18	Vienna: Artaria, 1819	yes	?	no	F, Sc, S, S/F	B♭, B♭, f♯, B♭	405, 175, 187, 400
Op 109		B & H 16/30	1820	Berlin: Schlesinger, 1821	yes	yes	1965	F, VF, Va	E, e, E	102, 177, 203
Op 110		B & H 16/31	1820–22	Paris: Schlesinger, 1822	yes	yes	1967	M, VF, S/F	A♭, f, a♭/A♭	116, 158, 25/186
Op 111		B & H 16/32	1821–22	Paris: Schlesinger, 1823	yes	yes	1952	S/F, Va	c, C	158, 177

CHART 2. THIRTY-TWO OTHER WORKS FOR SOLO PIANO

Number	Name	Collected edition	Composed	Original edition	Sketches extant	Autograph extant	Facsimile published	Key, variations per piece, no. of measures
Twenty Sets of Variations								
WoO 63	"March by Dressler"	NGA VII/5	1782	Mannheim: Götz, 1782	no	no	no	c, 9, 176
WoO 64	"Swiss Song"	NGA VII/5	ca. 1790	Bonn: Simrock, ca 1798	no	yes	no	F, 6, 79
WoO 65	"Venni amore"	NGA VII/5	1790	Mannheim: Götz, 1791	no	no	no	D, 24, 584
WoO 66	"Es war einmal ein alter Mann"	NGA VII/5	1792	Bonn: Simrock, 1793	no	no	no	A, 13, 537
WoO 68	"Menuett à la Vigano"	NGA VII/5	1795	Vienna: Artaria, 1796	no	no	no	F, 12, 275
WoO 69	"Quant è più bello"	NGA VII/5	1795	Vienna: Traeg, 1795	no	no	no	A, 9, 268
WoO 70	"Nel cor più non mi sento"	NGA VII/5	1795	Vienna: Traeg, 1796	yes	no	no	G, 6, 167
WoO 71	"Das Waldmädchen"	NGA VII/5	1796	Vienna: Artaria, 1797	no	no	no	A, 12, 371
WoO 72	"Une fièvre brûlante"	NGA VII/5	1796–97	Vienna: Traeg, 1798	yes	no	no	C, 8, 363
WoO 73	"La stessa, la stessissima"	NGA VII/5	1799	Vienna: Artaria, 1799	yes	no	no	B♭, 10, 373
WoO 75	"Kind, willst du ruhig schlafen"	NGA VII/5	1799	Vienna: Mollo, 1799	yes	no	no	F, 7, 519
WoO 76	"Tändeln und Scherzen"	NGA VII/5	1799	Vienna: Eder, 1799	yes	no	no	F, 6, 316
WoO 77	". . . on an original theme"	NGA VII/5	1800	Vienna: Traeg, 1800	no	no	no	G, 6, 142
Op 34	(dedicated to Princess Odescalchi)	NGA VII/5	1802	Leipzig: B & H, 1803	yes	lost	no	F, 6, 802
Op 35	"Eroica Variations"	NGA VII/5	1802	Leipzig: B & H, 1803	yes	yes	no	E♭, 15, 575
WoO 78	"God Save the King"	NGA VII/5	1803	Vienna: Bureau, 1804	no	no	no	C, 7, 156
WoO 79	"Rule Britannia"	NGA VII/5	1803	Vienna: Bureau, 1804	yes	no	no	D, 5, 234
WoO 80	"32 Vars." on an original theme	NGA VII/5	1806	Vienna: Im Kunst, 1807	yes	no	no	c, 32, 306
Op 76	(dedicated to Franz Oliva)	NGA VII/5	1809	Leipzig: B & H, 1810	yes	lost	no	D, 6, 178
Op 120	"Diabelli Variations"	NGA VII/5	1819–23	Vienna: Cappi, 1823	yes	yes	no	C, 33, 1157
Twelve Diverse Piano Pieces								
Op 129	"Rage Over a Lost Penny"	B & H 18/9	1795–98	Vienna: Diabelli, 1828	yes	yes	no	G, 1, 446
Op 51/1	Rondo	B & H 18/3	1796–97	Vienna: Artaria, 1797	no	no	no	C, 1, 135

Number	Name	Collected edition	Composed	Original edition	Sketches extant	Autograph extant	Facsimile published	Key, variations per piece, no. of measures
WoO 53	"Allegretto"	B & H 25/36	ca. 1796	[see collected edition]	yes	yes	no	c, 1, 170
Op 51/2	Rondo	B & H 18/4	1798	Vienna: Artaria, 1802	yes	no	no	G, 1, 254
Op 33	[7] Bagatelles	B & H 18/1	1802	Vienna: Bureau, 1803	yes	yes	no	7 pieces
WoO 57	"Andante favori," in Op 53	B & H 18/10	1803–04	Vienna: Bureau, 1805	yes	no	no	F, 1, 205
Op 77	Fantasie	B & H 18/5	1809	Leipzig: B & H, 1810	yes	yes	no	g/D♭, 1, 245
WoO 59	"Für Elise [Therese?]"	B & H 25/35	1810	Leipzig: Duncker, 1867	yes	?	1867	a, 1, 103
Op 89	Polonaise	B & H 18/6	1814	Vienna: Mechetti, 1815	yes	no	no	C, 1, 169
WoO 60	"Für Marie Szymanowska"	B & H 25/38	1818	Berlin: AMZ 49, 1824	yes	yes	no	B♭, 1, 39
Op 119	[11] Bagatelles (#12 = Hess A/21)	B & H 18/7	1820–22	Vienna, 1821; London, 1823	yes	yes	no	6 + 5 pieces
Op 126	[6] Bagatelles	B & H 18/8	1823–24	Mainz: Schott, 1825	yes	yes	no	6 pieces

CHART 3. FORTY-SIX CHAMBER WORKS WITH PIANO

Number	Title	Collected edition	Composed	Original edition	Sketches extant	Autograph extant	Facsimile published	Movements		
								Tempos or types	Keys	Measures
Four Works for Piano Four Hands										
Op 6	Sonata in D	NGA VII/1	1796–97?	Vienna: Artaria, 1797	no	no	no	F, Ro	D, D	157, 89
WoO 67	Vars "Waldstein"	NGA VII/1	1791–92	Bonn: Simrock, 1794	no	yes	no	M	C	206; 8 vars
WoO 74	Vars "Lied"	NGA VII/1	1799–1804	Vienna: Kunst, 1805	yes	yes	no	M	D	130; 6 vars
Op 134	"Grosse" Fuge	NGA VII/1	1826	Vienna: Artaria, 1827	no	lost	no	F	Bb	741
Ten Sonatas for Piano and Violin										
Op 12/1		NGA V/1	1797–98?	Vienna: Artaria, 1798	no	no	no	F, Va, Ro	D, A, D	236, 137, 230
Op 12/2		NGA V/1	1797–98?	Vienna: Artaria, 1798	yes	no	no	VF, M, F	A, a, A	245, 129, 350
Op 12/3		NGA V/1	1797–98?	Vienna: Artaria, 1798	yes	no	no	F, S, Ro	Eb, C, Eb	173, 71, 278
Op 23		NGA V/1	1800	Vienna: Mollo, 1801	yes	no	no	VF, M, VF	a, A, a	252, 207, 332
Op 24	"Spring Sonata"	NGA V/1	1800–01	Vienna: Mollo, 1801	yes	i–iii	no	F, S, Sc, Ro	F, Bb, F, F	247, 73, 43, 243
Op 30/1		NGA V/2	1802	Vienna: Bureau, 1803	yes	yes	no	F, S, Va	A, D, A	249, 105, 86
Op 30/2		NGA V/2	1802	Vienna: Bureau, 1803	yes	yes	no	F, S, Sc, F	c, Ab, C, c	254, 114, 84, 328
Op 30/3		NGA V/2	1802	Vienna: Bureau, 1803	yes	yes	1980	F, Mi, VF	G, Eb, G	202, 196, 221
Op 47	"Kreutzer Sonata"	NGA V/2	1802–03	Bonn: Simrock, 1805	yes	no	no	S/VF, Va, VF	A/a, F, A	599, 235, 539
Op 96		NGA V/2	1812	Vienna: Steiner, 1816	yes	yes	1977	F, S, Sc, M	G, Eb, g, G	281, 67, 97, 295
Seven Sonatas or Variations for Piano and Cello (or Horn)										
Op 5/1	*Grande Sonate*	NGA V/3	1796	Vienna: Artaria, 1797	yes	no	no	S/F, Ro	F, F	400, 290
Op 5/2	*Grande Sonate*	NGA V/3	1796	Vienna: Artaria, 1797	yes	no	no	S/F, Ro	g, G	553, 304
Op 17	Sonata (P & Hn/Vc)	B & H 14/1	1800	Vienna: Mollo, 1801	yes	no	no	F, S, Ro	F, f, F	180, 17, 184
WoO 46	Vars. on "bej Männern"	NGA V/3	1801?	Vienna: Mollo, 1802	no	yes	no	M	Eb	169; 7 variations
Op 69	Sonata	NGA V/3	1807	Leipzig: B & H, 1809	yes	i only	1970	F, Sc, S/VF	A, a, E/A	280, 519, 220
Op 102/1	"Deux Sonates" No 1	NGA V/3	1815	Bonn: Simrock, 1817	yes	yes	no	M/VF, S/VF	C, C	154, 249
Op 102/2	"Deux Sonates" No 2	NGA V/3	1815	Bonn: Simrock, 1817	yes	yes	no	VF, S, F	D, d, D	147, 85, 244

Fourteen Piano Trios (with Violin, Cello or Other Instruments)

Number	Title	Collected edition	Composed	Original edition	Sketches extant	Autograph extant	Facsimile published	Movements		
								Tempos or types	Keys	Measures
Hess 48	(Single movement)	NGA IV/3	ca 1784	London: Elkin, 1955		yes	no	F	Bb	122
WoO 37	Trio concertant	NGA IV/3	1786–90	B & H 25/31 (1888)	no	yes	no	F, S, Va	G, g, G	244, 73, 150
WoO 38	Trio	NGA IV/3	1790–91	Frankfurt: Dunst, 1830	no	lost	no	F, Sc, Ro	Eb, Eb, Eb	191, 110, 193
Op 44	Variations	NGA IV/3	1792–1803?	Leipzig: Hoffm., 1804	yes	no	no	M	Eb	401; 14 variations
Op 1/1	Trois Trios No 1	B & H XI/1	1793–94	Vienna: Artaria, 1795	no	no	no	F, S, Sc, VF	Eb, Ab, Eb, Eb	293, 123, 215, 478
Op 1/2	Trois Trios No 2	B & H XI/2	1793–94	Vienna: Artaria, 1795	yes	no	no	S/F, S, Sc, VF	G, E, G, G	462, 124, 130, 455
Op 1/3	Trois Trios No 3	B & H XI/3	1793–94	Vienna: Artaria, 1795	yes	no	no	VF, Va, Mi, VF	c, Eb, c, c	360, 131, 77, 420
Op 11	Grande Trio (Cl/Vn)	B & H XI/11	1797	Vienna: Mollo, 1798	yes	no	no	F, S, Va	Bb, Eb, Bb	254, 64, 211
Op 38	(Arr. of Septet Op 20)	NGA IV/3	1802?–03	Vienna: Bureau, 1805	no	inc.	no	S/VF+5mvmts	Eb+5 keys	943 total
Op 121a	"Schneider Kakadu"	NGA IV/3	by 1803?	Vienna: Steiner, 1824	no	yes	no	S/F	g/G	547; 10 vars
Op 70/1	"Ghost Trio" No 1	B & H XI/4	1808	Leipzig: B & H, 1809	yes	yes	no	VF, S, VF	D, d, D	270, 96, 411
Op 70/2	Trio No. 2	B & H XI/5	1808	Leipzig: B & H, 1809	yes	yes	no	S/F, M, F, F	Eb, C, Ab, Eb	243, 439, 189, 401
Op 97	"Archduke Trio"	B & H XI/6	1810–11	Vienna: Steiner, 1816	yes	yes	no	F, Sc, M, F	Bb, Bb, D, Bb	287, 335, 194, 410
WoO 39	"Brentano" (1 mvt)	NGA IV/3	1812	Frankfurt: Dunst, 1830	no	yes	inc.	F	Bb	124

One Quintet for Piano and Winds

Number	Title	Collected edition	Composed	Original edition	Sketches extant	Autograph extant	Facsimile published	Movements		
								Tempos or types	Keys	Measures
Op 16	Grand Quintetto	NGA IV/1	1796–97	Vienna: Mollo, 1801	yes	no	no	S/F, M, Ro	Eb, Bb, Eb	416, 112, 257

CHART 4. TEN WORKS WITH ORCHESTRA OR ORCHESTRA AND CHORUS

								Movements		
Number	Title	Collected edition	Composed	Original edition	Sketches extant	Autograph extant	Facsimile published	Tempos or types	Keys	Measures
WoO 4	Concert	B & H 25/47	1784	Leipzig: B & H, 1890	yes	no	no	F, S, Ro	E♭, B♭, E♭	263, 82, 280
WoO 6	Rondo	B & H 11/9	ca. 1795	Vienna: Diabelli, 1829	yes	yes	no	F (Ro)	B♭	378
Op. 19	Concert "2"	NGA III/2	1794, 98	Vienna: Hoffmeister, 1801	yes	yes	no	F, S, Ro	B♭, E♭, B♭	479, 91, 327
Op. 15	Concerto "1"	NGA III/2	1795, 98	Vienna: Mollo, 1801	yes	yes	no	VF, S, Ro	C, A♭, C	478, 119, 571
Op. 37	Concerto "3"	NGA III/2	1800	Vienna: Bureau, 1804	yes	yes	no	VF, S, Ro	c, E, c	507, 89, 463
Op. 56	P, Vn, Vc, & Orch	NGA III/1	1803, 04	Vienna: Bureau, 1807	yes	no	no	F, S, Ro	C, A♭, C	531, 53, 475
Op. 58	Concert "4"	B & H 9/4	1805, 06	Vienna: Kunst, 1808	yes	?	no	F, M, Ro	G, e, G	370, 72, 600
Op. 61	Vn Concerto transcribed	Hess X/1	1807	Vienna: Bureau, 1808	no	no	no	F, S, R	D, G, D	535, 91, 359
Op. 80	Fantasie, + chorus	B & H 9/8	1808	London: Clementi, 1810	yes	partly	no	S, F/M	c, c/C	26, 576
Op. 73	Grand Concerto "5"	B & H 9/5	1809	London: Clementi, 1810	yes	yes	no	F, S, Ro	E♭, B, E♭	582, 82, 431

INDEX

NOTE: All names and principal topics (including short titles in the Bibliography) are listed when they get more than passing mention. Italics indicate main discussions; quotation marks indicate statements by the person listed.